MARY of GALILEE

VOLUME II:
WOMAN OF ISRAEL — DAUGHTER OF ZION

prayers!

Fr. Bert Buby, Sm.

PERMISSIONS

Excerpts from the New Revised Standard Version Bible, copyright © 1989, by the Division of Christian Education of the National Council of the Churches of Christ in the United States of America.

Excerpts from the English translation of the Lectionary for *Masses of the Blessed Virgin Mary* © 1989, International Committee on English in the Liturgy, Inc. All rights reserved.

Excerpts from the English translation of the *Catechism of the Catholic Church* for the United States of America copyright © 1994, United States Catholic Conference, Inc. — Libreria Editrice Vaticana.

MARY *of* GALILEE

VOLUME II

Woman of Israel — Daughter of Zion

A Biblical, Liturgical, and Catechetical
Celebration of the Mother of Jesus

Bertrand Buby, SM

ALBA·HOUSE   **NEW·YORK**

SOCIETY OF ST. PAUL, 2187 VICTORY BLVD., STATEN ISLAND, NEW YORK 10314

Library of Congress Cataloging-in-Publication Data

Buby, Bertrand.
    Mary of Galilee: a trilogy of Marian studies: Mary in the New Testament,
    Mary in the Hebrew Scripture, Mary in the Apocrypha and the sub-apostolic
    writers / Bertrand Buby.
        p.   cm.
    Includes bibliographical references.
    Contents: v. 1. The Scripture texts. v. 2. The Hebrew texts.
    ISBN 0-8189-0697-9
    1. Mary, Blessed Virgin, Saint. I. Title.
  BT602.B79   1995
  232.91 — dc20   94-10788
                                      CIP

Nihil Obstat:
Reverend Robert L. Hagedorn
May 1, 1995

Imprimatur:
Most Reverend Carl K. Moeddel
Vicar General and Auxiliary Bishop of the Archdiocese of Cincinnati
May 4, 1995

The Nihil Obstat and Imprimatur are official declarations
that a book or pamphlet is free of doctrinal or moral
error. No implication is contained therein that those
who have granted the Nihil Obstat and Imprimatur agree
with the contents, opinions or statements expressed.

Produced and designed in the United States of America by the
Fathers and Brothers of the Society of St. Paul,
2187 Victory Boulevard, Staten Island, New York 10314,
as part of their communications apostolate.

ISBN: 0-8189-0697-9

Printing Information:

Current Printing - first digit	1	2	3	4	5	6	7	8	9	10

Year of Current Printing - first year shown

1995	1996	1997	1998	1999

TABLE OF CONTENTS

ACKNOWLEDGMENTS

Volume II of *Mary of Galilee* is due to the careful assistance of Marjorie Yefchak. I am indebted to Eileen Moorman for her corrections of style and expression of thought. Together with Dr. Ron Novotny and Brother Don Sullivan, SM, Marjorie and Eileen were also involved in proofreading the text.

The sketch of the earliest fresco of Mary was done by the artist Bev Stoller of Theotokos studio. I am deeply appreciative for her help with this sketch.

Father Johann Roten, SM, the President of the International Marian Research Institute at the University of Dayton, provided constant support and assistance in this endeavor.

To my brothers and sisters in the Society of Mary and the Daughters of Mary, and to the entire Family of Mary, I am also indebted. My own Marianist Community provided the space and atmosphere that I needed to accomplish this work.

Biblical Abbreviations

OLD TESTAMENT

Genesis	Gn	Nehemiah	Ne	Baruch	Ba
Exodus	Ex	Tobit	Tb	Ezekiel	Ezk
Leviticus	Lv	Judith	Jdt	Daniel	Dn
Numbers	Nb	Esther	Est	Hosea	Ho
Deuteronomy	Dt	1 Maccabees	1 M	Joel	Jl
Joshua	Jos	2 Maccabees	2 M	Amos	Am
Judges	Jg	Job	Jb	Obadiah	Ob
Ruth	Rt	Psalms	Ps	Jonah	Jon
1 Samuel	1 S	Proverbs	Pr	Micah	Mi
2 Samuel	2 S	Ecclesiastes	Ec	Nahum	Na
1 Kings	1 K	Song of Songs	Sg	Habakkuk	Hab
2 Kings	2 K	Wisdom	Ws	Zephaniah	Zp
1 Chronicles	1 Ch	Sirach	Si	Haggai	Hg
2 Chronicles	2 Ch	Isaiah	Is	Malachi	Ml
Ezra	Ezr	Jeremiah	Jr	Zechariah	Zc
		Lamentations	Lm		

NEW TESTAMENT

Matthew	Mt	Ephesians	Eph	Hebrews	Heb
Mark	Mk	Philippians	Ph	James	Jm
Luke	Lk	Colossians	Col	1 Peter	1 P
John	Jn	1 Thessalonians	1 Th	2 Peter	2 P
Acts	Ac	2 Thessalonians	2 Th	1 John	1 Jn
Romans	Rm	1 Timothy	1 Tm	2 John	2 Jn
1 Corinthians	1 Cor	2 Timothy	2 Tm	3 John	3 Jn
2 Corinthians	2 Cor	Titus	Tt	Jude	Jude
Galatians	Gal	Philemon	Phm	Revelation	Rv

MARY of GALILEE

VOLUME II:
WOMAN OF ISRAEL — DAUGHTER OF ZION

Chapter One

MARY: WOMAN OF ISRAEL

An Introduction

The four-volume *Testi Mariani del Primo Millennio*, published in Rome 1988-1991,[1] is a monumental edition of Marian texts from the first millennium. The first volume commences with forty-two pages of readings from the Hebrew Scriptures. These scriptural selections provide a background for experiencing the Catholic accommodated use of certain Hebrew texts when studying the Marian tradition of the early Christian theologians and pastors. Perhaps there is no better way of understanding their devotion and teaching about Mary than by reading these biblical texts. Though some Catholic scholars may wish to limit the Marian tradition which arises from the Church's use of the Hebrew Scriptures, the fact that the Hebrew Bible was God's revealed word for Jesus and his mother cannot be contested. To appreciate the Jewishness of both Jesus and Mary, these texts are indispensable. A certain ethos is experienced by studying the person of Mary in the history and growth of her own people, Israel. Paul can be understood so much the better through knowing the Scriptures of Israel; his own writings show that for him the Hebrew Scriptures were a source of life and inspiration. Would not these same writings have formed and influenced the person Mary of Nazareth in Galilee?

   Testi Mariani del Primo Millennio is a gold mine for Marian studies. The scriptural references provided have been taken from this work and supplemented in Appendix 1. The texts presented emanate from the feasts and memorials of the Virgin Mary and from scriptural readings, hymns, and homilies in the primitive Church and early Christianity. Early pastors and theologians of the Church used these texts in a broad, comprehensive, and accommodated way rather than taking a literal and historical approach. Thereby they discovered a rich symbolic and type-like meaning hidden within the texts. Wolfgang Beinert gives us a good insight about the texts:

> The Authors using these texts place great importance in their statements. They show how Mary has a very important role in the history of salvation which has reached its culmination in Christ. Inasmuch as these pericopes do not allow us to know a lot about the Mary of history, they do, however, allow us to know more clearly the kerygmatic Mary, that is, her place within the salvific plan of God which constitutes the true and proper object of New Testament preaching.[2]

It is suggested that the scriptural texts be read in the order given and in a meditative, reflective, and imaginative way for becoming better. acquainted with the living traditions of the early Church and for a better understanding of the Marian tradition.

The Approach

This book is the second volume of a trilogy which studies biblical references that are used in Mariology. There are Marian texts in the New Testament (*Mary of Galilee*, Volume I) which emanate from the Hebrew Scriptures either through their being cited in the New Testament or through their use in the tradition of the Catholic Church. There are also appropriations of the Hebrew Scriptures in the New Testament Apocrypha of the second and third centuries (*Mary of Galilee*, Volume III). Thus there are references which are directly from the Scriptures about Mary through the New Testament authors using the Old Testament, there are texts which are accommodated, and there are also symbols and images taken from the Old Testament that help us to see Mary in the light of the Scriptures. This study will examine such texts to see what has been said about Mary of Nazareth in the Church. Use will be made of valuable information garnered by the historical-critical method in the texts selected by the Italian editors as the living testimony of the Church at prayer. The task is to read, understand, and enjoy the Word of God in wider horizons of thought, and to deepen faith perceptions by creative intuitions and associations with that living Word of God.

The Scriptures are primarily the gift of God within the Church. In the Book of the Church (God's people) God speaks to all of us, especially whenever the Bible is read and proclaimed in the Church. From its very origin the Church celebrated readings from both testaments which were seen as completing each other. The First Testament (Old Testament/Hebrew) and the Second Testament (New Testament/Greek) were and are read together in the gatherings of God's people. The "Bible" for Jesus and Mary was the Old Testament. In turn, the life and words of Jesus inspired others to write a second testament under the guidance and light of the Hebrew Scriptures. The Scriptures are proclaimed by the Church in a canonical manner with the full range of all texts of the Bible being read and clarified. The Church and the New Testament writers had recourse to the Septuagint, the Greek translation of the Hebrew Scriptures (rather than the canonical Hebrew texts) and considered it an inspired text. *Koine* Greek was the *lingua franca* in the emerging and primitive Church. With the Septuagint, books now considered Apocrypha by some non-Catholics were (and are) read by the Church as part of the inspired Scriptures. Mary was explained and preached from the texts of these deuterocanonical books (Tobit, Judith, Wisdom, Sirach, Baruch, 1 Maccabees, 2 Maccabees, and some Greek passages found only in Daniel and Esther).

In the Church's tradition of explaining these texts, both exegetical and ecclesial criteria and principles have always been a part of her interpretation of the Bible. Moreover, a twofold hermeneutic is used by the Church in understanding the texts presented within the Marian tradition:

1) the Bible is interpreted in light of the faith of members of Christ's Resurrected body, the Church. Creeds, which emanated from the Scriptures, evidence the bulwark of that faith and belief with which the Church defended orthodoxy.
2) both the Hebrew Scriptures and the New Testament are read in the light of the Christ event. They comprise one book which is inspired and revealed by a living, loving personal God.

Often the Old Testament is seen as prefiguring and preparing for the New Testament. In order to understand the New Testament, the early pastors turned to the Old Testament for illumination and clarification. With God (through the Holy Spirit) as the principal author and inspirer of these books, the Church's use, understanding, and proclamation goes beyond a literal and historical understanding of the texts. A constant theological and pastoral approach was and is used by the Church. It is true that for the exegete the historical-critical study of the texts is primary, but for the Church and its believers, the spiritual and fuller sense is primordial.

The typological sense of understanding these texts was one of the earliest methodologies used within the Church for interpreting the Bible. This presented many of the symbols, themes, and persons in the light of the events of Jesus' life, death, resurrection, ascension and exaltation at God's right hand. The texts were also seen within the events of the birthing of the Church which came about on Calvary and at Pentecost. There is also the accommodated sense, which is developed chiefly in the Patristic writings and in the liturgy. In this volume, an effort will be made to discover how scholars used typology in their studies about Mary. Symbolism which is now being discovered in new ways in the Scriptures has an important place in research and teaching about Mary today.

Another, but less fortuitous, interpretation was that of the school of Alexandria, which emphasized the search for a more profound sense or even a mystical interpretation. Such a method consisted of allegorizing the texts by reading the facts and events as symbols of a higher reality. Often the literal and historical meaning was neglected. Such a moralizing sense of interpretation tried to find examples for a holy life within the Scriptures, and Mary became an important model and source for holiness.

The New Testament: A Window for the Old Testament

The principal Marian texts and themes are found in the New Testament writings which treat of Mary in relationship to her son. However, there are parallels to or citations from the Hebrew Scriptures with symbols such as Daughter of Zion, virgin, Davidic lineage, ark of the covenant, etc., which are common to both testaments. In addition to these writings there exists an oral tradition which continued side by side with the written Gospels and can only be recovered through a form-critical study of the texts of the New Testament and through the scriptural reflections of the leaders, theologians and pastors of the early Church. The use of these additional approaches provides a more ecclesial sense of the two testaments.[3] Within such a rich approach the singular privileges of Mary, such as the Immaculate Conception and the Assumption, can be studied.[4] In turn, the Fathers of the Church wrote in a pastoral manner for the people and culture in which they lived. Hence, Mary, as a follower of her son Jesus, is Virgin-Mother, *Panta Hagia* (All Holy) and *Theotokos* (God-bearer), who is a model for their lives and for the Church.

The infancy narratives are the point of departure for many of the Marian themes in the Church. It is in these areas of Scripture that the Old Testament is most frequently cited or recalled through use of a similar language, parallel ideas, and matching symbols. Parallels can be found in the Annunciation accounts to Mary and to Joseph. There are also parallels to the visitation, to the Magi, and to the shepherds. The Johannine texts were not used in the earliest years in patristic reflections on Mary but soon they, too, came into their own use. Texts from Genesis, Exodus, and the prophet Isaiah were used by the early Church theologians in their sermons, essays, homilies, and teachings about Mary. Among the preferred texts from the First or Old Testament were the initial account of Adam and Eve, the garden, the fall, their punishment, and their offspring who repeat a similar pattern. The Exodus Event was especially highlighted by the presence of God (walking with and leading the people of Israel; hence, the importance of the column of smoke and the cloud, the tabernacle, the ark, the altar, the candelabra). Such symbols lead us to an understanding of why these pastors and theologians referred to these texts in their presentation of Mary in the context of a history of a living tradition and a believing community. The prophetic references for Mary are few; her presence is rarely seen in the Psalms where it is rather an indirect one such as seeing her among the poor of God. Liturgical expressions went beyond the more explicit texts in search for a deeper devotion to and understanding of the mystery of Mary. The Scriptures were seen primarily through their use in the churches and synagogues. In these communities of faith a living and perennial tradition influenced an understanding of the faith; for Catholics this faith tradition involves the person of Mary of Nazareth. The Scriptures as read and applied in the Church are a basis for this study of Mary in relationship to Christ and the Church (Christology and Ecclesiology) with an awareness of the Holy Spirit working within communities of faith and illuminating those who study, teach, and preach the doctrines held within the tradition.

The Jewishness of Mary

Since Mary was born into Judaism, she experienced the Hebrew Scriptures both in her prayer and her mode of life as a woman of Nazareth. A principal objective within this book will be to put Mary back into a Judaic context. Various sources are available for such an effort. The richness of Aristide Serra's collection of essays on the Marian biblical texts, *E C'era la Madre di Gesù,* will be explored. A collection of Marian Masses which reflects the use of the Hebrew Scriptures in the liturgy offers more symbolic language about Mary and some biblical images taken from the Hebrew Bible.[5]

Both the Hebrew Scriptures and the Christian Scriptures are believed to be covenantal revelation, containing the history of the liberation and salvation of believing peoples. In this study, the covenanted history of salvation is essential to a knowledge of the First and Last Testaments.

This Jewish background of study helps render the meaning of Mary today through the Hebrew Scriptures and within the context of their use in the Catholic Church. It is necessary to have an understanding based not only on the scientific study of the Bible (the historical-critical method), but also one based on the living faith of the Church expressed through the Apostles' Creed, and the Creeds of Nicea, 325 C.E., and Constantinople, 387 C.E. These Creeds give the fundamentals of Catholic-Christian faith as professed and transmitted by the Church universal. Early within the councils and in the teaching of the theologians and pastors of the Church, both the Old and New Testaments were accepted as divinely inspired Scriptures. The unity of God's revelation through both testaments was stressed. The Christian dispensation reads both testaments in the light of Christ as the revealing Word.

Some of the earlier methods of interpreting the Scriptures have to be understood and have to be considered in pursuing a study of Mary in the Scriptures. The spiritual, analogical, symbolic, and typological senses are important developments within the Catholic tradition. As indicated above, the Alexandrian School presented its theological reflections through the use of analogy and symbolism, through the spiritual meaning and moral meaning of the Scriptures, and through allegory. The Alexandrian theologians emphasized *theoria* as their method. On the other hand, the Antiochene School emphasized a literal, historical, and philological meaning in their study of the texts in a method more associated with *praxis*. Other schools of thought such as the Cappadocians and Jerusalemites may have used a *via media* by having both *theoria* and *praxis* in their explanations of the Scriptures and Mary's role within them.[6]

A Marian Rereading of the Hebrew Scriptures

Through the references of the Old Testament used within the New Testament texts about Mary, one can see that her person and mission are read back into the Hebrew Scriptures. This Christian rereading is demonstrated by always starting with texts from the New Testament. Here Mary can be perceived in the shadow of the persons and institutions of the Old Testament. This type of an interpretation or hermeneutic enables an understanding of her as the complement to Israel, the People of God, in its pilgrimage towards a redeeming Messiah of the house of David. This rereading of the Marian texts of Matthew, Luke, and John in the light of pages from the Old Testament enables us to understand this Jewish woman from Nazareth in Galilee.

Mary is heiress to Israel's faith at Sinai:

> Moses went up the mountain to God. Then the Lord called to him and said, "Thus shall you say to the house of Jacob; tell the Israelites: you have seen for yourselves how I treated the Egyptians and how I bore you up on eagle wings and brought you here to myself. Therefore, if you hearken to my voice and keep my covenant, you shall be my special possession, dearer to me than all other people, though all the earth is mine. You shall be to me a kingdom of priests, a holy nation. That is what you must tell the Israelites." So Moses went and summoned the elders of the people. When he set before them all that the Lord had ordered him to tell them, the people all answered together, "Everything the Lord has said, we will do." Then Moses brought back to the Lord the response of the people (Ex 19:3-8).

The "yes" response or "amen" of Israel to God is the heart of the Old Testament message. Moses, the Mediator of God's message, inaugurates Israel's "yes":

> "That is what you must tell the Israelites." So Moses went and summoned the elders of the people. When he set before them

all that the Lord had ordered him to tell them, the people all
answered together, "Everything the Lord has said, we will do."
Then Moses brought back to the Lord the response of the
people (Ex 19:6b-8).

Israel is given a free choice for accepting the stipulations of the
covenant. The people affirmatively give their "yes" in Exodus 19:8a:

the people all answered together, "Everything the Lord has
said, we will do."

Compare:

When Moses came to the people and related all the words and
ordinances of the Lord, they all answered with one voice, "We
will do everything that the Lord has told us. . . ." Taking the
book of the covenant, he read it aloud to the people, who
answered, "All that the Lord has said, we will heed and do" (Ex
24:3, 7).

This is also symbolized in the spouse's "yes" in Ezekiel 16:8:

Again I passed by you and saw that you were now old enough
for love. So I spread the corner of my cloak over you to cover
your nakedness; I swore an oath to you and entered into a
covenant with you; you became mine, says the Lord God.

As a result, God is pleased and blesses Israel and her children:

"I have heard the words these people have spoken to you,
which are all well said. Would that they might always be of
such a mind, to fear me and to keep all my commandments!
Then they and their descendants would prosper forever" (Dt
5:28b-29; cf. Dt 5:23-28a).

Today at the Passover Haggadah this contract-covenant continues
and is sacramentally present to the Jewish believer:

"There was the day on which you stood before the Lord, your God, at Horeb, and he said to me, 'Assemble the people for me; I will have them hear my words, that they may learn to fear me as long as they live in the land and may so teach their children'" (Dt 4:10).

At Sinai Israel was born (Pentecost). Then new mediators after Moses kept this same covenant and spiritual rebirth of Israel in front of God's people (Jr 42). Joshua (Jos 24:1-28) renewed the covenant; kings like Josiah (2 K 23:1-3) and Asa (2 Ch 15:9-15) kept it alive, as did Nehemiah and Ezra (Ne 5:1-3; Ezr 10:10-12; Ne 9, 10) and Simon, likewise (1 M 13:1-9). Even later in Philo, and Qumran and the rabbinic literature, this Sinai covenant is celebrated and renewed with great emotion.

Mary's Covenantal Response

Mary's "yes" is seen both at the Annunciation (Lk 1:26-38) and at Cana (Jn 2:1-11). In the light of the Hebrew texts about the covenant and the "yes" of Israel, Mary's response at the Annunciation and at Cana can be better understood.

The Annunciation narrative is analogous to the Sinai covenant (cf. p. 8):

In the sixth month, the angel Gabriel was sent from God to a town of Galilee called Nazareth, to a virgin betrothed to a man named Joseph, of the house of David, and the virgin's name was Mary. And coming to her, he said, "Hail, favored one! The Lord is with you." But she was greatly troubled at what was said and pondered what sort of greeting this might be. Then the angel said to her, "Do not be afraid, Mary, for you have found favor with God. Behold, you will conceive in your womb and bear a son, and you shall name him Jesus. He will be great and will be called Son of the Most High, and the Lord God will give him the throne of David his father, and he will rule over the house of Jacob forever, and of his Kingdom there will be no end." But Mary said to the angel, "How can this be, since I have no relations with a man?" And the angel said to her in reply, "The Holy Spirit will come upon you, and the power of the Most High will overshadow you. Therefore the child to be born will be called holy, the Son of God. And behold, Elizabeth, your relative, has also conceived a son in her old age, and this is the sixth month for her who was called barren; for nothing will be impossible for God." Mary said, "Behold, I am the handmaid of the Lord. May it be done to me according to your word." Then the angel departed from her (Lk 1:26-38).

Gabriel is the Mediator just as Moses was. Mary is called by a special name *kécharitôménê* or the one who has been found already graced or favored by God. In the promise made to her a child is to be born who is the Holy One or Son of God. She will inherit a new house of Israel (Jacob), the Church. This is similar to the promises made to David:

"Now then, speak thus to my servant David, 'The Lord of hosts has this to say: It was I who took you from the pasture and from the care of the flock to be commander of my people Israel. I have been with you wherever you went, and I have destroyed all your enemies before you. And I will make you famous like the great ones of the earth. I will fix a place for my people Israel; I will plant them so that they may dwell in their place without further disturbance. Neither shall the wicked continue to afflict them as they did of old, since the time I first appointed judges over my people Israel. I will give you rest from all your enemies. The Lord also reveals to you that he will establish a house for you. And when your time comes and you rest with your ancestors, I will raise up your heir after you, sprung from your loins, and I will make his kingdom firm. It is he who shall build a house for my name. And I will make his royal throne firm forever. I will be a father to him, and he shall be a son to me. And if he does wrong, I will correct him with the rod of men and with human chastisements; but I will not withdraw my favor from him as I withdrew it from your predecessor Saul, whom I removed from my presence. Your house and your kingdom shall endure forever before me; your throne shall stand firm forever'" (2 S 7:8-16).

Mary's *fiat* is like that of her people Israel:

> "Therefore, you shall love the Lord, your God, with all your heart, and with all your soul, and with all your strength" (Dt 6:5).

She enters into a free, intelligent, and wise dialogue with Gabriel the mediator-messenger just as Moses carefully and clearly explained to his people God's designs and demands before the covenant was ratified. At Nazareth, the angel addresses Mary three times (Lk 1:28, 30-33, 35-37). Mary's reaction is recorded three times (Lk 1:29, 34, 38). The "yes" of Israel is also repeated (Ex 19:8; 24:3, 7; Jos 24:24; Ezr 10:12; Ne 5:12; 1 M 13:9). Mary's faith has matured through her response just as has that of the people of Israel. Both Gabriel and Moses bring back good news to God (Lk 1:38 and Ex 19:8).

In the Cana account the importance of the third day is highlighted:

> On the third day there was a wedding in Cana in Galilee, and the mother of Jesus was there (Jn 2:1).

just as it is in the Exodus covenant narrative:

> The Lord added, "Go to the people and have them sanctify themselves today and tomorrow. Make them wash their garments and be ready for the third day; for on the third day the Lord will come down on Mount Sinai before the eyes of all the people. Set limits for the people all around the mountain, and tell them: Take care not to go up the mountain, or even to touch its base. If anyone touches the mountain, he must be put to death. No hand shall touch him; he must be stoned to death or killed with arrows. Such a one, man or beast, must not be allowed to live. Only when the ram's horn resounds may they go up to the mountain." Then Moses came down from the mountain to the people and had them sanctify themselves and wash their garments. He warned them, "Be ready for the third day" (Ex 19:10-15).

The new wine is the symbol of the Good News of the Messianic times which results with Jesus' disciples believing in him: "Jesus did this as the beginning of his signs in Cana in Galilee and so revealed his glory, and his disciples began to believe in him" (Jn 2:11). A remarkable mutual recall of Sinai is seen in the Cana account in that his Mother's words to the servers:

"Do whatever he tells you" (Jn 2:5).

parallels:

the people all answered together, "Everything the Lord has said, we will do" (Ex 19:8a).

and:

When Moses came to the people and related all the words and ordinances of the Lord, they all answered with one voice, "We will do everything that the Lord has told us." . . . Taking the book of the covenant, he read it aloud to the people, who answered, "All that the Lord has said, we will heed and do" (Ex 24:3, 7).

There is an identity between Mary's "yes" and that of Israel, an identity between the community of Israel and the Church. Israel is frequently presented to God as a "spouse," a "woman." This word "woman" with its unusual connotation is also used at Cana and Calvary for Mary:

When the wine ran short, the mother of Jesus said to him, "They have no wine." [And] Jesus said to her, "Woman, how does your concern affect me? My hour has not yet come" (Jn 2:3-4).

Standing by the cross of Jesus were his mother and his mother's sister, Mary the wife of Clopas, and Mary of Magdala. When Jesus saw his mother and the disciple there whom he loved, he said to his mother, "Woman, behold, your son." Then he said

to the disciple, "Behold, your mother." And from that hour the
disciple took her into his home (Jn 19:25-27).

The Fourth Evangelist parallels Luke's notion of Mary as the
Daughter of Zion, another symbolic name for the Church. In more
explicit language, Paul sees in Jesus' mother the ideal incarnation of
ancient Israel joined to the fullness of time:

> But when the fullness of time had come, God sent his Son,
> born of a woman, born under the law (Gal 4:4).

In Luke Mary is symbolized as the Ark of the New Covenant. In the
Hebrew Scriptures there is a strict relationship between the covenant and the ark at Sinai. The ark symbolizes the Presence of God
among his people:

> "You shall make an ark of acacia wood, two and a half cubits
> long, one and a half cubits wide, and one and a half cubits high"
> (Ex 25:10).

The two tablets of the Ten Words or the Decalogue are part of the
revelation of God's holiness code for the People:

> "In the ark you are to put the commandments which I will give
> you" (Ex 25:16).

> When the Lord had finished speaking to Moses on Mount
> Sinai, he gave him the two tablets of the commandments, the
> stone tablets inscribed by God's own finger (Ex 31:18).

> "At that time the Lord said to me, 'Cut two tablets of stone like
> the former; then come up the mountain to me. Also make an
> ark of wood. I will write upon the tablets the commandments
> that were on the former tablets that you broke, and you shall
> place them in the ark.' So I made an ark of acacia wood, and cut
> two tablets of stone like the former, and went up the mountain
> carrying the two tablets. The Lord then wrote on them, as he
> had written before, the ten commandments which he spoke to
> you on the mountain from the midst of the fire on the day of

the assembly. After the Lord had given them to me, I turned and came down the mountain, and placed the tablets in the ark I had made. There they have remained, in keeping with the command the Lord gave me" (Dt 10:1-5).

This Presence of God (the Shekinah) and the use of the cloud and fire to symbolize this presence are important to the revelation of God's covenant with Israel. God descends and lives on Mount Sinai:

> The glory of the Lord settled upon Mount Sinai. The cloud covered it for six days, and on the seventh day he called to Moses from the midst of the cloud (Ex 24:16).

> Then the cloud covered the meeting tent, and the glory of the Lord [the Shekinah] filled the Dwelling. Moses could not enter the meeting tent, because the cloud settled down upon it and the glory of the Lord filled the Dwelling (Ex 40:34-35).

Finally, this Presence of God is perceived in the Holy of Holies in the Temple at Jerusalem where the ark is deposited:

> When the priests left the holy place, the cloud filled the temple of the Lord so that the priests could no longer minister because of the cloud, since the Lord's glory had filled the temple of the Lord. Then Solomon said, "The Lord intends to dwell in the dark cloud; I have truly built you a princely house, a dwelling where you may abide forever" (1 K 8:10-13; cf. 2 Ch 5:13).

This Annunciation parallels these Hebrew narratives making the analogy and symbolism apparent in Mary as the living ark of the covenant. Luke, using Septuagintal language in his Infancy Narrative, guides us in a rereading of the Old Testament through this symbolism of the ark and its relation to Mary. The same verb (*episkiazein*) is used for overshadowing the ark and overshadowing Mary:

> And the angel said to her in reply, "The Holy Spirit will come upon you, and the power of the Most High will overshadow

you. Therefore the child to be born will be called holy, the Son of God" (Lk 1:35).

and

Then the cloud covered the meeting tent, and the glory of the Lord filled the Dwelling. Moses could not enter the meeting tent, because the cloud settled down upon it and the glory of the Lord filled the Dwelling (Ex 40:34-35).

The one born of Mary is the Holy One.

In the Visitation pericope there is a resemblance to the transfer of the ark by David from Baala of Judah to Jerusalem. This is the same geographically in both Luke and Samuel:

During those days Mary set out and traveled to the hill country in haste to a town of Judah, where she entered the house of Zechariah and greeted Elizabeth. When Elizabeth heard Mary's greeting, the infant leaped in her womb, and Elizabeth, filled with the Holy Spirit, cried out in a loud voice and said, "Most blessed are you among women, and blessed is the fruit of your womb. And how does this happen to me, that the mother of my Lord should come to me? For at the moment the sound of your greeting reached my ears, the infant in my womb leaped for joy. Blessed are you who believed that what was spoken to you by the Lord would be fulfilled" (Lk 1:39-45).

David again assembled all the picked men of Israel, thirty thousand in number. Then David and all the people who were with him set out for Baala of Judah to bring up from there the ark of God, which bears the name of the Lord of hosts enthroned above the cherubim (2 S 6:1-2).

David's dancing may be compared with the Baptist's leaping for joy within the womb of Elizabeth (2 S 6:5, 12, 14, 16 and Lk 1:41-44). There are special blessings on Obed-edom just as Elizabeth blessed Mary:

The ark of the Lord remained in the house of Obed-edom the Gittite for three months, and the Lord blessed Obed-edom and his whole house. When it was reported to King David that the Lord had blessed the family of Obed-edom and all that belonged to him, David went to bring up the ark of God from the house of Obed-edom into the City of David amid festivities (2 S 6:11-12).

When Elizabeth heard Mary's greeting, the infant leaped in her womb, and Elizabeth, filled with the Holy Spirit, cried out in a loud voice and said, "Most blessed are you among women, and blessed is the fruit of your womb" (Lk 1:41-42).

The words of David and Elizabeth are equivalent in symbolism ("ark of the Lord" and "mother of my Lord"):

David feared the Lord that day and said, "How can the ark of the Lord come to me?" (2 S 6:9).

"And how does this happen to me, that the mother of my Lord should come to me?" (Lk 1:43).

Mary is the symbolic ark of the covenant. Elizabeth's respect for Mary and the reverence of the people toward the ark are other comparisons between the Hebrew account and that of Luke. The ark remains for a period of three months within Obed-edom's home (2 S 6:11), while Mary stays three months in the home of Elizabeth and Zechariah: "Mary remained with her about three months and then returned to her home" (Lk 1:56). Mary's "yes" accomplishes a new covenant with God. Jesus reposes in the new ark and is God present among the people of a renewed Israel.

Daughter of Zion

The comparison of Jerusalem to Mary is a typological application of the Scriptures, showing her as the Daughter of Zion and as universal Mother. This theme is the title for an important study of Mary by Ignace de la Potterie entitled *Mary in the Mystery of the*

Covenant. Both René Laurentin and Stanislaus Lyonnet, not, however, Raymond E. Brown,[7] see a Marian application and an echo from the above texts in the angelic salutation: "And coming to her, he said, 'Hail, favored one! The Lord is with you'" (Lk 1:28). Laurentin and Lyonnet see in texts which Luke applies to Mary a play on words and an allusion coming from four prophetic texts (Is 66:7; Jl 2:21-23; Zp 3:14; Zc 9:9) which speak of God's dwelling within the city of Jerusalem:

> "Do not be afraid, Mary, for you have found favor with God" (Lk 1:30).
>
> "Behold, you will conceive in your womb and bear a son, and you shall name him Jesus. He will be great and will be called Son of the Most High" (Lk 1:31-32a).
>
> "and the Lord God will give him the throne of David his father, and he will rule over the house of Jacob forever, and of his Kingdom there will be no end" (Lk 1:32b-33).
>
> "For today in the city of David a savior has been born for you who is Messiah and Lord" (Lk 2:11).

Such a penetration of prophetic texts on the part of Luke is based on his reading of the Hebrew Scriptures through the Septuagintal version. He used them in a Christian midrash identifying Mary as the Daughter of Zion, that is with Jerusalem and all of the people of Israel, purified through the Exile experience and now heiress to the promises of salvation. Mary, as part of the poor of Yahweh (*anawîm*), is also the remnant of Israel, that is, the poor and the humble: "But I will leave as a remnant in your midst a people humble and lowly, who shall take refuge in the name of the Lord; the remnant of Israel" (Zp 3:12-13). Ancient Israel on pilgrimage towards its messianic redemption realizes itself in this her daughter, a woman of Israel. The Lucan narrative echoes Exodus theology: God leading the people out through the desert to the promised land. In the Marian dimension of Luke this rereading of the prophets takes on an ecclesial and eschatological meaning.

In the matter of Mary/Jerusalem as universal Mother, the

prophets associated Jerusalem with the notion of universal mother to the nations, especially after the Babylonian Exile. The Exile occurred because of the infidelity of Israel to the covenant:

> "When you have children and grandchildren, and have grown old in the land, should you then degrade yourselves by fashioning an idol in any form and by this evil done in his sight provoke the Lord, your God, I call heaven and earth this day to witness against you, that you shall all quickly perish from the land which you will occupy when you cross the Jordan. You shall not live in it for any length of time but shall be promptly wiped out. The Lord will scatter you among the nations, and there shall remain but a handful of you among the nations to which the Lord will lead you" (Dt 4:25-27).

> "Of you who were numerous as the stars in the sky, only a few will be left, because you would not hearken to the voice of the Lord, your God. Just as the Lord once took delight in making you grow and prosper, so will he now take delight in ruining and destroying you, and you will be plucked out of the land you are now entering to occupy. The Lord will scatter you among all the nations from one end of the earth to the other, and there you will serve strange gods of wood and stone, such as you and your fathers have not known. Among these nations you will find no repose, not a foot of ground to stand upon, for there the Lord will give you an anguished heart and wasted eyes and a dismayed spirit. You will lived in constant suspense and stand in dread both day and night, never sure of your existence" (Dt 28:62-66).

Despite the dispersion and dismemberment, God does not abandon Israel:

> "Yet there too you shall seek the Lord, your God; and you shall indeed find him when you search after him with your whole heart and your whole soul. In your distress, when all these things shall have come upon you, you shall finally return to the Lord, your God, and heed his voice. Since the Lord, your God, is a merciful God, he will not abandon and destroy you, nor

forget the covenant which under oath he made with your fathers" (Dt 4:29-31).

"When all these things which I have set before you, the blessings and the curses, are fulfilled in you, and from among whatever nations the Lord, your God, may have dispersed you, you ponder them in your heart: then, provided that you and your children return to the Lord, your God, and heed his voice with all your heart and all your soul, just as I now command you, the Lord, your God, will change your lot; and taking pity on you, he will again gather you from all the nations wherein he has scattered you. Though you may have been driven to the farthest corner of the world, even from there will the Lord, your God, gather you; even from there will he bring you back. The Lord, your God, will then bring you into the land which your fathers once occupied, that you too may occupy it, and he will make you more prosperous and numerous than your fathers. The Lord, your God, will circumcise your hearts and the hearts of your descendants, that you may love the Lord, your God, with all your heart and all your soul, and so may live" (Dt 30:1-6).

Israel returns to the Land, to Jerusalem, being brought back by God in a second Exodus:

For now the Lord has spoken who formed me as his servant from the womb, that Jacob may be brought back to him and Israel gathered to him; and I am made glorious in the sight of the Lord, and my God is now my strength! It is too little, he says, for you to be my servant, to raise up the tribes of Jacob, and restore the survivors of Israel; I will make you a light to the nations, that my salvation may reach to the ends of the earth (Is 49:5-6).

"As the Lord lives, who brought the descendants of the house of Israel up from the land of the north" — and from all the lands to which I banished them; they shall again live on their own land (Jr 23:8).

They shall forget their disgrace and all the times they broke faith with me, when they live in security on their land with no one to frighten them. When I bring them back from among the peoples, I will gather them from the lands of their enemies, and will prove my holiness through them in the sight of many nations. Thus they shall know that I, the Lord, am their God, since I, who exiled them among the nations, will gather them back on their land, not leaving any of them behind. No longer will I hide my face from them, for I have poured out my spirit upon the house of Israel, says the Lord God (Ezk 39:26-29).

Israel will lead back to God even the pagan nations:

When the Lord has pity on Jacob and again chooses Israel and settles them on their own soil, the aliens will join them and be counted with the house of Jacob (Is 14:1).

Rise up in splendor! Your light has come, the glory of the Lord shines upon you. See, darkness covers the earth, and thick clouds cover the peoples; but upon you the Lord shines, and over you appears his glory. Nations shall walk by your light, and kings by your shining radiance. Raise your eyes and look about; they all gather and come to you: your sons come from afar, and your daughters in the arms of their nurses. Then you shall be radiant at what you see, your heart shall throb and overflow, for the riches of the sea shall be emptied out before you, the wealth of nations shall be brought to you. Caravans of camels shall fill you, dromedaries from Midian and Ephah; all from Sheba shall come bearing gold and frankincense, and proclaiming the praises of the Lord, all the flocks of Kedar shall be gathered for you, the rams of Nebaioth shall be your sacrifices; they will be acceptable offerings on my altar, and I will enhance the splendor of my house. What are these that fly along like clouds, like doves to their cotes? All the vessels of the sea are assembled, with the ships of Tarshish in the lead, to bring your children from afar with their silver and gold, in the name of the Lord, your God, the Holy One of Israel, who has glorified you (Is 60:1-9).

At that time they will call Jerusalem the Lord's throne; there all nations will be gathered together to honor the name of the

Lord at Jerusalem, and they will walk no longer in their
hardhearted wickedness (Jr 3:17).

The Temple becomes the privileged place of restoration:

Tell them: Thus speaks the Lord God: I will take the Israelites
from among the nations to which they have come, and gather
them from all sides to bring them back to their land (Ezk
37:21).

I will make them a covenant of peace; it shall be an everlasting
covenant with them, and I will multiply them, and put my
sanctuary among them forever. My dwelling shall be with
them; I will be their God, and they shall be my people. Thus
the nations shall know that it is I, the Lord, who make Israel
holy, when my sanctuary shall be set up among them forever
(Ezk 37:26-28).

Gather together our scattered people, free those who are the
slaves of the Gentiles, look kindly on those who are despised
and detested, and let the Gentiles know that you are our God.
Punish those who tyrannize over us and arrogantly mistreat us.
Plant your people in your holy place, as Moses promised (2 M
1:27-29).

We trust in God, that he will soon have mercy on us and gather
us together from everywhere under the heavens to his holy
Place, for he has rescued us from great perils and has purified
his Place (2 M 2:18).

All become members of the covenant:

the aliens will join them and be counted with the house of
Jacob (Is 14:1b).

And the foreigners who join themselves to the Lord, minister-
ing to him, loving the name of the Lord, and becoming his
servants — all who keep the Sabbath free from profanation
and hold to my covenant, them I will bring to my holy mountain and make joyful in my house of prayer; their holocausts
and sacrifices will be acceptable on my altar, for my house shall
be called a house of prayer for all peoples (Is 56:6-7).

I come to gather nations of every language; they shall come and see my glory. I will set a sign among them; from them I will send fugitives to the nations: to Tarshish, Put and Lud, Mosoch, Tubal and Javan, to the distant coastlands that have never heard of my fame, or seen my glory; and they shall proclaim my glory among the nations. They shall bring all your brethren from all the nations as an offering to the Lord, on horses and in chariots, in carts, upon mules and dromedaries, to Jerusalem, my holy mountain, says the Lord, just as the Israelites bring their offering to the house of the Lord in clean vessels. Some of these I will take as priests and Levites, says the Lord (Is 66:18-21).

See especially:

Many nations shall join themselves to the Lord on that day, and they shall be his people, and he will dwell among you, and you shall know that the Lord of hosts has sent me to you (Zc 2:15).

Jerusalem is hailed as "mother" of these nations and peoples; they are her children:

You shall ask yourself: "Who has borne me these? I was bereft and barren [exiled and repudiated]; who has reared them: I was left all alone; where then do these come from?" (Is 49:21).

A psalm of the Korahites. A song.

i

The Lord loves the city founded on holy mountains, loves the gates of Zion more than any dwelling in Jacob. Glorious things are said of you, O city of God! *Selah.*

ii

From Babylon and Egypt I count those who acknowledge the Lord. Philistia, Ethiopia, Tyre, of them it can be said: "This one was born there." But of Zion it must be said: "They all were born here." The Most High confirms this; the Lord notes in the register of the peoples: "This one was born here." *Selah.*

So all sing in their festive dance: "Within you is my true home"
(Ps 87).

A bright light will shine to all parts of the earth; many nations
shall come to you from afar, and the inhabitants of all the limits
of the earth, drawn to you by the name of the Lord God,
bearing in their hands their gifts for the King of heaven. Every
generation shall give joyful praise in you, and shall call you the
chosen one, through all ages forever. Accursed are all who
speak a harsh word against you; accursed are all who destroy
you and pull down your walls, and all who overthrow your
towers and set fire to your homes; but forever blessed are all
those who build you up. Go, then, rejoice over the children of
the righteous, who shall all be gathered together and shall
bless the Lord of the ages (Tb 13:11-13).

Jerusalem's surrounding walls, in reality, are similar to a womb
which encloses the Temple and all those who come back there to
adore the one true God.

This Marian rereading in a Christological-Marian manner for
salvation is especially apparent in John's Gospel. In the text of John
11:51-52 not only the dispersed of Israel but all children are reunited
(Jn 10:16; 16:32). There is need to listen to the words of Jesus and
to commit oneself to him in his reality as a person:

Simon Peter answered him, "Master, to whom shall we go?
You have the words of eternal life" (Jn 6:68).

Christ, the Lamb of God, the Suffering Servant (Jn 1:29, 36) brings
back dispersed humanity in another Temple and in another Jerusalem. Jesus himself is the true Temple:

Jesus answered and said to them, "Destroy this temple and in
three days I will raise it up." The Jews said, "This temple has
been under construction for forty-six years, and you will raise
it up in three days?" But he was speaking about the temple of
his body. Therefore, when he was raised from the dead, his
disciples remembered that he had said this, and they came to

believe the scripture and the word Jesus had spoken (Jn 2:19-22).

The Father and the Son are one:

> "The Father and I are one" (Jn 10:30).
>
> I saw no temple in the city, for its temple is the Lord God almighty and the Lamb (Rv 21:22).

The Church is gathered as one (Jn 10:16; 11:51-52; 12:32-33). Mary is the new Jerusalem and the universal mother, the ideal personification and model of Jerusalem. The Beloved Disciple represents the disciples of every age and time in John 19:26 (cf. Is 60:4; Ba 4:37; 5:4-5).[8]

In messianic terms, the Virgin is the universal woman and mother of the disciples of Jesus, that is, of the dispersed ones of God's children. They are united in the mystical temple of the person of Christ, to whom she has given human flesh and blood in her womb. The womb of Jerusalem is now the womb of Mary in the new creation and new redemption.

Mary: The Memory of Israel

In a remarkable book by Walter Brennan, *The Sacred Memory of Mary*, the theme of remembering is carefully developed. Mary is the memory of her people Israel. She ponders over and remembers God's promises (Lk 2:19, 51). She preserves her Jewish heritage and the messianic hopes of her people. Remembering is an important response of God's people throughout the Scriptures from the Torah to the Gospels. Remembering involves the significant events that have been accomplished in the midst of God's people and also the covenant given to them freely by the mercy (*hesed*) of God (Dt 4:9-10, 23, 32). This remembering (*anamnesis*) is universal (Dt 4:32a; 32:7a); it happened in the past generations (Dt 32:7b), from past times even from the beginning of creation (Ps 78:2; Is 46:8; Dt 4:32).

Hope and memory are related. Memory and Wisdom are related. Wisdom is remembering God's salvific acts (Jdt 8:26, 29; Si 39:1-7; 44:1-50:21, 27-28).

In Judaism the prodigious acts of God are seen as real today. In Judaic belief these events have almost the same significance as sacraments. Memory actualizes in the present; it motivates, it re-enacts through the liturgy, especially at the celebration of Passover. The faith of God's people both today and in the future comes about inasmuch as it is verified in the times gone by. The midrashic method of scriptural interpretation demonstrates such faith and actualization of faith in the commentaries and sermons based on the Hebrew texts. Even from the beginning of time the Exodus Event was foreseen (cf. *De Vita Moysis* 11:288 of Philo). Deuteronomy in its sermons and *pareneses* is a book of hopeful remembering for God's children and people (Dt 5:14-15; 8:2, 5; 9:4-7; 15:12-15; 24:17-22; Ezk 20:43-44; 36:31-32; Mi 6:3-5).

Memory stimulates hope in moments and times of persecution and personal suffering. Israel's memory helps her to realize her salvation:

> In you our ancestors trusted; they trusted and you rescued them. To you they cried out and they escaped; in you they trusted and were not disappointed (Ps 22:5-6).

> O God, we have heard with our own ears; our ancestors have told us the deeds you did in their days, with your own hand in days of old (Ps 44:2).

> I consider the days of old; the years long past I remember. In the night I meditate in my heart; I ponder and my spirit broods (Ps 77:6-7).

> I will remember the deeds of the Lord; yes, your wonders of old I will remember (Ps 77:12).

> I remember the days of old; I ponder all your deeds; the works of your hands I recall (Ps 143:5).

> Then they remembered the days of old and Moses, his servant; Where is he who brought up out of the sea the shepherd of his

flock? Where is he who put his holy spirit in their midst? (Is 63:11).

Study the generations long past and understand; has anyone hoped in the Lord and been disappointed? Has anyone perse-vered in his fear and been forsaken? has anyone called upon him and been rebuffed? (Si 2:10).

But then I remembered the mercies of the Lord, his kindness through ages past; for he saves those who take refuge in him, and rescues them from every evil (Si 51:8).

And so, consider this from generation to generation, that none who hope in him shall fail in strength (1 M 2:61).

The Exodus Event is especially bound up with memory:

"Perhaps you will say to yourselves, 'These nations are greater than we. How can we dispossess them?' But do not be afraid of them. Rather, call to mind what the Lord, your God, did to Pharaoh and to all Egypt: the great testings which your own eyes have seen, the signs and wonders, his strong hand and outstretched arm with which the Lord, your God, brought you out. The same also will he do to all the nations of whom you are now afraid" (Dt 7:17-19).

i

Praise the Lord, who is so good; God's love endures forever; Praise the God of gods; God's love endures forever; Praise the Lord of lords; God's love endures forever;

ii

Who alone has done great wonders, God's love endures forever; Who skillfully made the heavens, God's love endures forever; Who spread the earth upon the waters, God's love endures forever; Who made the great lights, God's love endures forever; The sun to rule the day, God's love endures forever; The moon and stars to rule the night, God's love endures forever;

iii

Who struck down the firstborn of Egypt, God's love endures forever; And led Israel from their midst, God's love endures forever; With mighty hand and outstretched arm, God's love endures forever; Who split in two the Red Sea, God's love endures forever; And led Israel through, God's love endures forever; But swept Pharaoh and his army into the Red Sea, God's love endures forever; Who led the people through the desert, God's love endures forever;

iv

Who struck down great kings, God's love endures forever; Slew powerful kings, God's love endures forever; Sihon, king of the Amorites, God's love endures forever; Og, king of Bashan, God's love endures forever; And made their lands a heritage, God's love endures forever; A heritage for Israel, God's servant, God's love endures forever.

v

The Lord remembered us in our misery, God's love endures forever; Freed us from our foes, God's love endures forever; And gives food to all flesh, God's love endures forever.

vi

Praise the God of heaven, God's love endures forever (Ps 136).

Israel remembers both the events and persons of the past:

In you our ancestors trusted; they trusted and you rescued them. To you they cried out and they escaped; in you they trusted and were not disappointed (Ps 22:5-6).

Then Zechariah his father, filled with the Holy Spirit, prophesied, saying: "Blessed be the Lord, the God of Israel, for he has visited and brought redemption to his people. He has raised up a horn for our salvation within the house of David his servant" (Lk 1:67-69).

Mary as a woman of Israel and daughter of Zion remembers and ponders over the words and events of God. The word *symballousa* used of her in Luke means to turn over and over again in one's mind and heart in order to face what is happening either through life's experiences or God's revelation:

And Mary kept all these things, reflecting on them in her heart (Lk 2:19).

He went down with them and came to Nazareth, and was obedient to them; and his mother kept all these things in her heart (Lk 2:51).

Symballousa can mean to interpret, to give the correct meaning to something, to think about and consider. In Greek literature the word *symballein* means revelation through an oracle (cf. the Oracle of Delphi from Michelangelo's painting in the Sistine Chapel). There is a dynamic development of Mary's faith through her memory.[9]

Mary is likewise prophetically foreshadowed in the Old Testament. There are several references in the Infancy Narratives and in the Johannine literature that explicitly and implicitly cite certain passages from the Old Testament. These texts are also referred to in *Lumen Gentium*, 55 (cf. Gn 3:15; Is 7:14; Mi 5:2).

Isaiah 7:14

Matthew's use of Isaiah 7:14 is the most important text of the Hebrew Scriptures for the Church's mariological reflections of the first centuries. The text formed part of the chains of Scripture (*catenae*) which were used during the patristic period to explain the role of Mary in her virginity and in the history of salvation. In the early Christian writings she is always presented in relationship to the primary purpose of the New Testament which has a Christological and soteriological focus. Incidentally, one of the earliest Christian paintings of this prophecy is found in the catacombs (*Catechism of the Catholic Church*, p. 13).

Isaiah 7:14 as a Hebrew text is not speaking of Mary but of the immediate historical situation during the time of Ahaz. For the historical background the time described in Isaiah 7:14 is reflected in 2 Kings 16:1-17, 2 Chronicles 28:5-25, and Isaiah 7:1-16. The *'almâ* is the young wife of Achaz the King. The son to be born will be the great and holy king Hezekiah who is probably the "Emmanuel" promised to the Davidic and messianic line of southern Israel, Judah. Thanks to Hezekiah, the House of David would not vanish. His birth between 733-732 BC.E. (Is 7:22-25) occurred while the country was already ravaged by wars, and, within a short time, Tiglat-Pilezer would defeat the kings at Damascus in 732 when Hezekiah would be born — "Bread and honey he would eat" — this happens at the time he is able to say *abbah* and *immah* or "daddy" and "mommy" — Is 8:4. (Gn 4:11 helps for understanding that the child spoken of is reaching the age of reason).

Matthew 1:23 cites the verse of Isaiah 7:14 in the context of the Annunciation to Joseph through a dream. The text, likewise, has to be seen within the context of the genealogy just given and in the background of Joseph belonging to the royal line of David. To interpret it ecclesially the use of the *sensus plenior* (the fullness of a Scripture passage in the light of all the Scriptures) is the preferred method for its citation in conciliar texts. Canonical criticism sees the final redaction of a scriptural passage such as Isaiah 7:14 as the one that gives us the intended interpretation or inspiration of the writer. In Matthew 1:23, Jesus is identified with the name Emmanuel. This name Emmanuel is a most special and unique use of a title; a *hapax* (one time only) appearance in the New Testament. In an extended sense and by looking at further passages in Matthew 16:18 and Matthew 28:20 (cf. Lk 1:32-33) an ecclesial dimension to this Christological title can be seen, for it speaks of Jesus being present to the community even to the end of time.

The writers of the New Testament had more frequent recourse to the Greek translation of the Old Testament called the Septuagint, and Matthew 1:23 refers to this translation calling the young maiden who is to be the mother of Emmanuel "O Parthenos" (the Virgin). The New Testament is in harmony and complementarity with the Old Testament (Mt 5:17), that is, Jesus comes to fulfill not do away with. The later Greek translations done by Symmachus and Theodoton remove *parthenos* from the Greek of Isaiah 7:14 and place a word meaning a young maiden (*neanis*) who is not necessarily a virgin. There may have been a Jewish concern about Mary, the

Mother of Jesus, being known as a virgin in these changes. The text from Isaiah would be a dangerous "proof text" in the hands of the Jewish-Christians if left as the Septuagint reads. This concern about the intended meaning of Isaiah 7:14 continues today. A leading Jewish scholar (Harry Orlinsky) is pursuing the background of the term *parthenos* as well as all of the other surrounding texts and information about it (*The Interpreter's Dictionary of the Bible*, suppl. vol.). Catholic scholars, basing their work on the Septuagint and Matthew 1:23, interpret the text as speaking of the virginity of Mary. Other exegetes situate the text more in a Christological interpretation than in a mariological one.[10] Some of the earliest uses of Isaiah 7:14 outside the Old Testament are found in Justin Martyr. The patristic literature from the fourth century abounds in use of the text to demonstrate the virginity of Mary.[11]

Micah 5:2

The original text of Micah 5:1-5 has to be seen in the light of the promise that Jerusalem, the Daughter of Zion, will be rescued from the Babylonian captivity. The symbolic "Daughter of Zion" becomes important in later Mariological reflection, but its Marian rereading is based on the accurate historical foundations of this expression in the Bible. The *ophel* or high place known as Zion is where David, a messianic king, had his ancient throne (Mi 4:8). The text speaks of a commander being born in Bethlehem-Ephrathah, that is from the ancient House of David (Mi 5:1b and Mi 4:8; 2 S 5:4-10; 7:1-17). Further reflections on this text are seen in Micah 5:1-4, John 7:40-42 and Matthew 2:5-6. There also may be a more delicate and subtle use of the idea from the text in Luke 2:6-7. There seems to be an echo of the fuller text of Micah in Luke. See the parallels:

Micah 5	Luke 2:4-14
v. 1 Bethlehem	v. 4 Bethlehem, Judah
v. 2 time. . . give birth	vv. 6-7 days. . . birth
v. 3 glory of Lord	vv. 8-9 glory of the Lord
v. 4 peace	v. 14 peace[12]

Genesis 3:15

To understand the context of Genesis 3:15 it is necessary to read Genesis 2:18-3:21 in which Eve is the "woman" of Genesis. There is also the presence of the serpent or the "deceiver" (cf. Ws 2:24; Jn 8:44) or those who become followers of the deceiver. The contrast between the seed of the serpent and that of the woman is important; also whether "seed" is used singularly or in a collective sense. There may be a relationship with John 3:14-15 as well. Some of the Aramaic texts which comment on Genesis (the Targums of Neofiti and Pseudo-Jonathan) have the notion of an individual messianic figure crushing the head of the serpent. The Targum on Genesis 3:15 is very important. According to a reading of the Targum, one sees that the woman of Genesis 3:15 not only represents humanity in general, but also the community of Israel in pilgrimage towards a messianic redemption. In a word, the Elect People are seen with their Messiah. The readings from the Jewish Targums help with a realization that the notion of a promised salvation and hope in that salvation was known to the early Jewish community.[13]

In the book of Revelation (the Apocalypse) there is a reference to the serpent within a definite Christological and ecclesiological symbolism. Reminiscences of Genesis 3:15 are echoed in Revelation 12:9 which identifies the serpent with the Devil, Satan. Other significant verses for consideration in Revelation are 12:4, 5, 12, 15, 16, 17. The Targum for Genesis 3:15 reads:

> I will place enmities between thee and the woman, between the descendants of your children and her children, and it will come about that when the woman's children observe the precepts of the Torah, they will take aim and crush your head. Whenever, however, they forget the precepts of the Torah, you will be the one who lays the snares and bites their heels. Nevertheless, there is a remedy for them, while for you there is none. They will find a remedy (or cure) for the heel in the time of the Messiah.

This text is found in a recension of the Targum Pseudo-Jonathan which is substantially the same in the foundational codices and fragments of Neofiti Targum.

E. Hoskyns (1920), A.-M. Dubarle (1951), P. Gächter (1953), F.-M. Braun (1953), and A. Feuillet (1964) see in the scene at the foot of the Cross (Jn 19:25-27) Mary as the antitype to Eve who, side by side with the new Adam (Jesus), is in conflict with the serpent (Gn 3:15: Gächter, Braun and possibly Dubarle), and Mary becomes the mother of all the living as Eve had been (Gn 3:20: Hoskyns, Dubarle, Feuillet) with the help of the Lord (Gn 4:1: Feuillet).

Raymond E. Brown in his commentary on John says:

> By way of summary, then, we may say that the Johannine picture of Jesus' mother becoming the mother of the Beloved Disciple seems to evoke the OT themes of Lady Zion's giving birth to a new people in the messianic age, and of Eve and her offspring. The imagery flows over into the imagery of the Church who brings forth children modeled after Jesus and the relationship of loving care that must bind the children to their mother. We do not wish to press the details of this symbolism or to pretend that it is without obscurity. But there are enough confirmations to give reasonable assurance that we are on the right track.[14]

The notion of hope is also present in Romans 16:20: "then the God of peace will quickly crush Satan under your feet. The grace of our Lord Jesus be with you" where it seems that Paul is reflecting on Genesis 3:15.

Revelation 12 is full of ecclesial symbolism in its imaging of the woman clothed with the sun. Who is the woman? In the context of the whole Bible she is the People of God both of Old Testament and New Testament; she is therefore the Church, the Synagogue, the Spouse of God. The twelve stars represent both the twelve tribes (Judaism) and the twelve apostles of Jesus (Christianity):

The wall of the city had twelve courses of stones as its

foundation, on which were inscribed the twelve names of the twelve apostles of the Lamb (Rv 21:14).

The birth pangs are not those of the initial birth or Incarnation, but rather sufferings of the Messiah in the Paschal/Passover Mystery. Compare texts from Revelation and John:

> She gave birth to a son, a male child, destined to rule all the nations with an iron rod. Her child was caught up to God and his throne (Rv 12:5).

> "When a woman is in labor, she is in anguish because her hour has arrived; but when she has given birth to a child, she no longer remembers the pain because of her joy that a child has been born into the world. So you also are now in anguish. But I will see you again, and your hearts will rejoice, and no one will take your joy away from you" (Jn 16:21-22).

> Jesus answered and said to him, "Amen, amen, I say to you, no one can see the Kingdom of God without being born from above." Nicodemus said to him, "How can a person once grown old be born again? Surely he cannot reenter his mother's womb and be born again, can he?" Jesus answered, "Amen, amen, I say to you, no one can enter the Kingdom of God without being born of water and Spirit. What is born of flesh is flesh and what is born of spirit is spirit. Do not be amazed that I told you, 'You must be born from above'" (Jn 3:3-7).

The "generation" or offspring recalls:

> I will proclaim the decree of the Lord, who said to me, "You are my son; today I am your father" (Ps 2:7).

and

> "We ourselves are proclaiming this good news to you that what God promised our ancestors he has brought to fulfillment for us, [their] children, by raising up Jesus, as it is written in the second psalm, 'You are my son; this day I have begotten

you.' And that he raised him from the dead never to return to corruption he declared in this way, 'I shall give you the benefits assured to David'" (Ac 13:32-34).

The texts summoned up are a rich source of messianic references:

> Only ask it of me, and I will make your inheritance the nations, your possession the ends of the earth. With an iron rod you shall shepherd them, like a clay pot you will shatter them (Ps 2:8-9).
>
> *A psalm of David.*
>
> The Lord says to you, my lord: "Take your throne at my right hand, while I make your enemies your footstool" (Ps 110:1).
>
> She gave birth to a son, a male child, destined to rule all the nations with an iron rod (Rv 12:5a).

These texts of the Psalms are also used in Acts as referring to the Resurrection of Jesus.

Satan has a limited time for his persecution and his temptation of the People of God:

> When the Dragon saw that it had been thrown down to the earth, it pursued the woman who had given birth to the male child. But the woman was given the two wings of the great eagle, so that she could fly to her place in the desert, where, far from the serpent, she was taken care of for a year, two years, and a half-year. The serpent, however, spewed a torrent of water out of his mouth after the woman to sweep her away with the current. But the earth helped the woman and opened its mouth and swallowed the flood that the Dragon spewed out of its mouth. Then the Dragon became angry with the woman and went off to wage war against the rest of her offspring, those who keep God's commandments and bear witness to Jesus. It took its position on the sand of the sea (Rv 12:13-18).

The woman becomes the spouse of the Lamb:

I also saw the holy city, a new Jerusalem, coming down out of
heaven from God, prepared as a bride adorned for her husband
(Rv 21:2).

She is the New Jerusalem:

He took me in spirit to a great, high mountain and showed me
the holy city Jerusalem coming down out of heaven from God
(Rv 21:10).

Also:

No longer shall your sun go down, or your moon withdraw, for
the Lord will be your light forever, and the days of your
mourning shall be at an end (Is 60:20).

Thus Revelation 12 transcribes through a symbolic code the Paschal
Mystery of Jesus Christ, which is realized, that is, actualized in the
Church.

Is Mary also the Woman of Revelation 12? Most exegetes
favor Mary being the Church or both peoples of Old Testament and
New Testament. In John 19:25-27 Mary has a mother's role for the
Beloved Disciple (cf. Rv 12:17). Mary is already filled with God's
grace (Lk 1:28, 47-49). She is called *kécharitôménê*. Mary in reality
gives birth to the Messiah as the Daughter of Zion, the People of
God (Rv 12:5) seen in a wider secondary and accommodated sense.
Mary is in pain while presenting the Gospel on the part of the
Church. She, too, advances in a pilgrimage of faith (*Lumen Gentium*,
58; Lk 2:48, 50, 51b; 8:19-21; 11:27-28) and is part of the Jerusalem
Church which suffered (Ac 1:14; 4:5-31; 5:17-41; 6:9-7:60; 8:1-3;
9:1-2; 12:1-9). Mary is also the spouse of the Lamb (Rv 21:1-22:5).
This passage has been symbolically used in the liturgy for the
mystery of the Assumption.

The complementarity of the two Testaments is seen through
an important text: "Do not think that I have come to abolish the law
or the prophets. I have come not to abolish but to fulfill" (Mt 5:17).
Luke's Gospel becomes clearer by looking at it in the expressions

paralleled in the Septuagint version of the Old Testament.[15] Both textually, structurally, and content-wise Luke's dependency on the Septuagint is seen; it is especially apparent in the Marian references of the Infancy Narrative.

Endnotes

[1] Georges Gharib, Ermanno M. Toniolo, Luigi Gambero, and Gerardo Di Nola, eds., *Testi Mariani del Primo Millennio* (Roma: Città Nuova Editrice, 4 volumes, 1988-1991).

[2] Wolfgang Beinert, *Parlare di Maria oggi?* (Catania, Italy: Edizioni Paoline, 1975) 24-25.

[3] Read Vatican II Dogmatic Constitution on Divine Revelation, *Dei verbum*, for some contemporary ecclesial understanding of these texts: Austin Flannery, gen. ed., *Vatican Council II: The Conciliar and Post Conciliar Documents*, new rev. ed., vol. 1 (Collegeville, MN: Liturgical Press, 1992).

[4] Refer to: Ignace de la Potterie, *Mary in the Mystery of the Covenant*, trans. Bertrand Buby (New York: Alba House, 1992); John Macquarrie, *Mary for All Christians* (Grand Rapids, MI: Eerdmans, 1990); Aristide Serra, *E C'era la Madre di Gesù. . . (Gv 2, 1): saggi di esegesi biblico-mariana, 1978-1988* (Milano: Edizioni Cens-Marianum, 1989).

[5] Numerous studies on this topic are available in Marian periodicals, including *Marian Studies, Marianum, Nuovo Dizionario di Mariologia, Nuovo Dizionario di Teologia, Marian Library Studies* (doctoral theses of European and American scholars), *Bulletin de la Societé Francaises d'Etudes Mariales* or *Etudes Mariales, Testi Mariani del Primo Millennio* in four volumes, *Ephemeridies Mariolgicae, Maria, Etudes sur la Sainte Vierge* (by J.Du Manoir), *Maria in Sacra Scriptura: Acta Congressus Mariologici-Mariani*, 1967, volumes 1-6, *Virgo Immaculata: Acta Congressus Mariologici-Mariani, 1955-58*, volumes 1-18. Selections from these resource materials speak to the richness of Marian inspiration from the Sacred Scriptures. Eamon Carroll reviews these collections each year at the Mariological Society of America and in its acta in *Marian Studies*.

[6] See Bertrand Buby, "Research on the Biblical Approach and the Method of Exegesis Appearing in the Greek Homiletic Texts of the Late Fourth and Early Fifth Centuries, Emphasizing the Incarnation Especially the Nativity and Mary's Place Within It," *Marian Library Studies*, 13-14 (1981-82).

[7] René Laurentin, *Structure et Théologie de Luc I-II* (Paris: Gabalda, 1957). Stanislaus Lyonnet, "Chaire Kécharitôméné," *Biblica* 20 (1939): 131-141. Raymond E. Brown, *The Birth of the Messiah: A Commentary on the Infancy Narratives in the Gospels of Matthew and Luke*, new updated edition (New York: Doubleday, 1993) 320-328, 353n45, 465, 637, 639-640, 648, 688.

[8] See Theodore Koehler's summary of the interpretation of these verses in his *Les principales interprétations traditionelles de Jn. 19, 25-27 pendant les douze premiers siècles, Etudes Mariales* 16 (1959) 119-155. Also note the commentary of Rudolph Bultmann in his *The Gospel of John* (Philadelphia: Westminster, 1971) 671-673.

[9] See Bertrand Buby, "The Biblical Prayer of Mary (Luke 2:19, 51)," *Review for Religion* 39 (1980): 577-581. Also, Walter Brennan, *The Sacred Memory of Mary* (New York: Paulist, 1988) and Ben F. Meyer, "'But Mary Kept All These Things. . .' (Luke 2, 19.51)," *Catholic Biblical Quarterly* 26 (1964): 31-49. Mary ponders over, realizes, interprets. She turns to

the Old Testament in her Magnificat just as a wise scribe would do (Si 39:1-11). She does this because she doesn't understand the mystery in its fullness — Jesus in the Temple (cf. Lk 2:48, 51b; *Lumen Gentium* 58). Mary was attentive to the works and words of Jesus her son (Lk 8:19-21; Lk 11:27-28). Various texts in Acts show the preaching about Jesus centered on salvation history (Ac 2:22-36; 3:13, 14-15; 5:30; 7:52; 10:38; 13:26-43). It is Mary who was also a participant in this salvific action of her son.

[10] The word *'almah* does not mean virgin, but a marriageable young girl. The word for virgin in Hebrew is *betbulah*; it is used 3 times in the Old Testament, out of its 51 appearances, to mean explicitly "virgin" (Lv 21:13f.; Dt 22:19; Ezk 44:22). The entire list of passages is studied in the *Theological Dictionary of the Old Testament*, vol. II (Grand Rapids, MI: Eerdmans, 1975) 338-343.

[11] For the best modern exegetical information consult: Raymond Brown, *The Birth of the Messiah*; René Laurentin, *A Short Treatise on the Blessed Virgin Mary* (Washington, NJ: AMI Press, 1991) and *The Truth of Christmas Beyond the Myths: The Gospels of the Infancy of Christ* (Petersham, MA: Bede, 1986).

[12] For a critique of the use of Micah 5:2-3, Genesis 3:15, and Isaiah 7:14 in *Lumen Gentium* of Vatican II see Charles H. Miller's thesis: *"As It Is Written": The Use of Old Testament References in the Documents of Vatican Council II* (St Louis, MO: Marianist Communications Center, 1973) 49-60.

[13] This goes against what modern scholars, primarily German ones, are saying about this text. See Charles Miller's thesis, pp. 49-56, to have the latter opinion in distinction to that of the Targums.

[14] Raymond E. Brown, intro. and trans., *The Gospel According to John* (xiii-xxi), Anchor Bible 29A (Garden City, NY: Doubleday, 1970) 926.

[15] Klemens Stock, "La Vocazione di Maria Lc 1,26-38," *Marianum* XLV (1983): 112-113 n41.

Chapter Two

MARY: MOTHER OF JESUS

Mary of Nazareth was a Jewish woman who gave birth to Jesus the Jew; both Mary and Jesus were born into Judaism, the Judaism of the first century. In the book of Esther (C:16) a woman of Israel prays to God: "As a child I was wont to hear from the people of the land of my forefathers that you, O Lord, chose Israel from among all peoples, and our fathers from among all their ancestors, as a lasting heritage, and that you fulfilled all your promises to them." Mary prayed in her Magnificat in that same spirit, continuing the faith and dedication to the God of Israel; therefore: "We can look upon Mary as she who stands at the crossroads of salvation history where the two traditions meet and whose presence there enables us to recognize what is common to them both, thereby calling us to an even deeper dialogue."[16]

There are important considerations to keep in mind in an approach to a study of Mary, the Galilean Jew, and her son Jesus. What is known about Mary, the mother of Jesus, from an historical point of view? Are the Gospels our primary source for seeing her in her Jewishness as a woman from Nazareth? How do we get a true image of her when we are removed from her by almost twenty centuries? We know Mary from a particular religious image in the Roman Catholic Church and even a more specific image in the Marian devotions. With all of the layers of tradition and the erudition of Mariologists, is it still possible to find the Mary of

Nazareth who was an ordinary Jewish woman of the first century of our common era?

First of all, the Gospels are not in any sense of the term historical chronicles or biographies of Jesus — much less a biography of Mary. The four "canonical" Gospels are the preached, the proclaimed, and the faith-witnessed accounts about Jesus Christ, the hero of the Christian world. Even though less can be known of Mary from these same Gospels, they are, nevertheless, the primary sources for a person named Mary of Nazareth, the Mother of Jesus. The Gospels were written by four evangelists, some of whom surely were Jewish. Most of our information about Mary comes from an anthropology and socio-religious perspective that was largely male-dominated, and from a Jewish and early Christian environment that was patriarchal and Mediterranean.

Fortunately, with the advances in biblical methodologies and historical-critical analysis, it is possible to get *behind* the texts of the New Testament which mention Mary and see in the sparse references to her a faith-filled woman of Israel spoken of within the context of the Christian *kerygma* or proclamation which was entirely centered on Jesus, the Christ. Moreover, recent sociological and anthropological studies have helped us to see the ethos, mores, and patterns of behavior that were characteristic of the world from which Jesus and Mary came, namely the eastern and Semitic part of the Mediterranean.[17]

Recent studies offer fresh insights for contemporary scholars regarding Mary. One book, *The Galilee in Late Antiquity*, centers on Galilean society and culture. It was composed by a gathering of scholars from America, Israel and Europe, including Jews and Christians, historians, sociologists, as well as New Testament and rabbinic scholars. By the term "Late Antiquity" the scholars meant events and sources from the first century C.E. to the Arab conquest of the seventh century. One of the chief scholars is Harold Clark Kee, who challenges a number of common assumptions in New Testament research. He claims that the synagogue in the time of Jesus was not a definable structure but a group of people who used private dwellings or small public halls for prayer and the reading of Scripture. Jesus' associations were with a wide range of peoples, including Gentiles and Roman officials, reflecting the heterogeneous society at the time. The cultural background of the Gospels was bilingual, reflecting a large degree of Greek and Aramaic influence.[18]

In these new studies the Gospel of Matthew emerges as a Galilean document of a deviant group that considered itself Jewish but was not regarded as such by the main Jewish community. This could also apply to the Pseudo-Clementine literature, which may belong to the Galilee of the second century. To understand Mary of Nazareth, such studies are imperative. It is by building the framework of a larger picture puzzle that the pieces are eventually put together for discovery of her portrait.

The Gospels indicate that Mary's son, Jesus, taught in synagogues. Recent studies in archeology and in epigraphy assert that the term *synagogue* refers to Jewish and Christian gatherings rather than to a structure. Jesus then would be teaching not in a synagogue as a place, but rather in a gathering designated for prayer. This is consistent with Joseph Gutmann's inference from archeological evidence that no synagogue buildings from Palestine in the first century can be positively identified. He concluded further that the synagogue began to develop as an institution housed in a definable structure only after the destruction of the Temple and with the Pharisaic-rabbinic assumption of authority within the Jewish community, i.e., 40-50 years after the death of Jesus of Nazareth.[19]

The manner in which Mark speaks of "their" synagogues seems to contrast with "ours" or the Christian synagogues. Matthew goes further, changing the term "synagogue" to "*ekklesia*" or church (cf. Mt 16:18; 18:17). "The consistent picture is that the Christian counterpart of the synagogue — that is, the ekklesia — is the gathered community of those who saw themselves as God's people."[20]

Private homes or privately owned buildings were places used for the gatherings in which Jesus found himself teaching and healing in Galilee. This is important for our reflections on Mary of Nazareth for she appears for the first time in Mark 3:31-35. She is seeking Jesus, her son, who is teaching at a gathering in a home not far from Nazareth:

> His mother and his brothers arrived. Standing outside they sent word to him and called him. A crowd seated around him told him, "Your mother and your brothers [and your sisters] are outside asking for you." But he said to them in reply, "Who are my mother and [my] brothers?" And looking around at those seated in the circle he said, "Here are my mother and my brothers. [For] whoever does the will of God is my brother and sister and mother."

Nazareth

Contrary to what was taught and studied in the 1950's through the '80's, Nazareth is now considered an important village overlooking the main route that led south and west from Sepphoris to Caesarea and was only a short distance from Japhia. In other words, Jesus grew up in one of the busiest trade centers in northern Israel or Galilee. Even though only 1500-2000 people lived there, they were probably in contact with the dominant Greco-Roman culture.

Recent excavations are taking place at Sepphoris, a little village just northwest of, and three to five miles from, Nazareth. It was one of the four major centers of Greco-Roman culture and Roman administration for all of Galilee, having a theater, a hippodrome and temples. Although the reported occupation of Jesus as a *tekton* has traditionally been rendered as "carpenter," it means "builder" and could well have included masonry. This opens the possibility that Jesus and his father, of similar trade according to Matthew 13:55, may have worked in the building of the adjacent Greco-Roman style city of Sepphoris. "To assume that Jesus and his first followers in Galilee were unaffected by or out of communication with Hellenistic culture is historically untenable."[21]

In the Galilee of Jesus, Palestinian Aramaic would have been his mother tongue, but certainly Jesus also knew Greek. "... for Jesus to have conversed with inhabitants of cities in the Galilee, and especially of cities of the Decapolis and the Phoenician region, he would have had to have known Greek, certainly at the conversational level."[22] At the trial of Jesus before Pilate, Pilate would have been speaking colloquial Greek, not the Aramaic language of Jesus.

It is conceivable that many women, especially strong leaders, knew how to read and write and most likely taught their children, both boys and girls, these communication skills. Jezebel wrote and signed letters for the king. Such precedents lead to an assumption that women would easily want to learn and use these skills which would have been the equivalent of computer literacy in those days.

The Bible is over 95% male-oriented. Of 1,426 names in the Bible only 111 names are women's. This enormous gap between the number of women's and of men's names signals the male-centered concerns of biblical literature. Mary of Nazareth, however, is among the women most mentioned in the Bible, that is, in the New Testament. She is an exception to the rule and almost for that reason an exceptional woman. The disparity between normative text and daily existence is particularly characteristic of gender.[23] Hence, very little is said of the actual experience of women in daily life and especially in the private life of the home. The silent years of Nazareth are all so true!

Nazareth in the first century was a village. As such, its people were farmers. (Even today the Israeli kibbutzim are corporate farms which are most successful in the Galilee district.) The "family household" remained the determinative location for most Israelite women, men, and children. Joseph and Mary with their child Jesus were a "family household." Usually extended families of several generations made up a family household. It was particularly difficult for a newlywed bride to feel accepted in such complexity. The stresses of a complex family had to be carefully managed in order for the viability of a family household to be preserved. This could account for Mary seeking out Jesus early in the story of Mark.

The women worked very hard. They put in at least five hours

in the fields of grain — barley and wheat. Near their household they looked after children while caring for vines, gardens, and fruit trees. They were the clothes makers, the food gatherers and preservers. One can catch a glimpse of such labor in a description of the valiant woman:

> When one finds a worthy wife, her value is far beyond pearls. Her husband, entrusting his heart to her, has an unfailing prize. She brings him good, and not evil, all the days of her life. She obtains wool and flax and makes cloth with skillful hands. Like merchant ships, she secures her provisions from afar. She rises while it is still night, and distributes food to her household. She picks out a field to purchase; out of her earnings she plants a vineyard. She is girt about with strength, and sturdy are her arms. She enjoys the success of her dealings; at night her lamp is undimmed. She puts her hands to the distaff, and her fingers ply the spindle. She reaches out her hands to the poor, and extends her arms to the needy. She fears not the snow for her household; all her charges are doubly clothed. She makes her own coverlets; fine linen and purple are her clothing. Her husband is prominent at the city gates as he sits with the elders of the land. She makes garments and sells them, and stocks the merchants with belts. She is clothed with strength and dignity, and she laughs at the days to come. She opens her mouth in wisdom, and on her tongue is kindly counsel. She watches the conduct of her household, and eats not her food in idleness. Her children rise up and praise her; her husband, too, extols her: "Many are the women of proven worth, but you have excelled them all." Charm is deceptive and beauty fleeting; the woman who fears the Lord is to be praised. Give her a reward of her labors, and let her works praise her at the city gates (Pr 31:10-31).

One can learn about Mary's household through the simple imagery and metaphorical language about this valiant woman. More about Mary of Nazareth can be learned through the simple metaphors and parables in the language of Jesus in his home. Pottery, textiles, and basketmaking were part of a woman's skilled and artful labor. Two points can be made here. First, is the extraordinary amount of time, at least in comparison to modern life, involved in carrying out life-supporting daily activities.[24] Second, is the degree of technological expertise involved in all of these household skills and chores. Often the woman because of her skills in planning and experience was in control over the critical aspects of household life.[25]

In her maternal role of parenting, a woman normally would have nearly double the amount of pregnancies in order to bear the desired number of children to carry on the chores and responsibilities of the household.[26] Jesus is named a *tekton* in Mark's Gospel. He may have been, after Joseph's death, Mary's hope for the future. He would have been a skilled builder like Joseph, his foster-father who is named a *tekton* as well: "Is he not the carpenter, the son of Mary, and the brother of James and Joses and Judas and Simon?" (Mk 6:3a). Because of the strain and tension of work, childbearing, and all the incumbent responsibilities of a household, women normally lived to the age of thirty; men, since they didn't encounter the danger of birthing children, to forty years.[27] There is an apocryphal work which has many men die at age 49.

Women spent much time with children of both genders. Boys as well as girls learned responsibilities from their mother. An example of how mothers had a role of a wisdom figure is seen in Proverbs 4:1-9; 6:20; 8:1-36; 31:10-31. They cared for, educated, and socialized their children. Whereas some ancient Near Eastern societies apparently favored men over women in the relegation of authority over offspring, Israel exhibited parity of mothers and fathers in this respect (e.g. Ex 20:12). Mary thus exercised clear authority over Jesus in his years at Nazareth in the household: "He went down with them and came to Nazareth, and was obedient to them; and his mother kept all these things in her heart" (Lk 2:51). In fact the household with its family laws served as the primary locus of community justice. Mary's presence at Cana attests that a woman had extra-household concerns. Usually the mother managed and planned and was also responsible for interfamily arrangements and, probably, most marriages.[28]

Archeological discoveries in households attest to devotions of a religious nature in the home. Carol Meyers writes that women's modes of prayer during this first century may even have influenced some of the formal liturgical experiences preserved in the Psalter. There were probably few gender-based restrictions, except for the possibility of serving as priests, which hereditary office was also not available to most men. The Scriptures also attest to women's special role in funerals, in music composition, dance, and even in major public events (Ex 15:20-21; Jg 5; Jg 21:21; 1 S 18:6-7; 2 Ch 35:25; Jr 9:17).[29] Meyers continues her observations, stating that ". . . while God is presented largely through male imagery, the prevailing monotheism of scripture, along with the nonsexual nature of divine creativity and the occasional female metaphors for God, may have contributed toward the relative social unity of male and female in household settings."[30] Once again, this can be noticed in the description of the finding of the Child Jesus in the Temple:

> The child grew and became strong, filled with wisdom; and the favor of God was upon him. Each year his parents went to Jerusalem for the feast of Passover, and when he was twelve years old, they went up according to festival custom. After they had completed its days, as they were returning, the boy Jesus remained behind in Jerusalem, but his parents did not know it. Thinking that he was in the caravan, they journeyed for a day and looked for him among their relatives and acquaintances, but not finding him, they returned to Jerusalem to look for him. After three days they found him in the temple, sitting in the midst of the teachers, listening to them and asking them questions, and all who heard him were astounded at his understanding and his answers. When his parents saw him, they were astonished, and his mother said to him, "Son, why have you done this to us? Your father and I have been looking for you with great anxiety." And he said to them, "Why were you looking for me? Did you not know that I must be in my Father's house?" But they did not understand what he said to them. He went down with them and came to Nazareth, and was obedient to them, and his mother kept all these things in her heart (Lk 2:40-51).

Mary the Jew

Both Matthew's and Luke's New Testament Infancy Narratives indicate that Joseph and Mary were faithful observers of the law; they, undoubtedly, were Pharisees who believed in angels, the prophetical writings, and the commandments of the law. We find Joseph struggling with the question of Mary's pregnancy and what mode of divorce he would pursue (Mt 1:18-25). In Luke Mary observed the law of purification when presenting Jesus in the Temple (Lk 2:22-24). She was one among many Jewish women who could have been so described. Paul in his cryptic statement that involves mention of a woman who had to be Mary, says, "But when the fullness of time had come, God sent his Son, born of a woman, born under the law, to ransom those under the law, so that we might receive adoption" (Gal 4:4-5). It would seem then that the approach of both Jewish scholars, and Christian scholars who wrote an excursus of Mary in the New Testament, was to describe first century Judaism and women within that religious and sociological milieu. Preachers, poets, and Mariologists would have to complete the portrait with their gifts of mind and touch. Ann Johnson has given us a remarkable book in *Miryam of Judah*. Through collaboration with a rabbi, along with her own biblical meditation on the text of Matthew's genealogy, she has captured with beautiful prose the life and thought of Jewish women and refracted that life and light into a portrait of Mary. Reading her book provides a sense of the Jewishness of Mary and an appreciation of her woman forerunners, some of whom were Jewish. Reading or, better, praying this book immerses one into the Jewishness of Miryam of Judah, the mother of Jesus.[31]

A Jewish woman faithful to the law did not participate in public life. Even her chin was covered by the veil which she wore so that none of her traits were distinguished. The fact that in Mark's Gospel Mary is searching for Jesus and is familiar with his whereabouts leads to an almost certain conclusion that she is then a widow and has possession of all that Joseph owned. It seems that she is concerned about keeping the good reputation of the family and name of Joseph. She searches for Jesus either to rescue him from troublesome crowds or to preserve the good name of the family. Jesus' public activity and his preaching were jeopardizing that for which she and Joseph had worked so long and hard.

In view of a society wherein a man was not normally permitted to speak with a woman in public and a married man could not look at another married woman, one can appreciate how startled the disciples were when Jesus spoke with the Samaritan woman. Failures of this type could result in the woman being divorced. Thus there is understanding of the Baptist's severity toward Herod's living with his brother's wife or the shock that Antipater brought upon the people because of his behavior towards Salome. Young girls were kept confined within certain quarters of the house while the mother was permitted to be seen at the door that led to the courtyard. It was even more severe for the Alexandrian Jewish women. In a work written in Alexandria, the mother of the seven martyred sons attests, "I was a chaste maiden and did not leave my father's house. . ." (4 M).[32] Twice a year on certain occasions (the 15 of Ab and the Day of Atonement) there were religious dances when girls could dance in the surrounding vineyards of Jerusalem.

Among the lower classes a woman could assist her husband in his trade. Removed from the holy city of Jerusalem, the country woman could fetch water at a well, could work with her husband and children in the fields, sell olives at her door and serve at table. Only when a young woman was $12\frac{1}{2}$ could she receive money for what she had sold; her father dispensed her then of the vow to give everything to him. He still retained the right to approve her husband and did so more often than not. Mention of these few circumstances surrounding Jewish women during the time of Jesus makes for an understanding of how restrictive life was for women. The great freedom that we see Mary having at the wedding feast of Cana or in searching for Jesus shows that she was now the only survivor. This also may attest that Jesus was the only child, for a pattern of confinement would have been more appropriate if there were other children in the home with Mary. (See Volume I, *Mary of*

Galilee: Mary in the New Testament, pp. 43-44, for the question of the brothers and sisters of Jesus.)

Education

Mary's education as a woman consisted of listening to the readings of the Torah and the Prophets in the synagogue (cf. Lk 4:16f). While Joseph was alive Mary apparently went with him to the Temple for the celebration of the three pilgrimage feasts of Passover, Pentecost, and Tabernacles. In the public life of Judaism within the synagogue and the Temple, women played an enthusiastic part. They edified most of the men. Though they were not counted among the ten (*minyan*) necessary for a prayer group on a Sabbath, they were permitted to read the lesson (Tosefta Mezilla IV, III, II, Babylonian Talmud, Myella 23a). Women attended the synagogue not only on Friday eve and the Sabbath but also during the week when prayer and study took place. (What a remarkable experience for those in the Galilean synagogue who heard Mary read a lesson.)

Probably during the time of Jesus the separation of men from women in the synagogue was not strict. From Acts 1:14 it can be seen how Mary at Pentecost (Shevuoth) was gathered with a large crowd of men and women including the apostles who are named. In Acts there are many references to women present in the synagogues of the Diaspora.

Mary's hymn of praise (Lk 1:46-55) was a spontaneous prayer that she could also have voiced in the synagogue or the Temple, for Hannah uttered her own hymn in the Temple after the birth of Samuel. In the Temple women could offer sacrifices but not in the detailed manner of men. Women could not enter the sanctuary from which they were removed by the Court of Israelites and by fifteen steps leading down to the Court of Women. If a woman wished to participate in the sacrifice, the victim could be taken out to the Court of Women (Babylonian Talmud Hagigah).

In the area of almsgiving and charity, two of the highest

obligations under religious law (Mt 7; Lk 21:1-4), there are many references in Judaism to the outstanding generosity of women. One of the inscriptions calls a certain woman "Mother of the synagogue." Most fathers taught their daughters the Torah as they did their sons. There are even recorded instances of women scholars who were listened to because of the wisdom of their opinions. It is possible to picture Mary of Nazareth in her own village synagogue having such a role (Mk 3:20-35; Lk 2; Jn 2:1-12).

In Judaism during the time of Jesus, man and woman were regarded as being equally created in the image of God (Gn 1:27); together they are called "humankind" (Gn 5:2) and form one unit. The rabbis would say "He who is not married is not a man" (Yev. 63a). In many spheres rabbinic law recognized the equality of men and women; they were subject to many of the same laws, religious prohibitions and penalties (Kidd. 35a) and could offer sacrifices in the Temple (Maimonides, Moasch ha Korbanat 2:3). Yet in many areas it was taken for granted that men and women are meant to be different in status, rights, and obligations and to complement rather than equal one another.

The passivity, hiddenness, and receptivity of women were emphasized. Women were especially blessed by men when they bore many children:

> Children too are a gift from the Lord, the fruit of the womb, a reward. Like arrows in the hand of a warrior are the children born in one's youth. Blessed are they whose quivers are full, they will never be shamed contending with foes at the gate (Ps 127:3-5).

> Like a fruitful vine your wife within your home, like olive plants your children around your table. Just so will they be blessed who fear the Lord (Ps 128:3-4).

A woman's virtues, as listed in the Talmud, were superior compassion, charity, chastity, piety, and primacy in educating their children and keeping their husbands from sin. Vices listed for women in the Talmud were gossip, superstition, and light-mindedness.

Marriage of Women

What is quite outstanding about the marriage of Jewish women is the frequency of marriage within the same family. It often happened that the daughter of one's brother or especially one's sister — a niece — was one's spouse. This is especially evident in the lists given to us by Josephus for the royal family of Herod, and this practice was acceptable by the Talmud. There was strong insistence on being from the same tribe and family. In Mary and Joseph's espousal, they were not; she was from the priestly line, he from the Davidic or royal line.

Like most young girls, Mary probably entered her espousal with Joseph in her thirteenth year. At 12½ years a young girl normally married and passed from the control of her father to that of her husband. If her father were dead, normally a legal guardian (her mother or brothers) who was a close relative of the family would arrange her contract (cf. Sg 8:8-10). The word used for designating a young girl was *q'tannah* "little one." Think of the phrase *talitha kum*, "little girl, I say to you, get up," found in Mark 5:41. The expression *talitha* would correspond in Aramaic with *q'tannah*. This age of a minor continued until 12 years and 1 day, after which the young girl became eligible for marriage and was called *na'arah*; after 12½ years she was called *bogêrêt*. Up to the age of 12½ a young girl did not have the right to refuse a marriage set up by the father; the acceptation or refusal was exclusively under the power of the father. Upon becoming 12½ years old she was then autonomous in choice, but his consent was still necessary. The future husband had to pay the father on the occasion of the espousal.

The engagement was a legal stage toward marriage where the girl passed from the authority of her father to that of her intended spouse. There were two steps in the marriage process: (1) a formal exchange of consent before witnesses — the man read or pronounced the consent while the woman agreed in a receptive mode (Ml 2:14; Mt 1:18). This was the betrothal or the *'erûsîn*; in reality it was a legal marriage contract and gave the young man rights over the girl. For Mary, Matthew's account presumes the expectation of virginity on the part of Joseph before taking her to his house. In parts of Judea interim marital relations during the espousal or engagement period were not unusual. In Galilee no such leniency was tolerated and the wife had to be taken to her husband's home as a virgin. Any infringement of the husband's marital rights during the period of espousal could be punished as adultery if perpetrated by someone other than her fiancé. Normally the girl continued to live with her parents for a year before entering her husband's home. The transferral was called the *nîsû'în* and marked the moment when he assumed her support with: (2) the taking of the young woman into his home. This entering into her husband's home was often a painful and enduring time of hardship, because she was introduced into his family which was not at all familiar and often hostile to the new young bride.

Once they were married the woman had the right to be provided for by her husband and even could bring this before the court. He had to assure her of nourishment, clothing and lodging, and the marriage act. He had to ransom her if she were captured, procure medicine for her if she were sick, assure burial on death with at least two flute players and a mourner in the funeral cortege (in some instances he was required to give her eulogy).

Mary's responsibilities are described well in the last chapter (31) of the Book of Proverbs which is read on the Sabbath and also at a woman's death. She had to mill grain, cook, wash and feed her children; she also made her husband's bed, cleaned and pressed his linen, provided his drink, and washed his face, hands and feet. He could sell what she made and even annul her marriage vows to him. Her obedience to her husband was a religious mandate. This extended to the children where they were to be more obedient to the father. If they were in danger of death she had to save her husband first.

Divorce was exclusively the prerogative of the husband. If one followed the liberal school of Hillel, a husband could dismiss his wife when she no longer pleased him with her comeliness or if she burnt his supper. Shammai was closer to Matthew's condition for divorce, namely, that the woman be guilty of lewd conduct — normally adultery; this was the most likely situation in which Mary found herself. Joseph's reaction shows that he may have been quite an exceptional man. If a woman was divorced she usually returned to her parents; thus we can see why it was considered natural to marry a niece. Children normally belonged to the father. The greatest gift a woman could give her husband was a male child.

Reflection

The great strength of Mary amidst all of the religious and social obstacles she encountered as a woman in the first century world of Judaism only emphasizes how true was her blessedness and her valor. She is a remarkably valiant woman who, while conforming to the requirements of her society and religion, surmounts them with the inward strength of her spirit.

In considering such a "low-Mariology" we are struck by her ability to do more than simply cope with difficult circumstances and tragic situations. Mary's personality shines through strongly in the accounts of the Gospels, whether it be in her setting out to help Elizabeth, or her going out to save Jesus and the family reputation (Mk 3:31-35). Her capacity to be present to God and to her son is remarkable. She as mother is the only believing disciple of Jesus who is with him from conception, to birth, to his active ministry, his presence at a wedding and then his tragic death on a cross. This dynamic presence of Mary of Nazareth is a strong characteristic of her in the pages of the New Testament.

Reflection on Mary brings realization that she accomplished what was required of her by the Law and what was required of her through the powerful and tragic events of her son's life by being present to all persons and to every event with the fullness of her womanhood. The pattern of faith in God seen in the history of her ancestry is consistent with the strength which enabled her to be so present in moments of joy, sadness, and tragic separations, even death. We saw her "pondering over all of these things" and thereby being present while passing through them. Good strength doesn't come by manipulation but by conviction, fidelity, and penetrating perspective on the events of life with its ups and downs. In her as in other witnesses of Jesus in the New Testament, the words of the Song of Songs resound: "For stern as death is love" (8:6b).

Mary experienced holiness as a Jew. Within Judaism holiness is bound to a place and to a definite time and is called forth through a definite activity; it is an integral part of the Jewish religious system.[33] Mary is a woman of courage, faith, and holiness. From the outset she reversed the pattern of expected passivity and turned her life's forces into concentrated action by means of prayer and in her social and religious life as a Jewish mother. We are speaking of a real, human, loving Jewish woman of faith. Both Judaism and Christianity are religions whose points of departure are from historical facts and a living tradition. The historicity of Mary and the reality of her glory and her suffering are the foundation for devotion to her. This Mater Dolorosa is a woman who experiences in an uninterrupted way the suffering of her people, the Jews. Mary is a real person who inspires us by her joy and encourages us by never being defeated by her unspeakable pain.[34]

The name Miriam (the Jewish form of Mary) was very common during the time in which she lived. This, too, brings out the humanness of her appearance in and among her people; her name is a symbol of her connectedness with the ordinary people of her time.

There is need to ponder more fully the Jewish atmosphere surrounding Mary in the New Testament, especially in the Infancy Narratives of Matthew and Luke. Almost the opposite has happened to Mary. Some early Christian heretics, following Marcion, wanted to expunge everything that was Jewish out of the New Testament. Mary, too, would have been eliminated. The more the Jewishness of the Gospels is better understood, then the persons who are historically there (Mary, Joseph, Jesus, Magdalene, and the apostles) are more real in their Mediterranean culture.

David Flusser says that:

The more Mary was understood to be human, the more she became a model for them. The belief in her virginity need not lead to an unnatural asceticism but can protect the believer from unchasteness and lead toward a spotless and shining purity. Mary became simultaneously symbolic of the pure mother and through devotion to her one can understand and preserve the divine element in the birth of every child.[35]

Josephine Massyngberde Ford suggests that Mary meditated only on the stories of the Hebrew Bible. She feels that Mary pondered over the word of God and exercised the role of a prophet in the sense that she reinterpreted the Scriptures through prayer and meditation as did Daniel (Dn 9), the Teacher of Righteousness at Qumran (1pHab 2:8-9), and Matthew.[36]

Mary belonged to a society and religion in which the Torah was spiritually and culturally alive. She belonged to the People of the Book in which visions and prophecies were experienced. In Luke 1-2 she can be seen as the recipient of some of these forms of God's revelation. ". . . even before the birth of Jesus she was among those who entertained a lively messianic expectation and were profoundly interested in the Jewish cult."[37]

We are encouraged to interpret Scripture in the light of current events and in the context of our own human experiences. At Qumran, in the Gospels, and in the synagogues this was a normal method called *pesher*. Coupled with the midrash haggadah the Scripture becomes alive and active as a two-edged sword in the hand of the user. Twice in Luke we are told that Mary pondered over the events (*rhemata*), the "things" which had occurred in her heart (Lk 2:19, 51). The word *diaterio* means a type of ruminating on spiritual truths. The most striking example of this is in Scripture itself in the Letter to the Hebrews. Mary's thoughts would have been quite similar to those of the author of this epistle who ponders, under the shadow of the Spirit of God, over the meaning of certain messianic texts, especially in the most repeated psalms in the Jewish Christian communities (Ps 2 and Ps 110).

Texts which are associated with the Birth of the Messiah have the possibility of stemming from Mary through the oral tradition of the early Jewish Christian community. Probably no evangelist spoke with her directly, but the community itself had preserved her recollections in memory of her Son. The Epistle to the Hebrews also has to be added to those writings which form a Christology based on the birth of Jesus. If so, then Mary the Mother is associated with all these birth narratives and Old Testament prophetic and psalmic texts.

Endnotes

[16] Avital Wohlmann, "Mary of Nazareth," *Sidic* 20.2 (1987): 9-14.

[17] "Mary — Woman of the Mediterranean: A Special Issue," *Biblical Theological Bulletin* 20 (1990): 45-94.

[18] Lee I. Levine, ed., *The Galilee in Late Antiquity* (Hoboken, NJ: Ktav, 1992) xix.

[19] Joseph Gutmann, *The Synagogue: Studies in Origins, Archaeology and Architecture* (New York: Ktav, 1975) 40.

[20] Levine, 12.

[21] Ibid., 15.

[22] Ibid., 21.

[23] Carol L. Meyers, "Everyday Life: Women in the Period of the Hebrew Bible," *The Women's Bible Commentary*, eds. Carol A. Newsom and Sharon H. Ringe (Louisville: Westminster/John Knox, 1992) 245.

[24] Ibid., 247.

[25] Ibid., 248.

[26] Ibid.

[27] Ibid.

[28] Ibid., 248-249.

[29] Ibid., 249.

[30] Ibid, 250.

[31] Ann Johnson, *Miryam of Judah: Witness in Truth & Tradition* (Notre Dame, IN: Ave Maria, 1987).

[32] James H. Charlesworth, *The Old Testament Pseudepigrapha*, vol. 2 (New York: Doubleday, 1985) 563.

[33] David Flusser, "Mary and Israel," *Mary: Images of the Mother of Jesus in Jewish and Christian Perspective* (Philadelphia: Fortress, 1986) 8.

[34] Ibid., 8-9.

[35] Ibid., 14.

[36] J. Massyngberde Ford, "The Mother of Jesus and the Authorship of the Epistle to the Hebrews," *The Bible Today* 82 (1976): 685.

[37] Ibid., 686.

Chapter Three

DAUGHTER OF ZION

The Use of the Hebrew Scriptures in Early Marian Tradition

In this chapter Mary is studied in the light of a Christian rereading of texts from the Hebrew Scriptures. Some of these texts are the citations of the Hebrew Scriptures by the authors of the Christian Scriptures, others are images or symbols taken from the Hebrew Scriptures and applied to Mary. This is especially true in the Catholic tradition which has maintained a strong devotion to the person of Mary and has reread certain Hebrew Scripture texts for an accommodated sense in a Marian perspective rather than a strict historical-critical exegesis. Mary was born after the formation of the Hebrew Scriptures and is not historically present in them. She was not intended within them *prima facie* by the authors of the texts. Only through a Christian rereading and application of certain symbols from the Hebrew Scriptures to Mary is it possible to approach this study.

In the document called the Dogmatic Constitution on the Church (*Lumen Gentium*), Chapter VIII, section II, which is entitled "The Function of the Blessed Virgin Mary in the Plan of Salvation," Vatican II placed Mary within a Christological and ecclesiological frame of reference in the texts considered to have a Marian implication. This principle should help the reader to understand Mary's subordination to Christ, and her role as a model believer within the context of the Church and its members. Only in paragraph 55 of the document are certain texts of the Hebrew Scriptures mentioned as having significance for understanding the person of Mary. The perspective with which the texts should be read and used is carefully and clearly stated:

> The sacred writings of the Old and the New Testaments, as well as venerable tradition, show the role of the Mother of the Savior in the plan of salvation in an ever clearer light and call our attention to it. The books of the Old Testament describe the history of salvation, by which the coming of Christ into the world was slowly prepared. The earliest documents, as they are read in the Church and are understood in the light of a further and full revelation, bring the figure of a woman, Mother of the Redeemer, into a gradually clearer light. Considered in this light, she is already prophetically foreshadowed in the promise of victory over the serpent which was given to our first parents after their fall into sin (cf. Gn 3:15). Likewise she is the virgin who shall conceive and bear a son, whose name shall be called Emmanuel (cf. Is 7:14; Mi 5:2-3; Mt 1:22-23). She stands out among the poor and humble of the Lord, who confidently hope for and receive salvation from him. After a long period of waiting, the times are fulfilled in her, the exalted Daughter of Zion and the new plan of salvation is established when the Son of God has taken a new nature from her, that he might in the mysteries of his flesh free man from sin.[38]

In addition to the above references to the Hebrew Scriptures, Vatican II also uses the symbol of Mary as the New Eve taking Genesis 3 into account. Irenaeus developed this more fully, seeing it as an image of Mary and her role in the Church.

Mary as Daughter of Zion

"Zion" is a symbol that has significance in Marian studies, both in exegetical work and in Marian theology espoused by the Second Vatican Council and in its connection with the biblical expression

"Daughter of Zion" or "Daughter Zion." The Western Wall of Jerusalem is considered as Zion by all Jewish people today. "Daughter of Zion" is applied by Catholics to Mary, the Jewish mother of Jesus, and the area of Jerusalem designated as Zion, according to Catholic tradition, is the location of the upper room where Mary gathered with the apostles and relatives of Jesus to pray for the coming of the Spirit. Catholic scholars speak of the person of Mary as representative of Israel's perfect response to the covenant established by God on Sinai. For Catholics the title "Daughter of Zion" has been within the Church since the sixth century (in the Visigoth Liturgy) and was highlighted in the Vatican II statement (about Mary) in paragraph 55 of *Lumen Gentium* above. Historically the word "Zion" appears as the name of the first stronghold of the city seized by David from the Jebusites. In the Psalms and the Prophets the word is associated with Jerusalem, the city of David.

Several Protestant and many Catholic exegetes see the symbol of "Daughter of Zion" as an appropriate title from the Hebrew Scriptures which proves helpful in understanding the role of the Mother of the Messiah in the history of salvation. It is especially from Luke's Annunciation narrative, from the Visitation, and from the Magnificat that the relationship of Mary to the Daughter of Zion is noticed by these exegetical theologians. Both the historical and prophetical books of the Hebrew Scriptures make use of the image and help for understanding of the significance of the word "Zion" and the symbol "Daughter of Zion."

Among the Protestant scholars who see this title as appropriate for Mary are A. G. Herbert, H. Sahlin, and M. Thurian. Among the many Catholic scholars who support this theme for Mary are R. Laurentin, L. Deiss, J. McHugh, T. Koehler, A. Serra, S. Lyonnet, E. Mori, B. Rigaux and P. Benoit.[39] More recently, A. Serra[40] and I. de la Potterie[41] have developed significant insights on the title "Daughter of Zion." These exegetes make use of a canonical, traditional, and thematic method for seeing Mary as the Daughter of Zion. The symbolism is not accepted by all Catholic exegetes and certainly Protestant scholarship would see no symbolism at all, except for the Protestant scholars mentioned above. Most North

American scholars follow the method of R. Brown in critiquing the title from a historical-critical methodology.[42] The presentation of the theme in this writing will use both the insights and results of Brown as well as the suggestions from Vatican II and a host of other scholars for gaining greater perception into the use of the title for Mary. This will help the reader to appreciate both the value of the Catholic tradition about Mary as reflected in Vatican II and the importance of not exaggerating certain texts or titles in reference to Mary.

The Church in referring to Mary as Daughter of Zion in *Lumen Gentium* is concerned with both a Scriptural foundation for Mariology and a pastoral concern for all believers. Vatican Council II presents a moderate and balanced faith-tradition approach to the texts and titles used for Mary from the Hebrew Scriptures. The texts primarily are used in a liturgical setting. Both the Church and the exegetes work from certain presuppositions. The exegetes go directly to the texts and explain their meaning from their historical context and their philological dimension. The Church uses both the long tradition of other commentators as well as the liturgical expression so necessary for the life of the faithful while reading these texts. Basically, the scientific approach to the Scriptures is more logical and objective since it is highly analytical, and is exclusively based on the exegesis flowing directly from the texts in their historical setting. The faith-tradition approach of the Church is more intuitive and works towards a synthesis through themes and images.

Both an analysis and a synthesis are important for creating a good tension within the thought and dialogue between scholars, readers, and believers for study and meditation on the sacred texts. Therefore, both methods are helpful in this particular study of Mary as Daughter of Zion within the Scriptures. Perhaps, formerly, Catholics (even scholars) lost sight of the centrality of Christ while presenting Mary, but in the light of the teachings of Vatican II Mary is now seen within the context of the Christology of the New Testament and within the rereading of the Hebrew Scriptures now so abundantly presented in the liturgical readings. This mode was present in the writers of the New Testament or Christian Scriptures as they pondered over the events and words of Christ in the context of the Hebrew Scriptures, the only Bible for Jesus and for them. Both approaches of the Church and of the scholars are useful in learning from one another while critiquing each other. The traditional approach freely uses the texts in the context of pastoral and liturgical concerns; hence the fuller sense of the Scriptures, the symbolic and even the allegorical, is part of the Church's interpretative voice. Here a canonical reading of the entire Bible allows for a moving from book to book in search of an explanation for a theme. The scientific pursuit of the exegete remains within the limits of each book of the Bible, interpreting the texts from their historical setting and from the intention of the author. The Western mind is fond of this latter approach because there are facts, results, and a certainty about what is said. Although the faith dimension is not always present in the historical-critical approach, through such studies, together with the presentation of the Scriptures by the Church (as faithful interpreter and carrier), a wholesome and ecclesial understanding of the Bible is achieved.

What Do the Scriptures Tell Us About Zion and the Daughter of Zion?

Turning to the more factual information available about Zion, a historical event brought the name of Zion into the Scriptures. Once that event was established, a rich development of Zion took place having powerful meanings, events, and extended symbolism for the Hebrew people. The historical account of 2 Samuel 5:7 is clear and concise: "But David did take the stronghold of Zion which is the City of David" (cf. 1 Ch 11:5). Zion was the Jebusite stronghold or rock fortress (which had a water source) captured by David and made the center and symbol of his own kingdom. In meeting the taunts of the Jebusites and capturing their city, David brought unity, strength, and a theocracy to the site of Zion. Zion is the cornerstone, the stronghold, and the symbol for an emerging nation under David, its messianic king.

Scholars today are convinced that the original Zion was on the east hill above Gihon.[43] In the Septuagint this stronghold is called the "citadel"; in the Hebrew text it is *millo*, rampart or earthwork. The site has been identified by archeologists with the triangular hill between the Tyropoeon and Kedron valleys. The stronghold was called "Jebus" during the time of its first occupants: "The man, however, refused to stay another night; he and his concubine set out with a pair of saddled asses, and traveled till they came opposite Jebus, which is Jerusalem" (Jg 19:10). The Jebusites probably were permitted to continue to live within the city after its capture by David. David brought the ark of the covenant to Zion, thus making it a sacred city. The symbolism of Zion continued to grow when Solomon built the temple and took the ark from Zion to the temple: "At Solomon's order the elders of Israel and all the leaders of the tribes, the princes of the Israelite ancestral houses, came to Jerusalem to bring up the ark of the Lord's covenant from the City of David (which is Zion)" (2 Ch 5:2).

The next historical reference of significance to Zion is during the reign of Hezekiah (715-687 BC.E.) while Isaiah was prophet. Here the expression "virgin daughter Zion" is used as the name of the area which the Assyrians under Sennacherib are threatening: "She despises you, laughs you to scorn, the virgin daughter Zion; Behind you she wags her head, daughter Jerusalem" (Is 37:22). This text shows that Daughter Zion is also called Jerusalem; she is the collective symbol for the people under the Davidic king Hezekiah. In the same Isaian tradition is an indication of a "remnant" of this people who will survive: "The remaining survivors of the house of Judah shall again strike root below and bear fruit above. For out of Jerusalem shall come a remnant, and from Mount Zion, survivors. The zeal of the Lord of hosts shall do this" (Is 37:31-32). This parallels an earlier expression from Isaiah 2:3: "For from Zion shall go forth instruction, and the word of the Lord from Jerusalem."

Zion in the Psalms

There are many references to Zion in the Psalms and all of them are positive and enthusiastic expressions about the city. Within Christian tradition several of these Zion Psalms are also considered to be messianic and are used in the Christian Scriptures to affirm Jesus as the Christ or the Messiah.[44]

Turning now to the more symbolic meaning of "Daughter of Zion," Catholic and Protestant scholars are found using it for Mary. The insight of Stanislaus Lyonnet gave impetus to studies connecting Mary, the mother of Jesus, with Virgin Daughter Zion.[45] The Annunciation narrative from Luke (1:26-38) is his point of departure. He finds in Gabriel's salutation and dialogue resonances in the minor prophets. The salutation in the Gospel of Luke reads "*Chaire, kécharitôménê.* " This is interpreted by Lyonnet to mean "Rejoice, O highly favored one." He leaves aside the banal "Hail, full of grace" for this more prophetic address that has an echo in Zephaniah 3:14-17 which parallels in similar thought and symbolism the structure used by Luke in the Annunciation. First:

> Shout for joy, O daughter Zion! Sing joyfully, O Israel! Be glad and exult with all your heart, O daughter Jerusalem! The Lord has removed the judgment against you, he has turned away your enemies; the King of Israel, the Lord, is in your midst, you have no further misfortune to fear. On that day, it shall be said to Jerusalem: Fear not, O Zion, be not discouraged! The Lord, your God, is in your midst, a mighty savior; he will rejoice over you with gladness, and renew you in his love, he will sing joyfully because of you, as one sings at festivals (Zp 3:14-18a).

In Luke's account is Mary's response to God's call in her Magnificat. She praises God as a daughter of Israel, and as the personification of her people rejoices in her God:

> "My soul proclaims the greatness of the Lord; my spirit rejoices in God my savior. For he has looked upon his

handmaid's lowliness; behold, from now on will all ages call
me blessed. The Mighty One has done great things for me,
and holy is his name. His mercy is from age to age to those who
fear him. He has shown might with his arm, dispersed the
arrogant of mind and heart. He has thrown down the rulers
from their thrones but lifted up the lowly. The hungry he has
filled with good things; the rich he has sent away empty. He
has helped Israel his servant, remembering his mercy, according to his promise to our fathers, to Abraham and to his
descendants forever" (Lk 1:46-55).

Luke may have been aware of the words of Zephaniah in the
Annunciation account for there are some signs of similarity and
parallelism:

"Hail [*Chaire*], favored one! The Lord is with you.".... "Do not
be afraid, Mary, for you have found favor with God. Behold,
you will conceive in your womb and bear a son. . ." (Lk 1:28,
30-31).

The same expressions are also found in Zechariah:

Sing and rejoice, O daughter Zion! See, I am coming to dwell
among you, says the Lord. Many nations shall join themselves
to the Lord on that day, and they shall be his people, and he
will dwell among you, and you shall know that the Lord of
hosts has sent me to you. The Lord will possess Judah as his
portion of the holy land, and he will again choose Jerusalem
(Zc 2:14-16).

Zechariah returns to the same theme in chapter 9. This is also taken
up in the Christian Scriptures upon Jesus' entry into Jerusalem (cf.
Mt 21:5 and Jn 12:15). Zechariah states:

Rejoice heartily, O daughter Zion, shout for joy, O daughter
Jerusalem! See, your king shall come to you; a just savior is he,
meek, and riding on an ass, on a colt, the foal of an ass (Zc 9:9).

In Joel are similar texts:

> Fear not, O land! exult and rejoice! for the Lord has done great things (Jl 2:21).

> And do you, O children of Zion, exult and rejoice in the Lord, your God! (Jl 2:23).

> And you shall know that I am in the midst of Israel; I am the Lord, your God, and there is no other; my people shall nevermore be put to shame (Jl 2:27).

> Then everyone shall be rescued who calls on the name of the Lord; for on Mount Zion there shall be a remnant, as the Lord has said, and in Jerusalem survivors whom the Lord shall call (Jl 3:5).

More recently Aristide Serra has discovered similar parallels to these prophetic announcements in the Dead Sea Scrolls and in the Tosephta Targum for Zechariah 2:14-15. In 1QM XII:13-14, we read:

> Rejoice greatly, Zion! Break forth with songs of joy, Jerusalem. Exult all you cities of Judah.[46]

René Laurentin took up the study of Lyonnet and saw in the Annunciation a remarkable similarity to Zephaniah 3:14-17, in which he found five parallels:

1. *Chaire* (Rejoice!) (Zp 3:14; Jl 2:21, cf. v. 23; Zc 2:2-14a; Zc 9:9).
2. Do not fear (Zp 3:16, cf. v. 15; Jl 2:21, cf. v. 22).
3. Yahweh is in the midst of Israel (Zp 3:15b, 17a; Jl 2:27; Zc 2:14; Zc 9:9).
4. Yahweh as King (Zp 3:15b; Zc 9:9).
5. Yahweh as Savior (Zp 3:17a; Zc 9:9).

Laurentin presents his thesis in this manner: ". . . the narrative of the Annunciation (Luke 1:28-33) beckons an echo of the series of three prophecies in uncovering the following essentials from Zephaniah 3:14-17, Joel 2:21-27, and Zechariah 9:9-10. All three (1) address the Daughter of Zion; (2) that is, Israel personified. They have as their purpose to announce messianic joy which is expressed by the word "Rejoice!" (3) These words are followed by the common expression: Do not fear. (4) The object of the message is the same: Yahweh comes to dwell within Zion (5) as King and (6) as Savior. All of these traits are found in the account of the Annunciation with two transpositions: (1) The message is addressed to Mary who is called *"kécharitôménê,"* and no longer Daughter of Zion. (2) It is Jesus, son of the Most High who comes to live within her as King and Savior. Is Luke's account an echo of one of the prophecies or a synthesis of all three? It is difficult to say. What is certain is that he has a great number of parallels or contacts with Zephaniah who is the most ancient of the prophets mentioned, and beyond question the source for the others."[47]

In the most recent study of these texts, Aristide Serra chooses Zechariah 9:9 as the source for his conclusions about the Daughter of Zion. Serra states that Zechariah polarizes one's attention more exclusively than Zephaniah or Joel. Moreover, the text is used in Matthew 21:5 and John 12:15. Serra sees Zephaniah used as a complementary illustration of what Zechariah is saying in 2:14-15. Serra establishes other texts from rabbinic literature and from the Targums and the Dead Sea Scrolls as an amplification of the text of Zechariah 9:9. His conclusion is that Luke did, at least indirectly, refer to these biblical prophecies of Joel, Zechariah, and Zephaniah. In fact, from the second century before Christ, the passages of Zechariah 2:14-15 and especially Zechariah 9:9 had become a *locus classicus* both for Judaism in its eschatological-messianic hope and Christianity which realized perfectly this eschatological-messianic hope in Jesus. Serra gives evidence that the commentaries on these passages are not only Palestinian, but also Egyptian and Babylonian thus enabling the universalist Luke to be familiar with such an interpretation. He also thinks that Luke's listeners would be attuned to such a message from the prophets. His conclusions parallel the points of contact that Lyonnet and Laurentin posited. Serra summarizes his analysis in this manner: "In the eyes of the first generation of Christians, the Mother of Jesus was configured as the ideal incarnation of the Daughter of Zion. In her, an individual person, the vocation of Zion-Jerusalem and of all Israel as the People of the Covenant matured in an exemplary fashion."[48]

Those authors who favor the symbolism of Mary as Daughter of Zion or Israel personified see the possibility of Luke having been inspired by these prophetic texts to compose the Annunciation to Mary. No one, of course, can be certain that this was the case, but there are certainly echoes and words in Luke that resemble the above texts from Zephaniah, Zechariah, and Joel. These passages of the prophetic literature are similar to what was said about Zion in the more historical books and in the Psalms. Zion becomes a powerful symbol for the presence of God in Israel. Holiness, security, salvation, and joy are all embodied in the theme and symbol of Zion.

Endnotes

[38] Flannery, *Lumen Gentium*, (55).

[39] Nunzio Lemmo, "Maria, 'Figlia di Sion,' a partire da Lc 1, 26-38, Bilancio esegetico dal 1939 al 1982," *Marianum* XLV (1983) 175-258. This doctoral dissertation contains an excellent bibliography on the topic of "Daughter of Zion" while listing all the Catholic and Protestant scholars who have written on this title. The more complete bibliography is contained in the thesis (cf. No. 37 Pontificia Facultatis Theologicae "Marianum," Romae, 1985).

[40] Aristide Serra, *E C'era la Madre di Gesù...(Gv. 2, 1) saggi di esegesi biblico-mariana, 1978-1988* (Roma: Edizioni Cens-Marianum, 1989). See especially "'Esulta, Figlia di Sion!' Principali riletture di Zc 2,14-15 E 9, 9a-c nel Giudaismo Antico e nel Cristianesimo del I-II secolo," pp. 3-43, and "'Lo Spirito Santo Scenderà su di te...' Aspetti Mariologici della Pneumatologia di Lc 1, 35a," pp. 44-54.

[41] Ignace de la Potterie, *Mary in the Mystery of the Covenant*, xxxviii. This is the most recent book to treat of the "Daughter of Zion" within the Catholic tradition. The eminent exegete, professor emeritus of the Biblicum in Rome, states:

Biblically speaking, then, where must we truly situate Mary? Is it in the Old Testament's perspective or that of the New Testament? Or is it in the perspective of both testaments at the same time? She is found exactly at the threshold, and thus can be considered from both sides at the same time. She is the "Figure of the Synagogue," but she is also the "Type of the Church," or as the Fathers of the

Church like to call her, she is the archetype and icon of the Church. Precisely because it is in her that the Old Testament image of the eschatological and messianic "Daughter of Zion" is realized, Mary is the personification of the new messianic people, the Church.

[42] Raymond Brown, *The Birth of the Messiah*, 320-328.

[43] Bargil Pixner, "Church of the Apostles Found on Mount Zion," *Biblical Archaeological Review* 16:3 (1990): 16+.

[44] Here is a survey of the Zion psalms:

The following psalms make mention of Zion: 2:6; 9:12, 15; 20:3; 48:3, 12, 13; 50:2; 51:20; 53:7; 65:2; 69:36; 74:2; 76:3; 78:68; 84:8; 87:2, 5; 97:8; 99:2; 102:14, 17, 22; 110:2; 125:1; 126:1; 128:5; 129:5; 132:13, 15; 133:3; 134:3; 135:21; 137:1, 3; 146:10; 147:12; 149:2.

This indicates that Zion is mentioned about forty times within the Psalms. Each psalm continues with great praise for Zion and it is extolled as a city of security, peace, and holiness. It is also the city of King David. These psalms have both royal and theocratic meaning. God is the true king of Israel; David is servant-king. These ideas are repetitive and continue what the historical books began in reference to Zion. Never in the psalms is there a negative connotation to Zion. Perhaps, it is helpful to remember this when considering the prophetic literature.

Briefly, we may summarize these psalms through the following themes:

1. The abiding presence of God dwelling within the walls of Zion: Psalm 9:12; 48:12; 50:2; 65:2; 69:36; 74:2; 76:3; 84:8; 99:2; 102:22; 110:2; 125:1; 128:5; 132:13; 134:3; 135:21; 146:10; 147:12. These references are mentioned here because in the Annunciation of Luke, the abiding presence of the Son of God who is also from the Davidic line will live within the womb of Mary. Thus the symbolism of the ark of the covenant within Zion is also used within the Catholic tradition and especially in its liturgy in reference to Mary, the new ark of the covenant.

2. Another strong motif within the psalms is that of rejoicing in God and praising God: Psalms 14:7; 48:3, 13; 65:2; 97:8; 137:1, 3; 146:10; 147:12. Again, in the Annunciation, Gabriel, the protector of Israel, announces to Mary ("*Chaire, kécharitôméné*": Lk 1:28) this joy. Mary in her own song of praise (Magnificat: Lk 1:46-55) praises God through whom salvation and deliverance into freedom come about. Psalms 9:15; 14:7; 53:7; 69:36; 102:14 do the same.

3. Prosperity and strength in Zion are found in Psalms 48:13; 84:8; 125:1; 129:5. These themes have a similar refrain in the Magnificat (Lk 1:53).

4. Messianic kingship and the reign of God are found in the Zion psalms: 2:6; 48:3, 12; 110:2; 146:10. It is especially in Psalm 2:6 that the royal messianism appears. This text is used in the New Testament in reference to Jesus as Messiah: "I myself have installed my king on Zion, my holy mountain." It is a psalm that is closely linked with the opening of the psalms as well. The Christian community reread these inspirations as divine revelation about Jesus. Through them they saw the Davidic and messianic qualities attributed to him. In the post-exilic period this psalm takes on an eschatological meaning which brings hope to the remnant of the people of Israel. Together with Psalm 110 it is used more often in the New Testament than the other psalms (cf. Ac 4:25-26; 13:33; Heb 1:5; 5:5).

Psalm 110 is the most often cited psalm in the New Testament. It, too, is a royal messianic psalm which may be connected historically with the succession of the Davidic monarch to the former status of the Jebusite king of Zion. There is also a priestly element in the psalm through the mention of the King of Salem, Melchizedek. He is eventually blessed by Abraham. This is interesting in the light of the Dead Sea Scrolls where mention is made of a messiah who is both king and priest or of two separate messianic figures, one who is priestly, the other who is kingly.

[45] Stanislaus Lyonnet, "*Chaire Kécharitôménê*," 131-141.

[46] Aristide Serra, *E C'era la Madre di Gesù*, 17.

[47] René Laurentin, *Structure et Théologie de Luc I-II*, 66-67.

[48] Serra, 43.

Chapter Four

A WOMAN OF FAITH
BLESSED AMONG WOMEN

The purpose of this chapter is twofold: first, to focus on women of faith and courage in the Hebrew Scriptures whose exemplary lives are seen in their individuality and their belonging to a community, and second, to show the mother of Jesus in continuity with these women. In the Hebrew Scriptures Abraham and Sarah are the initiators of a complete response in faith. Together they begin a lineage of believers who precede Mary, the mother of Jesus. She, in turn, renews their lively faith in God by her own "yes" and by her pilgrimage of faith.

This chapter will reflect upon Abraham and Sarah, upon Eve, and then take up the role of some of the important heroines in the Hebrew Scriptures. These selections from the Bible are enlivened today by their use in liturgical feasts and celebrations as well as through a personal reading of their colorful and exciting stories.

God's loving-kindness commences with the call of Abram and extends throughout the two testaments in the vocation stories of the followers of Abraham and Sarah. Mary, the mother of Jesus, is first called as a disciple of Jesus in the pilgrimage of faith towards the realm of God. Both Testaments are revelations from the same God and the same Holy Spirit who inspires these Sacred Scriptures, which are meant to be read and lived. This teaching from Vatican II on revelation is found in the decree *Dei verbum*. Emphasis is upon complementarity and continuity as well as promise and fulfillment which takes place in the totality of the Scriptures from Genesis to the Apocalypse. Exegetes from the earliest of Christian centuries, as well as modern commentators, perceive the necessity of knowing and relating to both Testaments as narratives of salvation history.

The formation of the Christian Scriptures came about through the Church's need to proclaim the Gospel message that Jesus Christ is Lord. The preaching or *kerygma* of the early inspired apostolic witnesses and their successors brought about the collection we call the New Testament or Christian Scriptures. The Hebrew Scriptures, through their translation into the koine Greek of the Septuagint, were the context and faith-filled writings for Jewish Christians in their proclamation and witness to Jesus, his words, and actions. The themes, symbols, types, and stories in the Hebrew Scriptures were retold and modeled in the fabric and dynamism about Jesus of Nazareth. The Hebrew Scriptures were a backdrop for the canvas of his own picturesque words, his parables, metaphors, fulfillment texts, and typological parallels. They were then handed on faithfully by inspired writers who proclaimed Jesus as Lord and Messiah.

God, therefore, is the author of both the Hebrew Scriptures and Christian Scriptures. One of the starting points in both Testaments is the positive and faithful response of God's chosen ones like Abraham, Moses, and Mary. There are countless other vocation narratives in the Scriptures, but the focus and purpose in this chapter is to treat the most significant calls of the matriarchs and holy women intimately bound up with divine providence. The exposition of the parallel lines and common features that appear in the call of these women and of the virgin Mary of Nazareth is the purpose of this chapter.

Our Father and Our Mother in Faith: Abraham and Sarah

Abraham is the archetype for responding in faith to God; together with Sarah, this patriarch responds to the divine initiative. Through him God promises the future of the People of God. The tension produced for Abraham, in a testing of his faith, is an important pedagogical and spiritual model for our own pilgrimage and our growth in faith. He was chosen and he freely responded in an affirmative way to Divine Providence, to salvation, and to the future of a People. Abraham is rightly called "our father in faith."

Abraham is not alone in responding to the call of God. His wife Sarah and then a continuing line of women respond to God. They help us understand the meaning of vocation especially in our reflections on Mary's call. Sarah, Hannah, and the women mentioned in Matthew's genealogy come to mind. Tamar, Rahab, Ruth, and Bathsheba are all mentioned in the Davidic lineage that leads to Jesus who was born of Mary (Mt 1:1-17).

Ruth, Esther, and Judith are women involved in the liberation of the chosen people and are seen as mediators of God's plan. In Ruth, the Davidic lineage, the family origins, and faith are emphasized. Esther is an exemplary woman of prayer — intercessory prayer accompanied by deeds in time of danger. Judith, through the power of God, destroys the enemy of Israel.

To understand Mary's vocation and participation in her son's life, the content of the calling of specific women from the Hebrew Scriptures along with the literary genres and patterns are studied and reread in order to discover how God called Mary to a mission for the Christian people. *Dei verbum*, 12 is helpful for understanding these passages:

> Seeing that, in sacred Scripture, God speaks through men [people] in human fashion, it follows that the interpreter of sacred Scriptures, if he [or she] is to ascertain what God has wished to communicate to us, should carefully search out the meaning which the sacred writers really had in mind, that meaning which God had thought well to manifest through the medium of their words.

> In determining the intention of the sacred writers, attention must be paid, *inter alia*, to "literary forms for the fact is that truth is differently presented and expressed in the various types of historical writing, in prophetical and poetical texts," and in other forms of literary expression. Hence the exegete must look for that meaning which the sacred writer, in a determined

situation and given the circumstances of [that] time and culture, intended to express and did in fact express, through the medium of a contemporary literary form. Rightly to understand what the sacred author wanted to affirm in his work, due attention must be paid both to the customary and characteristic patterns of perception, speech, and narrative which prevailed at the age of the sacred writer, and to the conventions which the people of [that] time followed in their dealings with one another.

But since sacred Scripture must be read and interpreted with its divine authorship in mind, no less attention must be devoted to the content and unity of the whole Scripture, taking into account the Tradition of the entire Church and the analogy of faith, if we are to derive their true meaning from the sacred texts. It is the task of exegetes to work, according to these rules, towards a better understanding and explanation of the meaning of the sacred Scripture in order that their research may help the Church to form a firmer judgment. For, of course, all that has been said about the manner of interpreting Scripture is ultimately subject to the judgment of the Church which exercises the divinely conferred commission and ministry of watching over and interpreting the Word of God.

Liturgical Use of These Narratives

The continuation of these biblical accounts of women of faith in the Synagogue and Church enlivens these writings (narratives usually) with their themes to illuminate the present realities of faith in the community. The evangelists, too, used similar biblical structures and elements (e.g., to describe the birth of the Messiah Jesus Christ or the announcement of the birth to Mary and Joseph in the Annunciation pattern) yet, they give a new meaning and hermeneutic to these stories and events found in the Hebrew Scriptures. Their profound reflection and their retelling of such narratives, their development of the constants and continuity of the salvific message of these accounts, and the progress of their own preaching and teaching, resulted in the finished canonical Scriptures we call the New Testament. There is both faithfulness to handing down a tradition (*paradosis*) and progress or development in these writings. Luke's Gospel introduction reminds us of this faithfulness to a tradition:

> Since many have undertaken to compile a narrative of the events that have been fulfilled among us, just as those who were eyewitnesses from the beginning and ministers of the word have handed them down to us, I too have decided, after investigating everything accurately anew, to write it down in an orderly sequence for you, most excellent Theophilus, so that you may realize the certainty of the teachings you have received (Lk 1:1-4).

Luke's introductory chapters show his familiarity with the Hebrew method of interpretation called Midrash. Christian Midrash consists in the rereading of a current event in the community and its life of faith in the light of the Sacred Scriptures (Jesus himself attests to this in Lk 4:16-30, as does Paul in 1 Cor 5:7-8).[49] Luke takes events surrounding the historical life of Jesus, his mother, and his disciples and explains them through the use of this method; this is especially true of Luke 1 and 2. Midrash is not a rigid historical and literal chronicle but rather a searching of the Scriptures and its events in the light of God's revelation both in the Hebrew Scriptures and in the events of Jesus' life and sayings. Midrash is taken from the Hebrew word Darash which means to interpret, to search out the meaning, to do exegesis of the events and facts of the Hebrew Scriptures and Christian Scriptures in the light of God's promises to faithful people.[50]

Another development within Midrash is the notion of a person's call. Vocation or call in the Hebrew Scriptures is neither a theoretical theme nor a doctrine, but simply concerns a religious experience of certain people called by God. It is a significant experience for, as Gabriel Marcel says, "A vocation means a particular calling directed to this special individual to obtain free consent and cooperation in the immense symphony which prepares and progressively realizes the human community."

Vocation is a total personal experience through which the individual comes to realize the bigger picture of life. It involves an intimate relationship with God as Person, and, yet, it is quite natural to our experience, giving meaning to the whole of life.

Analogous to all vocations or calls is the history of salvation, the divine initiative, and the same God who calls Abram and later Mary. There is a pattern in the Bible as to how God calls Israel both collectively as a people and also as individuals like Jacob who is then named Israel.

Each biblical vocation is theocentric or christocentric and soteriological. Abram's call prepares a people for the coming promises of salvation. Jesus himself was aware of the saying, "salvation is from the Jews" (Jn 4:22). "Only from God is Israel's salvation" is a theme common to Psalms. The Word of God becomes flesh and reveals the words of God. There is also the revelatory word(s) of the Hebrew Scriptures that Jesus himself used. From the fuller sense and from a canonical reading of the Bible, Christians see an implicit christological aspect to the Hebrew Scriptures as used and cited by the writers and preachers of the New Testament.

Mary's call is also to be seen in the light of the larger biblical context that has just been elucidated. The difference is the gratuitousness of this call and Mary's free response. Her vocation is within the context of a biblical call; it is singular, intimate, graced, but also within the salvific plan of God and the history of salvation. It is part of the promises and prophecies of God to the people. It involves the liberating activity of God through the Exodus Event and through the Resurrection Event of Jesus. Mary's vocation always has an orientation towards the People of God who are redeemed, chosen, and loved. John 3:16 says it so well: "For God so loved the world that he gave his only Son, so that everyone who believes in him might not perish but might have eternal life." Mary is the human instrument and mother of God's Son.

John Paul II addresses this idea through the teaching tradition of the Church in his encyclical *Redemptoris Mater*:

Mary's faith can also be *compared to that of Abraham*, whom St. Paul calls "our father in faith" (cf. Rm 4:12). In the salvific economy of God's revelation, Abraham's faith constitutes the beginning of the Old Covenant; Mary's faith at the Annunciation inaugurates the New Covenant. Just as Abraham *"in hope believed against hope*, that he should become the father of many nations" (cf. Rm 4:18), so Mary, at the Annunciation, having professed her virginity ("How shall this be, since I have no husband?") *believed* that through the power of the Most High, by the power of the Holy Spirit, she would become the Mother of God's Son in accordance with the angel's revelation: "The child to be born will be called holy, the Son of God" (Lk. 1:35).

However, Elizabeth's words "And blessed is she who believed" do not apply only to that particular moment of the Annunciation. Certainly the Annunciation is the culminating moment of Mary's faith in her awaiting of Christ, but it is also the point of departure from which her whole "journey towards God" begins, her whole pilgrimage of faith. And on this road, in an eminent and truly heroic manner — indeed with an ever greater heroism of faith — the "obedience" which she professes to the word of divine revelation will be fulfilled. Mary's "obedience of faith" during the whole of her pilgrimage will show surprising similarities to the faith of Abraham. Just like the Patriarch of the People of God, so too Mary, during the pilgrimage of her filial and maternal *fiat*, "in hope believed against hope." Especially during certain stages of this journey the blessing granted to her "who believed" will be revealed with particular vividness. To believe means "to abandon oneself" to the truth of the word of the living God, knowing and humbly recognizing "how unsearchable are his judgments and how *inscrutable his ways*" (Rm 11:33). Mary, who by the eternal will of the Most High stands, one may say, at the very center of those "inscrutable ways" and "unsearchable judgments" of God, conforms herself to them in the dim light of faith, accepting fully and with a ready heart everything that is decreed in the divine plan (*Redemptoris Mater*, 14).

As for the vocation of Abraham (Gn 11:27-25:11), it can be seen from the narrative that Abraham is faithful to the call of God. Mary's call is similar both explicitly and implicitly (Lk 1:52; Lk 1:37). Abraham is the icon — the image of Israel in its "roots" — receiving the promise through his response to God's call. His call takes on a universal aspect (Rm 4:11-12, 16).

Abraham was called forth from his father's house (Gn 12:1). The rupture from his ancestral land and its culture and environment was like unto a death for him (Gn 15:5-7; 2 S 14:14). The future seemed closed and empty (Gn 11:30; 12:1).

The end or goal of Abraham's call is seen in the fruitful effects of his faithfulness:

> "May God Almighty bless you and make you fertile, multiply you that you may become an assembly of peoples" (Gn 28:3; cf. Ex 3:6; Gn 15:6; Rm 4:3, 18-22).

> "I am the God of your father," he continued, "the God of Abraham, the God of Isaac, the God of Jacob." Moses hid his face, for he was afraid to look at God (Ex 3:6).

> Abram put his faith in the Lord, who credited it to him as an act of righteousness (Gn 15:6).

> For what does the scripture say? "Abraham believed God, and it was credited to him as righteousness" . . . . He believed, hoping against hope, that he would become "the father of many nations," according to what was said, "Thus shall your descendants be." He did not weaken in faith when he considered his own body as [already] dead (for he was almost a hundred years old) and the dead womb of Sarah. He did not doubt God's promise in unbelief; rather, he was empowered by faith and gave glory to God and was fully convinced that what he had promised he was also able to do. That is why "it was credited to him as righteousness" (Rm 4:3, 18-22; cf. Heb 11:8-19).

His vocation is in view of others, the multitude:

"I will make of you a great nation, and I will bless you; I will make your name great, so that you will be a blessing. I will bless those who bless you and curse those who curse you. All the communities of the earth shall find blessing in you" (Gn 12:2-3).

Though Abraham's call is an individual's call it is realized universally for all God's people.

Sarah: First Princess of Faith

It is Sarah, Abraham's wife, who brings the promise to fruition and helps Abraham to live out his faith in God. Sarai, the beautiful and dominant wife of Abram, has her name changed by God thereby signifying her election and vocation to be the mother of Isaac and the mother of believers. Her story commences in Genesis 12 and ends with her burial in the cave of Machpelah (Gn 23:19; 25:10; 49:31). John L. McKenzie notes: "The promise of a son to Abraham and Sarah appears in the J cycle (Gn 18:6-17); here Sarah laughs at the promise, thus furnishing an occasion to explain the name of her son Isaac."[51] In the Bible she is described as beautiful, generous in hospitality, and faith-filled accompanied by a sense of humor! The New Testament Epistles mention her four times (Rm 4:19; 9:9; Heb 11:11; and 1 P 3:6). These passages show how God worked through her to bear a son despite her barrenness; she is the believing wife and mother of the promise, and is also compared to the heavenly Jerusalem (Gal 4:21-30). Her faith and her obedience are extolled in Hebrews 11:11 and 1 Peter 3:6, respectively. Sarah initiates the matriarchs of the Hebrew Scriptures (Rebekah and Rachel). Her story is presented in the narrative form of traditional literature.[52]

Sarah's only appearance in the reading of the liturgy for masses in honor of the Virgin is in the Mass called "The Blessed Virgin Mary, Chosen Daughter of Israel." This mention of Sarah points out

Mary's continuity with the great matriarch who, through faith, overcomes her barrenness. Mary conceives Jesus because of her faith. The other points of comparison are the fact that Isaac, the son of promise, must issue only from Sarah, not a surrogate.[53] It is these unusual and often initially infertile women who have special births.[54] Sarah's barrenness is ended with the Lord saying to Abraham, "Is anything too marvelous for the Lord to do? At the appointed time, about this time next year, I will return to you, and Sarah will have a son" (Gn 18:14). Mary is told something similar by Gabriel, the messenger of God: "The Holy Spirit will come upon you, and the power of the Most High will overshadow you. Therefore the child to be born will be called holy, the Son of God. . . for nothing will be impossible for God" (Lk 1:35, 37).

Sarah/Mary

Sarah is a vivacious and dominant woman in the narratives of the Bible which came from three traditions: the Yahwist, the Elohist, and the Priestly. Her faith, hospitality, and freedom are evident in these narratives. McKenzie continues, summing up her personality:

> She is represented in the J narratives with a vivacious and well defined character, proud, quick to anger, hardly the submissive and demure wife, a bustling and generous hostess and easily amused, ready for the give and take of conversation with her man and his guests. These are not necessarily traits of the historical Sarah; she is described as the kind of wife whom the Bedu chieftain finds attractive, except for the curse of sterility. This curse is removed by the blessing which is conferred upon her husband.[55]

Mary has Sarah's trait of generous hospitality seen in her visit to Elizabeth (Lk 1:39-45). Mary is also blessed by God with a son despite the problem of her status as a virgin. She also is a model in faith seen throughout her whole life in the few events recorded about her in the New Testament.

Mary, a Model of Faith Among the Heroines of the Bible

In the celebration of Marian feasts, passages from the Hebrew Scriptures which narrate the lives and events of the great women heroines of Judaism are chosen. These great matriarchs, heroines, prophets, judges, and courageous women can be considered types and figures of Mary. A tradition about them continues both in Judaism after the formation of the Hebrew canon and in the Christian Church which attributes the gifts of these women to, and sees them mirrored in Mary.

There are significant studies of the life of Mary as prefigured by these women. A. Serra in his monumental essays on biblical-Marian exegesis shows the development of the Jewish tradition surrounding these biblical persons. In a spiritual and poetic reflective series, A. Johnson writes of these women in her trilogy: *Miryam of Nazareth, Miryam of Judah,* and *Miryam of Jerusalem.*

The early Christian writers like Justin, Irenaeus, and Tertullian likewise made use of a scriptural typology in their comparisons of Mary with the women of the Bible, especially with Eve, the mother of the living.

Johnson presents a good many of the women in her studies and spiritual writings about Mary. She is presenting them under the guidance of several rabbis in order to truly represent the Jewish tradition of which Mary is a part. She refers to Deborah, Judith, Esther, Ruth and Miryam (Moses' sister) in *Miryam of Nazareth.* In *Miryam of Judah* she refers to Bathsheba, Ruth, Rahab, and Tamar. In *Miryam of Jerusalem,* Eve, Sarah, Hannah, and a symbolic Queen Shalom-Zion are reflected and developed with a Marian purpose to better present the Jewish experience of holiness in the context of their lives seen in the Bible.

R. Brown's *The Birth of the Messiah* has references to various women within his research. His focus is upon Jesus Christ as Messiah; nevertheless, there are many points of reference and research which apply to Mary in relationship to these women, seen in the perspective of the mother of the Messiah. Who are these women? They are Eve, Judith, Esther, the bride of the Canticle, Rachel, Leah, Jochebed (mother of Moses), Deborah, the mother of the Maccabees, Ruth, and Miriam.

By a Christian faith-filled reading of the Hebrew Scriptures, many of Mary's women predecessors are remembered in her own commemoration in the liturgy of the Western Church. With the liturgical addition of 46 thematic masses in her honor, which include the regular Marian feasts of the Church, a selection of passages from the pages which highlight the illustrious feats and words of these heroines of Israel are often recalled in the first reading on the Marian feasts. Such a choice again confirms Mary as part of a long history of courageous God-centered women from that same covenant of loving-kindness between God and Israel.

An Evaluation of Earlier Interpretations of Genesis 1-3 and Eve as Mother of All the Living

J. H. Cardinal Newman and J. Lebon suggested that the idea of Mary as a new or second Eve was current during the time of the apostles. Contemporary exegetes concur with this notion especially through the text of the Fourth Gospel:

> Standing by the cross of Jesus were his mother and his mother's sister, Mary the wife of Clopas, and Mary of Magdala. When Jesus saw his mother and the disciple there whom he loved, he said to his mother, "Woman, behold, your son." Then he said to the disciple, "Behold, your mother." And from that hour the disciple took her into his home (Jn 19:25-27).

The Pauline mention of Christ as a second Adam also led early writers to compare Mary with Eve. St. Irenaeus is considered to be the founder of Mariology; he stamped the comparison of Eve and Mary in the mind of Christendom. The Eve-Mary parallel and contrast continued to appear in medieval writing. In recent times this theme appears to have become on a near-fundamental principle in Mariological studies.

Pius IX in the Bull *Ineffabilis Deus* states that the Fathers compared Mary with Eve "to demonstrate the original innocence and sanctity of the Mother of God," recalling that "they have also exalted her above Eve with a wonderful variety of expressions." Principal papal contributions to this teaching were made by Pius XII who brought together the two traditions of Mary as the new Eve and as the Woman in Genesis 3:15, setting the Eve-Mary parallel in Calvary and seeing it as a basis for Mary's part in our salvation. Vatican II in *Lumen Gentium* recalled the theme in the biblical setting of the Annunciation and mentioned it in the context of the Mary-Church typology.

Other than in the early chapters of Genesis, Eve is not mentioned in the Hebrew Bible. She seems to be alluded to by Ben Sira (Si 25:23) when he says, "In woman was sin's beginning, and because of her we all die." Ben Sira, who probably was taking a minority position, was the first known author to state that the negative results of a woman's acts are sin and death. This reading from Sirach was taken up a century later in the pseudepigraphical work called the Books of Adam and Eve wherein Eve relates and confesses her sinfulness. Later the cause and effect of sin was placed on Eve especially in the Apocalypse of Moses, written early in the century before Christ. Carol Meyers writes that these attitudes which entered Christian tradition are found in 1 Timothy 2:13-14: "For Adam was formed first, then Eve. Further, Adam was not deceived, but the woman was deceived and transgressed," wherein Eve is not only associated with sin but her creation is viewed as secondary with the implication that it was of lesser importance. Meyers contends that by the early centuries of the Christian era, the association of Eve and sin with sexuality and lust became common in religious literature. It was expanded in both Christian and ancient

Jewish postbiblical sources, with the serpent playing an increasingly satanic and phallic role. She writes of problems with ancient translations which possibly suffer from bias and distortion, including small and subtle examples of antifemale bias in St. Jerome's Vulgate. She also discusses distortion of biblical material in John Milton's *Paradise Lost* which can have far-reaching consequences. With interpretations of the Hebrew narrative of Genesis 2-3 becoming common after the formation of the canon, variations on themes of female sin and inferiority which were not part of the original text became endless. The more Eve was identified as the source of sin, the more urgent the need to control, subdue, and dominate her since she was seen as representative of her sex.[56]

With respect to God or humans, Hebrew is a gendered language. Certain words may be rendered as masculine in places where they are not meant to specify gender. An example is the generic word for human, *'adam*, which is usually translated as "man," and which Meyers sees as implying a priority for male existence. The word for that from which the first human being is formed is *'adamah*, usually translated as "ground" or "earth." Although the words for "human" and for "ground" are thus connected phonetically (and perhaps etymologically), in their traditional renderings they do not communicate either the generic nature of "man" or the integral connection of humanity with its earthly matrix. Meyers suggests that the Revised Standard Version of Genesis 2:7 be rendered differently. It reads:

> Then the Lord God formed man of dust from the ground and breathed into his nostrils the breath of life and man became a living being.

She says a better rendition is:

> Then God Yahweh formed an *earthling* of clods from the *earth* and breathed into its nostril the breath of life; and the *earthling* became a living being.
>
> or:

Then God Yahweh formed a *human* from clods of the *humus* and
breathed into its nostrils the breath of life, and the *human*
became a living being.

These last two translations capture the flavor and meaning of the
original text as well as the pun and assonance of the Hebrew. She
explains that names or substantives are not simply labels but are also
indicators of the essence of those things or beings designated. The
term *'adam* tells that the essence of human life is not its eventual
classification into gender categories (the first creature is not inher-
ently gendered) but rather its organic connection to the earth. The
earth here is not unspecified but is *'adamah*, that reddish brown
substance (humus) capable of absorbing water, being cultivated,
and supporting life.

Meyers reaches beyond Genesis 1 with its pairing of male and
female for procreative purposes to Genesis 2 with its presentation
of humans as social beings. Here before Eve is named as "mother of
all the living" in Genesis 3:20, the nonhierarchical relationship
aspect of the unifying bond of a couple precedes the parent-child
relationship which is an intrinsically hierarchal one.[57]

Eve: First Mother of All the Living

Eve's name in Hebrew means "life." She is called *Chavvah* (in
the Septuagint, *Eva;* in the Vulgate, *Heva*) because she is the mother
of all the living (Gn 3:20). Her initial appearance in the Hebrew
Scriptures is one of beauty, goodness, wisdom, and life. Why is it
that she has been contrasted with the first man in the Hebrew
Scriptures and then paralleled antithetically with Mary in the early
Christian writers Justin (100/110-165 C.E.) and Irenaeus (140-202
C.E.)? It is more appropriate for both the Church and the Synagogue to return to the positive and dynamic image of Eve that we
have in the earliest references to her in the Bible and the early
rabbinic literature where her beauty is extolled.

Phyllis Trible in her groundbreaking article on Genesis takes

us back to the Hebrew text and retrieves the positive image of Eve
that had been eradicated by the patriarchal rereading of the same
texts.[58]

One of the earliest texts from the Talmud comments on the
moment of creation:

> In the past Adam was created from the earth and Eve was
> created from "Adam" "in our image after our likeness" (Gn
> 1:26)
> "Neither man without woman
> nor woman without man,
>   nor the two of them without Divine Presence."

The word used for Divine Presence is *shekhinah* — both the divine
presence in the world and also the divine presence dwelling among
us humans.

In Genesis 2:7 (Yahwist tradition) there is a play on words that
suggests both man and woman were initially created from the earth
(*ha-'adamâ*) as earth creature (*ha-'adam*). This would show equality
and that sexual differentiation does not appear until the creation of
woman in Genesis 2:22.[59]

In Genesis 1:26-27 we read:

> And God said, "Let us make the earth-creatures (Adam) in our
> image and likeness and let them rule over the fish of the sea and
> the winged creatures of the heavens and over all living
> creatures and creeping things upon the earth." And God then
> created the earth-creature (*ha 'adam*) in the image (of God) —
> in the image of God God created them; male and female God
> created them. [My translation]

Susan Niditch comments:

> Without establishing relative rank or worth of the genders, the
> spinner of this creation tale indicates that humankind is found
> in two varieties, the male and the female, and this humanity in
> its complementarity is a reflection of the deity. For feminist

readers of scriptures, no more interesting and telegraphic comment exists on the nature of being human and on the nature of God. The male aspect and the female aspect implicitly are part of the first human and a reflection of the Creator. . . . In reading the Hebrew Scriptures as a narrative whole, including both Genesis 1:27 and Leviticus, one may receive the message that the genders were meant to be equal at the beginning.[60]

The culpability of the Fall (original sin) is due to the failure of *ha 'adam* seen as both male and female. Too often in Judaism and Christianity the blame is predominantly foisted on the woman Eve. By retrieving the more accurate and non-patriarchal interpretation of Genesis 1-3 a better understanding of the equality of all persons — including the original pair — is achieved without the blatant sexism that these chapters spawned among male interpreters for centuries.

In the more earthly theology of the Yahwist, Eve is depicted as the catalyst for the plot. She appears as one more curious, more alert, risking and testing the waters of one's choice as suggested by the cunning serpent. She is the protagonist and heroine of the story, not "Adam." Niditch says: "Eve, as she is named in 3:20, is the protagonist, not her husband. This is an important point, as is the realization that to be the curious one, the seeker of knowledge, the tester of limits is to be quintessentially human — to evidence traits of many of the culture-bringing heroes and heroines of Genesis."[61]

In understanding both the Church's and the Synagogue's image of Eve, there is need to look at the sources which comment on the second and third chapters of Genesis. Christians are aware of the contrast of Eve with Mary ("Eva" — "Ave" contrasts). However, it is from ancient Judaism that we first learn about the image of Eve. This literature from 200 B.C.E. to 400 C.E. includes such documents as the Apocrypha of the Old Testament, Philo (20 B.C.E.-54 C.E.), Josephus (37-103 C.E.), the Dead Sea Scrolls, the Targums, the Talmud, the Tosephta, the Midrashim and the Samaritan tradition of Memar Margah.[62] These writings comprise what, in general, can be called the *Torah b'al peh*, the living voice or living tradition, which comments on and applies the canonical Scriptures to the real situations of daily life.

Aristide Serra in his celebrated book *E C'era la madre di Gesù* tells us: "when ancient Israel speaks of the above mothers (Eve, Sarah, Rebeccah, Rachel, Bila, Leah, Zilpa, Jochebed, the mother of Moses, Miriam, Deborah, Ruth, Anna. . .) I have noticed that themes and doctrines are expressed that are very similar to what Christianity says about the mother of Jesus, starting already with the authors of the New Testament."[63]

Eve: The First and Most Beautiful Mother of Israel

The rabbinic writings praise the beauty and adornment of Eve while commenting on Genesis 2:22: "The Lord God then built up into a woman the rib that he had taken from man." For example, Rabbi Chama ben Chanina (260 C.E.) wrote that certainly God first clothed her (Eve) with twenty-four precious decorations (those which describe the women of Israel in Isaiah 3:18-24) and then God brings her to the man. Therefore the Lord through the mouth of Ezekiel applies the following (which was originally addressed to the prince of Tyre) to her:

> In Eden, the garden of God, you were, and every precious stone was your covering [carnelian, topaz, and beryl, chrysolite, onyx, and jasper, sapphire, garnet, and emerald]; of gold your pendants and jewels were made, on the day you were created (Ezk 28:13).

And

> You were stamped with the seal of perfection, of complete wisdom and perfect beauty (Ezk 28:12; cf. Genesis Rabbah 18, 1 and 2, 22 and the Babylonian Talmud, Baba Bathra 75a).[64]

As for Eve being called the mother of Israel, we have from Pseudo-Philo (100 C.E.):

> It was not unjustly that God took and formed a rib from you, knowing that from it Israel was born (*Liber Antiquitatum Biblicarum* 32, 15).

The Babylonian Talmud states:

> The image of Eve has been transmitted to the preeminent beautiful women of every age (Babylonian Talmud, Sotah 9B).

Other rabbis reflect that Eve's beauty was so outstanding that the serpent desired to have her for himself and, intending to kill Adam, tried to seduce her. A similar thought was also expressed by Gnostics of the second century, as related by Irenaeus: "Those who are called Angels — some of them arriving and seeing her beauty and calling her Eve desired to beget daughters with her" (*Adversus Haereses*, I. 30.7). Undoubtedly, this idea stems from Genesis 6:1-4, which recounts the legend of the appearance of giants upon the earth:

> When men began to multiply on earth and daughters were born to them, the sons of heaven saw how beautiful the daughters of man were, and so they took for their wives as many of them as they chose. Then the Lord said: "My spirit shall not remain in man forever, since he is but flesh. His days shall comprise one hundred and twenty years." At that time *the Nephilim appeared on earth* (as well as later), after the sons of heaven had intercourse with the daughters of man, who bore them sons. They were the heroes of old, the men of renown. [my italics]

Sarah also is praised in reference to her beauty and that of Eve (Genesis, Rabbah 40, 5a, 12, 14).

In intertestamental literature (Old Testament Pseudepigrapha) the mother of the seven sons refers to Eve. She addresses these righteous sayings to her children:

> I was a chaste maiden and did not leave my father's house, but I kept guard over the rib built into woman's body (Gn 2:22 in the Septuagint). No seducer of the desert nor deceiver in the field corrupted me, nor did the seducing and beguiling serpent defile my maidenly purity (IV Maccabees 18:7-9).[65]

Later Jewish writings contrast Eve's disobedience with the fidelity and obedience of the Israelites to God on Mount Sinai. These people, because of their positive response to the covenant and the Torah, take the place of Eve without losing their integrity. Rabbi R. Yochanan (279 C.E.) had this phrase: "When the serpent accosted Eve, he injected concupiscence within her. . . (while) the Israelites who stood opposite Mt. Sinai were no longer unchaste" (Babylonian Talmud, Shabbat 146a). In the same line "the Gentiles (*goyim*), however, who did not stand opposite Mt. Sinai never ceased in their unchastity."

In the New Testament, Eve is never mentioned in the Gospels. Adam is only mentioned in Luke's genealogy (Lk 3:38). Eve is mentioned in two Pauline writings:

> For I am jealous of you with the jealousy of God, since I betrothed you to one husband to present you as a chaste virgin to Christ. But I am afraid that, as the serpent deceived Eve by his cunning, your thoughts may be corrupted from a sincere [and pure] commitment to Christ (2 Cor 11:2-3).

> For Adam was formed first, then Eve. Further, Adam was not deceived, but the woman was deceived and transgressed. But she will be saved through motherhood, provided women persevere in faith and love and holiness, with self-control (1 Tm 2:13-15).

Both passages emphasize the denigration of Eve. This, too, would be taken up in Judaism. The beginnings of the negative aspects of

Eve appear. They will be overemphasized in Justin (100/110-165 C.E.), Irenaeus (140-202 C.E.) and Tertullian (137-228 C.E.). These Christian writers will contrast Mary's "yes" with Eve's fall — and within a biblical context. The beauty, the intelligence, the willingness to risk and explore found in Eve are not mentioned. She is denounced again and again in both Christian and Jewish interpretations of the texts of Genesis 3. Only through the retrieval of a more faithful interpretation of the Hebrew text can we come to an appreciation of the greatness of Israel's first mother Eve, the mother of the living. The Eve-Church typology is inaugurated by these three writers and then is taken up again by Augustine (354-430 C.E.). The texts of Genesis 3:15 and Isaiah 7:14 become leaders in a whole chain of texts that continue such a development of Mary-Church over against Eve. The good qualities of Eve are forgotten because of the seduction of the serpent.

Parallels are seen between Mary's dialogue with Gabriel and Eve's dialogue with the serpent (Gn 3:1-7, Lk 1:28-35). The text of Genesis 3:15 is also compared with the scene of Mary at the foot of the Cross (Jn 19:25-28a). Newman and Lebon suggested that Mary is seen as a new Eve by these early Church writers. In my opinion, such an interpretation did not belong to the earliest commentators in Christianity. Have not the Jewish commentators interpreted Eve in ambivalent ways, sometimes emphasizing her beauty and adornment and, at other times, her failure? A return to a positive presentation of Eve would take nothing away from the Synagogue or Church. The method of parallel typology is more a method of interpretation of the past and, possibly, a patriarchal tendency. Yet, the theory of Justin, Irenaeus, and Tertullian persists. Later writers would continue the development. Jerome says, "Death through Eve, life through Mary." St. Augustine is more tempered. Michael O'Carroll notes: "Reflecting constantly on the Church and Christ its head, he [Augustine] saw Eve as the figure of the Church, which he also called 'mother of the living.' Mary is the model for her sex. The death-life antithesis is for him 'through a *woman* death, through a woman life.'"[66]

Louis Billot as a dogmatic theologian states an extreme position: "It is generally to be held about the Virgin Mother that in the
order of restoration she holds the place that Eve held in the order
of perdition."[67]

Papal statements about Eve are not as negative as the ones
mentioned above. The Popes usually attribute the fall to Adam as
well as Eve. Notably Pius XII brings together the traditions about
Mary as a new Eve and as the Woman in Genesis 3:15. This latter
interpretation sets up the parallel of the garden (Gn 3) with Calvary
(Jn 19:25-28a).

Vatican II's *Lumen Gentium*, 56, mentions Eve while citing Irenaeus, Epiphanius, Jerome, and Augustine. Fortunately, the opening
paragraph in using both the text of Genesis 3:15 and Isaiah 7:14
counteracts this negativity within a context of salvation history or
redemption.

Conclusion

One could view the process of salvation history from Eve to
Mary as a double movement: first the breaking up of the human race
into many disparate individuals, and then the gradual concentration
of all expectations of salvation in the Messiah born of Mary, the
Mother of God. All the eminent women in the Old Testament are
concrete and partial realizations of the primal mother from ancient
times (Eve) who perdures and extends herself in them. As the new
Adam extends himself in the "Mystical Body" of Christ (the ecclesial
community of the new People of God), so also does Mary represent
all those "children of God, once dispersed, but now brought
together" by her Son.

Jesus' words on the cross, "There is your mother" (Jn 19:27),
may point to the popular etymological explanation of Eve's name in
Genesis 3:20: "The man called his wife Eve, because she became the
mother of all the living." Just as the Church is "the Jerusalem above
. . . our mother" (Gal 4:26), so also is Mary the mother of believers,

who, at the cross, were concretely present in the person "of the disciple whom Jesus loved."[68]

Comparisons can be odious. Perhaps it is more appropriate to refrain from building up one person at the expense of another. Eve, like Mary, has been redeemed. It is time to emphasize her positive human qualities as well as her lost preternatural ones. A delightful description of Eve speaks to these reflections and sounds just like the doctrine of the Catholic Church about the Immaculate Conception: "Being the first woman Eve had no inherited sin. Coming from the hand of God, Eve had an advantage no other woman has ever had — she was pure and holy, with the divine image unimpaired."[69]

Rebekah

Rebekah is the second matriarch of Israel. She is described in Genesis 24:16: "The girl was very beautiful, a virgin, untouched by man." Her story is the conclusion of the Abraham saga.

> She is the most clever and authoritative of the matriarchs, and yet she epitomizes womanly beauty and virtue, in her conduct (her virginity, her actions at the well), in her energetic speech, in her thoughtful courtesy, and in her self-assurance.[70]

Rebekah as a woman of Israel, in fact the mother of Jacob who is later called Israel, is presented as a virgin the first time she is mentioned in Genesis. As her story continues and she is married to Isaac, we discover she is sterile up to the moment that she prays God to deliver her from this situation. She gives birth to Esau and Jacob, but has a special preference for Jacob. It is through her mediation and cleverness that she wins for Jacob the blessing of the aging and blind Isaac. Jacob has to flee from Esau, thus creating a separation of the mother from her preferred child.

In Paul's letter to the Romans, the following theological insight displays Rebekah's role in the history of God's People, Israel:

> . . . when Rebecca had conceived children by one husband, our
> father Isaac — before they had yet been born or had done
> anything, good or bad, in order that God's elective plan might
> continue, not only by work but by his call — she was told,
> "The older shall serve the younger" (Rm 9:10-12).

Paul's marvelous commentary on the messianic promise, carried on in a more dramatic way in the history of salvation through Jacob, emphasizes the free election of God through the persons of faith, the great matriarchs and patriarchs of the Genesis account.

Mary's call comes to her through Gabriel and she, too, is eventually separated from her son both in the three days of searching for him and in the year or years of his active ministry. Her role in the messianic promise continues what had begun in her ancestors — Sarah, Rebekah, Rachel.

Carol Meyers shows the importance of the biblical women such as Rebekah when she states that women who occasionally appear in leadership roles in the biblical record should not be viewed as exceptions but as representatives of perhaps a larger group of publicly active females whose identity was lost because of the male-controlled canonical process; that the female prophets and wisdom figures could not have found their place in the canon if they were not part of an acknowledgment of female worth and authority.[71]

Teresa Okure, a Nigerian scholar, perceived a connection between Rebekah's role and that of Mary. Seen from the twentieth-century perspective, Rebekah's action of helping Jacob to steal the paternal blessing from Isaac would not be condoned. Yet, her action would be praised in the moral code of her time. Okure explains that what she did paralleled Abraham's giving out his wife, Sarah, to be his sister, thus bringing disaster on innocent Egyptians (Gn 12:10-29). Rebekah's case involved not ingenuity directed toward personal gain, but rather her cooperation with God in her own way to bring about realization of the divine plan, for God had revealed to her the destiny of her two children before they were born. The mother of Jesus cooperated with God in the final and greatest stage in salvation history.[72]

Rebekah/Mary

Rebekah is a virgin at the time of her marriage to Isaac. Her single-mindedness, fidelity, and love of predilection for Jacob are qualities that perdure in the narratives about her. She is creative in her manner of helping Jacob to steal the blessing of the firstborn from Isaac (Gn 22:23; 24; 26:6-11; 27).

Mary is a virgin in the accounts of Matthew (1:16; 18-25) and Luke (1:26-38). Her blessedness is extolled by Elizabeth (Lk 1:45). Her single-mindedness is seen in the events which relate her to her son Jesus on almost every occasion in which she is mentioned in the New Testament.

Rachel

It is from Rachel that the most genuine of the Israelite tribes issue, hence she is a woman of Israel *par excellence* since she is the mother of Joseph and Benjamin by Jacob. "The story of Rachel is a story of unparalleled love and devotion in the biblical narrative."[73]

Matthew 2:17-18 sees the fulfillment of the prophecy of Jeremiah which speaks of Rachel's great sorrow: "A voice was heard in Ramah, sobbing and loud lamentation; Rachel weeping for her children, and she would not be consoled, since they were no more." This citation from Jeremiah 31:15 refers to the taking of Israel by Assyria in 722-21 B.C.E. There is a parallel to the original narrative setting surrounding Rachel when she died in giving birth to her second son (Gn 35:16-19). Matthew, who is clearly speaking of the birth of the Messiah Jesus, uses the text from Jeremiah to show that the Holy Family escapes the slaughter of the children of Bethlehem.

In a recent presentation of Rachel by Jacob Neusner, Mary, the mother of Jesus, is compared to Rachel.[74] To show the powerful intercession Rachel has with God, Neusner uses a commentary on Lamentations in the work called Lamentations Rabbah. This is a midrash on Rachel with passages of the Torah, the Psalms and the Prophets which shows that it is a Pharisaic interpretation of Rachel. Perhaps Matthew too was a converted Pharisee and thought along these same lines but knew of the mother of Jesus. The format is more folkloric in Lamentations Rabbah while more soberly narrative in Matthew — more prosaic, if you will. The Hebrew commentary is a haggadah, i.e., a religious retelling of the story of innocent children with a culmination and resolution of their continued pain and suffering through Rachel who intercedes with God for the children of the future. All of the male heroes fail in interceding with God (Abraham, Isaac, Jacob and Moses) while Rachel succeeds. The author of the midrash works from a timeless perspective — a "kairos" reckoning in which all times and persons are present before God and one another, a concept close to the Catholic belief in the Communion of Saints.

Rachel gains God's ear because she speaks of love and of family relationships. There is a healing of blood relationships because she not only *speaks* of love but has lived out of love and experienced it throughout her life. "Rachel's message to God is to relate to Israel with the love that comes from within the family, the holy family" (Neusner's words).

Neusner intellectually presents the facts about Mary but admits he does not understand them. He admits of *analogy* on the human level, but not on the transcendent level of mystery. And this is how it should be. In our own reflections, we are dealing primarily with the historical person of Mary of Nazareth — the most revered woman of all times and the unique one who has appeared on the cover of many issues of *Time* magazine. The Marian Library in Dayton, Ohio, boasts of 80,000 volumes that touch some aspect of her; it is impossible to dismiss her from Jewish, Muslim, and Christian memory for she does appear in these Traditions.

Neusner begins with an incident of the Holy Family in Matthew's Gospel — the most Jewish of the Gospels and the one which immediately ties in the story of Jesus with texts from the Hebrew Scriptures which act as a scaffold for the building of the Jesus story in Matthew. More than any other Gospel, Matthew directly cites the Old Testament to describe or demonstrate a point Jesus is making or an event in his life. These are called fulfillment texts and Neusner has cited one of them which brings in an analogy with Rachel, a great woman and saint in the Hebrew Scriptures and Tradition. It is here that Neusner captures the "ethos" of Catholicism for Mary by demonstrating how a believing Jew has similar sentiments and devotion for Rachel.

Neusner notes that the Judaic Mary plays a role in the very passage in which Mary and Jesus figure as principals. That helps in understanding Mary at Cana (Jn 2:1-12) or Mary's intervention in Mark (3:31-35) or her illuminative presence in Chapters 1 and 2 of Luke's Infancy Narrative. The concluding paragraph of his own theologizing on the passage is found on page 99 and is worth citing: ". . . if I could do it, so can you. Why this excess of jealousy for idolatry, which is nothing, that 'you have sent my children into exile'?"

Neusner thus sees more than a parallel between Mary and Rachel. It is more of an analogy and thereby touches the components of faith and reason within two traditions which come very close to one another in understanding the significance of prayer and love, especially when it comes from saintly persons like Rachel and Mary. Neusner speaks of the need for *feeling, sensing;* for sympathy and even empathy if we are to make analogies like this. He sees his faith as a Jew leading him to God who is the same God for Christians and Muslims. When Jews say to God's covenant of Sinai, "We shall do and we shall obey," Christians understand that Mary tells them "Do whatever he (Jesus) tells you," and that God listens and even works miracles!

Neusner has understood the person of Mary. He has also shown that "formative emotions" are as constitutive of the social construction of reality as "formative ideas."

Rachel/Mary

Rachel overcomes her sterility through the help of God. She is clever in her stealing of the teraphim or household gods of Laban, her father, thereby securing her independence and the predominance of the heritage of Israel. Her sorrow is evident in the loss of Joseph her son. This is recalled by Jeremiah the prophet (Jr 31:15). She is the beloved bride of Jacob who labored extensively for her hand.

Mary's virginity is blessed through the overshadowing of the Holy Spirit and she gives birth to Jesus. Matthew recalls the incident of Rachel's weeping when narrating the slaughter of the Innocents. Mary like Rachel is a sorrowful mother who endures the death of her son Jesus on Calvary.

Leah

Leah is an important mother of the Israelites. She stems from Terah of Mesopotamia through Nahor and Bethuel. Her father is Laban, son of Bethuel and brother to Rebekah. Leah is the mother of Reuben, Simeon, Levi, Judah, Issachar, Zebulun, and Dinah. The sons of her slave are Gad and Asher who are also reckoned as her sons. Leah through divine Providence is the ancestor of two great figures in Israel, namely, Moses and David. This gift to her is from God despite Jacob's preference for Rachel. The last mention of Leah is Genesis 49:31: "There Abraham and his wife Sarah are buried, and so are Isaac and his wife Rebekah, and there, too, I buried Leah — the field and the cave in it had been purchased from the Hittites."

During the patriarchal age the marriage laws were not as strict as those prescribed in Leviticus 18:6-8. How does Leah fit into the Marian tradition? Through the fact that Judah, one of her sons, is the originator of the Davidic lineage. Though she is not mentioned in the genealogy of Matthew 1:1-17 there is a connection through Judah and through her unusual marriage to Jacob. She is the prolific mother of eight of the twelve tribes named after her sons.

Leah/Mary

Leah's fidelity to Jacob is among her strengths. She is the mother of the eight "Leah tribes." Her devotedness to family life and parents is among her virtues. She is a person who is no stranger to self-sacrifice.

Mary gives birth to Jesus who is a descendant of Judah (a son of Leah). Mary likewise is faithful to her family throughout the hidden years and in the public life of Jesus. Her presence in John's Gospel at the foot of the Cross attests to her compassion, her suffering, and her love.

Deborah and Jael

Deborah is one of the mothers of Israel who is honored both in the Scriptures and the Tradition of Israel. There are two Deborahs mentioned in the Hebrew Scriptures, the nurse of Rebekah who is buried near Bethel (Gn 35:8) and the prophetess Deborah, the wife of Lappidoth (Jg 4:4-5:31). Judges 5 is the important chapter for remembering her, while Pseudo-Philo offers fascinating information about her in the Tradition of Israel.

Deborah because of her leadership, courage, and prophetic-call is honored in the victory song over Jabin and Sisera, the Canaanite leaders. The victory song is one of the oldest pieces within the Hebrew Scriptures, perhaps going back to the epoch of the Judges (1200 B.C.E.).

Deborah's song consists of 106 lines. It is written or sung not by her but about her. The song is about water and glory — the mediation of God, Yahweh, through a storm brings about God's glory through the victory. Jael, another woman, finalizes the victory by killing Sisera the commander of the Canaanites. Blessings and curses make up the latter part of the poem. Jael is praised as "Blessed among women" (Jg 5:24).

In a rereading of the Hebrew Scriptures and of Pseudo-Philo

it can be seen by analogy how the Catholic Church has detected similarities in the Virgin Mary to both Deborah and Jael. First, Deborah as Mother of Israel calls her children to walk in the way of the Torah. (The information primarily comes from Pseudo-Philo.) Mary, likewise, exhorts the servants at Cana to do whatever Jesus tells them (Jn 2:1-5). Deborah is exhorting Israel to glory in the Lord. Water is the symbol or means of victory. This parallels Jesus changing the water into wine, thereby manifesting his glory (Jn 2:11).

In the victory song Jael, the wife of Heber, is praised: "Blessed among women be Jael, blessed among tent-dwelling women" (Jg 5:24). We read in Luke the beatitudes bestowed on Mary by Elizabeth (Lk 1:45), by Gabriel in the Annunciation (1:28), and also by the unknown woman in the crowd (Lk 11:27). Deborah is seen as Mother of Israel in spirit; Mary is the Mother of all believers represented by the beloved disciple at the foot of the Cross (Jn 19:25-27).

There is also the similarity of the Holy Spirit resting upon both Deborah and Mary. The prophetess is extolled in Tradition:

> What was Deborah's character that she should have judged Israel, and prophesied to them at a time when Phinehas son of Elazer was alive? I call heaven and earth to witness that whether it be Gentile or Israelite, man or woman, slave or handmaid, according to the deeds which he does, so will the Holy Spirit rest on him (Tan. d. b. El. p. 48).

Within Chapter 5 of Judges, Deborah spoke about Jael in verse 24 calling her "Blessed among women," a descriptive phrase left out of the prose version. It seems appropriate to mention Deborah's words about Jael in our discussion about Deborah since those words actually do find resonance in the Lucan presentation of the Visitation scene. On the side of the Hebrew tradition, the words of Deborah have also found resonance in Judith 13:18, in the words uttered by Uzziah to Judith, after she had liberated the city of Bethulia, by cutting off the head of the general of the invading force,

Holofernes. Uzziah said to her: "Blessed are you, daughter, by the Most High God, above all the women on earth."

Jewish commentators confirm the specific connections between the Lucan Mary and Jael and even the Lucan Mary and Judith, especially noting some of the visual and performance oriented artistic pieces based upon the images of these women of the Hebrew Testament. A question is whether there might be any additional possible associations between Deborah and Mary. The Jewish or Catholic sources do not mention any additional connections but a couple of additional possibilities will be considered.

There are certain traditions which give Mary a role in the discernment of heresy, true and false apostles, etc., within the life of the Church. This context of "judging" like Deborah, listening and responding to the cries of her people, might be an appropriate image and context to offer those who want to try to imagine the meaning of this traditional function of Mary in the Church. This image is a logical extrapolation of her continual pondering and sure adherence to the Mystery of Christ: "And Mary kept all these things, reflecting on them in her heart" (Lk 2:19, 51). Luke 11:28 reads: "Rather, blessed are those who hear the word of God and observe it."

Is it pushing the analogy too far to suggest that this same verse offers another possible connection between Deborah and Mary? Given the previous connection between Mary and Jael (Jg 4:21 and 5:24), one in which the Fathers of the Church read Genesis 3:15 as *a woman* crushing the head of the serpent, might we not see Deborah's and Jael's actions suggesting images for reflection upon Mary's role as "judge" and "prophetess" in relationship to the apostles who were sent out after the Resurrection to go to all nations in order to preach God's effective word of redemption from sin and thus be his "witnesses in Jerusalem, throughout Judea and Samaria, and to the ends of the earth" (Lk 24:44-49 and Ac 1:8)?

These comparisons, perhaps, might be supplemented by one additional reference from within the "core and center" of the Magnificat: "He has thrown down the rulers from their thrones but lifted up the lowly. The hungry he has filled with good things; the rich he has sent away empty" (Lk 1:52-53). These words of Mary have their resonances in Deborah's poetic description of the mother of Sisera who waits in vain for her son to return along with the spoils of victory (Jg 5:28-31).

One final word about Jael. In the Canticle of Deborah, Jael receives a blessing: "Blessed among women be Jael, blessed among tent-dwelling women." Similar words are used of Mary by Elizabeth; Mary, however, is more of a city-dwelling woman than a tent-dweller.

Deborah, Jael/Mary

Deborah is a remarkable leader who has the gifts of prophecy and wisdom. Her decisions result in victory for Israel at the hands of another courageous woman, Jael. Deborah, in her Canticle (Jg 5), shows total confidence in God and attributes the victory to God's power over the foreign kings.

Mary does not enter into the realm of judging and prophesying nor is she a leader in time of war. She does display a similar gift of practical wisdom and in her Magnificat Canticle sings of the power of God over Israel's enemies. Mary compares with Jael in sharing a similar macarism: "Blessed are you among women."

Jochebed

Jochebed, the mother of Moses, Miriam, and Aaron, is considered as a "Mother of Israel" in the Jewish tradition. She is a Levite and is mentioned in the genealogies of Exodus 6:20 as the wife of Amram and as the mother of Moses and Aaron. In Numbers 26:59 she is described as "of the tribe of Levi, born to the tribe in Egypt."

A. Serra presents the dismissal of Jochebed by her husband Amram from the haggadah Sotah 12a (200-300 C.E.). This story tells of the decision of Amram and all Israelites to cease having children because of the persecution of Pharaoh. Miriam, his daughter, convinces him to secretly take back Jochebed. Upon this renewal of their wedding ceremony Psalm 113:9 is sung. Miriam, true to her prophetic calling, then foresees the birth and destiny of Moses, her brother. She says, "My mother will give birth to a son who will be the savior of Israel" (Sothah 12b-13a). After the child's birth, it is Miriam who saves Moses from the waters of the Nile and has Moses' own mother, Jochebed, nurse him for the daughter of Pharaoh.

There are within the haggadah many similarities to Matthew's Annunciation to Joseph (Mt 1:18-25). We see this in the parallels to Joseph's struggle whether to be husband to Mary of Nazareth, the prophetic announcement of the birth by a divine messenger, and the miraculous circumstances in which Mary conceives. In the haggadah, Jochebed becomes youthful again and gives birth to Moses at 130 years of age! She also bears Moses with minimal pain and without any signs of having been pregnant. This quiet birth of Moses conceals him from the Egyptian spies. Rabbi Juda Zebina says that righteous women are excluded from the decree pronounced against Eve (Gn 3:16): "We are not in the presence of a gratuitous exception or a quirk in nature. In this event a divine plan is manifested, which concerns the people of Israel."[75] Moreover, such a birth has an eschatological meaning.

Matthew's account about the virgin birth is within the same theological framework and is at least two hundred years earlier than the Jewish haggadah. Within this tradition is the Apocalypse of Baruch (100-150 C.E.): "Women will no longer suffer during their pregnancies, and the anguish of child-bearing will be spared for the fruit of their womb" (2 Baruch 73:1-7; 74-1). Mary of Nazareth, the mother of Jesus, is not from the Davidic messianic line; since Elizabeth, the wife of Zechariah, is her cousin, Mary stems from the same lineage as Jochebed.

There are other "traditions" that have resonances in the Infancy Narratives of Matthew and Luke which R. E. Brown points out:

... the tradition of an angelic appearance to Miriam. ... In the

first-century A.D. work, the *Biblical Antiquities* of Pseudo-Philo
(ix 10), the Spirit of God came over Miriam, and a man (angel)
in linen garments appeared to her in a dream. She was told to
inform her parents that through the child to be born to them
God would save His people. Since Miriam is the Hebrew form
of Mary's name, alongside the tradition of an angelic appearance to the father of the savior (which has echoes in Matthew),
there was the tradition of an angelic appearance to a woman
named Mary (which has echoes in Luke). Le Déaut, "Miryam,"
points out that in the early Targum Neofiti on Exod 1:15,
Miryam of the tribe of Levi was considered to have received
the crown of royalty, for she was to be the ancestor of David.
Luke's Mary, who is betrothed to Joseph of the House of David
(1:27) has a relative, Elizabeth, who is of the House of Levi,
descended from Aaron (1:5, 36).[76]

In the Church's doctrine of the perpetual virginity of Mary,
one sees that such a condition of not suffering while giving birth (*in
partu*) is also present in Judaism in the haggadah surrounding
Jochebed. This is also seen as an eschatological theme in view of the
future liberation from the oppression of Egypt. Some exegetes in the
Christian tradition see a *virginitas in partu* through the variant text
given for John 1:13: "[He] who was born, not of blood nor of the will
of the flesh nor of the will of man, but of God." An important study
of this text from the Catholic doctrinal point of view was done by
I. de la Potterie.[77]

On the other hand Bruce Metzger points out the following:

Although a number of modern scholars (including Zahn,
Resch, Blass, Loisy, R. Seeburg, Burney, Büchsel, Bolismard,
Dupont, and F.M. Braun) have argued for the originality of the
singular number, it appeared to the Committee that, on the
basis of the overwhelming consensus of all Greek manuscripts,
the plural must be adopted, a reading which, moreover, is in
accord with the characteristic teaching of John. The singular
number may have arisen either from a desire to make the
Fourth Gospel allude explicitly to the virgin birth or from the

influence of the singular number of the immediately preceding αυτου.[78]

Jochebed is considered the mother of Moses and of all Israel. Rabbi Juda the Prince taught that:

> Yokebed [Jochebed], who gave birth to Moses; Moses was considered to be the equivalent of 600,000 persons, that is, all of Israel, for it is said, "Then Moses and all the Israelites sang" (Exodus 15:1) — and in another passage, "The Israelites carried out every thing just as the Lord had commanded Moses" (Exodus 39:32) — and yet another: "Since then no prophet has arisen in Israel like Moses" (Deuteronomy 34:10).[79]

True, this is a subtle way of interpretation which is demonstrating that Moses stands for all the people of Israel who, at that time, numbered 600,000 (Ex 12:37). As a consequence, Jochebed, the mother of Moses, is considered the mother of all Israel. The person of Mary especially in the Johannine tradition is also considered mother of all believers who are represented by the beloved disciple (Jn 19:26-27). From the corporate personality of Moses and his mother, Jochebed, Christianity moved towards an ecclesial unity seen in Mary as spiritual mother of all the faithful.

Jochebed/Mary

Jochebed is the mother of Moses the savior and liberator of Israel. Jewish tradition has her miraculously giving birth to him without pain. She also protects him from Pharaoh. She is considered as the Mother of Israel.

Mary is the mother of Jesus who is the Messiah and Savior in Christian belief. She gives birth to Jesus miraculously and together with her husband Joseph protects him from the murderous hands of Herod.

Miriam

Two significant studies about Miriam, the sister of Moses, help us understand why there has been a comparison between her and Mary of Nazareth, the mother of Jesus.[80] In all probability the women called Mary in the New Testament have been named after Miriam, the sister of Moses.[81]

Her name signifies "lady princess" or, if named after the place called Meribah, "waters of bitterness." Most likely Miriam, the sister of Moses, is the only person in the Hebrew Scriptures to have such a name excepting a Judahite who possesses a variant of this name. St. Luke uses Mariam, the Septuagintal form of Miriam in his Gospel.

O. Bardenhewer maintained there are at least 67 different etymologies connected with the name "Miriam"![82] Most likely the name describes a woman who is stately — hence, princess, and likewise, beautiful. If the name Miriam is seen as Egyptian, then the meaning of "dear" or *cherie* is best in translation. If we accept de la Potterie's interpretation of *kécharitôménê* in Luke 1:28, then it would refer to Mary as being a woman graced by God and one who is also graceful and beautiful.[83]

Miriam is considered a prophetess in Judaism. She also sings the victorious song about God the deliverer of her people during the Exodus:

> The prophetess Miriam, Aaron's sister, took a tambourine in her hand, while all the women went out after her with tambourines, dancing; and she led them in the refrain: "Sing to the Lord, for he is gloriously triumphant; horse and chariot he has cast into the sea" (Ex 15:20-21).

Her song begins with the same words of a long hymn attributed to Moses (Ex 15:1-18). F.M. Cross and D.N. Freedman attribute this "Song of the Sea" to Miriam.[84] In the Lucan Infancy Narrative the Magnificat is attributed to Mary with a few minor manuscripts ascribing it to Elizabeth. Both hymns have several themes in common.

Mary glorifies God as her Savior, while Moses or Miriam sing about the glory, *kabôd*, of God; both identify God as Lord and Savior. Abraham is the father in faith of both women; both exalt God in their triumph over the mighty ones; Pharaoh is cast down just as the proud and mighty ones are in Mary's Magnificat. The powerful right hand or arm of God is outstretched for both singers. The mighty works of God are extolled; God's steadfast love has saved and liberated Israel, the people. These parallels are more easily seen in a contextual reading of the "Song of the Sea" in the Septuagint with Mary's Magnificat in the Greek of St. Luke. Luke not only used this earliest Greek translation of the Hebrew text but also imitated its style, expression, and vocabulary.

The flight into Egypt by Mary and Joseph to avoid the tyranny and violence of Herod is a reversal of Moses', Miriam's, and Aaron's flight from Pharaoh. Mary of Nazareth, however, touches the same Egyptian soil as her matronymic Miriam (Mt 2:13-15).

The fact that there are seven distinct texts which speak of Miriam attest to her as a woman leader in Israel. The prophet Micah extols her: "For I brought you up from the land of Egypt, from the place of slavery I released you; and I sent before you Moses, Aaron, and Miriam" (Mi 6:4).

Miriam/Mary

Tracing the attributes of Miriam, the sister of Moses, we discover the following: she is a leader, a prophetess, a mediator, an initiator, a servant, a nurse, a caring person, a model of discretion and timing, a negotiator, and a woman who secretly and effectively works behind the scenes in the salvific history of the people.[85]

The Catholic Church uses such attributes for Mary of Galilee in its devotional hymns and litanies. The biblical sources for such expressions are taken from the Cana event (Jn 2:1-11) and from the Annunciation and Visitation accounts (Lk 1:28-45).

Judith

Judith is the heroine of the deuterocanonical book with the same name. She exemplifies the ideal woman of later Jewish piety (150-100 B.C.E.). In many of the events of her life she fits the description of a woman who was a Pharisee. In her victory over Holofernes she resembles Deborah and Jael in their victory over Sisera. She describes herself in Judith 11:17: "Your handmaid is, indeed, a God-fearing woman, serving the God of heaven night and day."

In her religious observance Judith is a righteous person. She observes the prescriptions of the Torah, is a chaste widow, observes the feasts and even eves of the feasts as well (8:6). She observes the laws of ritual purification and cleansing (12:2, 9, 19; 16:18). ". . . she is a model of Pharisaic religion. It is no wonder that her devotion is blessed — she is rich, she is beautiful, she is held in high repute by all (8:7-8) — though it may be noted there is no mention of her having children. The story centers round her courage, her initiative, her selflessness (13:20). . . ."[86]

Judith represents the entire faithful people of Israel. This is especially seen in her final hymn (16:1-17). Judith belongs to the poor of Yahweh (*tapenoi*) (6:19; 13:20; 16:11). A. Serra says, "The spiritual physiognomy of Judith is undoubtedly that of 'the poor in spirit.'"[87] In her actions Judith "serves as a paradigm for human liberation. Judith upholds the fundamental truths that faith does not depend on visible results (8:17-27) and that God's might is not in numbers (9:11)."[88]

Judith/Mary

In Mary of Nazareth there are similarities to Judith's absolute trust in God as one of the *'anawîm* or poor ones; there are the ritual observances to the laws of purification and celebration of the feasts, especially Passover. Both are exemplary in their prayer-life and in their religious participation.

In the liturgical readings of masses in honor of Mary, the blessing of Judith is similar to the angelic salutation of Luke: "Blessed are you, daughter, by the Most High God, above all the women on earth" (Jdt 13:18). Frequently in song and response the praise of Judith is celebrated also in Mary: "You are the glory of Jerusalem, the surpassing joy of Israel; You are the splendid boast of our people" (Jdt 15:9), and finally from her own hymn (Jdt 16:13-14):

> A new hymn I will sing to my God. O Lord, great are you and glorious, wonderful in power and unsurpassable. Let your every creature serve you; for you spoke, and they were made, you sent forth your spirit, and they were created; no one can resist your word.

Esther

Contemporary celebrations of the Book of Esther take place on the Jewish feast of Purim wherein the children reenact the scenes of the book while dressing in all kinds of costumes. The archenemy, Haman, is usually dressed in a black costume. In the celebration of Purim the two main ethical ideas are self-sacrifice and divine intervention. These two concepts are the themes which form the Book of Esther.[89]

In the celebration of Hebrew feasts the five scrolls are read. They are called the Five Megillot. Esther, however, is considered to be the "Megillah" *par excellence*. "Unless another of the five is indicated, 'Megillah' is taken to mean the Book of Esther."[90]

Esther is the heroine of the story and is a paradigm for a fully liberated woman who places all her confidence in God. Through prayer and fasting she is able to challenge the evil perpetrated in the Persian Empire and to intercede for her people Israel before King Ahasuerus. "Esther became involved in the fate of the Jews by becoming part of the public outcry regarding the decree by annihilation. She joined the fast of the Jews for three days in preparation for going to the king resolute that 'if I perish, I perish!' There is both resignation and liberation in her fasting and its certain measure of confidence for her that the public outcry will be successful."[91]

Esther/Mary

Mary, the mother of Jesus, is similar to Esther in prayer and in her intercessory power with God. She also advances the good of both Jewish people and of the Christian people through her role as Queen Mother.

Three selections from the Book of Esther are used in the Mariology of the early Christian writers and in the Catholic liturgy (Est 2:16-18; C:12, 14-15, 25, 30; and 8:3-8, 16-17).

Tamar

Tamar, "Palm Tree," is the first woman named in the genealogy of Matthew: "Judah became the father of Perez and Zerah, whose mother was Tamar" (Mt 1:3). The source for the mention of Tamar is Genesis 38. Judah, because of the death of two of his sons who were married successively to Tamar, fears for the third son Shelah. He sends Tamar away childless as a widow. Tamar, through a creative and deceptive disguise, has Judah, her father-in-law, solicit her as a prostitute. Before consenting she makes sure she has several signs of Judah, his seal, his stick, and a cord, so as to vindicate herself and assure his pledge. She conceives. After first condemning Tamar, Judah realizes he is the offender of God's law: "She is more in the right than I am, since I did not give her to my son Shelah" (Gn 38:26). She gives birth to twins, Perez and Zerah. Perez is the ancestor of David (Rt 4:18f), and, hence, of the eventual Messiah.

The entire story is illustrative of the law of the levirate:

> When brothers live together and one of them dies without a
> son, the widow of the deceased shall not marry anyone outside
> the family; but her husband's brother shall go to her and

perform the duty of a brother-in-law by marrying her. The first-born son she bears shall continue the line of the deceased brother, that his name may not be blotted out from Israel (Dt 25:5-6).

Elaine M. Wainwright comments:

She [Tamar] is an endangered woman in the hands of the patriarchal law. Because of Tamar's foresightedness, however, it becomes clear that the child Tamar bears is of Judah and she is therefore reincorporated into the patriarchal clan but in a way that has challenged its structures. . . . She has made possible the accomplishment of the levirate law, the continuation of the male line to the house of Judah; but she has also protected her own right to exercise her reproductive power and to bear children.[92]

Tamar/Mary

Why does Matthew start with Tamar in his genealogy? Because it is from the messianic line of Judah that David will spring. Tamar also demonstrates the anomalous situation of her being a widow and needing intervention from God to redeem her and to clarify her righteousness. Mary, the mother of Jesus, is likewise in an anomalous situation through a pregnancy which did not come about from Joseph her fiancé. Just as Tamar was vindicated as righteous before God, Mary, too, is seen to be innocent. Joseph discovers this through a dream.

Rahab

Just as Tamar is not condemned as a prostitute, neither is Rahab (Jos 2) who is praised for her faith, her ingenuity, and her hospitality — one of the greatest virtues extolled in the Scriptures. She is revered both in the New Testament (Heb 11:31; Jm 2:25) and in later traditions in Christianity (1 Clement 12:1) and in Judaism (Mek Ex 18:1; Midr. Ruth 2:1).

Her unusual sexual status is probably one of the reasons Matthew includes her in the genealogy of Jesus. R.E. Brown asserts that it is because of the fact of the irregular marital status of the women that they are included in the genealogy rather than the fact of their sinfulness or their being foreigners.[93]

Wainwright notes: "She is neither virginal daughter nor non-virginal wife and hence represents a danger to the patriarchal social structure, but as professional harlot she is also an endangered woman in the hands of this same system."[94]

The fact that she gains for herself and her family a place in the history of Israel is another factor in Matthew's inclusion of her in his genealogy. She is a woman open and sensitive to the power of God and creative in her use of God-given gifts. As such she is worthy to be noted among the mothers of Israel. Though bound within the patriarchal structure of her culture and society, she goes beyond them by her faith, her creative instincts, and her reading of the signs of God's activity in Israel's warriors. Rabbinic literature extols her as the Mother of Israel from whom eight priests and eight prophets descend.[95]

Wainwright points out that there is no male descendant from her and yet she is mentioned in the genealogy. Her faith and assistance to God's chosen one, Israel, may be the link in the genealogy from which the Messiah springs.[96]

Rahab/Mary

There are several points of convergence between the stories of Rahab and Mary; these help us gain a greater understanding of both women, and the faith that has linked them in the biblical tradition: sexuality is an issue in both stories; both women ran the risk of punishment (death); both were the means through which God took possession of the land and of human hearts; both were signs and exemplars of faith (Heb 11); both were mothers to the household of faith.

Ruth

Ruth is considered among the "Mothers of Israel." Targum on Ruth, 2, 12 translates: ". . . you are one who has arrived. . . . protected under the shadow of the Majesty of God and under God's glory, and thanks to this reward you will be liberated from the judgment of Gehenna because you have a place among Sarah, Rebeccah, Rachel and Leah — that is among the mothers of Israel." (Rabbah Ruth 5.5 at 2:13; Pesikta of Rob. Kohaha 26, 1.)

In this branch of literature Ruth is personified as Israel while Boaz her husband symbolizes God. The rabbinic literature parallels her relationship with Boaz to that of Israel in relationship to God apart from whom there shall be no other god (cf. Ex 20:3), and Israel is to glorify God (cf. Ex 15:2). This is intimately bound up with the Covenant between God and Israel which is similar to Ruth's spousal covenant with Boaz. From such a covenantal union springs the Anointed One, the Messiah.

The Church, too, in its earlier tradition continues the typology showing Boaz as a figure of Christ while Ruth images the Church. In the twelfth and thirteenth centuries Mary also is seen to be symbolized in Ruth. Peter of Cella (1115-1182) sees a parallel in Ruth's words, "I am Ruth, your handmaid," with Mary's, "Behold the handmaid of the Lord, be it done to me according to your word" (Lk 1:38).

Ruth is listed among the ancestors of Jesus in the magnificently patterned genealogy of Matthew. Mary is the last mother of Israel to be mentioned in this descending *toledoth Jeshua*, generations of Jesus. Just as in the Book of Ruth the narrator introduces the heroine through a passive third person approach, Matthew does the same throughout his Infancy Narrative.[97] The narrative of Matthew never allows these women (Tamar, Rahab, Ruth, Bathsheba and Mary) to speak, whereas Ruth speaks magnanimously in her beautiful statement of commitment and fidelity to Naomi.

Just as there was mention of an exodus from Judah and then a return in Ruth 1:1 and 7, so, too, does Matthew refer to the years in captivity and finally (through the genealogy) a return to the land of Israel. Bethlehem becomes the locus for the loving-kindness of God and for the promise of hope and salvation for the future through Ruth's offspring and (in Matthew) for Mary's child Jesus.

The fivefold Torah of Matthew seen through the five women in the genealogy is what the Book of Ruth has done through the starting with a man, Boaz, and ending with a woman, Ruth, who gives birth to the ancestor of David and the promise of a Messianic lineage. Torah is to be understood as the revelation of God, instruction of God, rather than as our bland and often prejudiced term "Law."

Just as in Ruth there is completion and then continuation so, too, in Matthew with the fourteen generations there is a certain completion and continuation.[98] Phyllis Trible's perception of Ruth's radical decision to choose to return to Bethlehem with Naomi gives insight into another possible reason for Matthew's including Ruth in his genealogy: "From a cultural perspective, Ruth has chosen death over life. She has disavowed the solidarity of family; she has abandoned national identity; and she has renounced religious affiliation. In the entire epic of Israel, only Abraham matches this radicality, but then he had a call from God (Gn 12:1-5)."[99]

Both Ruth and Mary are active respondents to God in their life stations. As such they represent their people Israel in its primordial covenant response on Sinai. Ruth anticipates the response, "All that the Lord has said, we will heed and do" (Ex 24:7). Ruth says to Boaz, "Why should I, a foreigner, be favored with your notice?" (Rt 2:10), and to Naomi she says, "I will do whatever you advise" (Rt 3:5). Mary, too, has been looked upon with favor: "Hail, favored one! The Lord is with you" (Lk 1:28). Mary affirms this in her own canticle, "For he has looked upon his handmaid's lowliness; behold, from now on, will all ages call me blessed" (Lk 1:48). Mary, too, like Israel on

Sinai responds to God's call, saying, "May it be done to me according to your word" (Lk 1:38). Both women have been looked upon with favor and both respond to this affirmatively. Ruth is named among the mothers of Israel in the final verses of the book!

The elders at the gate confirm the covenant of marriage between Boaz and Ruth:

> We do so. May the Lord make this wife come into your house like Rachel and Leah, who between them built the house of Israel. May you do well in Ephrathah and win fame in Bethlehem. With the offspring the Lord will give you from this girl, may your house become like the house of Perez, whom Tamar bore to Judah (Rt 4:11-12).

There are three important names in this prayer of the elders; Matthew, too, uses them in his Infancy Narrative: Ruth, understood in the blessing prayer; Tamar, mentioned also in the genealogy of Matthew; and, finally, the birthplace of Jesus, Bethlehem of Judah in Ephrathah (Mi 5:1; Mt 2:6). Matthew also drew his traditional material from Ruth 4:18-22 and 1 Chronicles 1-3 to formulate his genealogy.

The closing line of the Book of Ruth explains why she was chosen among the five women in Matthew's genealogy: "Obed was the father of Jesse, and Jesse became the father of David."[100]

One last reflection concerns the paradox of God's working within human history. Ruth's situation of being a foreigner without progeny is transformed through her loving-kindness (*hesed*) towards Naomi. In turn, Boaz acts as *go'el* or redeemer in order to restore the name of Elimelech for Naomi. Phyllis Trible shows that Ruth becomes the wife of Boaz but it is God who gives her the power to conceive. This, too, is suggested by Matthew in the paradox of Mary who is the last woman to be mentioned in the genealogy: "Of her was born Jesus who is called the Messiah" (Mt 1:16).[101]

Ruth/Mary

At the center of Mary's canticle is the loving-kindness of God. The Hebrew word *hesed* is at the basis of this disposition of God. In Elaine Mary Wainwright's study *hesed* is also at the heart of the story of Ruth. Wainwright says, "The Book of Ruth also celebrates the [*hesed*] of the woman (Ruth 1:8; 2:20; 3:10) and even though the innuendo of uncovering the feet of Boaz raises questions regarding the anomalous situation this action creates, there is no language of sin in relation to Ruth throughout the book."[102] This, too, is the evaluation we have with texts in Luke surrounding the Virgin Mother of Jesus. The traditions of both Synagogue and Church keep the sinlessness of both these mothers of Israel, respectively.

Bathsheba: Queen Mother (Gebîrâh)

In Matthew's genealogy (1:6) Bathsheba is described as the "wife of Uriah." In not mentioning her name, there is a break in the pattern of the women mentioned, namely, Tamar, Rahab, and Ruth. Bathsheba is, however, essential to the genealogy in Matthew's purpose and a similarity is seen in what at first is an irregular marital union with David. After Uriah's death she is the wife of David, and in a certain sense "Queen Mother" or *Gebîrâh*,[103] giving birth to four other sons after the death of her first son. Solomon succeeds David through her influence and that of the prophet Nathan (1 K 1:11-37). Wainwright astutely remarks, "It is important to note here that, according to the biblical tradition, it is not as wife of Uriah but as legal wife of David that Bathsheba becomes the mother of Solomon, her link into the Matthean genealogy."[104]

In the Jewish tradition contemporaneous with the formation of the New Testament, Bathsheba is seen as a noble woman of Israel. As Queen Mother, *Gebîrâh*, she had great influence both with David and his successor Solomon. As with the other women in the genealogy, Bathsheba is seen within the history of salvation for Israel and within the action and plan of God. This opens the way for seeing why Bathsheba would also be a key person who helps in understanding the final woman to be mentioned, Mary the mother of Jesus. Bathsheba, too, is involved in the action of the Spirit and in the history of salvation.

Wainwright cites an early rabbinic tradition showing how essential Bathsheba is in God's action in history: "It is revealed and known to thee that Bath-sheba was held ready for me from the six days of Creation, yet she was given to me for sorrow (Midr. Ps 3:5)." This tradition is further clarified: "Raba (d. ca. 247) expounded: . . . BathSheba, the daughter of Eliam, was predestined for David from the six days of Creation, but that she came to him with sorrow. And the school of R. Ishmael taught likewise: She was worthy [i.e. predestined] for David from the six days of Creation but that he enjoyed her before she was ripe (b. Sanh. 107a)."[105]

Bathsheba/Mary

In any comparison of Bathsheba with Mary, the mother of Jesus, the notion of "Queen Mother" perhaps can help with understanding that the theme came from the Hebrew Scriptures and later developed into the Queenship of Mary through devotion and liturgy. How may we understand Mary's Queenship in light of the Queen-Mother tradition? It has been said that some "powerful women" of the Hebrew Scriptures are types of Mary. Verses from Esther and Judith in particular have been used in reference to Mary in the Church's liturgy: "You are the glory of Jerusalem, the surpassing joy of Israel; you are the splendid boast of our people" (Jdt 15:9). The verse may express the sentiments of the Christian community.

The Queen Mother plays an active and assertive role in relation to her son. She is totally concerned with his kingdom. In a sense, Mary can be said to be responsible for her son's kingship by reason of her motherhood and real concern for the reign of God (*Lumen Gentium*, 56). It would be difficult to prove, however, that Mary was aware of any royal character to her assent at the time of the Annunciation. Mary did not seek the throne for her son as did other "Queen Mothers." On the contrary, she served the mystery of the redemption "in subordination to Christ" (*Lumen Gentium*, 56). Her service was one of self-effacement as was her son's. Both lived an experience of *kenosis*.

The Queen Mother had powerful influence in the kingdom. This power flowed from her status as mother of the king. If we compare this to Mary's mediation, we can see the relation of her mediation to her maternity. Mary's role is relative to the activity of Christ. She never ruled in Christ's place as would the Queen Mother.

The rule of Mary, like that of Christ, is not to be understood in terms of domination, except over evil. Her rule, like Christ's, is based on humility and obedience and is characterized by faith, hope and love. This is how she and Christ relate to the members of the faith.[106] Mary's activity as Queen Mother is her present role: she is faithful to God; she identifies with the community of those who follow Christ. Her influence is captured in the words, "Do whatever he tells you." Mary's influence is felt within the communion of saints. Her intercessory power is the same as any creature before God. Her maternal intercession, her "manifold intercession," (*Lumen Gentium*, 62) is what is close to, and expressive of, the *Gebîrâh* theme. One ancient song that praises Mary as queen, as mother, and as mediator is the *Regina Caeli*:

> Hail, holy Queen, mother of mercy, our life, our sweetness, and our hope.
> To you do we cry, poor banished children of Eve.
> To you do we send up our sighs, mourning and weeping in this vale of tears.
> Turn then, most gracious advocate,
> your eyes of mercy toward us,
> and after this our exile
> show us the blessed fruit of your womb, Jesus.
> O clement, O loving, O sweet Virgin Mary.

The Mother of the Sons of the Maccabees

This woman is not given a name in 2 Maccabees but she is identified as the "mother of the nation," vindicator of the Law, defender of piety, a holy and God-fearing mother, a mother who combats in God's favor because of her dedication (cf. 4 M 15:29; 16:12-14; 17:2, 4). The Church compares her admirable courage in the martyrdom of her seven sons to that of Mary at Calvary (Jn 19:25-27). Passages from 2 Maccabees are recalled in the liturgy and celebrated in the mass in honor of the Virgin Mary. A. Serra concludes: "The mother of the Maccabees and the mother of Jesus: two women, two mothers who are involved in the immolation of their sons, supported by the vigor of the faith of their ancestors."[107]

Endnotes

[49] Bertrand Buby, "A New Testament Passover Haggadah," *The Bible Today* 29 (1967): 2010-2016.

[50] Addison G. Wright, *Midrash* (Staten Island, NY: Alba House, 1967); Jacob Neusner, *Midrash in Context: Exegesis in Formative Judaism* (Philadelphia: Fortress, 1983); Renée Bloch, "Midrash," *Dictionnaire de la Bible*, Suppl. vol. V (Paris: Letouzey 1957) 1263-1282.

[51] John L. McKenzie, *Dictionary of the Bible* (New York: MacMillan, 1965) 773.

[52] Susan Niditch, "Genesis," *The Women's Bible Commentary*, eds. Carol A. Newsom and Sharon H. Ringe (Louisville, KY: Westminster/John Knox, 1992) 15.

[53] Ibid., 16.

[54] Ibid., 17.

[55] McKenzie, 773.

[56] Carol Meyers, *Discovering Eve: Ancient Israelite Women in Context* (New York: Oxford UP, 1988) 74-77.

[57] Ibid., 80-86.

[58] Phyllis Trible, "Depatriarchalizing in Bibical Interpretation," *Journal of the American Academy of Religion* 41 (1973): 30-48.

[59] Phyllis Trible, *God and the Rhetoric of Sexuality* (Philadelphia: Fortress, 1978) 77.

[60] Niditch, 12-13.

[61] Ibid., 13.

[62] Roger Le Déaut, *Judaisme* in *Dictionnaire de Spiritualite*, vol. VIII (Paris: Beauchesne, 1974) 1478-1495.

[63] Serra, *E C'era la Madre di Gesù*, 470.

[64] Ibid., 475.

[65] Charlesworth, *The Old Testament Pseudepigrapha*, 563.

[66] Michael O'Carroll, *Theotokos: A Theological Encyclopedia of the Blessed Virgin Mary* (Wilmington, Delaware: Glazier, 1982) 140.

[67] Louis Billot, *De Verbo Incarnato*, 6th ed., (Rome, 1922) 380.

[68] J. de Fraine, *Women of the Old Testament*, trans. Forrest L. Ingram (De Pere, WI: St. Norbert Abbey P, 1968) 3-8.

[69] Herbert Lockyer, *All the Women of the Bible* (Grand Rapids, MI: Zondervan, n.d.) 57.

[70] David Noel Freedman, ed-in-chief., *The Anchor Bible Dictionary*, vol. 5 (New York: Doubleday, 1992) 629.

[71] Meyers, *Discovering Eve*, 195-196.

[72] Teresa Okure, "Women in the Bible," *With Passion and Compassion: Third World Women Doing Theology* (New York: Maryknoll, 1988) 47-59.

[73] Freedman, *Anchor Bible*, vol. 5, 605.

[74] Jacob Neusner, "Can People Who Believe in Different Religions Talk Together?", *Journal of Ecumenical Studies* 28 (1991): 88-100.

[75] Serra, 439.

[76] Brown, *The Birth of the Messiah*, 116n45.

[77] Ignace de la Potterie, "La mère de Jésus et la conception virginale du Fils de Dieu," *Marianum* XL (1978): 41-90.

[78] Bruce Metzger, *A Textual Commentary on the Greek New Testament* (New York: United Bible Societies, 1971) 197.

[79] See Canticle Rabba 1, 15.3 and 4, 1.2.

[80] Phyllis Trible, "Bringing Miriam out of the Shadows," *Bible Review* 5.1 (1989): 14+. R. Le Déaut, "Miryam, soeur de Moïse, et Marie, mère du Messie," *Biblica* 45 (1964): 198-219.

[81] F. Zorrell, "Maria, soror Mosis, et Maria, Mater Dei," *Verbum Domini* 6 (1926): 257-263: "Undoubtedly, the name of the Blessed Virgin Mary was given to her by her parents honoring the great person of Miriam, the sister of Moses and Aaron (in the Old Testament). She, under Moses, her brother, was a prophetess, a leader of the people who brought them through the Red Sea and through the desert. Probably a desire for rebirthing the People Israel, another Mary, a divinely illuminated prophetess, and leader of people into the realm of God led Joachim and Anna to bestow this name, likewise the same for the parents of Mary Magdalene, Mary of Bethany, Mary the mother of James, the mother of Mark." [my translation]

[82] O. Bardenhewer, *Der Name Maria: Geschichte der Deutung Desselben* (Fribourg im Breisgau, 1895) 157-158.

[83] de la Potterie, *Mary in the Mystery of the Covenant*, 17-20.

[84] Frank M. Cross, Jr., and David Noel Freedman, "The Song of Miriam," *Journal of Near Eastern Studies* 14 (1955): 237-250. (Cf. P. Trible, "Bringing Miriam Out of the Shadows," 34n5: "In scholarly literature, Exodus 15:1-18 is more often called 'The Song of the Sea' and Exodus 15:21 the 'Song of Miriam.')" Following Cross and Freedman (see endnote 4), many scholars now attribute the Song of the Sea to Miriam (not to Moses, as tradition holds) and thus designate both Exodus 15:1-18 and Exodus 15:21 the Song of Miriam. By contrast, the Song of Moses is Deuteronomy 32:1-43, and the Blessing of Moses is Deuteronomy 33:2-29. Also, more recently in the *New Jerome Biblical Commentary* 3:50: "Verse 21 attributes the song to Miriam rather than to Moses — a more original attribution, since well-known figures in literary tradition tended to attract to themselves other's traditions."

[85] Trible, op. cit. These attributes are gleaned from her commentary on the prayers where Miriam is mentioned.

[86] Reginald C. Fuller, gen. ed., *A New Catholic Commentary on Holy Scripture*, rev. and updated (Nashville: Thomas Nelson, 1969) 404.

[87] Serra, 114.

[88] Raymond E. Brown, Joseph A. Fitzmyer, and Roland E. Murphy, eds., *The New Jerome Biblical Commentary* (Englewood Cliffs, NJ: Prentice, 1990) 573-574.

[89] C. G. Montefiore and H. Loewe, *A Rabbinic Anthology* (New York: Schocken, 1974) 99-101.

[90] Rufus Learsi, *Israel: A History of the Jewish People* (New York: Meridian, 1966) 120.

[91] John F. Craghan, "Esther: A Fully Liberated Woman," *The Bible Today* 24 (1986): 6-11.

[92] Elaine Mary Wainwright, *Towards a Feminist Critical Reading of the Gospel according to Matthew* (New York: Walter de Gruyter, 1991) 162.

[93] Brown, *The Birth of the Messiah*, 74.

[94] Wainwright, *Towards a Feminist Critical Reading of the Gospel According to Matthew*, 164:
> "The woman who is outsider to the patriarchal culture generally and outsider to the ethnic culture of Israel is incorporated into both (6:25). The "profession of faith" of Rahab (Jos 2:9-11) is linked closely to her securing a promise of safety from the spies (vv. 12-13) and hence it would seem that the ancient text is already hinting at the power of God which is associated with the extraordinary initiative taken by Rahab in the face of the powers of the patriarchal world."

[95] Ibid., 165.

[96] Ibid., 166.

[97] Trible, *God and the Rhetoric of Sexuality*, 166-167:
> "Third-person narration names the characters, specifies their relationships, and describes their plight, but it does not allow them to emerge as human beings. Subjects of verbs, they are objects of discourse; spoken about, they do not speak."

[98] Ibid., 168-169:
> "This double function of completion and continuation resolves the grammatical-existential tension between person and nonperson, between life and death. Resolution comes along sexual lines. The males die, they are nonpersons; their presence in the story ceases (though their absence continues). The females live; they are persons; their presence in the story continues. Indeed, their life is the life of the story. One set of opposites has worked its way to a resolution that in turn generates other sets of opposites."

[99] Ibid., 173.

[100] Donald Senior, gen. ed., *The Catholic Study Bible: New American Bible* (New York: Oxford UP, 1990) 282: "The father of Jesse, the father of David: indicating the place of Obed, Jesse, and David in the line of Judah and the ancestry of Christ, the Messiah; cf. Mt 1, 5f."

[101] Trible, op. cit., 193:
> "The gift of life resides neither in male nor in female, but in God. Only after this perspective is introduced do we read, 'she bore a son.' Intercourse between Ruth and Boaz is itself divine activity. That equation comes in both the structure and content of the report, and thereby the narrator announces that all is well. Ten years of a childless marriage in Moab (1:4-5) have been quickly redeemed in the union of Ruth and Boaz. Yahweh has given conception; blessing has transformed curse. This announcement of a private union for blessing mediates between public gatherings

which, on the one side, legitimate the union and, on the other, celebrate it."

[102] Wainwright, op. cit., 64 (cf. 166-168). David Daube, *The New Testament and Rabbinic Judaism* (London: Athlone, 1956) 27-36. J. Massingberd Ford, "Mary's Virginitas Post-Partum and Jewish Law," *Biblica* 54 (1973): 269-272.

[103] Niels-Erik A. Andreasen, "The Role of the Queen Mother in Israelite Society," *The Catholic Biblical Quarterly* 45 (1983): 179-194.

"A queen mother (*gebîrâ*) fills a clearly defined role in a number of ancient and modern societies. The omphalos-myth, pertaining to the earth with its life giving center and symbolized by the mother-goddess (divine mother), was suppressed by Old Testament prophets and historians. Her presence appears only in a modified form as wisdom (Pr 1-9). A role remained for Judean queen mothers which corresponded to a position of seniority in the court (lady counsellor) and fit the motif of Lady Wisdom in Proverbs. Bathsheba was not given a title of *gebîrâ* but did occupy a position from which she functioned as counsellor and as a source of wisdom, and with a concern as to succession and stability of the kingdom upon David's impending death. In an effort to secure the throne for her son she appealed directly to David. As queen mother she may have also performed as counsellor in political and judiciary affairs at court and as mediator between political factions in the nation. Her son Solomon did indeed give hearing to her counsel which demonstrates the regard to which the position of queen mother was held in Jerusalem. '. . . the queen mother was a "lady counsellor" whose role was reflected in the motif of "Lady Wisdom" in Proverbs' (*Anchor Bible*, vol. 5, 585)."

[104] Wainwright, op. cit., 168-170.

[105] Ibid., 169.

[106] George Francis Kirwin, "The Nature of the Queenship of Mary," diss., Catholic Univ. of America, 1973, 320.

[107] Serra, 460.

Chapter Five

THE HEBREW SCRIPTURES
AND VATICAN II

Chapter VIII of *Lumen Gentium*, the Dogmatic Constitution on the Church, treats of the Blessed Virgin Mary, and it is within paragraph 55 that the function of the Blessed Virgin in the plan of salvation is described.[108] Both the writings of the Hebrew Scriptures and the Christian Scriptures are considered part of the revelatory message about Mary's role in salvation history. In the document the books of the Hebrew Scriptures are seen as a preparation for the coming of the Messiah or the Christ. Mary, as Mother of the Messiah, is considered to be prophetically foreshadowed in certain texts of Genesis and the prophets Isaiah and Micah. She is also identified with the title "exalted Daughter of Sion." This title is a symbolism applied to Mary from a Christian tradition and from a rereading of these prophetic passages. It is to the more explicit references that we now turn in this chapter; they are Genesis 3:15, Isaiah 7:14, and Micah 5:2-3. The last two texts, cited in Matthew 1:23 and 2:6, show that the early reminiscences of Matthew's Jewish-Christian Church were carried over from the Hebrew Scriptures and applied or reread in the light of the birth of the Messiah whose Mother was Mary, the wife of Joseph, from the lineage of David and Judah.

Mary is described in *Lumen Gentium*, 55 as one who "stands out among the poor and humble of the Lord, who confidently hope for and receive salvation from him." This spiritual attitude is seen in the image of Mary portrayed in Luke's Magnificat where she is surely among the *'anawîm*, a title for those who are courageously and totally dependent upon God and often described in the Psalms and several of the prophets as the "poor of Yahweh."

This chapter will explore the traditional rereading of these texts in the light of their Messianic fulfillment in Jesus, who was born of Mary of Nazareth. An effort to understand these same texts from a historical-critical perspective as well as from modern critical assessment of their interpretive value will also be explored. We turn to the texts in the order they are presented in *Lumen Gentium, 55*.

Genesis 3:15

> "I will put enmity between you and the woman, and between your offspring and hers; he will strike at your head, while you strike at his heel" (Gn 3:15).

This text is strongly attested to in the tradition of the Catholic Church and is called the "Protoevangelium" or First Good News of a promise of victory over evil symbolized under the serpent who beguiled the first couple.[109] Unlike the texts of Isaiah and Micah in *Lumen Gentium, 55*, Genesis 3:15 is never directly cited in the New Testament. However, the symbolism of the Woman and the serpent (dragon) are insinuated in Revelation 12:1-5, 9, 17. R. E. Brown in his commentary on John 19:26 gives the following:

> Perhaps we may also relate Mary the new Eve to Gen. iii 15, a passage that describes a struggle between the offspring of Eve and the offspring of the serpent, for "the hour" of Jesus is the hour of the fall of the Prince of this world (John xii 23, 31). The symbolism of the Fourth Gospel has a certain resemblance to that of Rev xii 5, 17 where a woman gives birth to the Messiah in the presence of the Satanic dragon or ancient serpent of Genesis, and yet also has other offspring who are the targets of Satan's wrath after the Messiah has been taken to heaven.[110]

Both Justin (+165) and Irenaeus (+202) link Mary with the person of Eve, especially with regard to Genesis 3:15. Their use of the Scriptures is basically allegorical and typological in these comparisons, and contrasts Mary with Eve. They use the personalities and events of the Hebrew Scriptures as types for Christ and Mary. Since such typology with Mary is more frequent in Irenaeus, he is sometimes called the "father of Mariology."

Justin's Mariology is summed up this way: "Thus Eve and Mary — two women, two virgins — are considered responsible for the story of humankind, next to and subordinate to the two heads of humanity, Adam and Christ; Eve with Satan, Mary with God; Eve responsible for death, Mary for life, — especially through her virginal obedience, the only way this was possible."[111]

Irenaeus sees Mary as the Advocate of Eve (Adv. Haer. 5, 19, 1 SC 153, 249). He gives us one of the foundational texts for the intercession of Mary. Intercession is also an aspect of Mary's role reflected in the earliest Marian prayer, the *sub tuum praesidium*: "Under your mercy, we take refuge, Mother of God [*Theotokos*], do not reject our supplications in necessity. But deliver us from danger. [You] alone chaste, alone blessed."[112] The same intercessory prayer is implied in *Lumen Gentium*, 66: "From the earliest times the Blessed Virgin is honored under the title of Mother of God, whose protection the faithful take refuge together in prayer in all their perils and needs."

Irenaeus sees the birth of Jesus from Mary as the event which recapitulates creation because the human story begins on a new course initiated by Christ and by his very being and doing as the God-man. This for Irenaeus is the meaning of salvation history.

In the apocryphal *Gospel of Philip* this traditional understanding of Genesis 3:15 is implied: "Adam was made from two virgins: the Spirit and virgin earth. Through this Christ was born of the Virgin as a remedy against the sin from the beginning."[113]

In Judaism the text of Genesis 3:15 is interpreted in a Messianic promise. The earliest targums indicate a messianic meaning:

The *Targum of Onkelos*: And enmity I will put between you and between woman, and between your descendant and between her descendant. He shall be recalling (DeKHIR) what you did to him in the beginning; and you shall be observing (NATAR) him in the end ("head" was interpreted as "beginning," and "heel" as "end"). So "recalling" and "observing" are an interpretation, too, more than a translation.

The *Targum of Pseudo-Jonathan*: And enmity I will put between you and the woman, between your offspring-sons, and between her offspring-sons. And it shall happen that when the sons of the woman will be observing (NATeRIN) the precepts of the Law, they will be striving to strike (MACHYAN) you on the head; and when they will be forsaking the precepts of the Law, you will be striving to bite (NAKHITH) them in the heels. But for them there will be a remedy; whereas for you there will be no remedy. And they will be ready to make a crushing (SHePHIYUTHA') with the heel in the days of the Messiah King.

The *Targum of Jerusalem*: And it shall happen that when the sons of the woman will observe the Law and fulfill the commandments, they will strive to strike (MACHAYAN) you on the head and kill you; and when the sons of the woman will forsake the precepts of the Law and will not keep the commandments, you will strive to bite (NAKHITH) them in their heel and harm them. However, there will be a remedy for the sons of the woman, but to you, O serpent, there will be no remedy. Still, behold, they will be prepared to apply a remedy to each other in the heel, at the final of days, in the days of the Messiah King.

The dogmatic proclamation of the Immaculate Conception in 1854 led Catholic exegetes and theologians to study and interpret Genesis 3:15 in a Mariological sense. Cardinal Agostino Bea summed up these studies with an article entitled "Maria SS. nel Protoevangelo (Gen. 3, 15)." The article appeared in *Marianum*.[114]

We learn from Bea that, before the Council of Trent, Martin Luther complained about the prevalent Mariological interpretation. In his commentary on Genesis, Luther states that "all contemporary Catholic exegetes support a Mariological interpretation, they abuse the most holy Word (of the Protoevangelium) in favor of idolatry. This is done either by ignorance or by the pride of those who govern the Church. And since these are not opposed to idolatry, the sound doctrine is slowly but surely extinguished" (M. Luther, *Exeg. op. lat. t. I: Gen. I-IV*, pp. 242-243).

Bea shows that over 81% of Catholic theologians and exegetes between 1562-1600 gave Genesis 3:15 a Marian interpretation, that is, 77 out of 95. Even in a period of Catholic biblical decadence (1750-1820) 40 out of 47 authors still gave it a Marian interpretation. After the definition of the Immaculate Conception in 1854, 77.5% of Catholic exegetes continued to give it a Marian interpretation.

Bea's article ends with the conclusion that in the two doctrines of the Immaculate Conception and the Assumption, Genesis 3:15 has a Marian interpretation both in the Scriptures and in the tradition of the Catholic Church.

Exegetes who have followed the historical-critical method are not convinced of the validity of giving Marian interpretations to Old Testament texts. This is a correct judgment about the chronological character of such texts. It has enabled theologians and biblical scholars to explain what was "behind the text" in its historical and cultural setting. Texts are always revelatory of the times in which they were written. Moreover, the Hebrew Scriptures are the story of the Jewish people and of the heroes and heroines, kings and prophets, men and women before Jesus Christ. This is important for Mariologists. Their first task is to explore the meaning behind the text. To do this means to accept the Jewish scholarship that is, so to speak, the guardian of the authentic historic and revelatory nature of the texts in themselves. Scientific exegesis is a prerequisite for good Mariology and for a tempering of over-spiritualization and of reading everything in the Hebrew Scriptures in the light of Christian revelation.

Shortly after Vatican II, Charles Miller studied the use of

Hebrew texts in the Council. He especially noted the texts of *Lumen Gentium*.[115] We have to remember that at the outset interpretations of Genesis 3:15 did not have a Marian connotation. Perhaps the messianic implication in the promise led some early Christians to a Marian interpretation since Mary is the Mother of the Messiah according to Christian texts and traditions. St. Jerome's translation of the text was incorrect in changing the pronoun in Hebrew from "he" to "she." This translation of the Vulgate had a lasting and perduring influence on men and women of the Church. William Joseph Chaminade, Marianist founder, used the text for indicating Mary's victory over Satan and evil: "She shall crush thy head and will continue to do so." Chaminade was greatly influenced by the Vulgate and handed down that tradition to his congregations and to the Sodalities.

Today the correct translation of the text influences every serious student of the Bible to place the victory over evil with the Messiah rather than with the Mother of the Messiah. Earlier statements by Pope Pius IX were closer to the interpretation suggested by Jerome's translation. Pius IX said that Mary was closely united to Christ "with him and through him, eternally at enmity with the evil serpent, and most completely triumphed over him and thus crushed his head with her immaculate foot."[116] Such an interpretation is not based on the exact meaning of the text in its historical-critical and in its textual-critical evidence. In a sense devotion outran reason; heart went beyond mind. In the earliest interpretations neither a Marian nor a Messianic application appeared. Rather the struggle of the human race with evil predominated. When the collective connotation became singular, then Christ was the victor over evil. We can see such an influence on the writer of the Fourth Gospel as well as in the Pauline references to the New Adam.

In Miller's study we discover that there was a proposal to drop Genesis 3:15 from the statement about Mary's role in the mystery of Christ. Eventually, the final structure and the text appeared under the title *"De Matre Messiae in Vetere Testamento"* (Concerning the

Mother of the Messiah in the Old Testament). The explanation of the Council Fathers is:

> (B) The order of exposition of this first part follows the *history of salvation*, as it is narrated in Holy Scripture from the Old Testament on, *so that no discrepancy might appear* between the woman, the mother of Christ in the Gospels, and the figure of the B. Virgin as it is shown in the theological treatment or venerated by the Christian people. From the biblical documents a progress in revelation about Mary is illustrated; but it is expressly noted that the inspired books are read in the Catholic Church, as it is necessary, under the light of the full revelation and are understood according to the mind of Tradition.
>
> The first foreshadowing is found in the *Protoevangelium,* the *oracle* of Is 7:14, however, it is applied to the B. Mary in the strict sense in Mt 1:22-23. At the end of the Old Testament preparation, Mary, the daughter of Sion, excels among "the poor of the Lord," and with her, in the fullness of time, the new Economy is introduced, in which Christ redeemed the world "by the mysteries of his flesh"; this last indication means to insist upon the realism of the incarnation through Mary.[117]

The interpretive key in the Council's viewpoint is that the texts are read in the light of full revelation and within the Church. This *sensus plenior* is coupled with the ecclesial understanding of the text in its tradition and memory. Mariologists work within such a framework. Fortunately, they also are using the best of scientific exegesis and modern methods in order to interpret and explain "what is in front of the text," that is, current hermeneutics with an ecclesial and revelatory quality, and "what is behind the text" through philology, textual criticism and historical-critical exegesis. The overarching theme of such an interpretation is the history of salvation in God's plan. Christian feminist biblical scholars move us further through a method which liberates the text of any oppressive connotations. The history of salvation is explained not in Kingdom terminology but as "God's transformative dream for humanity."[118]

In article 54 of *Lumen Gentium* the Council did not intend to give a full teaching about Mary and certainly it did not intend to interpret the texts of the Hebrew Scriptures in a final way because of the exegetical questions which are raised. Pastorally the Council was concerned with seeing the Scriptures in the light of faith and its ongoing development. The statement of the Council about Mary is this: she is prophetically foreshadowed in Genesis 3:15 in the victory over the serpent. Miller points out that D.J. Unger would give an exclusive Jesus and Mary interpretation to the text, while Speiser would comment: "The passage does not justify eschatological expectations." Cassuto is somewhat in between these two positions, seeing the struggle as internal and allowing for a victory over sin similar to that of Cain in Genesis 4:7.[119]

Miller's conclusion is helpful in assessing where the Mariological interpretation is coming from:

> It seems clear that Vatican II's Mariological reference to Gn 3:15 in LG is really more an appeal to Tradition than to a proof text from the Old Testament. Literally, the text says nothing about the woman sharing in the victory of her "seed" over the serpent, if indeed there be such a victory. Even the patristic tradition itself, furthermore, is not unanimous on the Mariological significance of the passage. At most, it might be considered an example of *sensus plenior*.[120]

Genesis 3:15 also appears in *Dei verbum*, 3. There a promise of redemption and a hope of salvation are given to the "first parents."

In the most recent Catholic commentary on Genesis 3:15, the following is given:

> The snake is cursed, condemned to crawl on its belly, eat dirt, and be forever the enemy of the woman he deceived and of her offspring. *He shall strike your head*: "He" refers to offspring, which is masc. in Hebrew. Christian tradition has sometimes referred it to Christ, but the literal reference is to the human descendants of Eve, who will regard snakes as enemies.[121]

Genesis 3:15 in John Paul II's *Redemptoris Mater*

Throughout the Marian encyclical of John Paul II, the text of the Protogospel, the "first Good News" (Gn 3:15), is highlighted. The Pope sets it within the context of salvation history. The providence of God is always present in the revelation of the Scriptures and certain texts are filled with eschatological hopes, others with joy; Genesis 3:15 is such a text of promise.

In this text in the liturgy of the Easter Vigil the Exsultet proclaims the *felix culpa*, the happy fault of Adam. The atmosphere of this great liturgical celebration captures the ethos and impact which this famous text has within the Church.

Prior to John Paul's use of the text, Pius XII saw it as a prophetical oracle in *Munificentissimus Deus*: Mary the new Eve subject to the new Adam "is most intimately associated with him in that struggle against the infernal foe, which, as foretold in the Protoevangelium, would finally result in that most complete victory over sin and death which are always mentioned together in the writings of the Apostle of the Gentiles." Pius XII likewise wrote in *Fulgens Corona* that the biblical foundation of the doctrine of the Immaculate Conception was "in these words which not a few Fathers, Doctors of the Church, and many approved interpreters applied to the Virgin Mother of God: 'I will put enmities between thee and the woman, and thy seed and her seed.'"

The Papal Bull of Pius IX made direct application of the text to the victory of Jesus Christ over the deceitful serpent while Mary was prophetically *pointed out*. However, in the dogmatic formulation of the decree on the Immaculate Conception the text was not used (cf. "Woman in Genesis 3:15," *Theotokos*).

In Vatican II the statement found in paragraph 55 of *Lumen Gentium* was marked by a slight recession from the stronger and more explicit uses of the text by Pius IX and Pius XII. The word *designatam* was changed to *adumbratam* Mary was therefore prophetically "foreshadowed" rather than "pointed out."

In *Redemptoris Mater* (Mother of the Redeemer), John Paul II uses the text in paragraphs 7, 11, and 24 (two times).

In paragraph 7[122] Mary is the "woman" who is the Mother of him to whom the Father has entrusted the work of salvation. John Paul II emphasizes the divine plan of salvation and does not separate the text from an orchestration of other Marian texts: Isaiah 7:14, Galatians 4:4-5, and especially the Infancy Narratives of Matthew and Luke. Thus the Holy Father is pondering over the text in the light of fuller revelation, that is in the light of what today would be called canonical criticism, and in the interpretation which springs from a *sensus plenior*. Scripture explains Scripture and opens up the fullness of God's revelation. This means that if you are able to interpret in a clear manner the meaning of a given text within the Bible by means of other texts, then it is based on a sound method-ology. This would be, in my opinion, a stronger argument than one springing from a comparative study of religions — which seeks parallels outside the Judaeo-Christian tradition and the Bible.

In paragraph 11 of *Redemptoris Mater*[123] the text is interpreted more fully in the light of Revelation 12:1 and is presented as a confirmation of a *promise* made by God to us. Such a development in the interpretation of John Paul II in comparison with that of the Fathers who took the Vulgate's translation as *she shall crush* the head of the serpent is not to be minimized. Formerly the text had an exclusive Marian interpretation while being based on the faulty translation of Jerome.

Finally,[124] John Paul II raises the text of Genesis 3:15 to another level by uniting it with John 2:1-11 (Cana) and John 19:25-27 (Calvary). He also attaches the fourth and final mention of the Protoevangelium (Genesis 3:15) with Revelation 12:1. Mary is the woman who occupies a unique place in the whole economy of salvation. Her divine motherhood is to be poured out upon the whole Church.

The Marian sense in Genesis 3:15 is *implicit* in that it can only be understood in the light of other revelations both in Scripture and Tradition. With the help of other texts the Protoevangelium indi-cates the divine intention of envisioning the Messiah and his Mother in this announcement made to the Woman who vanquishes the Serpent/Evil; the text thereby renders a revelatory meaning that is more direct and personal.

In Catholic tradition the text of Genesis 3:15 has been given more attention than any other in the Pentateuch. In the light of Vatican II we can trace a methodology and an approach from what is called salvation history that enables us to see from our *faith* perspective a Marian implication. While being critical scientifically in exegesis, there is, at the same time, the wisdom of a living Tradition. The Church is seen as Wisdom-Teacher helping those who are believers to understand texts which were motivated by a profound spirit of faith in the divinely inspired writer as well as in the People of Faith for whom these texts were written.

Genesis 3:15 — The Protogospel in the Perspective of New Testament Revelation

French scholars of both Mariology and the Bible attach this text to the ecclesial Marian teaching by accommodation to Revelation 12 where the woman and the serpent are mentioned in the last book of the New Testament. Just as Genesis, though not chronologically first, opens the pages of the Torah so the Protoevangelium (Gn 3:15) opens the pages of Mariology in reflecting on Revelation 12.

The text of Genesis 3:15 focuses on a woman of the future other than Eve. The renowned Mariologist M-J Nicolas says: "It is the Woman as such, the same one who will undergo the sufferings of maternity, the Woman whose meaning seems to be that of the Mother who precedes humanity and ushers in Man." Whether we read the Vulgate, the Septuagint, or the Masoretic text, the passage implies the confrontation is between the Woman and the Serpent. It is she as Mother who will triumph over the serpent who intends to inflict death and evil on humankind, whom the woman has brought to birth. There seems to be an individualization more than collectivity that is implied in the text: a man, a woman, a victor, and the conquered serpent. It is within such a context that Vatican II in

Lumen Gentium, 55 interprets the Woman, her offspring and Evil. Scripture scholars are opposed to such a personal interpretation — especially those who are exclusively followers of the historical-critical method. However, the tradition of the Church, the liturgy, and other scholars will lead us to look more seriously at Vatican II's interpretation.

It is only in the light and perspective of New Testament revelation that we can speak of Mary in the Hebrew Scriptures. She is, however, a Jewish woman who was immersed within her culture which centrally made her a woman of the Torah. She belonged to the People of God, the Jews. She was familiar with the Temple, its rituals, and especially its prayers, the Psalms. But everything we know about her symbolically or factually comes only from the New Testament and the Tradition based on this Testament.

Certainly from the title "Mother of the Messiah" we recognize that she would have an influence on all Mariological teaching. This title springs from the New Testament which calls her Mother of Jesus, Mary, Mother of my Lord, and Woman. The title itself is *prophetic* because the entire New Testament message not only sees itself in the light of Jesus Christ (the way, truth, and life) but also, in the light of the New Testament, brings its own revelation to our eyes and ears through the marvelous utilization of the Hebrew Scriptures — the Torah, the *Khtuvim* (Writings) and the *Nebiim* (the Prophets). The Messiah himself in Luke's Resurrection Narrative underlines this:

> And he said to them, "Oh, how foolish you are! How slow of heart to believe all that the prophets spoke! Was it not necessary that the Messiah should suffer these things and enter into his glory?" Then beginning with Moses and all the prophets, he interpreted to them what referred to him in all the scriptures (Lk 24:25-27).

Conclusion About Genesis 3:15

Chapter VIII of *Lumen Gentium* was originally drawn up as a separate schema for a dogmatic constitution on Mary as Mother of God and Mother of humankind. The first paragraph contained references to Genesis 3:15 and Isaiah 7:14. Instead, in 1963 the Council voted to include the document on Mary in the Constitution on the Church. A final fascicle of the article appeared on November 28, 1965. As stated in paragraph 54, the Council did not intend to give a complete teaching about Mary nor to decide questions, particularly exegetical questions concerning the Old Testament, which have not yet been worked out by theologians. It did state in paragraph 55 its own rules of hermeneutics for reading the Hebrew Scriptures. The Council understood Mary to be "prophetically foreshadowed" in the victory over the serpent promised to our first parents after their fall into sin.

Isaiah 7:14/Vatican II

Matthew cites Isaiah 7:14, altering the text of the Septuagint and using it in the dream Annunciation to Joseph (Mt 1:23). In Catholic tradition this is the famous Emmanuel prophecy. It is an explicit text from the Hebrew Scriptures used within the New Testament. The text has a messianic import and Marian implication. The fact that it occurs immediately after the presentation of the Davidic lineage of Joseph, the foster-father of Jesus, demonstrates that the Jewish-Christian community of Matthew was concerned about the Jewish background of Jesus' parents and of the community's own Jewish roots. This is also the first text of a prophetic nature to appear in Matthew's Gospel which is one of divine and messianic accomplishment.

The pericope of Matthew 1:18-25 is an announcement to Joseph about the miraculous birth of Jesus Christ. This section can be called the "footnote" of the genealogy that Matthew has so carefully constructed as the introduction to his Gospel. Within the revelation to Joseph about the reality of Mary's pregnancy is the actual statement of the angelic messenger to Joseph. This announcement parallels and implements what Matthew sees as the prophetic fulfillment of the words of the prophet Isaiah (7:14). The content focuses upon the child to be named Jesus and is addressed to Joseph of the family of David, but Mary, mentioned in verse 20, is the only antecedent for the virgin who is the person to have within her womb the promised Emmanuel. Mary parallels the word "virgin"; Jesus parallels the name "Emmanuel." The name "Jesus" is explained: "for he shall save his people from their sins" and Matthew then gives the interpretation of the Hebrew word "Emmanuel," that is, "God is with us."

Matthew 1:18-25 is an example of instruction to a Jewish-Christian community about Jesus and the manner of his birth. R. Brown calls it a "teaching technique designed to offer background for those who already believe."[125]

Matthew uses his characteristic pattern for inserting a formula citation:

1:18-19	setting the scene
1:20-21	the command
1:22-23	formula citation
1:24-25	execution of the command

In 1:22-23 Matthew cites Isaiah 7:14 in a formula which differs from both the Hebrew text and the Septuagint. The Jews never have seen Isaiah 7:14 as a text which infers a birth from a virgin who remains virgin. In fact, they do not consider the text to be among the over 400 texts said to be messianic. Matthew 1:18-25 is unique in thought and content to the Matthean community; it is absolutely new to Jewish thought. In the second century this was pointed out to the Christians by Trypho, the Jew in Justin's *Dialogue* (IV, 31, 6-8). The statement that Jesus was born of a virgin mother is of Jewish Christian origin prior to Matthew's account; it is not based on a legend of Jewish derivation.

Lumen Gentium, 55 and John Paul II link the Isaian text with Genesis 3:15: Since the plan of salvation, which was assured by

Yahweh (Gn 3:15), comprised a woman in an important role, the opinion of those who see in Isaiah 7:14 an echo of Genesis 3:15 cannot be dismissed lightly. Vatican II describes Isaiah 7:14 as an "oracle" applied in the strict sense to Mary in Matthew 1:23.

The text has been seen to have messianic and Marian import in the history of its tradition within Christianity. R. Brown has an excellent insight in his summation of the study:

> Matthew has been trying to explain that Jesus is truly of the House of David, a Davidic descent that is not at all negated by the fact that Joseph begot him legally rather than naturally. And here [Mt 1:23] he has a text addressed to the House of David which speaks of a virgin being with child and giving birth to a son. Not only through the women mentioned in the genealogy, but also through this virgin *foretold* [my italics] in His word spoken by the prophet, God had prepared for the birth of Jesus the Messiah "in this way" (Mt 1:18). But Matthew has also been trying to explain that "this way," which involves the creative action of the Holy Spirit rather than the sexual action of a man, means that Jesus is God's Son as well as David's.[126]

Brown's remarks are similar in thought to one of the earliest references in the New Testament to Jesus' messianic origins. The reference in Romans 1:3-4 has both the Davidic/Messianic concept, as well as the divine origins of Jesus. Paul's text antedates that of Matthew by over 25 years:

> the Gospel about his Son, descended from David according to the flesh, but established as Son of God in power according to the Spirit of holiness through resurrection from the dead, Jesus Christ our Lord (Rm 1:3-4).

In this passage we have the earliest reference to Jesus as the promised Messiah who was born of the Davidic seed according to the flesh in his human existence. The lines can be paralleled with one another to show the humanness of Jesus which springs from Mary his Mother, and the graced-nature of the Christ who belongs to God:

Humanness:	Divine likeness:
the Messiah was *born* (of Mary)	and was made or designed
from the seed of David (through Joseph and Mary?)	Son of God in power
according to the flesh (again Mary)	according to the Spirit of holiness through resurrection from the dead

Biblical scholars assert that Paul is using a kerygmatic statement or proclamation about who Jesus is; this statement was already in use among those Christians before Paul knew them. Paul uses this credal statement in the introduction of this Epistle to express relationship by human descent or kinship in the Davidic Messianic line. We are at least certain of the parenting of Mary; Paul is not interested in her virginity; but, then again, he gives no evidence about a human father of Jesus. In chapter nine he returns to the ancestry of the Christ:

> For I could wish that I myself were accursed and separated from Christ for the sake of my brothers, my kin according to the flesh. . . theirs the patriarchs, and from them, according to the flesh, is the Messiah. God who is over all be blessed forever. Amen (Rm 9:3, 5).

We note that Paul is only interested in the Messiah, that is, the Christ, and not in his parents. But the fact that he does mention the Davidic lineage leads us to think of Mary and Joseph, especially through what we know from Matthew 1:18-25. The concepts of the human origins of the Messiah have always been expressed in the Christian understanding of the Messiah (*Mary of Galilee*, Volume I, pages 17-20).

Returning to Matthew 1:18-25, Bernard Lindars has an interesting suggestion that Isaiah 7:14 was first used by Christians in its Hebrew form to support the Davidic origins of Jesus, and only later in its Greek form to support the virginal conception of Jesus.

R.E. Brown also concludes that "Jesus is the final and once-for-all manifestation of God's presence with us, which is so much the work of the Spirit that for the first time in the genealogical record of the Messiah no human begetter can be listed."[127]

Paul Ricouer's expression "what the world behind the text is" refers to the historical events, the socio-economic and cultural setting that existed at the time a certain text was written. The exegetical task is to recover as much of these factors behind the text as is possible. Ricouer's other expression "what is in front of the text" refers to the methods and hermeneutics of today which enable both the interpreter and the reader to make the text meaningful and applicable to today's issues and needs whether personal or communitarian.

In selecting the text of Isaiah 7:14, Vatican II kept alive a Marian interpretation found within a Messianic text which contained a promise. Such an interpretation pertains to what is "in front of the text" for it is definitely an interpretation that originally did not belong to the historical event described in the text itself, nor to the meaning attached to the text which issued from the Hebrew (not the Christian) Scriptures some seven to eight hundred years later. Most likely the text is still more alive and meaningful within its Christian tradition of interpretation than in what lies behind the text in its Hebrew language and in Judaism. It is the tension and the controversy, the Matthaean rereading and use of the text, that keeps the text of Isaiah 7:14 alive today. The following is an example from the recent biblical parallels offered in six distinct official translations in English of Isaiah 7:14:

> Look, the young woman is with child and shall bear a son, and shall name him Immanuel. — *New Revised Standard Version*
>
> A young woman is with child, and she will give birth to a son and call him Immanuel. — *Revised English Bible*
>
> the virgin shall be with child, and bear a son, and shall name him Immanuel. — *New American Bible*
>
> the young woman is with child and will give birth to a son whom she will call Immanuel. — *New Jerusalem Bible*

Behold, a virgin shall conceive, and bear a son, and shall call his name Immanuel. — *King James Version*

the maiden is with child and will soon give birth to a son whom she will call Immanuel. — *Jerusalem Bible*

Since the text is also cited in Matthew 1:23, a similar excursus can be made to parallel the Hebrew text with the Christian text of the New Testament from these six different English translations:

"Look, the virgin shall conceive and bear a son, and they shall name him Emmanuel," which means "God is with us." — *New Revised Standard Version*

"A virgin will conceive and bear a son, and he shall be called Emmanuel," a name which means, "God is with us." — *Revised English Bible*

"Behold, the virgin shall be with child and bear a son, and they shall call him Emmanuel," which means "God is with us." — *New American Bible*

"Look! the virgin is with child and will give birth to a son whom they will call Immanuel," a name which means "God-is-with-us." — *New Jerusalem Bible*

Behold, a virgin shall be with child, and shall bring forth a son, and they shall call his name Emmanuel, which being interpreted is, God with us. —*King James Version*

The virgin will conceive and give birth to a son and they will call him Immanuel, a name which means "God-is-with-us." — *Jerusalem Bible*

One gets the impression that the text itself both in Isaiah 7:14 and Matthew 1:23 is referring to the same historical event during the time of Ahaz and then to the birth of Jesus in the manner in which Matthew uses the text. But in each of the six versions in English there are specific aspects which differ from the other five whether it be from the original Isaian text or that found in Matthew. This short excursus shows us the difficulties an exegete faces even in the simple task of establishing a translation which would correspond to the original Hebrew or to the Greek of the Septuagint which Matthew was probably relying upon.

This is but the first step in the process of discovering what is "behind the text." One can imagine how many different insights, applications, and special meanings could be garnered from any one of these translations. The value of this presentation of the text in six different English translations is that it shows that philological competency does not necessarily result in similarity in translation. These various translations show there are at least two original texts (the Hebrew and the Septuagint) at the basis for the school or community of Matthew. The Hebrew text dates from the time of Ahaz, king of Judah, and Isaiah, the prophet (735-715 B.C.E.). The Septuagint was written between 150-100 B.C.E., while Matthew was probably written 85 C.E. Understandably a complexity arises in the text because the Septuagint and Matthew are already interpretations which are, so to speak, "in front of the text." The exegete remains with the original Hebrew text and, likewise, proceeds to the other texts, the Septuagint and that of Matthew, but always with the purpose of discovering the "world in back of the text."

Since Vatican II, three excellent Catholic biblical commentaries have been published. They are: *A New Catholic Commentary on Holy Scripture* (1975 revised and updated), *The Jerome Biblical Commentary* (1968), and *The New Jerome Biblical Commentary* (1990). These commentaries give us the world behind the text from the perception of leading Catholic exegetes.

The *New Catholic Commentary* has a rather extended interpretation of Isaiah 7:14 but makes a strong point for a Messianic interpretation of it in its original context. The sign given to Ahaz is one of destruction for it means that the Assyrian invasion will last for a number of years, perhaps till the child promised to the maiden is able to distinguish right from wrong. "It should be noted that the sign is given to the Davidic dynasty more than to Ahaz alone. Hence it is above all the confirmation of the ancient oracle of Nathan (2 S 7:11-16). The older and more traditional view applied the prophecy direct to the Messiah." This viewpoint is not without its difficulties.[128]

The Jerome Biblical Commentary explanation on Isaiah 7:14 is the work of F.L. Moriarty, who options for an interpretation that is dependent upon the "great dynastic promise made to David's house" (2 S 7:12-16): "The child about to be born, therefore, may be the young Hezekiah in whose birth Judah would see the continuing presence of God among his people and another renewal of the promise made to David." He moves on, however, to give an eschatological perspective to Isaiah, hence, opening the way for a future Messianic promise as well. In this, Moriarty gives more visionary power to Isaiah than does A. Penna in the above *New Catholic Commentary*. Moriarty concludes:

> Nevertheless, the solemnity of the oracle and the name "Emmanuel" lend credence to the opinion that Isaiah's perspective does not stop at the birth of Hezekiah; it moves ahead to the ideal king of David's line through whose coming God could finally be said to be definitively with his people. This does not mean, of course, that Isaiah foresaw the fulfillment of this prophecy in Christ, but he expressed the hope that Christ perfectly realized. Matthew and the Church have seen in the birth of Christ from the Virgin Mother the perfect fulfillment of this prophecy.[129]

The Benedictine scholar Joseph Jensen gives us the latest commentary on Isaiah 7:14 in *The New Jerome Biblical Commentary*:

> *"the young woman"*: *Hā `almâ* is not the technical term for a virgin (*betûlâ*). This is best understood as a wife of Ahaz; the child promised will guarantee the dynasty's future (note again "the house of David" in v 13; cf. v 2 and for this reason can be called Immanuel ("with us is God").[130]

Jensen is more reserved in his statements about the text. He more strictly remains with the world behind the text. This is the primary task of the exegete.

The Interplay of Faith and Responsible Biblical Research

In rereading Isaiah 7:14 in the light of Matthew 1:18-25, it is seen that Matthew's central concern is the legitimacy of Jesus' birth as Messiah. Matthew carefully unfolded his genealogy in order to convince the reader that Jesus is the Messiah through Abraham and David. His aim in recounting the dream given to Joseph is to seal that claim. His use of Isaiah 7:14 is primarily a focus on the birth of the one promised in the oracle. He is not focusing on the sign which would be that of a marriageable young woman giving birth. The word he has chosen for this "young woman" is *parthenos*, "virgin." Being a virgin, this young woman had no intercourse with a man nor specifically with her espoused Joseph (Mt 1:18-25).

We may ask why Matthew uses the Isaiah 7:14 text within the context of a dream that explains the integrity and fidelity of Mary to whom Joseph was engaged. The Hebrew text of Isaiah uses the word *'almah* which does not in itself connote a virgin, but does not exclude the meaning. The fact that the Septuagint made such a translation demonstrates the more difficult reading of *'almah* as "virgin." O.J. Baab points out:

> An examination of the occurrences of [*'almah*] in the Old Testament does not remove the possibility of the meaning "virgin." E.g., Abraham's servant speaks of the "young woman" who comes out to draw water as the one appointed to be the bride of his master's son (Gn 24:43-44). From the context, it is certain that this [*'almah*] is a virgin. (Cf. Ex 2:8; Pr 30:18-19; Sg 1:3-4).[131]

S. Mowinckel sees that the woman of Isaiah 7:14 may be a supernatural woman who would give birth to a son who is the omen of a wonderful transformation.[132]

Parallels to Isaiah 7:14 have been found in the Nikkal poem written in Ugaritic and discovered at Ras Shamra in 1933. The important lines are: (a) 77:5: "a virgin [*bethulah*] will give birth"; (b) 77:7: "Lo, a young woman [*'almah*] bears a son." Argument can be made through such a similar subject of "virgin" and "young woman" that in Ugaritic an *'almah* is considered as a virgin. Nevertheless, the controversy over the text remains, for Koehler and Baumgarten point out that *'almah* means a "marriageable girl, young woman (until the birth of her first child)" (Lexicon, p. 709).[133] This could leave open the possibility of a pregnant woman being called a virgin until her first born sees the light of day. D. Moody demonstrates how a tradition about the virgin birth and a Messianic reference in Isaiah 7:14 developed:

> Since the time of Jerome a number of Christians, recognizing fully the immediate reference to a fulfillment in the time of Ahaz, have found it tenable to defend both the Messianic reference of Isa. 7:14 and the virgin birth of Jesus, by noting the use of typological interpretation in the Gospel of Matthew (e.g. 2:6, 15, 18, 23).[134]

Both Moody and Brown demonstrate that the text of Isaiah 7:14 does not prove the virgin birth nor is it necessary to the narrative. Matthew, however, as a skillful scribe, does keep bringing forth new treasures from his searching and using the prophets. This is especially the case in the Infancy Narrative from 1:18-2:23, a portion of his Gospel wherein he uses five citations from the Hebrew Scriptures.

H.M. Orlinsky, on the other hand, sees Christianity as developing an ideal of virginity not present in Judaism nor in the Near East during the time of Jesus. He states:

> When early Christianity developed the belief of virgin birth for Jesus, it was natural to point to a possible proof text in Isa. 7:14. The exclusive meaning "virgin" was assumed for παρθενος [*parthenos*] in the Septuagint, and consequently for the Hebrew term which is translated ['almah].[135]

Orlinsky makes the point that *'almah* does not mean "virgin" in almost every citation in which it is used. It is found four times in the singular and five times in the plural and means "young woman, girl, or maiden." His concluding paragraph is precisely the way Judaism would understand the Hebrew text and how they always have understood what was the "world behind the text." Here is the conclusion:

> Once the correct meaning of [*'almah*] in Is 7:14 is adhered to — and the force of adjective [*harah*] and of the participle [*yaldat*] given their natural due — it becomes clear that what the prophet Isaiah is saying to Ahaz is, "Behold, the young woman is with child and is about to give birth to a son. Let her name him Immanuel," i.e., before the baby that the pregnant woman will soon bear has grown significantly (vs. 16) the invaders will themselves be invaded. This is related to what the prophet says in the next chapter (8:1-4). As for the word order and intent of Is 7:14, Peters asserted bluntly: "There is a striking resemblance between this verse and Gn 16:11. Is there any proper ground for translating the tenses differently in the two verses?" Of the newer official translations, only the Jerusalem Bible and the New Jewish Version have rendered the entire Isaiah verse correctly.[136]

In his article on "Virgin Birth" in *The Interpreter's Dictionary of the Bible* (Supplementary Volume), R.E. Brown states:

> In terms of evidence, Is 7:14 currently has a less important role in the discussion: first it is widely agreed that it refers to a conception in the eighth century B.C. that somehow continued or supported the Davidic line of kings, rather than to the conception of Jesus; second, even the LXX [Septuagint] reading, "Behold, *the virgin* will conceive and bear a son," does not necessarily envisage a virginal conception, for the future tense may mean that a woman who is now a virgin will conceive; third, granted that in his infancy narrative Matthew himself probably added the "fulfillment citation" (1:22-23; 2:5-6, 15, 17-18, 23) to existing material, the citation of Is 7:14 did not create the idea that Jesus was virginally conceived but was used to illustrate it.[137]

Catholic Catechism and Isaiah 7:14

John Paul II signed the Apostolic Constitution "Deposit of Faith" for the publication of the *Catechism of the Catholic Church* on October 11, 1992.

The person of the Blessed Virgin Mary is treated in a contextual manner, that is, Mary is present in areas of the *Catechism* that are appropriate; for example, in the Creed or in the doctrine of the Incarnation. The text of Isaiah 7:14 occurs in chapter 2 under the title of the credal expression "I Believe in Jesus Christ, The Only Son of God" and under the subtitle "Mary's virginity". The text reads:

> The Gospel accounts understand the virginal conception of Jesus as a divine work that surpasses all human understanding and possibility: "That which is conceived in her is of the Holy Spirit," said the angel to Joseph about Mary his fiancée. The Church sees here the fulfillment of the divine promise given through the prophet Isaiah: "Behold, a virgin shall conceive and bear a son" (par. 497).

This is the sole reference to Isaiah 7:14 and it is given according to the Greek translation of Matthew 1:23. Within such a context we see the ecclesial interpretation given under the light of faith. The important contribution of the statement is that it unites the text with Matthew 1:23, one of the five fulfillment texts in the Infancy Narrative, and rereads Isaiah 7:14 under the Matthaean influence rather than as a Hebrew text taken in its historical setting. The *Catechism of the Catholic Church* is presenting an ecclesial, not a historical-critical, reading of the text. Fortuitously, Matthew's Gospel is the one that directly uses the term for Church (*ekklesia* in Mt 16:18 and 18:17). The presentation is one of faith within an ecclesial reading of the Gospel text. The overall context of Vatican II is also understood within the *Catechism*, hence, in *Lumen Gentium*, 55 where the text of Isaiah 7:14 appears, it is immediately followed by Matthew 1:22-23. There is no polemic involved per se; it is simply an apophatic statement made in faith, but within ecclesial and conciliar contexts.

The only other implicit mention of Matthew 1:23 in the *Catechism* is in chapter 3 entitled "I Believe in the Holy Spirit." The relevant passage is offered as part of the synthesis under the heading of "The Holy Spirit and the Church." The implied text of Galatians 4:4 introduces the text:

> In the fullness of time the Holy Spirit completes in Mary all the preparations for Christ's coming among the People of God. By the action of the Holy Spirit in her, the Father gives the world Emmanuel, "God-with-us" (Mt 1:23).

This statement complements what was said above while showing the importance of the Holy Spirit within the event of the Incarnation among the People of God, another ecclesial expression of Vatican II. The pneumatology that is described in the paragraph adds still another important manner of understanding Mary and her role within salvation history or the "fullness of time."

In the schema for *Lumen Gentium* on July 3, 1964, Isaiah 7:14 is used with Micah 5:2-3:

> But you, Bethlehem-Ephrathah, too small to be among the clans of Judah, from you shall come forth for me one who is to be ruler in Israel; whose origin is from of old, from ancient times. (Therefore the Lord will give them up, until the time when she who is to give birth has borne, and the rest of his brethren shall return to the children of Israel.)

C. Miller notes: "The passage from Micah seems to have been chosen for this Mariological context because of 'she that travaileth shall bring forth.'[138] It was the wish of twelve of the Council fathers that this text be given with Isaiah 7:14 and Matthew 1:22-23. They were aware that the exegetes were not in agreement with a literal interpretation of Isaiah 7:14 as applying to Mary, whereas, they were convinced Matthew 1:22-23 did apply to her. This is the only place where the Council went to so much trouble to insert even a second 'cfr.' in a series of references."[139]

In the *New Jerome Biblical Commentary* this text of Micah is confirmed as relating to Isaiah 7; 9; 11. "Allusions are made globally to the messianic texts of Isa. 7; 9; 11; 2 Sam 7; Ps 89. The Hebr text identifies this city of Ephrathah (see Josh 15:59; Ruth 4:11) as Bethlehem. It is the city of Jesse and of his son David, who was chosen to be king of the 12 tribes of Israel. Matt 2:5-6 shows how this text came to be interpreted."[140]

B. Renaud's interpretation makes of Micah's *yoleda* in v. 3 an allusion to Isaiah's *yoledet*, i.e., she who shall bring forth is similar to Isaiah's word. This word can be traced back to a line of individual miraculous births in the Hebrew Scriptures and a tradition which closely associates a woman with the work of salvation.[141] The Council also mentions the exalted daughter of Sion (a theme treated in this volume). This allows for the collective or corporate personality envisioned by certain Hebrew titles such as "daughter of Sion."

C. Miller summarizes his analysis of the Council's use of all the Old Testament references in *Lumen Gentium*, 55 in the following paragraph:

> Although *LG* explicitly bases its use of Is 7:14 and Mi 5:2-3 on tradition, the reference to Isaiah finds its primary basis in Mt 1:23. While the Isaiah prophecy was not in itself originally messianic in the full sense, it would seem to have acquired such a notion by the time of its *relecture* by the author of Mi 5:1-5, the latter passage being literally a messianic prophecy. *LG* interprets the Mican reference, then, as the fulfillment of a prophetic oracle.[142]

Endnotes

[108] *Lumen Gentium*, (55).

[109] O'Carroll, *Theotokos*, 139-141.

[110] Brown, *The Gospel According to John*, 926.

[111] Stefano De Fiores and Salvatore Meo, *Nuovo Dizionario di Mariologia*, 2a ed. (Milano: Edizioni Paoline, 1986) 1048.

[112] O'Carroll, 336.

[113] J.-E. Ménard, *L'Evangile selon Philippe* (Paris: Letouzey, 1967) 82, 87.

[114] Cardinal Agostino Bea, "Maria SS. nel Protoevangelo (Gen. 3, 15)," *Marianum* XV, 1953: 1-21.

[115] Miller, *"As It Is Written,"* 16-60.

[116] *Papal Teachings, Our Lady,* ed. at Solesmes (St. Paul Publications, Boston), 71, 72. Cf. Leo XIII, *Augustissimae Virginis,* AAS, 30 (1898), 129; Pius X, *Ad diem illum,* AAS 36 (1904), 462. Pius XI, *Divini Redemptoris,* AAS 29 (1937) 96; Biblical Commission, 1909, *Enchiridion Biblicum* 3, 38.

[117] Miller, 50-51.

[118] Elaine Wainwright, "But Who Do You Say That I Am?" unpublished, p. 24.

[119] Miller, 52-55.

[120] Ibid., 56.

[121] Brown, *New Jerome Biblical Commentary,* 2:5; 12.

[122] *Redemptoris Mater* 7: "'Blessed be the God and Father of our Lord Jesus Christ, who has blessed us in Christ with every spiritual blessing in the heavenly places' (Eph 1:3). These words of the *Letter to the Ephesians* reveal the eternal design of God the Father, his plan of man's salvation in Christ. It is a universal plan, which concerns all men and women created in the image and likeness of God (cf. Gn 1:26). Just as all are included in the creative work of God 'in the beginning,' so all are eternally included in the divine plan of salvation, which is to be completely revealed, in the 'fullness of time,' with the final coming of Christ. In fact, the God who is the 'Father of our Lord Jesus Christ' — these are the next words of the same Letter — 'chose us in him *before the foundation of the world,* that we should be holy and blameless before him. He destined us in love to be his sons through Jesus Christ, according to the purpose of his will, to the praise of his glorious grace, which he freely bestowed on us in *the Beloved.* In him we have redemption through his blood, the forgiveness of our trespasses, according to the riches of his grace' (Eph 1:4-7).

"*The divine plan of salvation* — which was fully revealed to us with the coming of Christ — is eternal. And according to the teaching contained in the Letter just quoted and in other Pauline Letters (cf. Col 1:12-14; Rm 3:24; Gal 3:13; 2 Cor 5:18-29), it is also *eternally linked to Christ.* It includes everyone, but it reserves a special place for the 'woman' who is the Mother of him to whom the Father has entrusted the work of salvation. As the Second Vatican Council says, 'she is already prophetically foreshadowed in that promise made to our first parents after their fall into sin' — according to the Book of Genesis (cf. 3:15). 'Likewise she is the Virgin who is to conceive and bear a son, whose name will be called Emmanuel' — according to the words of Isaiah (cf. 7:14). In this way the Old Testament prepares that 'fullness of time' when God 'sent forth his Son, born of woman. . . so that we might receive adoption as sons.' The coming into the world of the Son of God is an event recorded in the first chapters of the Gospels according to Luke and Matthew."

[123] *Redemptoris Mater* 11: "In the salvific design of the Most Holy Trinity, the mystery of the Incarnation constitutes the superabundant *fulfillment of the promise* made by God to man *after original sin,* after that first sin whose effects oppress the whole earthly history of man (cf. Gn 3:15). And so, there comes into the world a Son, 'the seed of the woman' who will crush the evil of sin in its very origins: 'he will crush the head of the serpent.' As we see from the words of the ProtoGospel, the victory of the woman's Son will not take place without a hard struggle, a struggle that is to extend to the whole of human history. The 'enmity,' foretold at the beginning, is confirmed in the Apocalypse (the book of the final events of the Church and the world), in which there recurs the sign

of the 'woman,' this time 'clothed with the sun' (Rv 12:1).

"Mary, Mother of the Incarnate Word, is placed *at the very center of that enmity*, that struggle which accompanies the history of humanity on earth and the history of salvation itself. In this central place, she who belongs to the 'weak and poor of the Lord' bears in herself, like no other member of the human race, that 'glory of grace' which the Father 'has bestowed on us in his beloved Son,' and this *grace determines the extraordinary greatness and beauty* of her whole being. Mary thus remains before God, and also before the whole of humanity, as the unchangeable and inviolable sign of God's election, spoken of in Paul's letter: 'in Christ. . . he chose us. . . before the foundation of the world. . . he destined us. . . to be his sons' (Eph 1:4,5). This election is more powerful than any experience of evil and sin, than all that 'enmity' which marks the history of man. In this history Mary remains a sign of sure hope."

[124] *Redemptoris Mater* 24: "Thus we find ourselves at the very center of the fulfillment of the promise contained in the ProtoGospel: the 'seed of the woman. . . will crush the head of the serpent' (cf. Gn 3:15). By his redemptive death Jesus Christ conquers the evil of sin and death at its very roots. It is significant that, as he speaks to his mother from the Cross, he calls her 'woman' and says to her: 'Woman, behold your son!' Moreover, he has addressed her by the same term at Cana too (cf. Jn 2:4). How can one doubt that especially now, on Golgotha, this expression goes to the very heart of the mystery of Mary, and indicates the unique place which she occupies *in the whole economy of salvation?* As the Council teaches, in Mary 'the exalted Daughter of Sion, and after a long expectation of the promise, the times were at length fulfilled and the new dispensation established. All this occurred when the Son of God took a human nature from her, that he might in the mysteries of his flesh free man from sin.'

"The words uttered by Jesus from the Cross signify that *the motherhood* of her who bore Christ finds a 'new' continuation *in the Church and through the Church*, symbolized and represented by John. In this way, she who as the one 'full of grace' was brought into the mystery of Christ in order to be his Mother and thus *the Holy Mother of God*, through the Church remains in that mystery as *'the woman'* spoken of by the Book of Genesis (3:15) at the beginning and by the Apocalypse [Rv] (12:1) at the end of the history of salvation. In accordance with the eternal plan of Providence, Mary's divine mother-hood is to be poured out upon the Church, as indicated by statements of Tradition, according to which Mary's 'motherhood' of the Church is the reflection and extension of her motherhood of the Son of God.

"According to the Council, the very moment of the Church's birth and full manifestation to the world enables us to glimpse this continuity of Mary's motherhood: 'Since it pleased God not to manifest solemnly the mystery of the salvation of the human race until he poured forth the Spirit promised by Christ, we see the *Apostles* before the day of Pentecost "continuing with one mind in prayer with the women and *Mary the mother of Jesus*, and with his brethren" (Acts 1:14). We see Mary prayerfully imploring the gift of the Spirit, who had already overshadowed her in the Annuncia-tion.'

"And so, in the redemptive economy of grace, brought about through the action of the Holy Spirit, there is a unique correspondence between the moment of the Incarnation of the Word and the moment of the birth of the Church. The person who links these two moments is Mary: *Mary at Nazareth* and *Mary in the Upper Room at Jerusalem*. In both cases her discreet yet essential presence indicates the path of 'birth from the Holy Spirit.' Thus she who is present in the mystery of Christ as Mother becomes — by the will of the Son and the power of the Holy Spirit —present in the mystery of the Church. In the Church too she continues to be *a maternal presence*, as is shown by the words spoken from the Cross: 'Woman, behold your son'; 'Behold, your mother.'"

125 Brown, *The Birth of the Messiah*, 144n30.

126 Ibid., 150.

127 Ibid., 153.

128 *A New Catholic Commentary on Holy Scripture*, 575-576.

129 Raymond E. Brown, Joseph A. Fitzmyer, and Roland E. Murphy, eds., *The Jerome Biblical Commentary* (Englewood, NJ: Prentice, 1968) 16:19-21; 271.

130 *The New Jerome Biblical Commentary*, 15:18-20; 235.

131 George Arthur Buttrick, ed., *The Interpreter's Dictionary of the Bible: An Illustrated Encyclopedia*, vol. 4 (New York: Abingdon, 1962) 787-788.

132 S. [Sigmund] Mowinckel, *He That Cometh*, trans. G. W. Anderson (New York: Abingdon, n.d) 110 ff., 184-185.

133 *Interpreter's Dictionary of the Bible*, vol. 4, 789-791.

134 Ibid., 789-791.

135 Keith Crim, gen. ed., *The Interpreter's Dictionary of the Bible: An Illustrated Encyclopedia*, suppl. vol., 939-940.

136 Ibid., 939-940.

137 Ibid., 940-941.

138 Miller, 58.

139 Ibid.

140 *The New Jerome Biblical Commentary*, 16:23-30; 253.

141 B. [Bernard] Renaud, "Cahiers de la Revue Biblique," *Structure et Attaches Littéraires de Michée IV — V*, vol. 2 (Paris: Gabalda, 1964) 71-72, 94.

142 Miller, 60.

Chapter Six

MARY IN BIBLICAL REFERENCES FROM THE HEBREW SCRIPTURES

For understanding the Church's use and interpretation of the texts of the Hebrew Scriptures, both the document of Vatican II on the Sacred Liturgy, *Sacrosanctum Concilium*, and the eighth chapter of *Lumen Gentium* are essential to reading, interpreting, and listening to the sacred texts in which Mary has a role in salvation history during the liturgical seasons. All liturgy is a celebration of the Paschal Mystery — an event which encompasses the suffering, death, resurrection, and ascension of Jesus, as well as the sending of the Spirit. Mary is always to be understood within the context of the Paschal Mystery of Christ and the history of salvation among the People of God, the Church.

I. de la Potterie recently expressed interest in looking at some important references that have been used from the Hebrew Scriptures regarding Mary. This interest and concern is both legitimate and scholarly for the texts are kept alive both by an ecclesial reading and interpretation as well as by the creative and scientific analysis that have been applied to the texts by scholars using new methods in approaching these texts. The continuity of a living tradition is a valid stratum within the new landscapes developed around these texts. In reflecting about the tension between the scholarly approaches and the more traditional ecclesial and liturgical appreciation of these texts, the following two citations from de la Potterie are insightful for the task of this chapter:

In the present development of Mariology, the Old Testament preparation for the New Testament's doctrine about Mary is not reduced to specific verses of the Scripture. It is rather a question of a general theme which is extended over numerous texts, most particularly texts in the prophetic literature. In our approach to the biblical background of the image of Mary, we will also adopt this method of study. We will approach several texts which present a symbolic feminine image in which the prophets discovered the symbol of the Messianic Zion. This "Daughter of Zion" is characterized as a woman who is at once spouse, mother, and virgin. It is within this context of Old Testament literature that present-day exegesis concerning Mary renews and develops itself.

Nevertheless, in this spousal relationship of a covenant, Mary is evidently not situated at the side of God or of Christ, but next to the human partner of the covenant: the people of God. During the epoch of the New Covenant, it is a woman who henceforth "represents among all of the creatures the Israel of God, the pre-redeemed humanity, that God could 'espouse' to divinize her in him." Mary thus becomes the personification of the people of God that Israel was; and she thereby becomes the image of the Church. That is why one could call her: "Mary, the First Church." And still for the same reason, the title "Daughter of Zion," which in the Old Testament designates Israel in its relations with God and which is then applied to the Church, is already in the Gospels (at least implicitly) applied to Mary. For the same reason, the Council called her "The Daughter of Zion par excellence" (*Lumen Gentium*, 55), and the Pope, in his encyclical *Mother of the Redeemer* (n. 3), speaks of "this hidden 'daughter of Zion'" (cf. Zp 3:14; Zc 2:14), that God had involved her in the accomplishment of the plan of salvation.[143]

From the earliest celebration of the Eucharist through prayers, institutional rites, and the Sacred Scriptures the Virgin Mary has been commemorated in the liturgy. Since Vatican II the choice of the Sacred Scriptures for Marian commemorations has been expanded and developed, offering to the faithful a rich biblical experience and appreciation of Mary, the mother of Jesus. We have already seen the foundational texts suggested by the Council itself in *Lumen Gentium*. This more comprehensive biblical approach continues in *Marialis cultus* of Paul VI in 1974, in the encyclical *Redemptoris Mater* of John Paul II, and in the *Collection of Masses of the Blessed Virgin Mary*. Since we are focusing upon Mary as a Woman of Israel and the Daughter of Zion, we now turn to the texts from the Hebrew Scriptures that are used in these documents.

In the Church's celebration of Mary since Vatican II, a careful attention to her ecclesial role, her relationship to Christ, and her cooperation in the mystery of salvation in history are essential to understanding Mary today. The Constitution on the Sacred Liturgy states: "In celebrating this annual cycle of the mysteries of Christ, Holy Church honors the Blessed Mary, Mother of God, with a special love. She is inseparably linked with her son's saving work."[144] This specific article had a major influence on both *Marialis cultus*, on the Roman Calendar, and on the special Collection of Masses in honor of Mary.[145]

On November 21, 1965, Pope Paul VI spoke of the "synthesis" which the Council presented on Mary. "It is. . . the first time, and it fills us with joy to say it, that an ecumenical council has presented so vast a synthesis of the Catholic doctrine on the place which Mary has in the mystery of Christ and the Church."[146] Despite Paul VI's enthusiasm and the Council's chapter on Mary in *Lumen Gentium*, a period of Marian crisis resulted from 1965-1974. Conciliar statements take time. Implementation requires careful planning and explanation. Perhaps experimentation was the way of coping with renewal within the Church, but after ten years new signs of a revitalized Marian presence would appear. Joseph Cardinal Suenens best described the critical period concerning Mary:

> . . . a time of considerable lessening of appreciation for Mary, if not among the faithful in general, at least in intellectual circles. There was a reaction against a Marian theology which was too essentialist, deductive, abstract, and concentrated on her privileges in a context that was not Christological. This

reaction was opposed to a Marian devotion that remained on the edge of liturgical renewal, was too dependent upon private revelations, and too remote from biblical theology.[147]

On February 2, 1974 Paul VI signed the document *Marialis cultus*. In this document the principles of how Mary is related to the central mystery of Christ are given:

1) Mary is to be seen as having a role in the history of salvation as God's providential presence among humankind through Jesus Christ.
2) Both the Theocentric and Christocentric focus are important wherever Mary is spoken of or celebrated.
3) An ecclesial emphasis on Mary's being in and among its members rather than separate and above them is also a working principle for Marian study and devotions.

As T.A. Thompson says:

All forms of Marian devotion gravitate "towards this worship [of Christ] as to their natural and necessary point of reference" (MC, Intro.). All devotion expressed toward Mary is ultimately given to Christ: "What is given to the Handmaid is referred to the Lord". . . A distinguishing trait of *Marialis cultus* is the language of bonding and of union used to describe the relation of Christ to Mary.[148]

The Sacred Scriptures are essential to this Marian renewal in the liturgy of the Church. Thompson, citing *Marialis cultus* 12, 14 says:

The Lectionary, with its rich and varied collection of Old and New Testament biblical texts concerning the Virgin Mary, sets forth "more completely the mystery of Christ." Scriptural readings with reference to Mary are not limited to the Marian feasts but are also part of the Sunday liturgy and the celebration of the sacraments. In this way, a Marian dimension can be part of the Sunday liturgies and the celebration of the sacraments.[149]

During the 1987-1988 Marian Year John Paul II insisted on Mary's being a part of the liturgical, sacramental, and biblical life of the Church. Even in the psalms or the Liturgy of the Hours an ecclesial and Marian perspective could be given. John Paul II strengthens the primary principle of Paul VI's *Marialis cultus*, namely, that an "inseparable bond" (*nexu indissolubili*) exists between Christ and Mary in the totality of his mystery.

Before Vatican II in the "age of Marian devotions" many pastors and theologians considered the biblical and Christocentric emphasis non-Marian. But since Vatican II there is a greater effort to reunite liturgy and Marian devotion both through a more expansive and rich use of Scripture as well as through the Church's emphasis on the indissoluble connection of the Mother with the Son. It is from the Bible that all devotion draws inspiration and gains new vigor and sure help (*Marialis cultus*, 30). Paul VI is the doctor of Mary's exemplarity: his emphasis on modelling our behavior on her virtues safeguards us within the Church from certain devotional deviations such as "vain credulity which substitutes reliance on merely external practices for serious commitment . . . and sterile and ephemeral sentimentality, so alien to the spirit of the Gospel that demands persevering and practical action" (*Marialis cultus*, 38).[150]

Biblical References from the Hebrew Scriptures
Used in the Liturgy for Feasts and Commemorations
of the Blessed Virgin Mary

The purpose of this chapter is to reflect upon the passages used in the liturgy on feasts of the Virgin Mary or memorials in her honor. These reflections will follow the universal Lectionary and the more recent Lectionary for *Collection of the Masses of the Blessed Virgin Mary* (1992). In recent studies of these texts, the focus is upon the mysteries of Christ and Mary's relationship to them. In her specific titles or privileges there is also an emphasis on her relationship to Christ; thus, Mariology is always seen in an ecclesial and Christological framework within the liturgy as well as in the Scriptures which are designated for particular mysteries of Christ and Mary.

Mary and the Advent Liturgy (Gn 3:9-15, 20; Is 7:14; Mi 5:1-4)

This season is one of the great blessings of the liturgical year. It is a season in which joy, hope, and patient waiting for the birth of Jesus are thriving within the texts, songs, and atmosphere of the sacred liturgy. There is an underlying history of salvation which begins with creation and continues through the formation and development of the People of God down to the moment of the Incarnation when Jesus Christ, Son of God, is born of the virgin Mary from Nazareth in Galilee.

Within the first novena of days in the Advent Season, the feast of the Immaculate Conception is celebrated. This is always on December 8th. It is from the Hebrew Scriptures of Genesis 3:9-15, 20 that our first reflection about the Scriptures and Mary arises. This text has already been commented upon, but we may also reflect upon it in the light of a Marian liturgical celebration. Though the dogma of Mary's Immaculate Conception was promulgated in 1854, the use of the text chosen from Genesis has a long tradition within the Catholic Church. Perhaps a new development which the dogma receives today is that Mary is intimately associated within the Church envisioned as the People of God. The special gift she enjoys as being conceived without sin in her person is entirely due to God's loving-kindness to her parents whose names we do not know from the Bible, but who are called Anne and Joachim in the *Protoevangelium Jacobi* or Protogospel of James. In recent documents such as *Redemptoris Mater*, our own predestination and calling to lead a sinless life are emphasized through a text from Ephesians which helps us to understand in a communitarian and ecclesial manner the Immaculate Conception. The text reads:

> Blessed be the God and Father of our Lord Jesus Christ, who has blessed us in Christ with every spiritual blessing in the heavens, as he chose us in him, before the foundation of the world, to be holy and without blemish before him. In love he destined us for adoption to himself through Jesus Christ, in accord with the favor of his will, for the praise of the glory of his grace that he granted us in his beloved (Eph 1:3-6).

Just as we are called to such unblemished holiness through the saving power of Jesus Christ's blood so, too, is Mary predestined and preserved from the evil of sin through God's loving-kindness. She, too, is dependent upon God and upon Christ for redemption. Her unique situation is one that models in her the reality of what we, too, hope for through our baptism and our spiritual lives.

The liturgy sees the promise of such a victory over sin and death in the Protoevangelium of Genesis 3:15. The text has traditionally been seen in the Church as the "first proclamation of the good news of salvation."[151] In the text of Genesis the woman referred to is Eve, the "mother of all the living," while an enmity between her descendants and the serpent with its repugnant yet tantalizing symbolism is predicted by the speaker in the narrative, God. Her descendants are read in a collective way, meaning the entire race, in the original inspired text of the Hebrew Scriptures. In the Septuagint the term for seed has a singular masculine antecedent; hence, it was easily used by the Christian theologians of the early Church as referring to Christ. Jerome's translation in the Vulgate easily leads to a Mariological interpretation, but this was not his intention. In fact he knew the Hebrew text was clearer in reference than the Old Latin text. Jerome says in his *Book on Genesis and Hebrew Questions*: "The Hebrew text reads better than the Old Latin, namely, 'He shall crush thy head, and you shall crush his heel,' because our steps shall proceed ahead from the heel, and the Lord will crush quickly Satan under our feet."[152]

Unfortunately there is no mention of Genesis 3:15 in the rest of the Hebrew Bible. It is Irenaeus who follows Justin in making it a personal messianic reference to Christ. However, most of the early theologians did not follow this interpretation. The direct Mariological reading of the text through *"she shall crush thy head"* is probably not due to Jerome but to his retaining of the antecedent "she" from Latin manuscripts. Where then did the feminine translation come from? Philo Judaeus (a contemporary of St. Paul) maintained that the pronoun should pair with "woman" rather than with "seed" since in rigid parallelism "the opposition in this member of the verse returned to that of the woman and the serpent." Ambrose also followed this interpretation but like Philo he applied it to Eve, not to a personal messianic victor.

Both Pius IX in *Ineffabilis Deus* (Dec. 8, 1854) and Pius XII in *Munificentissimus Deus* (Nov. 1, 1950) used the text in a Mariological and messianic sense for the proclamation of the dogmas of the Immaculate Conception and of the Assumption respectively.[153]

In conclusion, for the feast of the Immaculate Conception the Genesis text (Gn 3:9-15, 20) is paralleled with the New Testament's account of Mary's Annunciation. In an ecclesial and Marian reading this means that Mary will, by her *fiat*, give her free response in acceptance of the Divine Will to be the New Eve, the new Mother of the Living.[154] Just as Eve is the mother of all born into chronological time, Mary is the mother of all born into eternal life. B. Lazor points out that there is no mention of any such privilege as the Immaculate Conception in the Bible, but the expression used for Mary in the account of the Annunciation, "Hail, Full of Grace," or "Most Favored One," does help to obviate some of the difficulties. I. de la Potterie would also interpret the perfect passive participle used to describe Mary (*kécharitôménê*) as meaning the one who has already *been* transformed and favored by God's grace.[155]

Throughout Advent the classical prophet Isaiah is read within the liturgical readings. His theme of creative-redemption and hope inspires the Church to reflect upon the birth of Christ in the light of such a confident expectancy of God's coming among the people, especially Israel. During Advent, Isaiah is read as a whole. The timeless atmosphere of the liturgy (*kairos*) renders a prayerful reading of Isaiah as more fitting for the needs of a listening and believing people. During Advent over fifty selections are from Isaiah ranging from chapter one to chapter sixty-five.

The Immanuel prophecy of Isaiah 7:14 is central to our celebration of Advent in this season of surprise, fulfillment, and attentive awaiting. Carroll Stuhlmueller, a perceptive commentator on Isaiah, captures the ethos of Advent when he says:

> We too can be faced with puzzling and agonizing situations which seem to deny God's goodness and justice. God never

asks us to betray our human intelligence. God gives us a mind
and a store of ancestral wisdom by which to form prudent
decisions. Yet, within this human process God will intervene
at times and overwhelm us with the miraculous. We feel like
Mary the virgin who is with child. Without doing anything or
with a sweep of wonder reaching far beyond our human
activity, God will act. We can only exclaim, "Immanuel —
God is with us." We will call God "Yahweh Sidqenu," for he is
justly fulfilling his promises and our hopes far beyond all
expectation. The fulfillment will be like a tender shoot, grow-
ing from a hidden root. What is so miraculous, must be
surrounded with the most tender care.[156]

This text (Is 7:14), which has been traditionally accepted and
commented upon in a Mariological manner, has to be seen within
the total message of Isaiah. The text itself refers to a definite
historical event in the past — almost eight hundred years before
Mary ever existed. However, it was taken up by Matthew and used
in his Infancy Narrative to introduce a series of prophetic passages
that help explain the Christian's perception of the birth of Jesus
Christ, son of Abraham, son of David (Mt 1:1).

The background for this Emmanuel text of Isaiah 7:14 is the
entire Book of Emmanuel (Is 7:1-12:6). This section of Isaiah is a
commentary on the period of the Syro-Ephraimite War, 735-732
B.C.E. Emmanuel is "the messianic king, peace-loving, utterly just
and full of the gifts of the Spirit of Yahweh."[157]

Isaiah's prophecy to Ahaz is set within the context of absolute
faith in God rather than Ahaz's leaning towards a political solution
by joining with a dangerous political partner, Assyria. Nevertheless,
a sign is given: "Therefore the Lord himself will give you this sign:
the virgin [in the original Hebrew, the word virgin means a young
woman of marriageable age] shall be with child, and bear a son, and
shall name him Immanuel" (Is 7:14). We have noted how this text
has meaning within the historical context of Israel and that the child
could be one of the immediate successors to Ahaz, Hezekiah.
Pertinent to our reflection on why the earliest Christian writings

preferred Matthew's understanding of the text is the following commentary:

> The LXX [Septuagint] translation of Isaiah, made before 150 B.C., renders 'almâ by *parthenos*, 'virgin'; and the Old Latin, following the LXX, has *virgo*. Jerome adopted the same word in his version even though he was translating from the Heb. We may regard the LXX rendering as a witness to later Jewish tradition concerning the meaning of the prophecy. St. Matthew's Gospel of course unequivocally states the virginal conception where this prophecy is quoted (Mt 1:23; cf. Lk 1:35) using the word *'parthenos'*.[158]

This passage is an important one for paralleling the origins of David and the continuance of the Messianic lineage. Matthew's Gospel cites the passage while changing it to exalt Bethlehem because Jesus, a Davidic, is born in this town (Mt 2:6). The citation is a fulfillment text in Matthew. In the original Hebrew text of Micah there is hope for Judah because the rise of a ruler is promised. The passage recalls that of Isaiah 7:14. Isaiah was a contemporary of Micah. These passages also refer to the pregnant mother. The theme of peace closes the prophecy with the statement that the one born will himself be peace.

Ephrathah refers to the clan to which Jesse the father of David belonged; he resided in Bethlehem. René Laurentin sees within this Matthean passage a rereading which leads the Church to see Mary as the eschatological daughter of Zion; that is, she is the Mother of the Messiah and of the Church.[159] There are also innuendoes that lead one to see Isaiah 7:14 and its reference to Emmanuel as a parallel. Undoubtedly, this is the reasoning behind the text as used by Vatican II in *Lumen Gentium*, 58. It fits in well with the Advent season — a season of hope, peace, and of God's presence as Emmanuel in the person of Jesus who is born of the Virgin Mary.

Feast of Our Lady of Lourdes

The Catholic Church celebrates the Feast of Our Lady of Lourdes on February 11. Judith is only used twice within the sanctoral cycle, namely, for widows in the Common of Saints outside the Easter season and in the Common of the Blessed Virgin for readings outside the Easter season. The readings for the Feast of Our Lady of Lourdes are Isaiah 66:10-14, Judith 13:18-20, and John 2:1-11, the Cana account. Brief comment will be made upon these texts in the light of Paschal Mystery faith.

Isaiah 66:10-14 is used in the Liturgy of the Hours, Thursday Morning Prayer, Week IV. This powerful passage shows the compassionate love of God for Israel in its post-exilic period and its return to Mother Jerusalem. It is easy for the homilist and reader to see an ecclesial application of the text through the theme of Jerusalem as mother-city for her children. The outcome of the return to the Holy City is unparalleled joy and comfort for her faithful children. The feminine aspect of God is apparent. Yahweh comforts Israel as a mother comforts her sons and daughters.

The larger context of the passage is within the notion of passing from sorrow to a new heaven and a new earth (Is 63:1-6, 16). "Rejoice!" recalls the angelic salutation to Mary. In the light of paschal belief is the conviction that, through God's compassionate love, human beings have been redeemed from exile, sin, and death. The image of a child nursing at its mother's breast is a beautiful image of joy, peace, and contentment. This, of course, is also true of Mary's nurturing and joyful care of us as her children.

For further reflection on the New Jerusalem, study of the final two chapters (21 and 22) of the Book of Revelation concerning the New Heaven and the New Earth is recommended.

The Responsorial Psalm used for this feast is from Judith 13:18-20. This text is appropriate for reflecting upon Mary through a valiant Jewish prototype, Judith. Fortunately, liturgical sensitivity, shown in the removal of the lines of violence from this portion of Judith, makes it a response of praise of Mary similar to Gabriel's words at the Annunciation:

> . . . Blessed are you, daughter, by the Most High God, above all the women on earth; and blessed be the Lord God, the creator of heaven and earth. . . Your deed of hope will never be forgotten by those who tell of the might of God. May God make this redound to your everlasting honor, rewarding you with blessings. . . . .

For the celebration of Mary in Ordinary time there is only one text used on the Vigil of the Assumption, 1 Chronicles 15:3-4, 15, 16; 16:1-2. The ark of the covenant being brought into the tent David had pitched is the subject of this passage. James Turro gives the following comments for this reading:

> 1st Reading: I Chron. 15:3-4, 15, 16; 16:1-2.

> The choice of this account of the transfer of the Ark from Obededom's house to Jerusalem is surely meant to suggest the now widespread view that assimilates Mary to the Ark of the Covenant. As God was present over the Ark and carried about with the Ark, so God was present with and carried about by Mary. The holiness of the Ark in which God dwelt is intimated in several ways: 1) "David assembled *all* Israel in Jerusalem" (This was not an ordinary, quotidian happening; it was solemn and noteworthy.); 2) it is the Levites only who may presume to bear this sacred object; 3) the Ark is greeted with elaborate acclaim — chanters, musical instruments, harps, lyres and cymbals. In transfer, all this bespeaks the holiness of Mary, in whom God dwelt as on the Ark.[160]

Collection of the Masses of the Blessed Virgin Mary

On May 31, 1992, Feast of the Visitation, Daniel E. Pilarczyk, Archbishop of the Diocese of Cincinnati and President of the National Conference of Catholic Bishops, issued the decree establishing December 8, 1992, Solemnity of the Immaculate Conception, as the effective date for the use of the *Collection of Masses of the Blessed Virgin Mary* in the dioceses of the United States.

The titles of the Masses as well as the chapters and verses of the texts referenced in this chapter are listed in Volume 2, Lectionary, of the *Collection of Masses of the Blessed Virgin Mary* (Contents, pp. 7-8, and Indexes, pp. 236-240). Since Volume I of this trilogy concentrated on the texts of the New Testament, the focus here will be primarily on the Hebrew Scriptures. This commentary is meant to assist the reader and the homilist in seeing the traditional applicative and accommodative use of these texts from the Hebrew Bible. The sequence of scriptural references for the 46 Masses is given in the Lectionary Indexes.

Why a *Collection of Masses of the Blessed Virgin Mary*?

Thomas Thompson answers this question by giving the background of the *Collection*.

> The *Collection* was developed by a group within the Congregation of Divine Worship from 1984 to 1986. It includes texts from a number of sources: early sacramentaries, the *Missale Romanum*, and Mass formularies recently composed by religious congregations and dioceses and submitted to the Congregation. (Since 1970 the Congregation for Divine Worship approved over 200 Mass formularies of the Blessed Virgin in the various "propers" for dioceses and religious orders.) The origin of about half of the Mass formularies is mentioned in the introduction.

> The *Collection* was published in response to directors of Marian shrines and others who requested a greater selection of texts for Masses to commemorate the Virgin Mary. At Marian shrines, the Votive Mass of the Blessed Virgin may be celebrated for those on pilgrimage almost every day of the year (with the exception of Sundays, solemnities, and feasts of the Lord). To avoid excessive repetition of the same Mass and to present a larger view of the role of the Virgin Mary within the Church, the request for additional Votive Masses was made.[161]

In this chapter the forty readings from the Hebrew Scriptures together with the Psalms and Canticles taken from the Hebrew Scriptures are commented upon in the light of the Marian theme presented in the collection of Masses in honor of Mary. The overarching guide that the Church uses in these selected texts is that they are to be seen as part of a "single corpus that is permeated by the mystery of Christ."[162] This means that the Hebrew texts are being used with a Christian rereading of them in the context of the Christ-Event. The readings are, therefore, to be read with an ecclesial and faith viewpoint. The importance of an inspired Christian faith is what enables the Church to celebrate the Sacred Readings as part of the liturgy. Such an appreciation of the Scriptures can be enhanced by modern methods of explaining the Scriptures, but the latter are not able to declare, to proclaim, or to explain what the light of faith and prayer of a believing community can experience and celebrate through the Sacred Scriptures. It is within this ecclesial and faith-inspired perspective that the readings from the Hebrew Scriptures are chosen for the Masses in honor of Mary. Mary herself, as the Jewish mother of Jesus, would have been familiar with her own people's reading of the Tanach or Hebrew Bible. The Church sees Mary as her spiritual Mother and appreciates the Hebrew Scriptures which were familiar to Mary of Galilee.

Readings from the Hebrew Scriptures Used in the Collection

The regular biblical sequence of the Hebrew Scriptural readings are given with a brief commentary. The commemorative Mass is also mentioned.

1. *Genesis 3:1-6, 13-15 ("The Blessed Virgin Mary,*
   Help of Christians," #42B, pp. 181-182)

This reading is offered as an alternative to the selection from the Book of Revelation 12:1-3, 7-12ab, 17. With previous lengthy comment on this passage of Genesis, the reflection here will be brief. Mary is seen as the Woman whose offspring will conquer the wily serpent by crushing its head. We have seen that Mary is interpreted as a new Eve figure. This is one of the earliest texts to have been applied to Mary through typological and analogical rereading of this passage. Several exegetes, like Feuillet and Brown, have seen similarities to this passage in the text mentioned above from the Book of Revelation and from the scene on Calvary in John 19:25-28a.

2. Genesis 3:9-15, 20 ("The Blessed Virgin Mary, Image and Mother of the Church," #25, p. 118)

Pope Paul VI on November 21, 1964, proclaimed Mary "Mother of the Church, that is to say, of all Christian people, faithful and pastors who call her mother most loving."[163]

From a Catholic doctrinal perspective the Genesis text commences the history of salvation or God's creative redemption of the human race through the victory of the mother of the living (Eve/Mary) over the serpent through her offspring. The text begins with God speaking with Adam who is blaming Eve for his own sin. The Preface for this Mass turns more to the New Testament text of John 19:25-27 and Acts 1:12-14. There is a mention of Mary receiving God's word in her immaculate heart and thereby conceiving the Word in her virginal womb first through faith. This thought is present in Ambrose and Augustine. Mary contrasts with Adam who is not listening to God with a pure heart and conscience.

3. Genesis 12:1-7 ("The Blessed Virgin Mary, Chosen Daughter of Israel," #1A, p. 21)

This Advent Mass makes use of an excellent selection from Genesis 12 which recalls God's promise to Abraham that "all the communities of the earth shall find blessings in you." Mary like Abraham is a model of faith and absolute trust in God. She as the model of faith in the second Testament reflects her ancestor in faith, Abraham. Mary in her song proclaims: "He has helped Israel his servant, remembering his mercy, according to his promise to our fathers, to Abraham and to his descendants forever" (Lk 1:54-55). In the context of the reading from Genesis as well as those from Ruth

2:1-3, 8-11; 4:13, 17 and Matthew 1:1-17, Mary is seen within Israel
and its heritage as the People of God. Salvation comes from Israel:
"You people worship what you do not understand; we worship what
we understand, because salvation is from the Jews" (Jn 4:22). She is
a Daughter of Israel through birth and through her remarkable
living out of her Judaism in all its aspects. We see her in Christianity
as the Mother of the Messiah, Jesus Christ (Mt 1:1, 16, 18-25).

4. Genesis 22:1-2, 9-13, 15-18 *(Alternative Reading,* Appendix, Old Testament #1, pp. 199-200)

This alternate reading for a commemoration of Mary is the
text of the sacrifice of Isaac by Abraham and the blessing conferred
upon him by God. Undoubtedly, the parallel in Mary's seeing her
son Jesus crucified recalls this sacrifice of Isaac. The absolute trust
of both Abraham and Mary at the beginning of their call by God
continues at the supreme moment of sacrifice of both Isaac and
Jesus. The blessing given to Abraham is the seventh and the
climactic one. This is Abraham's greatest trial as well as Mary's (Jn
19:25-27). "The story is a masterpiece, presenting God as the Lord
whose demands are absolute, whose will is inscrutable, and whose
final word is grace."[164]

5. Genesis 28:10-17 *(Alternative Reading, Appendix,* Old Testament #2, p. 201)

This passage narrates the dream or vision of Jacob at Bethel,
and the stairway or ramp leading to heaven. Both the promise and
blessing of God upon the descendants of Israel and the origin of a
sacred dwelling place are part of the narrative. The vision indicates
a link between heaven and earth. In the Tradition of the Church,
Mary, too, is seen as the "Gate of Heaven" and a recipient of the
greatest of blessings bearing the Son of God in her womb.

6. Exodus 3:1-8 (*Alternative Reading, Appendix, Old Testament* #3, p. 203)

This is an alternate reading for a commemorative Mass in honor of Mary. The vision of the burning bush is the first miracle in which Moses is involved. In verse 2 an angel of the Lord is said to appear, then in verse 4 the angel is identified with God.

The Synagogue commentary says: "Here [in v. 2] Moses had not yet become fully conscious of his prophetic call and therefore saw *an angel of the LORD;* but when he turned aside to look at the burning bush, he caught a glimpse of the *Shekinah.*"[165]

The Catholic Tradition has seen Mary's virginity as symbolized by the burning bush which was not consumed. Both Gregory of Nyssa and Hesychius of Jerusalem use the symbol in their homilies for the Nativity.[166]

7. Exodus 19:3-8a ("*Our Lady of Cana,*" *Christmas Season,* #9, p. 54)

This passage is chosen because it presents Moses as the mediator of a special covenant of God with Israel. The people on hearing about this covenant reply, "Everything the Lord has said, we will do." In the Cana narrative Jesus is seen as commencing another covenant and Mary says, "Do whatever he shall tell you" (Jn 2:5). Her response is the same as that of Israel. This theme of covenant and the people's response is admirably developed by Aristide Serra in his monumental biblical and Marian work.[167]

8. Numbers 24:15-17a (*Alternative Reading, Appendix, Old Testament* #4, p. 205)

This is the only passage chosen from the Book of Numbers in the Masses in honor of the Virgin Mary. Amphilochius of Iconium uses Numbers 24:17 to speak of Jesus as the Messiah. The Dead Sea Scrolls use the text in a messianic sense. Coins of Simon ben Kosibah after the revolt against Rome carry a star.[168] The rabbinic literature witnesses to a messianic understanding of Numbers 24:17. The earliest Christian use of the text is found in Justin Martyr's *Apology* (Apol I, 32, 12). For Justin the Advent of Christ is the rising of a star. This is in harmony with the Jewish understanding of the text: "A prediction of the messiah whose advent will be like a star appearing in the heaven, and he will gather the dispersed people of Israel(N)."[169]

9. *Ruth* 2:1-2, 8-11; 4:13-17 (*Alternative Reading, Appendix, Old Testament #5, pp. 207-208*)

This text is used as an alternate first reading in the liturgy. Ruth is important as a link within the genealogy given by Matthew. She is also an example of commitment and fidelity. Like Ruth, Mary also says "yes" to God in her consent to Gabriel's message. Phyllis Trible says of Ruth, "There is no more radical decision in all the memories of Israel."[170] The final purpose for the book of Ruth seems to be the ending which treats of the origins of King David. Josephus also comments on the Book of Ruth: "This story of Ruth I have been constrained to relate, being desirous to show the power of God and how easy it is for Him to promote even ordinary folk to rank so illustrious as that to which he raised David, sprung from such ancestors" (Ant. 5.9.4. e 337).[171]

10. *1 Samuel* 1:24-28; 2:1-2, 4-8 (*"Holy Mary, Handmaid of the Lord," #22, pp. 105-106*)

This narrative about Hannah, the mother of Samuel, may have provided the framework for Luke's Infancy Narrative because of the many parallels to what he recounts about Mary. Numerous studies have been made on the hymn of Hannah which is echoed in Mary's Magnificat. The hymn of Hannah also resonates in several psalms, especially Psalm 113:7-9. The response for this Mass is the Magnificat of Mary! Both Hannah and Mary are humble servants of God who pray intensely and respond positively to the work of God in their lives.

11. 2 Samuel 7:1-5, 8b-11, 16 ("*The Blessed Virgin Mary, Chosen Daughter of Israel,*" #1B, p. 22)

The reading is chosen to give a distant background for Mary's being called the Daughter of Zion and the joy of Israel. The feast associates Mary with Adam and Eve, Abraham, Jesse and David. Vatican II in *Lumen Gentium*, 55 states:

> She stands out among the poor and humble of the Lord, who confidently await and receive salvation from Him. With her, *the exalted Daughter of Sion* [my italics], and after a long expectation of the promise, the times were at length fulfilled and the new dispensation established. All this occurred when the Son of God took a human nature from her, that He might in the mysteries of His flesh free man from sin.

The promise of God given to David through the prophet Nathan is central to the passage from 2 Samuel 7:16: "Your house and your Kingdom shall endure forever before me; your throne shall stand firm forever."

12. 1 Kings 8:1, 3-7, 9-11 ("*The Blessed Virgin Mary, Temple of the Lord,*" #23A, p. 109)

This Mass celebrates both the Divine maternity of Mary and the holiness of her life. She is considered a true temple of the Lord because she bore the Son of God within her womb.

The passage from 1 Kings contains a magnificent description of the sacredness of the Temple in Jerusalem built by Solomon. There are many of the sacred titles and symbols of God within the narrative: the ark of the covenant, the city of David called Zion, the wings of the Cherubim, the Holy of Holies, the two tables of the Law, and the cloud displaying the glory of the Lord. Perhaps the Presentation of Jesus within the Temple in Luke 1:21-38 contains similar symbols of a sacred nature. Both passages capture the ethos of the Temple in Jerusalem. It is important to remind ourselves that Vatican II does not separate Mary from us within the Church. She is there in the midst of us, her brothers and sisters in faith. The text from St. Paul's first letter to the Corinthians explains it well:

> Do you not know that you are the temple of God, and that the Spirit of God dwells in you? If anyone destroys God's temple, God will destroy that person; for the temple of God, which you are, is holy (1 Cor 3:16-17).

13. *1 Chronicles 15:3-4, 15-16; 16:1-2 ("Holy Mary, Mother of the Lord," #19A, p. 95)*

Several exegetes have seen a parallel in Mary's visit to Elizabeth with this selection from 1 Chronicles wherein David brings the ark of the covenant to the Temple and dances before the ark.[172] The passage narrates how David is preparing everything concerning the ark for the Lord. The term "Lord" is used at the beginning, verse 3; in the middle of the selection, verse 15; and at the end, chapter 16, verse 2. This parallels Elizabeth's exclamation: "And how does this happen to me, that the mother of my Lord should come to me?" (Lk 1:43).

14. *Judith 13:14, 17-20; 15:8-10; 16:13-14 ("The Blessed Virgin Mary, Pillar of Faith," #35, p. 152; "The Blessed Virgin Mary at the Foot of the Cross," #12A, Lenten Season, p. 67; "The Immaculate Heart of the Blessed Virgin Mary," #28, p. 126; "Our Lady of Ransom," #43, p. 184)*

The selections from Judith, one of the heroines of Israel, are significant for the Church's celebration of Mary in four distinct Masses. Since the readings are basically the same, they have been put under one heading.

The Book of Judith develops a series of reflections on the greatness of God seen in the marvels of the Exodus Event or in the Passover which is relived in each generation by the Jewish people. It is especially in times of great difficulties and oppression that the Book of Judith is understood: "The Book of Judith is a vivid story relating how, in a grave crisis, God delivered the Jewish people through the instrumentality of a woman."[173]

Judith's victory over Holofernes is recalled in the selection from chapter 13. She is praised in these words: "Blessed are you, daughter, by the Most High God, above all the women on earth" (Jdt 13:18). She is further praised by the people: "You are the glory of Jerusalem, the surpassing joy of Israel; you are the splendid boast of our people" (Jdt 15:9). Judith, in turn, praises the God of Israel:

> A new hymn I will sing to my God. O Lord, great are you and glorious, wonderful in power and unsurpassable. Let your every creature serve you; for you spoke, and they were made; you sent forth your spirit, and they were created; no one can resist your word (Jdt 16:13-14).

Our Christian tradition has made of these selections from Judith a Mariological allegory thereby taking away from the powerful emotion and passion that the original writer had for the Jewish people. Mary's victory is in the spiritual order, not the temporal.

15. *Esther C:12, 14-15, 25, 30; 8:3-8, 16-17a ("Holy Mary, Queen and Mother of Mercy," #39, p. 166; "The Blessed Virgin Mary, Mother and Mediatrix of Grace," #30, p. 133)*

The first selection from Esther is taken from the Vulgate and, hence, C:12, 14-15, 25, 30 presents the prayer of Esther for her people Israel. This humble prayer resonates with the outcry of the *'anawîm* or poor of Yahweh. She depends totally on the mercy, *hesed*, of God. The invocation to the God of Abraham, Isaac, and Jacob is particularly powerful for it is taken up also by Jesus (Mt 22:32; Lk 20:37-38). Just as Esther prays so poignantly for her people, so, too, does Mary pray for her people Israel and for all believers.

16. 2 Maccabees 7:1, 20-29 ("The Commending of the Blessed Virgin Mary," #13, Lenten Season, pp. 69-70)

This Mass centers on the scene at the foot of the Cross in John 19:25-27. It emphasizes the commendation of a filial relationship between Mary and the Beloved Disciple extending this relationship to all disciples of Christ. The commendation is part of the Paschal Mystery of Christ and the compassion of Mary.

The narrative of the holy mother of the martyrs of Israel serves as a model for such dedication to God. Mary as the Daughter of Zion *par excellence* likewise has such dedication to God and her sons and daughters that nothing can impede her intervention. In this account, the resurrection of the dead and the impetratory and expiatory value of the holy ones is understood and taught. In the text there is also a strong theology of martyrdom that became characteristic of the early Christians. In Maccabees there are strong didactic parallels to Psalm 139:13-16, Wisdom 7:1-2, and Ecclesiastes 11:5. Verse 28 is the first mention of God who creates out of nothing (*ex nihilo*). The mother is confident that God will restore her sons if they are faithful to their belief in God the Creator and Restorer of life.

17. Proverbs 8:17-21, 34-35; 8:22-31 ("The Blessed Virgin Mary, Mother and Teacher in the Spirit," #32A, p. 142; "The Blessed Virgin Mary, Seat of Wisdom," #24A, p. 113)

The remarkable poem of Proverbs 8 is a manifestation of God through the feminine image of Wisdom. The poem describes Wisdom's birth (Pr 8:22-31). Why would Wisdom's birth be described? Kathleen O'Connor, a scholar of Wisdom literature, gives us the answer:

> It is these origins before the birth of the world which establish the Wisdom Woman's authority. In the ancient world, the older the religious figures and traditions were believed to be, the more claim they had to reveal hidden truths. She is older than even the oldest thing we know, the earth itself. By placing her birth before creation, the author gives her unquestionable

authority to speak the truth. This Wisdom Woman is an
ancient power to be reckoned with.[174]

Both a relationship with God and the great dignity of human
beings are primary roles of Wisdom. The Church through the
liturgy has accommodated this text to Mary, Seat of Wisdom.

18. *Song of Songs* 2:8-14 *(4:6-7, 9, 12-15); Ezekiel 47:1-2, 8-9, 12
    ("The Visitation of the Blessed Virgin Mary," #3B, pp. 29-30;
    "The Blessed Virgin Mary, Fountain of Salvation," #31, p. 136)*

The first selection is a love song during springtime with a visit
from the maiden's lover. W. Rudolph says this is "the most beautiful
song to nature in the Old Testament." The theme and the season fit
well with the celebration of Mary's visit to Elizabeth which happens
in late spring (May 31) in the liturgical feast. The mention of the
swiftness of the gazelle recalls that Mary went with "haste" (*metá
spoudés*) to Elizabeth (Lk 1:39).

The second selection from Song of Songs 4 emphasizes both
the interior and exterior beauty of the bride in a poetic and not an
allegorical way. The fountain theme which runs through the final
verses is accommodated to Mary as the fountain or source of health
and salvation. There is a picture of ecstatic wholesomeness in the
description of the bride as a garden of delights which heals, soothes,
and intoxicates with joy the lover who suffers from being away from
the bride.

19. *Sirach* 24:1-4, 18-21; 24:9-12, 18-21; 24:17-21 *("The Blessed
    Virgin Mary, Seat of Wisdom," #24, p. 114; "The Blessed Virgin
    Mary, Mother of Divine Hope," #37, p. 158; "The Holy Name of
    the Blessed Virgin Mary," #21, p. 102; "The Blessed Virgin Mary,
    Mother of Fairest Love," #36, p. 155)*

The praise of Wisdom in Sirach parallels what we have seen in
Proverbs about Wisdom personified as Woman. Both the selection
from Proverbs and the one from Sirach are taken from among the
poetic verses that each book possesses.

We see in Mary several of the sacred themes and symbols of Israel within this famous chapter of Sirach; for example: Wisdom as Torah, Jerusalem the City of God, the People of God. There are angelic attendants to the throne of God, a divine activity of Wisdom between heaven and earth — serving as a type of mediatrix, and the pillar of cloud which symbolizes the Presence of God or the *Shekinah.* Themes of Zion and discipleship are also present.

The identification of Wisdom with Torah (Revelation, Instruction, and Law of God) is central to this praise of Wisdom. This is similar to the Fourth Evangelist's seeing all creation as dependent upon the Word of God whose revelation is in the very Person of Jesus (Jn 1:1-4, 14).

Many of these symbols and themes from Wisdom literature have been used for Mary throughout the liturgy.

20. Sirach 51:13-18, 20-22 *("Holy Mary, Disciple of the Lord," #10, Lenten Season, p. 61)*

This is the personal testimony of Sirach about his search for Wisdom. As a true pupil of Israel's Wisdom, the Torah, he has succeeded in sharing this search with the readers and believers. The selection chosen describes a true disciple of the Law (Torah) and the virtues necessary in order to discover Wisdom. This last chapter of Sirach, which is an alphabetical poem, forms an inclusion with the beginning of Sirach.

21. Isaiah 7:10-14; 8:10c *("The Blessed Virgin Mary and the Annunciation of the Lord," #2A, Advent Season, p. 26)*

The liturgy uses the theme of Emmanuel several times during the year: the Feast of the Annunciation, March 25; the 20th of December; and on the Fourth Sunday of Advent in Cycle B. The prophecy of Isaiah 7:14 is used in parallel with Luke 1:26-38 on this feast. It is a text which was predominant in the fourth and fifth century homilies of the Fathers of the Church.

22. *Isaiah 9:1-3, 5-6 ("The Blessed Virgin Mary, Mother of the Savior," #5A, Christmas Season, p. 39; "The Blessed Virgin Mary, Queen of All Creation," #29A, p. 129; "The Blessed Virgin Mary, Mother of Good Counsel," #33A, p. 145; "The Blessed Virgin Mary, Queen of Peace," #45, p. 191)*

The same text is used in all four Masses. The titles given to Emmanuel draw the attention of the Church to a messianic and Marian application to Christ and Mary. The verses are most familiar to us through the Advent and Christmas liturgy:

> For a child is born to us, a son is given us; upon his shoulder dominion rests. They name him Wonder-Counselor, God-Hero, Father-Forever, Prince of Peace. His dominion is vast and forever peaceful, from David's throne, and over his Kingdom, which he confirms and sustains by judgment and justice both now and forever. The zeal of the Lord of hosts will do this!

This is one of the most important messianic passages of the Old Testament. If an ideal king is meant, then the application to Jesus is easily made by the Christian reader. If it is an historical figure, then King Hezekiah of the royal Davidic line would be the best choice for whom it meant; however, there are chronological difficulties. The dynastic Davidic promise is meant by the verses which contain the mention of the birth of a son (verses 5-6). This promise is alive in such passages as 2 Samuel 7:14; Isaiah 7:14; and Psalm 2:7.

23. *Isaiah 11:1-5, 10 (Alternative Reading, Appendix, Old Testament #6, p. 209)*

The oracle is related to the above passages taken from Isaiah and also speaks of an ideal royal messianic leader of Israel. The Christian tradition has changed "fear of the Lord" into "piety" thereby giving the mystical seven gifts of the Holy Spirit. Mary as

Mother of the Messiah is related to the Church's understanding of this text.

24. Isaiah 53:1-5, 7-10 ("The Blessed Virgin Mary, Health of the Sick," #44, pp. 187-188)

The last four songs of the Suffering Servant, which have the theme of the Servant bearing our sufferings, are presented in this Mass which is especially appropriate for sacred Marian shrines of healing throughout the world.

Isaiah 53 is the most complex and difficult of the Servant Songs to interpret; however, its theological message is that the ultimate effect of the Servant's suffering is a sign of hope and success for the Servant. A. Penna concludes his commentary on this song in this manner: "Reflection on these passages was an important element in the early Church's understanding of the role of our Lord, and of his death as a vicarious expiation."[175]

25. Isaiah 56:1, 6-7 ("The Blessed Virgin Mary, Mother and Teacher in the Spirit," #32, pp. 142-143)

With chapter 56 of Isaiah we enter into the Book of Consolation (Trito-Isaiah), which extends to the final chapter (66) of Isaiah. This section is postexilic and centers on Jerusalem, which in a Christian rereading of Isaiah is a symbol of the Church. The Church is emphasized in the Christian rereading of this text as a "house of prayer for all peoples" (v. 7). Salvation is assured through the observance of the Sabbath and the keeping of God's revelatory laws. The key word "justice" is indicative of the spiritual life. Carroll Stuhlmueller writes: "The Temple receives its 'highest title' (Cheyne, *op. cit.*, 62), one that is frequently inscribed over synagogues today: 'house of prayer.'"[176]

26. Isaiah 60:1-6 *("The Blessed Virgin Mary and the
    Epiphany of the Lord," #6, Christmas Season, p. 42)*

The reading is the traditional one used for the Feast of
Epiphany. The section harmonizes well with Matthew's narrative
about the Magi and the gifts they bring — gold, frankincense, and
myrrh (v. 6 and Mt 2:11). These verses are a lyrical description of
the new Jerusalem.

Stuhlmueller says this about the expression "the glory of the
Lord shines": "This phrase always signals an extraordinary illumination, as though God were not wrapping splendor around Jerusalem
but rather, by his presence within the city, radiating a dazzling light
(Dt 33:2; Mal 3:19)."[177]

27. Isaiah 61:1-3, 10-11; 9-11 *("The Blessed Virgin Mary, Mother of
    Consolation," #41, p. 175; "The Blessed Virgin Mary, Cause of
    Our Joy," #34B, p. 149)*

In Luke's Gospel, in the account of Jesus' reading from the
scroll of Isaiah in the synagogue (Lk 4:18ff), Is 61:1-2 is cited. The
first three verses center on God's mission to the affected. Stuhlmueller
comments, "Here, as throughout the poem, metaphors are abundant, but the basic idea looks to the total salvation of God's people
— bodily, spiritually, individually, and socially (cf. Mt 11:4-6)."[178]

28. Isaiah 66:10-14 *("The Blessed Virgin Mary,
    Mother of Divine Providence," #40, p. 172)*

The gentle nourishment of Mother Zion is offered as consolation to her children in this last Isaian citation used in the liturgy
for a feast in honor of Mary. Perhaps, in an ecumenical spirit and
vision, these words of Isaiah offer the world of religion much hope.
Stuhlmueller remarks, "The Church of apostolic days, living in the
final age of the world and inaugurated by Christ's death and
resurrection, frequently quoted this chapter to settle internal quar-
rels with Judaizing groups and to argue against those Jews who
rejected Christianity."[179]

What better image for the providence of God than a mother nursing, caressing, and comforting her children?

29. Ezekiel 47:1-2, 8-9, 12 ("The Blessed Virgin Mary, Fountain of Salvation," #31, p. 136)

This dramatic and descriptive passage about the sacred waters flowing from the Temple and purifying all waters with their dynamic sanctifying action fits well with the title for this Mass. God is the source of these living waters which purify, strengthen, and save. The imagery is complemented by what the Fourth Evangelist says of Jesus:

> On the last and greatest day of the feast, Jesus stood up and exclaimed, "Let anyone who thirsts come to me and drink. Whoever believes in me, as Scripture says: 'Rivers of living water will flow from within him.'" He said this in reference to the Spirit that those who came to believe in him were to receive. There was, of course, no Spirit yet, because Jesus had not yet been glorified (Jn 7:37-39).

It is likewise complemented in the Gospel reading for this Mass, John 19:25-37. W. Robertson Smith notes, "Of all inanimate things that which has the best marked supernatural associations among the Semites is flowing (or, as the Hebrews say, 'living') water."[180]

30. Micah 5:1-4a (Alternative Reading, Appendix, Old Testament #7, p. 211)

This pericope is a messianic oracle which speaks of the origins of a Davidic ruler who shall shepherd the flock of God. Matthew 2:6 cites verse 1 of Micah in the narrative about the Magi and their inquiry into where the Messiah was to be born. In the Church's rereading of Micah in the light of Matthew, verse 2 which reads ". . .when she who is to give birth has borne. . ." is accommodated to the mother of the Messiah. R. Laurentin sees this verse as referring to Mary, the eschatological daughter of Zion and mother of the Messiah and the Church.[181]

31. *Zephaniah 3:14-18a; 3:14-20 ("The Visitation of the Blessed Virgin Mary," #3A, Advent Season, p. 29; "Holy Mary, Mother of Unity," #38A, p. 161)*

The setting for this selection is the restoration of daughter Zion, Jerusalem, through God. By means of a remnant people who are righteous and humble, this restoration is promised. A homecoming is to be celebrated which excludes none of those truly humble, poor, and dependent upon God. Jerusalem, the Daughter of Zion, is to rejoice and exult, for God is within her midst.

S. Lyonnet noticed that the expression "Rejoice," *Chaire* in the Septuagint, is also used in Gabriel's address to the Virgin Mary (Lk 1:28). With this insight, many Catholic exegetes and some Protestant exegetes have seen the theme of Mary as Daughter of Zion. This is an example of Old Testament symbolism attached to Mary. R.E. Brown states: "She is to be identified with those of low estate and the poor (the Magnificat); but she is not oppressed or violated, and is totally faithful (1:45) and obedient to God's word (1:38)."[182]

32. *Zechariah 2:14-17 ("The Blessed Virgin Mary, Cause of Our Joy," #34A, p. 149)*

This is another Daughter of Zion theme in the setting of a New Jerusalem. An extensive study on these verses, both in their original Hebrew setting and in the Christian rereading of them, is done by Aristide Serra. Serra attempts to discover whether Luke in the Annunciation account models the address to Mary as Daughter of Zion by a rereading and then an implicit use of Zephaniah 3:14-17; Joel 2:21-27; Zechariah 2:14-15; 9:9. He answers in a positive manner, both from Judaism's use of these texts for an eschatological-messianic era of hope and for Christianity by realizing this hope in Jesus the Messiah. His contention is that Luke would have been aware of the messianic use of such texts. The application to Mary as Mother of the Messiah would be a natural one for Luke. He further concludes, "In the eyes of the first generation of Christians, the Mother of Jesus was configured as the ideal incarnation of the 'Daughter of Zion.' In her, as an individual person, the vocation of Zion-Jerusalem and of all Israel, the people of the Covenant matured in an exemplary fashion."[183]

33. *Zechariah 9:9-10 (Alternative Reading, Appendix, Old Testament* #8, *p. 213)*

The Messiah will come in a humble way, not like a king riding in a chariot or upon a horse. "The Evangelists see a literal fulfillment of this prophecy in the Savior's triumphant entry into Jerusalem (Mt 21, 4f; Jn 12, 14f)."[184]

34. *Malachi 3:1-4 ("The Blessed Virgin Mary and the Presentation of the Lord,"* #7, *Christmas Season, p. 45)*

Malachi is used for the celebration of the Feast of February 2, formerly known as the Purification. In the early Church the Feast was also called *Hypapante* in the East or the Feast of the Meeting. The scene centers on the Messenger of God coming to the Temple. Stuhlmueller states:

> In 3:1, therefore, he seems to be presenting the eschatological moment in the language of God's great interventions in sacred history: God's speaking to the Patriarchs (Gn 16:7ff; 22:11) and to Moses (Ex 3:2); God's leading the way through the Red Sea (Ex 23:20) and giving the covenant (Jgs 2:1-5; Ac 7:53; Gal 3:19. . .).[185]

Verse 3 helps for a Christian rereading of the text in light of Mary's presenting Jesus in the Temple.

35. *1 Samuel* 2:1, 4-5, 6-7, *8abcd, Canticle (Responsorial: Appendix, Old Testament #5, p. 208)*

This is a hymn attributed to Hannah, the mother of Samuel. It has a similarity to Mary's Magnificat and to several psalms. Frequently psalms are attributed to a person by the redactor.

36. *Judith* 16:13, 14, 15 *(Responsorial: "The Blessed Virgin Mary, Help of Christians," #42, p. 182)*

The Canticle of Judith chants the praises of God through creation in the verses chosen for this feast. P. Giffin describes these lines in the following words: "A mosaic of phrases from many psalms with a firm statement or prophetic lines that fear of the Lord must underline all outward observance, cf. Hos 6:6; Ps 51(50):18."[186] Judith throughout the book and especially in this hymn (16:1-17) is a model of a woman transformed through her freedom and courage. The Synagogue formerly celebrated this book during Hanukkah. Catholics apply such powerful help to Mary.

37. *Sirach* 14:20, 21-22, 23-25, 26-27 *(Responsorial: "The Blessed Virgin Mary, Mother of Good Counsel," #33, pp. 146-147)*

This passage treats of the search for Wisdom and its blessings. One of the principles of good living and of the spiritual life is to seek direction and to be open to counsel. Every effort is made by the just person to pursue Wisdom which contains understanding and counsel. There are parallels to Proverbs 3:13; 8:34; 9:1-6 where Wisdom is personified.

38. *Isaiah* 12:2-3, *4bcd, 5-6; 12:1, 2-3, 4bcd, 5-6 (Responsorial: "The Visitation of the Blessed Virgin Mary," #3, p. 30; Responsorial: "The Blessed Virgin Mary, Image and Mother of the Church" (III), #27, pp. 123-124; Responsorial: "The Blessed Virgin Mary, Fountain of Salvation," #31, p. 137; Responsorial: "The Blessed Virgin Mary, Mother of Consolation," #41, pp. 176-177)*

This short chapter of Isaiah is a song of thanksgiving in six verses. It is one of the favorite choices for Masses honoring the Virgin Mary. Another reference to Zion makes it appropriate for the Church and Mary, the image of the Church, when this song is reread with Christian faith and devotion. Verse 3 contains the expression "fountain of salvation" (Mass #31). The chapter is a synthesis of Isaiah's key ideas and themes; it also is a hymn of thanksgiving after the great deeds God has accomplished as the Holy One of Israel. Israel and the Church are redeemed communities. The term "salvation," *Jeshuah* (*yesû'â*), is used three times in the short song.[187]

39. *Isaiah 61:10a-d and f, 11; 62:2-3 (Responsorial: "Holy Mary, The New Eve," #20, pp. 98-99)*

The predominant image is that of a bride adorned for her husband. The blessings of righteousness and salvation are the ornaments of the bride. The city of Jerusalem and especially its sacred stronghold and holy place, Zion, is vindicated and renewed (Is 62:2-3). As we have seen throughout this book, Zion has been a symbol both for the Church and for Mary. The reference to the bride and the garden in Isaiah 61:10-11 makes one recall the garden of Genesis and the first woman, the mother of all the living, Eve. The new name indicated in Isaiah 62:2 is applied to Jerusalem and by Christians to the Church; by Catholics to Mary as the New Eve.

40. *Jeremiah 31:10, 11-12ab, 13-14 (Responsorial: "Holy Mary, Mother of Unity," #38, pp. 162-163)*

This passage speaks of the ingathering of Israel by God who is compared to a shepherd. In reality, Israel is experiencing another liberating Exodus.

Wisdom Literature and Mary/Reflection on Proverbs 8 and Ecclesiasticus 24

In a recent team-taught course with Dr. Eric Friedland on the topic of Jewish Thought and Christian Response, several passages were selected from Wisdom literature, especially Proverbs 8 and Sirach or Ecclesiasticus 24. These texts manifest the Wisdom of God and God's *Shekinah* or Glory dwelling among us. These same texts are used in the feasts and memorials of Mary. It is through the symbolism and imagery of Wisdom that a divine feminine dimension is seen in Judaism; Catholic tradition and liturgy have applied the same texts to Mary.

The class taught was composed of Catholics, Protestants, and Jews. Care was taken to point out that only Proverbs was considered to be a canonical Scripture for the Jews and Protestants, while the original Greek texts of Wisdom and Sirach are canonical for Catholics and the Orthodox Church.

Wisdom literature is used frequently in the liturgy; for example, Sirach or Ecclesiasticus thirty-seven times and Wisdom nineteen times. In the Jewish services one might hear a conservative or reform rabbi read at a funeral the comforting words from the Wisdom of Solomon (3:1-9). Proverbs is used in nine different liturgical readings.

The Wisdom texts used for Marian feasts and commemorations throughout the year are the following:

Proverbs	8:22-31
Ecclesiasticus	3:2-6, 12-14
	24:1, 3-4, 8-12, 19-21
	44:1, 10-15
	51:17-30
Song of Songs	2:8-14
	5:2-5

Proverbs 8:22-31

Wisdom is personified in this poem which consists of seven stanzas. The selection for Marian feasts is taken from the fifth and sixth stanzas. These verses show Wisdom's priority to all things and her presence at Creation. The notion of a model or living symbol is expressed in the Hebrew word *Re'sît* which indicates the origin of wisdom. The liturgical application of this text to Mary, the Seat of Wisdom, is a felicitous one since it relates her to the divine intelligence of God which plans all things for the good of all creation. The text also fits in well with the prologue of John's Gospel which emphasizes the Word or *Logos* as the source of all creation. The incarnational impact of the prologue is also related to the Word born of Mary.[188] By accommodation the Church sees Wisdom as a complement to the Word made flesh. In relation to the Second Person of the Trinity we can see why the Church uses the text for Mary. We have to realize that Wisdom is primarily posited of God and then of Christ:

> Wisdom is, indeed, an expression of the creative action of God, not an eternal existence; yet she is the decisive act in which the meaning of all God's creative acts is disclosed. The identification of this Wisdom with the Word of God [*Logos*], with the Law (Sir. 24:23), Spirit (Exod. 28:3; Job 32:8, Wis. 1:7, 9:17, 11:20), and with Christ (1 C. 1:24, 30) always includes this element of the decisive action of God. . . . God made the cosmos for Wisdom, and with Wisdom as pattern. This affirmative view of material existence corresponds to Gen. 1, 'it was good'.[189]

The selection Proverbs 8:22-31 is used in the Common of the Blessed Virgin for a reading outside of the Easter Season. The *Catholic Catechism* uses this text for its catechesis on creation, referring it exclusively to God.[190]

Ecclesiasticus or Sirach 24:1, 3-4, 8-12, 19-21

This favored chapter of Sirach is in praise of Wisdom. The verses selected for a Marian commemoration tie in with the salvific plan of God and with Israel's spiritual inheritance as a people. Mary is part of that spiritual inheritance, being a Daughter of Israel as well as Daughter of Zion (cf vv. 8-10). This chapter is the high point of the book and is modeled on Proverbs 8. Sirach has skillfully adapted this form [an aretalogy] to his concept of divine Wisdom which he can personify as a female figure, conveying the Lord's gracious will to humankind. The image is a natural one, since both Hebrew and Greek words for "wisdom" are feminine nouns: *hokmah* and *sophia*.[191]

In the former Latin Liturgy, a gloss for verse 18 (vv. 24f) was used as a popular refrain honoring Mary the Mother of Jesus: "I am the mother of fair love, of fear, of knowledge and of holy hope. In me is all grace of the way and of the truth; in me is all hope of life and of virtue." Matthew 11:28-30 is also an echo of verses 19-21.

The *Catholic Catechism* uses Sirach 24 along with Proverbs 8 in explaining how Mary is the dwelling place of the Holy Spirit and the Son: "In this sense the Church's Tradition has often applied the most beautiful texts on wisdom in relation to Mary. Mary is acclaimed and represented in the liturgy as the 'Seat of Wisdom.'"[192]

The Song of Songs and Mary

This canticle of erotic love songs has been mystically interpreted within Judaism as well as within the Church. So strong are the images and language of love that the rabbis strongly advised that only those over twenty-eight years of age could approach its pages. On the other hand, both the Synagogue and Church transformed the Song's eroticism into the love of God for the individual, or the love of God towards the collective Israel or the Church. God was the partner in a nuptial relationship based on a Covenant of love that is stronger than death. It is no doubt from Paul's knowledge of the Song that he idealizes married love between husband and wife. By using the love relationship, he sees the love God has for the Church as a continuation of God's covenant with Israel (Eph 5:32-33; Rm 9:4-5, 13).

Though modern scholars insist on its literal meaning as a collection of erotic love songs, there is a rising current of new hermeneutics within the world of biblical scholarship that has its merits. As Roland Murphy says, "Modern hermeneutical theory recognizes that any text has an afterlife, that it acquires meaning as it lives on in the community that treasures it."[193] Phyllis Trible sees the Canticle as commentary on Genesis 2 and 3.[194]

The Church celebrates Mary through the use of the following selections from the Song of Songs: 2:8-14; 4:6-7; 4:9 and 4:12-15:

> Hark! my lover — here he comes
>   springing across the mountains,
>   leaping across the hills.
> My lover is like a gazelle
>   or a young stag.
> Here he stands behind our wall,
>   gazing through the windows,
>   peering through the lattices.
> My lover speaks; he says to me,
>   "Arise, my beloved, my beautiful
>   one,
>   and come!
> "For see, the winter is past,
>   the rains are over and gone.
> The flowers appear on the earth,
>   the time of pruning the vines has
>   come,
>   and the song of the dove is heard
>   in our land.
> The fig tree puts forth its figs,
>   and the vines, in bloom, give forth
>   fragrance.
> Arise, my beloved, my beautiful one,
>   and come!
>
> "O my dove in the clefts of the rock,
>   in the secret recesses of the cliff,

Let me see you,
> let me hear your voice,
For your voice is sweet,
> and you are lovely" (Sg 2:8-14).

Until the day breathes cool and the
> shadows lengthen,
> I will go to the mountain of myrrh,
> to the hill of incense.
You are all-beautiful, my beloved,
> and there is no blemish in you (Sg 4:6-7).

You have ravished my heart, my
> sister, my bride;
> you have ravished my heart with
> one glance of your eyes,
> with one bead of your necklace (Sg 4:9).

You are an enclosed garden, my
> sister, my bride,
> an enclosed garden, a fountain
> sealed.
You are a park that puts forth pome-
> granates,
> with all choice fruits;
Nard and saffron, calamus and cin-
> namon,
> with all kinds of incense;
Myrrh and aloes,
> with all the finest spices.
You are a garden fountain, a well
> of water
> flowing fresh from Lebanon (Sg 4:12-15).

In other liturgical celebrations, the Song is used for the feast of Mary Magdalene, for the celebration of the sacrament of marriage, and for the consecration of those entering religious life.

Though the allegorical interpretation of the Song presents its difficulties, it is easily accommodated to the symbolic language of love which is best expressed in poetry and song. Origen was the first to comment allegorically on the Song of Songs. St. Bernard also used the Song and was its chief expositor in the Middle Ages. A recent thesis from the International Marian Research Institute, sister to the Marianum in Rome, has treated of Rupert of Deutz's commentary on the Song of Songs.[195]

St. Ambrose is the first to give a Mariological interpretation by comparing Mary with the Church (Sg 1:1, 2, 4; 3:11; 7:1, 2). St. Jerome saw Mary's virginity in the light of Song 4:21 and 4:13; so, too, Epiphanius for 4:12; likewise, St. Isidore. Germanus of Constantinople uses Song 3:6 and 4:8 for his homily for the Purification, while the passionate Marian writer, St. John of Damascus uses 1:2, 12, 13; 1:1, 2, 3, 5, 11, 12; 3:6, 11; 4:7, 8, 9, 10, 12, 13, 14; 5:1, 3; 6:8, 9.

The Mariological interpretation of the Song of Songs is a constant in the history of the Church from Origen to the most recent liturgical use of texts in the Masses in honor of the Blessed Virgin. "Not only is the Virgin Mary the holiest of all the members of the Church, but she also concurred in the accomplishment of the mystical union of the Son of God with humanity."[196]

Since love is the language of the mystics, the Song was a favored source for the reflection and spiritual life of the saints. M. O'Carroll sums it up very well: "If to the Christian S. expresses Christ's love for his Church, then since Mary is a type of the Church, the figurative Marian interpretation is valid and may powerfully help those with true mystical endowment."[197]

Psalms Used in the Collection of Masses of the Blessed Virgin Mary

The Psalms used in the Masses of the Blessed Virgin Mary are nineteen in number. They are given in chronological order with a reference to the Mass title and the page(s) on which they are found in the Lectionary of the Collection.

1. Psalm 2:7-8, 10-11ab (Responsorial: Alternative Reading Micah 5:1-4a, Appendix, Old Testament #7, pp. 211-212)

This Psalm is the response to the first reading from Micah 5:1-4a. Since Micah is speaking of a birth in Bethlehem the response takes up the theme of a Messianic birth, "You are my Son; today I am your father." The other verses show the dominion of the Messianic King over the nations and over kings. The Psalm is also used at Christmas, midnight Mass (cf. Heb 1:5; 5:5). In Christian tradition this is one of the most important and the first of the Messianic royal Psalms applied to Jesus Christ (cf. Ps 18, 20, 21, 45, 101, 110, and 132).

2. Psalm 8:4-5, 6-7a, 7b-9 (Responsorial: Alternative Reading Romans 8:28-30, Appendix, NT #10, p. 217)

The selections from this Psalm of praise fit against the background of Creation (Gn 1-2). Of interest to us is the expression "son of man" or creature of the earth (Adam) which is one of the favorite titles for Jesus in the Gospels. This is the Psalm which was cited after the landing on the moon. The *Name* of God is both a sacred way of speaking about God and a reverent acknowledgment of God. Both Paul and contemporary Judaism use *Name* as an expression for God, for example in the blessing *Baruch ha Shem*, "Blessed be the Name."

3. Psalm 13:6 (Used for Birth of Mary in Roman Missal Celebrated on September 8)

Verse 6 is the final verse of Psalm 13, an individual lamentation which ends in great confidence because of God's fidelity to the promises to David. This response echoes both Mary's "yes" to God and her beautiful song of praise, the Magnificat. The emphasis on the *hesed* or loving-kindness of God is the reason for confidence and for the exultant response. The Church also rejoices in the birth of Mary, the Virgin of Nazareth, on this feast.

4. Psalm 15:2-3a, 3bc-4, 5 (Responsorial: "The Blessed Virgin Mary, Mother and Teacher in the Spirit" Proverbs 8:17-21, 34-35; Isaiah 56:1, 6-7, #32, p. 143)

Psalm 15 is used as a response for the Mass entitled "The Blessed Virgin Mary, Mother and Spiritual Teacher" (*Magistra*). As a response, it pertains more to the believer listening to the Wisdom of Mary. This is characteristic of Wisdom literature which is bound to practical everyday experiences. The wise person seeks God, and Mary is seen as the Teacher of Wisdom in the light of Proverbs 8:17-21, 34-35 and Isaiah 56:1, 6-7. Paul refers to verse 3 of this Psalm in Romans 3:10-12 showing that all are sinners, often not listening to Wisdom. The verses chosen are the virtues a wise person lives out: justice, truth, clean speech, charity towards neighbor and generosity.

5. Psalm 16:5 and 8, 9-10, 11 (Responsorial: Alternative Reading Genesis 22:1-2, 9-13, 15-18; 1 Corinthians 15:20-26, Appendix, Old Testament #1, p. 200 and NT #12, pp. 220-221)

This Psalm is used as a response to Genesis 22:1-2, 9-13, 15-18 and to 1 Corinthians 15:20-26 in the Lectionary. It is the expression of a just person responding to God. Such an attitude enables the person to approach God in the Temple. The selection of verses emphasizes an I-thou dialogue between the believer and God.

6. Psalm 18:2-3, 5-6, 7, 19-20 (Responsorial: "The Blessed Virgin Mary at the Foot of the Cross" (I) Romans 8:31b-39, #11A, p. 65; "The Commending of the Blessed Virgin Mary" 2 Maccabees 7:1, 20-29, #13, pp. 70-71)

Used in the new votive Masses in honor of the Virgin Mary, this Psalm is a royal hymn of thanksgiving and one of the largest Psalms comprising 51 verses. It is used five times in the entire liturgical cycle outside of this special commemoration of Mary. It reflects both the suffering of Jesus on the Cross and the compassion of Mary at that solemn moment (Jn 19:25-28a). God the Savior is praised; the distress of the one who is suffering and God's deliverance of the victim ends with a crowning theophany. As such, the selection of John's Gospel account of Jesus' death is an appropriate one. Jesus at the moment of death is exalted on the Cross as Victor over death.

7. *Psalm 19:8-9, 10-11, 15 (Responsorial: "Holy Mary, Disciple of the Lord" Sirach 51:13-18, 20-22, #10, pp. 61-62)*

This didactic poem is part two of Psalm 19 and probably a separate Psalm celebrating the Torah as wisdom and perfection. It fits well with the disposition of a disciple of Jesus — listening, following, searching for God and Wisdom. Mary, too, is a disciple of the Lord especially in the Gospel of Luke.

8. *Psalm 22:4-6, 10-11, 23-24 (Responsorial: "Holy Mary, Mother of God" Galatians 4:4-7, #4, pp. 37-38)*

This Psalm is an individual lament. It is cited by Jesus on the Cross (Mt 27:46; Mk 15:34). The cry of anguish ends in victory at the end of the Psalm. In the Masses in honor of the Virgin Mary, Psalm 22 is used for her title "Holy Mary, Mother of God." The verses chosen emphasize that God is present from the moment of birth. This response admirably corresponds to the selection from Paul, Galatians 4:4-7, where the children of God cry out "Abba!" and with the Gospel which shows Jesus in the manger. Joseph and Mary are there with the child. Verses 10 and 11 are perfect for recalling God's maternal care experienced for a newborn.

9. *Psalm 24:7, 8, 9, 10 (Responsorial: "The Blessed Virgin Mary and the Presentation of the Lord" Malachi 3:1-4, #7, pp. 45-46)*

The latter part of this Psalm is used for the votive Mass called "The Blessed Virgin Mary and the Presentation of the Lord." It is a refrain that is found in the Hebrew Psalm as a pilgrim believer approaches the Temple: "Lift up your heads, O gates; rise up, you ancient portals, that the king of glory may enter." This Psalm is a magnificent hymn of praise to God which includes an entrance liturgy. The choice of it corresponds perfectly to the Presentation of the Lord in the Temple — Feast of the Presentation of the Lord (February 2). The texts are the same for the reading from the Prophet (Ml 3:1-4) and the Gospel of Luke is shortened to focus on Simeon and Mary in the Temple (Lk 2:27-35).

10. *Psalm 24:1-2, 3-4ab, 5-6 (Responsorial: Alternative Reading Genesis 28:10-17, Appendix, Old Testament #2, p. 202)*

The Psalm is the response to Genesis 28:10-17 which treats of Jacob's dream of the "ladder" or "stair" to the heavens. Here is the meeting place between God and people, between heaven and earth. The Psalm completes the scene since it is a hymn about Zion and the Temple, God's chosen dwelling place. The connection with Genesis is found in verse 6: "Such are the people that love the Lord, that seek the face of the God of Jacob."

11. *Psalm 27:1, 3, 4, 5 (Responsorial: "The Blessed Virgin Mary, Pillar of Faith" Judith 13:14, 17-20, #35, p. 153)*

Celebrated as part of the feast of "The Blessed Virgin Mary, Pillar of Faith," Psalm 27 is one of trust (vv. 1-6). "The Temple was the place of refuge *par excellence.*"[198] The Psalm serves as a response to the reading from Judith 13:14, 17-20 which is centered on God who reduces all enemies to nothingness.

12. *Psalm 31:2-3b, 3c-4, 5-6, 15-16, 20 (Responsorial: Alternative Reading Hebrews 5:7-9, Appendix, NT #16, pp. 227-228)*

The response is composed of verses from the three parts of a Psalm. The choice comes from the prayer of confidence (vv. 2-9), from a Psalm of distress (vv. 10-19), and from a hymn of God's goodness (vv. 20-25). The poignant prayer of Jesus as he breathes his last is from this Psalm: "Into your hands I commend my spirit; you will redeem me, Lord, faithful God" (cf. Lk 23:46; Ac 7:59).

The response mirrors the selection from Hebrews 5:7-9 which echoes the final outcry of Jesus. The humanity of Jesus through being born of Mary is what is intended in this response.

13. *Psalm 34:2-3, 6-7, 8, 9 (Responsorial: "Holy Mary, Fountain of Light and Life" Acts of the Apostles 2:14a, 36-40a, 41-42, #16, pp. 82-83)*

Mass #16 in honor of Mary is entitled "Holy Mary, Fountain of Light and Life." The senses of sight, hearing, and taste are centered upon God, the source of light and life in this Psalm. The Psalm is a didactic one using the 22 letters of the Hebrew alphabet to complete its meaning. Mary's song, the Magnificat, echoes the exuberant and confident praise in this Psalm. The senses represent life given to Mary and all believers by God.

14. *Psalm 40:7-8a, 8b-9, 10, 11 (Responsorial: "The Blessed Virgin and the Annunciation of the Lord" Isaiah 7:10-14; 8:10c, #2A, pp. 26-27)*

This response pertains to the feast of the Annunciation. It echoes both Mary's "yes" and the "yes" of Jesus to assuming flesh from her. It also contains an ecclesial (*qahal*) reference in verses 10 and 11 thus fulfilling what *Lumen Gentium* calls for in our veneration of Mary: a Christocentric and ecclesial emphasis.

15. *Psalm 45:11-12, 14-15, 16-17, 18 (Responsorial: "The Blessed Virgin Mary, Queen of All Creation" Isaiah 9:1-3, 5-6, #29A, pp. 129-130)*

The regal character of this Psalm complements the theme for the Mass entitled "The Blessed Virgin Mary, Queen of All Creation." The verses chosen are addressed to a woman who has been chosen to be queen of Israel supposedly during King Solomon's era.

This is one of the Psalms that has messianic and royal meaning both within Judaism and within the Christian Church, which has accommodated this to Jesus the Christ and King. Mary's queenship would follow upon her association with Christ. In a fuller sense she is likened to the *Gebîrâh* or Queen Mother.[199] "For us Christians the psalm looks forward to the messianic fulfillment begun with Christ, so that it came to be understood of the 'nuptials of the Lamb' when Christ weds his spouse the Church, the 'new Jerusalem' (Apoc [Rv] 21:2, 9)."[200]

16. *Psalm* 67:2-3, 4-5, 6-7 (*Responsorial: "The Blessed Virgin Mary, Mother and Mediatrix of Grace" Esther* 8:3-8, 16-17a, #30, p. 134)

This is an appropriate response to the Mass entitled "The Blessed Virgin Mary, Mother and Mediatrix of Grace." The Psalm indicates that all grace is from God: "May God be gracious to us and bless us; may God's face shine upon us" (v. 2). This Psalm is familiar to us as an alternate invitatory in the daily "Prayer for Christians" (breviary). It is a refrain that fits the first reading from the Book of Esther wherein Esther succeeds in convincing King Ahasuerus to spare and vindicate the People of God, Israel (Est 8:3-8, 16-17a). The Gospel is well chosen. It is the wedding feast of Cana (Jn 2:1-11) wherein Mary successfully rescues a young couple from their embarrassment about a shortage of wine.

17. *Psalm* 72:1-2, 7-8, 10-11, 12-13 (*Responsorial: "The Blessed Virgin Mary and the Epiphany of the Lord" Isaiah* 60:1-6, #6, pp. 42-43)

This Psalm is associated with the feast of Epiphany. The readings in the Mass in honor of the Blessed Virgin Mary are taken from this Mass (#6, "The Blessed Virgin Mary and the Epiphany of the Lord"). It is also used in response to a reading from the Book of Numbers in the Appendix of alternate selections from the Hebrew

Scriptures (Nb 24:15-17a). The selection speaks of a star rising out of Jacob and a staff springing forth from Israel. Another reading emphasizing the Daughter of Zion (Zc 9:9-10) has this same response with verse 17 of the Psalm added. Verse 17 shows the role of Mary within creation and the history of salvation: "May his name be blessed forever; as long as the sun, may his name endure. May the tribes of the earth give blessings with his name; may all the nations regard him as favored." Another alternate reading is from Isaiah 11:1-5, 10 in which the root of Jesse is extolled. Mary may be seen as the Mother of the Messiah who springs from the root of Jesse through the Davidic lineage. She is the Daughter of Zion *par excellence*.

18. *Psalm 84:2-3, 5-6, 9-10; Psalm 84:3, 4, 5, and 10, 11*
    (Responsorial: "Our Lady of Nazareth" (II) Colossians 3:12-17,
    #8, pp. 51-52; "The Blessed Virgin Mary, Temple of the Lord"
    1 Kings 8:1, 3-7, 9-11, #23A, pp. 110-111)

The response of the Psalm is to the veneration of "Our Lady of Nazareth" (#8). The reading is from Colossians 3:12-17 which emphasizes the virtues and disposition of the follower of Christ. The Gospel is the selection from Matthew indicating that Jesus' origins are from Nazareth (Mt 2:13-15, 19-23). The second Mass entitled "The Blessed Virgin Mary, Temple of the Lord" also makes use of this same Psalm which focuses both upon the home and the Temple. We can see that the Jewish origins of mother and child are important to the feast. In Matthew the fifth of the prophetic announcements brings his Infancy Narrative to a close: "He shall be called a Nazorean." There is no such prophecy found in the Hebrew Scriptures. This is carefully explained in *The Catholic Study Bible*: "The vague expression 'through the prophets' may be due to Matthew's seeing a connection between Nazareth and certain texts in which there are words with a remote similarity to the name of that town."[201] One should also note that in the second Mass the stronghold of Zion derives from 1 Kings 8:1, 3-7, 9-11.

19. Psalm 85:9ab-10, 11-12, 13-14 *(Responsorial: "The Blessed Virgin Mary, Queen of Peace" Isaiah 9:1-3, 5-6, #45, pp. 191-192)*

Under the title "The Blessed Virgin Mary, Queen of Peace" (#45), this Psalm centers on the peace (*shalom*) that God brings to the people (v. 9). The response is ideal for the season of Advent. This passage is therefore a prayer that God's personal presence may come to dwell in our land in the ideal messianic age; for Christians, this is fulfilled in the Incarnation. This Psalm calms the believer within an atmosphere of peace, the peace God's presence brings. It is a tranquil and balanced part of the Psalter. This prayer originally could have been said after the Exile or in thanksgiving for the harvest after the autumn rains. The rain touching the earth symbolizes the Incarnation in the Church's use of Isaiah as well as in this Psalm. A Jewish commentary on the Psalms says of the concluding verse: "God marks out the path for Israel to traverse, leading to salvation and happiness. Otherwise, the subject is pictured as a herald clearing a way for God's Advent, who brings with Him safety and happiness for the nation."[202]

20. Psalm 87:1-2, 3 and 5, 6-7 *(Responsorial: "Our Lady of the Cenacle" Acts of the Apostles 1:6-14, #17, p. 86; "The Blessed Virgin Mary, Queen of Apostles" Acts of the Apostles 1:12-14; 2:1-4, #18, pp. 88-89; "The Blessed Virgin Mary, Image and Mother of the Church" (II) Acts of the Apostles 1:12-14, #26, pp. 120-121)*

The Psalm is used in three Masses in Honor of the Virgin: "Our Lady of the Cenacle," "The Blessed Virgin Mary, Queen of Apostles," and "The Blessed Virgin Mary, Image and Mother of the Church". The first celebration couples the Psalm with the Apostles gathered in the upper room (Ac 1:12-14) before the descent of the Holy Spirit, and the scene at the foot of the Cross (Jn 19:25-27). The Psalm centers on an image of Mary and the Church, namely, Zion and its gates and dwelling place for the Lord. Since Mary is present in both scenes with the Apostles and, at least, with the Beloved

Disciple and the Holy Women, she is better seen as Daughter of Zion in this Mass. In the second Mass, however, Zion as an image of the Church is suggested. The symbol of Zion is polyvalent especially within the context of liturgical celebrations. The Masses selected are from the same evangelists, Luke and John. The latter feast chooses Cana, which is a mirror of what happens at Calvary in its symbolism and in its ecclesial as well as sacramental meanings.

21. *Psalm 96:1-2a, 2b-3, 11-12, 13 (Responsorial: "The Blessed Virgin Mary, Mother of the Savior" Isaiah 9:1-3, 5-6, #5A, p. 40)*

This response occurs in a Mass during the Christmas season under the title "The Blessed Virgin Mary, Mother of the Savior." The Psalm is a hymn of praise which calls all peoples to worship God. It is among the greatest of Psalms which emphasize monotheism. It fits admirably with the era of peace, Pax Augustana, suggested by Luke's Gospel for the feast (Lk 2:1-14). "Not only the nations but all creation is called to join in joyfully receiving the good news of Yahweh's universal reign."[203]

22. *Psalm 103:1-2, 3-4, 6-7, 8 and 10; 103:1-2, 3-4, 6-7, 8 and 11; 103:1-2, 3-4, 6 and 8, 13 and 17; 103:1-2, 3-4, 8-9, 13-14, 17-18a (Responsorial: "The Blessed Virgin Mary, Health of the Sick" Isaiah 53:1-4, 7-10, #44. pp. 188-189; Alternative Reading Exodus 3:1-8, Appendix, Old Testament #3, p. 204; "Holy Mary, Queen and Mother of Mercy" (II) Ephesians 2:4-10, #39, pp. 169-170; "The Blessed Virgin Mary, Mother of Reconciliation" 2 Corinthians 5:17-21; #14, pp. 72-73)*

This Psalm is used in four different selections of the Masses in honor of Mary: "The Blessed Virgin Mary, Health of the Sick" (#44); as a response to the reading from Exodus concerning the burning bush—a symbol for Mary's virginity (Ex 3:1-8); in the Mass entitled "Holy Mary, Queen and Mother of Mercy" (#39); and "The Blessed Virgin Mary, Mother of Reconciliation" (#14).

The Psalm is beautiful in its composition. The superabundant and magnanimous compassion and loving-kindness of God are present throughout the Psalm, giving confidence and comfort to those who sing or pray it.

Both the individual and the community are heard in this Psalm. The most far-reaching attributes of God are felt within this hymn of praise: *hesed* (loving-kindness), *tsedakah* (acts of holy justice), and *rahamim* (tender-mercies). Roland Murphy has this important note: "It is such lines as these that give the lie to the popular travesty of the OT as a testament of fear."[204]

23. *Psalm 113:1-2, 3-4, 5-6, 7-8 (Responsorial: "The Blessed Virgin Mary, Chosen Daughter of Israel" Genesis 12:1-7, #1A, p. 23)*

This familial Psalm suits the Mass of the "The Blessed Virgin Mary, Chosen Daughter of Israel" (#1). As a descendant of Abraham (Gn 12:1-7) Mary is among the elect believers. The response bridges the account of Abraham, our ancestor in faith, and the genealogy from Matthew 1:1-17 wherein Jesus is seen as a son of David and son of Abraham. The Jewishness of Jesus and Mary is central to this commemoration during Advent. The Psalm also is one of the first in a series of three Hallel sections of the Psalter: Psalms 112-117, 120-136, and 146-150 — great hymns of praise. There is also a hint of God's reversing the plight of the poor and the childless which suggests Mary's conception of Jesus by the over-shadowing of the Spirit. One exegete sees a connection with the Song of Hannah in 1 Samuel 2:1-10; which, in turn, seems to influence Mary's Magnificat.[205] This is the magnificent "family" hymn which is used to show the origins and family tree of the Messiah — and his Mother.

24. *Psalm 116:12-13, 15-16bc, 17-18 (Responsorial: Alternative Reading Colossians 1:21-24, Appendix, NT #15, pp. 225-226)*

This response is used with a selection from Colossians 1:21-24 which emphasizes our fulfilling in life the sufferings of Christ through our union with his body which is the Church. There is a suggestion of our spiritual relationship to Mary through verse 16: "Lord, I am your servant, your servant, the child of your maidservant."[206]

The same use is made of this Psalm in the Evening Prayer of Sunday, Week III, followed by a prayer that is dependent on Colossians 1:21-24: "Father, precious in your sight is the death of the saints, but precious above all is the love with which Christ suffered to redeem us. In this life we fill up in our own flesh what is still lacking in the suffering of Christ; accept this as our sacrifice of praise, and we shall even now taste the joy of the new Jerusalem."

25. *Psalm 118:14-15, 16-17, 19-21 (Responsorial: Alternative Reading 1 Corinthians 15:54-57, Appendix NT #13, p. 222)*

This responsorial Psalm is one of thanksgiving. It is used as a response to a reading from 1 Corinthians 15:54-57 which shows Christ's ultimate victory over death. The Psalm also is a victory hymn for deliverance from death through the graciousness of God. "The psalmist acknowledges his previous pitiful situation, but the Lord demonstrated his covenantal fidelity by helping him. Verse 15, the start of the victory song, links the psalmist's experience with that of the community."[207]

26. *Psalm 119:1-2, 10-11, 12 and 14, 15-16 (Responsorial: "Our Lady of Cana" Exodus 19:3-8a, #9, pp. 54-55)*

This response is to the Mass entitled "Our Lady of Cana." The Psalm is the longest in the Psalter and is entirely dedicated to the Torah. Torah is the living Word of God; Torah is revelation and life. We can see Mary responding to Jesus with an expression that a devout Jew would have, "Do whatever he tells you" (Jn 2:5). This is the spirit of response that both Jesus and Mary had to the Torah as prayerful and devout Jews.

The composer of this Psalm was probably a scribe from the school of Ezra. He carefully constructed the Psalm by going through the 22 letters of the Hebrew alphabet, and in sequences of eight lines began a new thought with each of the letters of the alphabet. Wisdom is equated with Torah. The final book of the New Testament, Revelation calls Jesus the Alpha and the Omega, the first and the last of the Greek alphabet including all of the letters in-between. Mary at Cana has the disposition that the Psalm suggests: "With all my heart I seek you; do not let me stray from your commands. In my heart I treasure your promise, that I may not sin against you" (Ps 119:10-11).

27. *Psalm 122:1-2, 3-4, 8-9 (Responsorial: "The Blessed Virgin Mary, Gate of Heaven" Revelation 21:1-5a, #46A, pp. 194-195)*

This is the responsorial Psalm used for the Mass entitled "The Blessed Virgin Mary, Gate of Heaven." It is one of the Hallel Psalms used during Passover and is called a song of ascents attributed to David. In reality the vocabulary and grammar point to a much later date than the era of David. The Psalm is analogous to what is being said of Mary as Gate of Heaven, for the Psalm expresses the joy of a pilgrim entering and leaving the porticoes of the Temple. The Psalm is also classified as a Zion hymn. Mary, of course, is the Daughter of Zion. An important exegetical insight is offered for verse three: "If the meaning is that Jerusalem is 'joined together in unity' (compact, ordered), it may be an allusion to the inviolability of the city; note the references to gates (v 2), walls, and battlements (v 7)."[208] A Jewish commentary also addresses this important verse three: "A more satisfactory interpretation does not see in the words a description of the city's material condition, but of its religious and national purpose. The verb 'compact' (*chabar*) is used of human association, and yields the noun *chabar* 'companion.' Difficult to translate, the phrase has the meaning: 'as a city in which companionship together was fostered.' It was the centre which held the scattered tribes together in a coherent body."[209] Mary as spiritual Mother of the Church is a model for its unity and peace.

28. *Psalm 131:1, 2, 3 (Responsorial: "Our Lady of Nazareth"*
Galatians 4:4-7, #8, pp. 48-49; "The Blessed Virgin Mary,
Mother of Divine Providence" Isaiah 66:10-14, #40, pp. 172-173;
Alternative Reading Romans 12:9-16a, Appendix, NT #11, pp.
218-219)

Responsorial Psalm 131 is used in the commemoration called
"Our Lady of Nazareth" (#8). It is also the refrain for the Mass
entitled "The Blessed Virgin Mary, Mother of Divine Providence,"
and, finally, as the responsorial for an alternate first reading from St.
Paul's epistle to the Romans 12:9-16a. "The Psalm is a literary gem
of exquisite beauty and surpassing spirituality."[210] It consists of three
verses and is the third shortest Psalm after Psalms 117 and 134.
Mary's being an ordinary Jewish woman who lives a simple lifestyle
is mirrored by this response. We are reminded of the beautiful
beatitude given to Mary from a woman: "Blessed is the womb that
carried you and the breasts at which you nursed." Jesus replied,
"Rather, blessed are those who hear the word of God and observe
it" (Lk 11:27-28). The Psalm corresponds to the piety of the "poor
of Yahweh," the 'anawîm.

29. *Psalm 132:11, 13-14, 17-18 (Responsorial: "Holy Mary,*
Mother of the Lord" 1 Chronicles 15:3-4, 15-16; 16:1-2,
#19A, pp. 95-96)

This Psalm contains several of the sacred symbols which the
Church applies to Mary: the ark of the covenant, Zion as the
dwelling place of God, and the promise of endurance to David's
lineage. Mary is the Jewish Mother of Jesus the Messiah. Mary is
seen as Zion, both mother of God's people and safe dwelling for the
ark of the covenant.

The Psalm in its entirety recaptures the intimate relationship
of God to David represented in the sacred sites of Jerusalem (Zion)
and Bethlehem, the city of David and later the birthplace of Jesus.

30. *Psalm 145:1-2, 4-6, 8-9 (Responsorial: "The Blessed Virgin Mary at the Foot of the Cross" (II) Judith 13:17-20, #12A, pp. 67-68)*

This Psalm is the response for a second commemoration of "The Blessed Virgin Mary at the Foot of the Cross" (#12A). It follows upon a reading from the book of Judith (13:17-20). The Gospel is the scene at the foot of the Cross in John 19:25-27. The Psalm praises the greatness and goodness of God and emphasizes God's compassion and mercy. We can learn much from the Jewish appreciation of this Psalm, for it occurs three times each day in their liturgy. One rabbi declares, "Whoever recites this psalm thrice daily may be assured that he is a son of the World to Come, because it contains the verse, *Thou openest thy hand and satisfiest every living thing with favour*, i.e., an acknowledgment of man's dependence upon God's grace."[211] Undoubtedly, the Psalm is used in such a solemn commemoration as the death of Jesus in order to help us to meditate, ponder, and contemplate the awesome greatness of God so far beyond our understanding and comprehension (cf. v. 3).

31. *Psalm 147:12-13, 14-15, 19-20 (Responsorial: "The Blessed Virgin Mary, Seat of Wisdom" Proverbs 8:22-31; Sirach 24:1-4, 18-21, #24A, #24B, pp. 114-115)*

The last responsorial Psalm pertains to the Mass entitled "The Blessed Virgin Mary, Seat of Wisdom." Proverbs 8:22-31 and Sirach 24:1-4, 18-21 are alternate first readings for this Mass. The contemplation of God's wisdom is present throughout the liturgical readings. The Psalm response encourages Zion and Jerusalem to praise God because of God's word which runs swiftly and is proclaimed to Jacob. God's commands and laws are the fabric of Wisdom. Acknowledging one's total dependence upon God and prioritizing God's word and commands are Wisdom. Mary exemplifies this through her pondering over of the events and words of God in her life (Lk 2:19, 51). God as Creator is emphasized throughout the Psalm.

Endnotes

[143] de la Potterie, *Mary in the Mystery of the Covenant*, xxiii-xxiv, xviii.

[144] *Sacrosanctum concilium*, (103).

[145] Cf. Thomas A. Thompson, "The Virgin Mary in the Liturgy: 1963-1988," *Marian Studies* XL (1989): 77-104.

[146] Ibid.

[147] Léon Joseph Cardinal Suenens, *A New Pentecost?* (New York: Seabury, 1975) 183.

[148] Thompson, 77-104.

[149] Ibid.

[150] Ibid.

[151] *New Catholic Commentary on Holy Scripture*, 181.

[152] *Liber hebraicarum questionum in Genesim* (PL 23, 981).

[153] cf. *New Catholic Commentary*, 181-182.

[154] Bernard A. Lazor, "Mary in the Mysteries of Christ from Advent to the Baptism of the Lord: Biblical References," *Marian Studies*, XLI (1990): 31-48.

[155] de la Potterie, 18.

[156] Carroll Stuhlmueller, *Biblical Meditations for Advent and the Christmas Season* (New York: Paulist, 1980) 64.

[157] *New Catholic Commentary*, 575.

[158] Ibid., 576.

[159] Laurentin, *Structure et Théologie de Luc I-II*, 152-162.

[160] James C. Turro, "Mary in Ordinary Time: Biblical References," *Marian Studies* XLIII (1992): 60-71.

[161] Thompson, 77-104.

[162] *Collection of Masses of the Blessed Virgin Mary*, vol. 2, Lectionary, Introduction (New York: Catholic Book, 1992) 13.

[163] *Acta Apostolica Sanctae Sedis* (AAS) 56 (1965): 1015.

[164] *New Jerome Biblical Commentary*, 2:34-35; 25.

[165] A. Cohen, ed., *The Soncino Chumash: The Five Books of Moses with Haphtaroth* (London: Soncino, 1966) 328.

[166] PG 46: 1136c; Michel Aubineau, *Les Homélies Festales d'Hésychius de Jérusalem*, vol. I (Bruxelles: Société des Bollandistes, 1978) 121.

[167] A. Serra, *E C'era la Madre di Gesù*.

[168] 1QM 11:5-7; CD 7:19-20; cf. *Jerome Biblical Commentary*, 75:168-171; 702.

[169] Cohen, 926.

[170] Trible, *God and the Rhetoric of Sexuality*, 173.

[171] Wainwright, *Towards a Feminist Critical Reading of the Gospel According to Matthew*, 166-168.

[172] Richard D. Nelson, "David: A Model for Mary in Luke?" *Biblical Theology Bulletin* 18 (1988): 138-142.

[173] *New American Bible* (Collins World, 1970) 590.

[174] Kathleen M. O'Connor, *The Wisdom Literature* (Wilmington, DE: Glazer, 1988) 66.

[175] *New Catholic Commentary*, 595.

[176] *Jerome Biblical Commentary*, 22:52-54; 381.

[177] Ibid., 22:55-58; 382.

[178] Ibid., 22:59-61; 383.

[179] Ibid., 22:66-69; 385.

[180] W. Robertson Smith, *The Religion of the Semites: The Fundamental Institutions* (New York: Schocken, 1972) 135.

[181] Laurentin, 152-162.

[182] Brown, *The Birth of the Messiah*, 321; cf. 320-327.

[183] Serra, 3-43.

[184] D. Senior, ed., *The Catholic Study Bible*, 1165n9.9.

[185] *Jerome Biblical Commentary*, 23:64-67; 400.

[186] *New Catholic Commentary*, 406.

[187] Cf. *New Jerome Biblical Commentary*, 15:27-29; 238.

[188] Cf. John 1:13 and some ancient Latin renderings of the text. See *Mary of Galilee: Volume I*, pp. 115-116.

[189] Matthew Black and H.H. Rowey, eds., *Peake's Commentary on the Bible* (London: Nelson, 1964) 449.

[190] *Catechism of the Catholic Church* (Boston, MA: Pauline Books and Media, 1994) par. 288; 75n127.

[191] R.A.F. MacKenzie, *Sirach* (Wilmington, DE: Glazier, 1983) 100-101.

[192] *Catechism*, par. 721; 191.

[193] *New Jerome Biblical Commentary*, 29:6-13; 463.

[194] Trible, 144-162.

[195] Peter Winston Gittens, "Magistra Apostolorum in the Writings of Rupert of Deutz," diss., Pontifical Theological Faculty, The Marianum, Rome, and the International Marianum Research Institute, University of Dayton, 1991, 78-138.

[196] *New Catholic Commentary*, 524.

[197] O'Carroll, *Theotokos*, 328.

[198] *New Jerome Biblical Commentary*, 34:40-46; 530.

[199] Kirwin, "The Nature of the Queenship of Mary," 312.

[200] *New Catholic Commentary*, 456.

[201] Isaiah 11:1 and Judges 13:5, 7: *neser* and *nazîr*. Senior, *Catholic Study Bible*, 10 (NT section).

[202] A. Cohen, *The Psalms* (London: Soncino Press, 1971) 85.

[203] *New Jerome Biblical Commentary*, 34:109-114; 542.

[204] *Jerome Biblical Commentary*, 35:114-119; 594.

[205] cf. *New Jerome Biblical Commentary*, 34:128-135; 546. See especially 1 Samuel 2:8 and Luke 1:52.

[206] cf. Psalm 86:16; Wisdom 9:5; Psalm 143:12.

[207] J.F. Craghan, *Yesterday's Word Today* (Collegeville, MN: Liturgical, 1982) 339.

[208] *New Jerome Biblical Commentary*, 34:140-147; 548.

[209] Cohen, 422.

[210] Ibid., 435.

[211] Ibid., 467.

Chapter Seven

MARY IN THE CATECHISM
OF THE CATHOLIC CHURCH

John Paul II promulgated the *Catechism of the Catholic Church* in his Apostolic Constitution *Fidei Depositum* (The Deposit of Faith) on October 11, 1992. Formerly October 11 was celebrated as the Feast of the Holy Mother of God. Thirty years prior, the Council of Vatican II opened. The Pope stated:

> The principal task entrusted to the Council by Pope John XXIII was to guard and present better the precious deposit of Christian doctrine in order to make it more accessible to the Christian faithful and to people of good will.[212]

John Paul II views the *Catechism* as a presentation of the mysteries of God's loving-kindness through the history of salvation. It is within that overarching theme that we can see the role of the Virgin Mother, the favorite title for Mary in the *Catechism*. In fact, she is important throughout the *Catechism* rather than in one concentrated section. Her presence is seen within the whole context of the *Catechism* and not in isolation from the four principal parts: The Profession of Faith; The Celebration of the Christian Mystery; Life in Christ; and Christian Prayer. In the *Catechism* there are 121 references to Mary, plus two found in the decree *Fidei Depositum* and one in the prologue presented through the earliest fresco from the catacomb of Priscilla in Rome dating from 200 C.E. (Appendix 4).

In the Apostolic Constitution *Fidei Depositum*, John Paul II summarizes both how he envisions the *Catechism* and how he understands Mary's role:

> In reading the *Catechism of the Catholic Church* we can perceive the wonderful unity of the mystery of God, his saving will, as well as the central place of Jesus Christ, the only-begotten Son of God, sent by the Father, made man in the womb of the Blessed Virgin Mary by the power of the Holy Spirit, to be our Savior. Having died and risen, Christ is always present in his Church, especially in the sacraments; he is the source of our faith, the model of Christian conduct, and the Teacher of our prayer.[213]

His concluding paragraph contains a prayer to Mary:

> I beseech the Blessed Virgin Mary, Mother of the Incarnate Word and Mother of the Church, to support with her powerful intercession the catechetical work of the entire Church on every level, at this time when she is called to a new effort of evangelization.[214]

For the reader, Mary will be presented within the following five-fold order which is characteristic of Vatican II and which is used within the curricula of two of the best institutes of Mariology[215]: Mary and the Trinity Especially in Relation to God as Creator; Mary and Jesus, the Christ; Mary's Call and Mission Under the Guidance and Overshadowing of the Holy Spirit; Mary and the Church; and Mary's Life of Faith and Prayer.

Mary and the Trinity Especially in Relation to God as Creator

The key reference to Mary and the Trinity in the *Catechism of the Catholic Church* is found in the explanation offered for Article 12 of the Apostles' Creed,[216] "I Believe in Life Everlasting."[217] This belief leads all human beings, who are made in the image and likeness of God, to their common goal which is a communion of life and love with the most Holy Trinity. Mary as a human achieved this union with God within the mystery of the Trinity because of her courageous faith, her undaunted hope, and her burning charity. She lived out her pilgrimage of faith and fulfilled the deepest human longings. The *Catechism* states:

> **1024** This perfect life with the Most Holy Trinity — this communion of life and love with the Trinity, with the Virgin Mary, the angels and all the blessed — is called "heaven." Heaven is the ultimate end and fulfillment of the deepest human longings, the state of supreme, definitive happiness.

Mary through her being conceived without sin is the most perfect *image* of God ever created and redeemed in a special manner by her son, Jesus. Through her life of faith, hope, and charity which related her to the Trinity she also perfected her *likeness* to God. She is taken up into heaven (her glorious Assumption) because of her conformity to her son. As creature she offered perfect adoration to God both through her words and her life-giving example:

> **2097** To adore God is to acknowledge, in respect and abso-lute submission, the "nothingness of the creature" who would not exist but for God. To adore God is to praise and exalt him and to humble oneself, as Mary did in the Magnificat, confess-ing with gratitude that he has done great things and holy is his name.[218] The worship of the one God sets man free from turning in on himself, from the slavery of sin and the idolatry of the world.

Paragraph 369 is included within this section because it speaks of our being made in the image of God (Gn 2:7, 22 and also Gn 1:26-27). Mary is not directly mentioned, but the import of the paragraph shows us as images of God. Through both the mystery of her Immaculate Conception and her glorious Assumption, Mary is an exemplar for us of what it means to be created in the image and likeness of God:

> **369** Man and woman have been *created*, which is to say, *willed* by God: on the one hand, in perfect equality as human

persons; on the other, in their respective beings as man and woman. "Being man" or "being woman" is a reality which is good and willed by God: man and woman possess an inalienable dignity which comes to them immediately from God their Creator.[219] Man and woman are both with one and the same dignity "in the image of God." In their "being-man" and "being-woman," they reflect the Creator's wisdom and goodness.

Mary's Immaculate Conception is mentioned in the *Catechism* in paragraphs 490, 491, 492 and 493. The Assumption is mentioned in paragraphs 966, 974, 2177 (Feasts of Mary) and 2853. Paragraph 2853 has eschatological importance and is an excellent summary of the two mysteries of Mary in the light of Jesus' victory over the "prince of this world, Satan," and reads:

> **2853** Victory over the "prince of this world"[220] was won once for all at the Hour when Jesus freely gave himself up to death to give us his life. This is the judgment of this world, and the prince of this world is "cast out."[221] "He pursued the woman"[222] but had no hold on her: the new Eve, "full of grace" of the Holy Spirit, is preserved from sin and the corruption of death (the Immaculate Conception and the Assumption of the Most Holy Mother of God, Mary, ever virgin). "Then the dragon was angry with the woman, and went off to make war on the rest of her offspring."[223] Therefore the Spirit and the Church pray: "Come, Lord Jesus,"[224] since his coming will deliver us from the Evil One.

Mary and Jesus, the Christ

John Paul II emphasizes the centrality of Jesus Christ in the unity of the mystery of God. Both the Apostles' Creed, which is the Creed used for explaining the faith in the *Catechism*, and the Nicene Creed declare the redemption as the mission of Jesus Christ. In fact, in one of the most insightful paragraphs in the *Catechism* we learn that Jesus Christ is at the heart of catechesis:

426 "At the heart of catechesis we find, in essence, a Person, the Person of Jesus of Nazareth, the only Son from the Father . . . who suffered and died for us and who now, after rising, is living with us forever."[225] To catechize is "to reveal in the Person of Christ the whole of God's eternal design reaching fulfillment in that Person. It is to seek to understand the meaning of Christ's actions and words and of the signs worked by him."[226] Catechesis aims at putting "people. . . in communion. . . with Jesus Christ: only he can lead us to the love of the Father in the Spirit and make us share in the life of the Holy Trinity."[227]

Mary is the Mother of the Redeemer. She it is who gave birth to Jesus the Redeemer, and cooperated in the mystery of our salvation. Mary is within God's plan of salvation for all:

502 The eyes of faith can discover in the context of the whole of Revelation the mysterious reasons why God in his saving plan wanted his Son to be born of a virgin. These reasons touch both on the person of Christ and his redemptive mission, and on the welcome Mary gave that mission on behalf of all men.

The initiative of God is involved in the plan and history of salvation:

503 Mary's virginity manifests God's absolute initiative in the Incarnation. Jesus has only God as Father. "He was never estranged from the Father because of the human nature which he assumed. . . . He is naturally Son of the Father as to his divinity and naturally son of his mother as to his humanity, but properly Son of the Father in both natures."[228]

Mary cooperated throughout her life and also from heaven in the mystery of God's redemptive plan:

969 "This motherhood of Mary in the order of grace continues uninterruptedly from the consent which she loyally gave at the Annunciation and which she sustained without wavering beneath the cross, until the eternal fulfillment of all the

elect. Taken up to heaven she did not lay aside this saving office but by her manifold intercession continues to bring us the gifts of eternal salvation. . . . Therefore the Blessed Virgin is invoked in the Church under the titles of Advocate, Helper, Benefactress, and Mediatrix."[229]

Paragraph 2617 likewise infers Mary's role in the redemption.

The *Catechism* carefully distinguishes Mary's secondary role in relationship to Christ who is the one mediator between God and ourselves:

> **570** "Mary's function as mother of men in no way obscures or diminishes this unique mediation of Christ, but rather shows its power. But the Blessed Virgin's salutary influence on men . . . flows forth from the superabundance of the merits of Christ, rests on his mediation, depends entirely on it, and draws all its power from it."[230] "No creature could ever be counted along with the Incarnate Word and Redeemer; but just as the priesthood of Christ is shared in various ways both by his ministers and the faithful, and as the one goodness of God is radiated in different ways among his creatures, so also the unique mediation of the Redeemer does not exclude but rather gives rise to a manifold cooperation which is but a sharing in this one source."[231]

Other paragraphs that refer to Mary's relationship to Christ are: 437, 467, 469, 726, 1138, 2665.

Mary, Mother of the Messiah

The title *Christos* means "the anointed one." The Hebrew equivalent is "Messiah." Mary is introduced into this title as the Jewish woman who is the Mother of the Messiah. Jesus as Messiah is seen in Luke's Gospel as the promised one who will save Israel (Lk 2:11). Jesus is the holy one who is born of the Virgin Mary (Lk 1:35). It is through the overshadowing of the Holy Spirit that Jesus was conceived and born of Mary (Mt 1:20). She is espoused to Joseph of the house of David through whom the messianic promises were made (Mt 1:16). Article 3 of the Nicene Creed, cited in *Catechism* par. 456, expresses in a faith statement what the Gospels attest, namely, " . . . by the power of the Holy Spirit, he became incarnate of the Virgin Mary. . . . "

The *Catechism* emphasizes the divinity and humanity of Jesus Christ within the context of Scripture, Conciliar Christology, and Tradition. It is especially through Jesus' humanity that Mary assures us that she is his human Jewish mother. Jesus is a Divine Person. The Word, having assumed the totality of our humanness in Jesus, asserts that his mother Mary is also intimately bound up with him as a Divine Person. At the third ecumenical Council of Ephesus in 431 C.E., Mary is described as *Theotokos*, that is, "the God-bearer." In the Western Church this title is translated as *Mater Dei*, "Mother of God" or *Dei Genitrix*, "Begetter of God." The emphasis of the Council of Ephesus is upon Jesus Christ. Mary, however, as a human person who became the Mother of Jesus through her free consent at the Annunciation assures what is most human in Jesus. He is a real historical figure in world history precisely because he was "born of a woman." The Johannine expression, "And the Word became flesh and made his dwelling among us" (Jn 1:14), is what the Council of Ephesus was explaining against any form of Docetism or Nestorianism which would divide the Person of Christ.

This same teaching is reaffirmed by the fourth ecumenical Council at Chalcedon in 451 C.E. against any form of Monophysitism which again would divide Jesus Christ by leaving aside his human nature and the limitations it imposes. The *Catechism* (pars. 465-468) clearly summarizes the statements made in the early Councils about Jesus in order to help instruct the faithful in the living Tradition of the Church concerning the Incarnation. Without mentioning Mary, Christ's humanity would be neglected. He is like to us in all things except sin (cf. Heb 4:15).

Jesus is our brother because Mary his mother is the giver of what we all possess — our human nature and its limitations. The union of Jesus as Word, his divinity, is emphasized at the Council of Constantinople in 553 C.E. and his union with God the Father and with the Holy Spirit is affirmed. The *Catechism* uses both the Council's statement and the liturgy to describe this Trinitarian belief. The following citation from the Byzantine Liturgy is used to explain more concretely the mystery:

> **469** And the liturgy of St. John Chrysostom proclaims and sings: "O only-begotten Son and Word of God, immortal being, you who deigned for our salvation to become incarnate of the holy Mother of God and ever-virgin Mary, you who without change became man and were crucified, O Christ our God, you who by your death have crushed death, you who are one of the Holy Trinity, glorified with the Father and the Holy Spirit, save us!"[232]

Vatican II in *Gaudium et spes* also affirms the Second Person of the Blessed Trinity in the Person of Jesus, the Word become flesh. Again Mary is seen as a human person who has assented fully to this mystery of her Son: "He worked with human hands, he thought with a human mind. He acted with a human will, and with a human heart he loved. Born of the Virgin Mary, he has truly been made one of us, like to us in all things except sin."[233]

In summary, in the *Catechism* the third part under paragraph 1 of Article 3, "He was Conceived by the Power of the Holy Spirit, and Was Born of the Virgin Mary,"[234] is entitled "True God and True Man."[235] This section is a summary and a synthesis of the great Councils of the Church from the fourth century through the sixth which carefully define the human and divine natures of Christ in the one Person, the Word, Jesus Christ who was born of the Virgin Mary.

Mary's Call and Mission under the Guidance and Overshadowing of the Holy Spirit

There are a considerable number of references to Mary and the Holy Spirit in Part One of the *Catechism* (pars. 721-725). Her cooperation with the work of the Spirit is seen in her because: (1)

the Father found the *dwelling place* where his Son and his Spirit could dwell among men (par. 721); (2) the Holy Spirit *prepared* Mary by his grace (par. 722); (3) in Mary, the Holy Spirit *fulfills* the plan of the Father's loving goodness (par. 723); (4) in Mary, the Holy Spirit *manifests* the Son of the Father, now become the Son of the Virgin (par. 724); and (5) finally, through Mary, the Holy Spirit begins to bring men, the objects of God's merciful love, *into communion* with Christ (par. 725). Several of the symbols of the Holy Spirit are also presented in a Marian dimension — especially the *anointing* and the symbol of the *cloud* and *light* (pars. 695, 697). Other paragraphs which mention Mary in relationship to the Holy Spirit are: 485, 486, 504, 726, 744, 2673, 2676, 2682.

Perhaps the section (par. 2, Chapter Two, Article 3) entitled "Conceived by the Power of the Holy Spirit and Born of the Virgin Mary"[236] is the centerpiece in the Marian teaching of the *Catechism*. Commencing with Paul's announcement of the Christ-event in the fullness of time (Gal 4:4), and then showing how the Holy Spirit descends upon Mary at the Annunciation (Lk 1:35), it is learned that the mission of the Holy Spirit is conjoined and ordered to that of the Son (par. 485). Through the operation of the Holy Spirit, Mary conceives the eternal Son. The Christ, that is the Anointed One of the Holy Spirit, progressively manifests himself to the shepherds, the Magi, the Baptist, and to the disciples. ". . . God anointed Jesus of Nazareth with the holy Spirit and power" (Ac 10:38). Mary's response to God and the action of the Spirit results in the birth of Jesus. Her faith has made this possible.

Mary was already foreseen in the Divine plan. This is emphasized in the section of Vatican II's *Lumen Gentium* dedicated to Mary: "The Father of mercies willed that the Incarnation should be preceded by assent on the part of the predestined mother, so that just as a woman had a share in bringing about death, so also a woman should contribute to life."[237]

The singular grace of Mary's Immaculate Conception is also due to the presence and operation of the Holy Spirit. Her redemption is also due to her Son but in view of his merits. In the Eastern Tradition Mary is called the All-Holy one, *Panagia*. She is celebrated as "free from every stain of sin, as though fashioned by the Holy Spirit and formed as a new creature."[238] Moved by the Holy Spirit, Elizabeth praises Mary for her faith and professes her as "the mother of my Lord" (Lk 1:43).

Mary and the Church

Paragraph 963 of the *Catechism* logically follows up on Mary's motherhood with Jesus to her spiritual motherhood with the Church: "She is 'clearly the mother of the members of Christ'. ... since she has by her charity joined in bringing about the birth of believers in the Church, who are members of its head." This role of Mary as Mother of the Church flows from her motherhood to Christ. Paul VI stated, "Mary, the Mother of Christ, is the Mother of the Church" (Paul VI, Discourse of Nov. 21, 1964).

For scriptural foundation the text of John 19:26, "Woman, behold, your son," is used for her spiritual motherhood in the Church and its members. This text has long been used for this teaching about Mary, perhaps as early as the fourth century. Her presence with Jesus from the moment of his conception, through infancy, childhood, and adulthood, as well as her involvement in the Paschal Mysteries and the coming of the Spirit at Pentecost, enables Mary to be a model for the Church — in fact, to be Mother of the Church. Her own Assumption into heaven is an anticipatory sign for what all Christians are called to experience in their own resurrection.

Mary is the Mother of the Church, that is mother of the faithful in the order of grace. She lived out a life of faith and love, two responses to life experiences seen in John's Gospel. In chapters 1-12 the virtue of faith is emphasized, "to believe in Jesus" (*pisteuein eis Iesoun*); in chapters 13-21 love (*agapan*) is emphasized. Mary truly is the type and model of the Church. This aspect of Marian influence is the teaching of Vatican II wherein Mary as type of the Church is presented.[239] Because of her faith, obedience, hope, and charity as she cooperated with the redemptive plan of her Son, she is seen and established as the Mother of us all in the order of grace. And since this maternity of Mary is carried out after her Assumption through her intercession for us, she also is invoked within the Church as Advocate, Helper, Benefactress, and Mediatrix.[240]

As John Paul II carefully explains how this maternal function of Mary in no way diminishes the mediation of Jesus her son (*Redemptoris Mater*, Part III, par. 38), so does the *Catechism* indicate Mary's helping and subordinate role to Christ. Vatican II was equally careful on the unique mediator role of Jesus:

> . . . the Blessed Virgin is invoked in the Church under the titles of Advocate, Helper, Benefactress, and Mediatrix. This, however, is so understood that it neither takes away anything from nor adds anything to the dignity and efficacy of Christ the one Mediator.

> No creature could ever be counted along with the Incarnate Word and Redeemer; but just as the priesthood of Christ is shared in various ways both by his ministers and the faithful, and as the one goodness of God is radiated in different ways among his creatures, so also the unique mediation of the Redeemer does not exclude but rather gives rise to a manifold cooperation which is but a sharing in this one source.

> The Church does not hesitate to profess this subordinate role of Mary, which it constantly experiences and recommends to the heartfelt attention of the faithful, so that encouraged by this maternal help they may the more closely adhere to the Mediator and Redeemer.[241]

Care is taken to demonstrate that there is no aspect of adoration in the Marian devotions and festival celebrations given in her honor throughout the liturgical year. Nevertheless, as Paul VI said in *Marialis cultus* (Devotion to the Blessed Virgin Mary): "The Church's devotion to the Blessed Virgin is an intrinsic element of Christian worship."[242]

Finally, Mary is the eschatological icon of the Church in its mission of being a pilgrim people of faith:

. . . the Mother of Jesus in the glory which she possesses in body and soul in heaven is the image and beginning of the Church as it is to be perfected in the world to come. Likewise she shines forth on earth, until the day of the Lord shall come (cf. 2 P 3:10), a sign of certain hope and comfort to the pilgrim People of God.[243]

Paul VI said it so well in his brief statement: "We believe that the most holy Mother of God, the New Eve, Mother of the Church, continues in heaven her maternal role towards the members of Christ."

Vatican II establishes the most advanced notion in Mariology by placing Mary within the eighth chapter of *Lumen Gentium*, the Dogmatic Constitution on the Church. The *Catechism* renders this relationship in several articles which make her role more explicit (cf. par. 963). The Church has always been related to the person of Christ as spouse; the feminine dimension of the Church is a characteristic of Mary's role within the Church. Here are a few examples:

773 In the Church this communion of men with God, in the "love [that] never ends," is the purpose which governs everything in her that is a sacramental means, tied to this passing world.[244] "[The Church's] structure is totally ordered to the holiness of Christ's members. And holiness is measured according to the 'great mystery' in which the Bride responds with the gift of love to the gift of the Bridegroom."[245] Mary goes before us all in the holiness that is the Church's mystery as "the bride without spot or wrinkle."[246] This is why the "Marian" dimension of the Church precedes the "Petrine."[247]

829 "But while in the most Blessed Virgin the Church has already reached that perfection whereby she exists without spot or wrinkle, the faithful still strive to conquer sin and increase in holiness. And so they turn their eyes to Mary":[248] in her, the Church is already the "all holy."

507 At once virgin and mother, Mary is the symbol and the most perfect realization of the Church: "the Church indeed

. . . by receiving the word of God in faith becomes herself a mother. By preaching and Baptism she brings forth sons, who are conceived by the Holy Spirit and born of God, to a new and immortal life. She herself is a virgin, who keeps in its entirety and purity the faith she pledged to her spouse."[249]

Clement of Alexandria had a glimpse of this realization of the Church when he said,

813 What an astonishing mystery! There is one Father of the universe, one Logos of the universe, and also one Holy Spirit, everywhere one and the same; there is also one virgin become mother, and I should like to call her "Church."[250]

Mary is called the eschatological icon of the Church. This is beautifully portrayed in the *Catechism*:

972 After speaking of the Church, her origin, mission, and destiny, we can find no better way to conclude than by looking to Mary. In her we contemplate what the Church already is in her mystery on her own "pilgrimage of faith," and what she will be in the homeland at the end of her journey. There, "in the glory of the Most Holy and Undivided Trinity," "in the communion of all the saints,"[251] the Church is awaited by the one she venerates as Mother of her Lord and as her own mother.

In the meantime the Mother of Jesus, in the glory which she possesses in body and soul in heaven, is the image and beginning of the Church as it is to be perfected in the world to come. Likewise she shines forth on earth, until the day of the Lord shall come, a sign of certain hope and comfort to the pilgrim People of God.[252]

Mary is the symbol and most perfect realization of the Church (par. 507). She is a preeminent and wholly unique member of the Church, indeed, the exemplary realization, *typus*, of the Church (par. 967). She is the model and source for the Church as Mother and teacher (par. 2030). Mary is the figure and model for the Church at prayer; the one who sustains the prayer of the Church (par. 2679).

The Scriptures also are used to point out Mary's relationship to Christ in the Church. Perhaps the passage in the *Catechism* most descriptive of her relationship to Christ and also of the origin of the Church is:

> 964 Mary's role in the Church is inseparable from her union with Christ and flows directly from it. "This union of the mother with the Son in the work of salvation is made manifest from the time of Christ's virginal conception up to his death";[253] it is made manifest above all at the hour of his Passion:
>
>> Thus the Blessed Virgin advanced in her pilgrimage of faith, and faithfully persevered in her union with her Son unto the cross. There she stood, in keeping with the divine plan, enduring with her only begotten Son the intensity of his suffering, joining herself with his sacrifice in her mother's heart, and lovingly consenting to the immolation of this victim, born of her: to be given, by the same Christ Jesus dying on the cross, as a mother to his disciple, with these words: "Woman, behold your son."[254]

Other paragraphs which may be consulted for Mary and the Church are: 766, 867, 968, 969, 972-975, 1138, 1172, 1370, 1419, 1477, 1655, 1717, 2030, 2827.

The title of Mary as New Eve is not directly found in the Scriptures, but is seen both by the theologians of the early Church as well as by some contemporary scholars as emanating from several scriptural references. These are the scene at the foot of the Cross (Jn 19:25-28a) and from those references where Christ is called a second or New Adam (cf. Rm 5:19-20). Mary is often reflected upon as a second or New Eve in association with her son Jesus as the New Adam. The first perceptions of this association come in the second century C.E. from Justin the Martyr and Irenaeus of Lyons.

The *Catechism* (pars. 410-411) introduces the theme of the New Eve in the section of the Creed showing Christ's victory over the origin of sin as well as over death itself. The text used for the victorious promise made to Adam and Eve is Genesis 3:15: "I will put enmity between you and the woman, and between your offspring and hers; he will strike at your head, while you strike at his heel." This passage is called the Protoevangelium for it is the first announcement of a redeemer Messiah involving a conflict between the Woman and the serpent in which her descendant will be the victor. Christian Tradition has seen Jesus the Christ as the New Adam while many Fathers and Doctors of the Church have seen the Mother of Christ as a New Eve. Her having been already transformed by grace enables Mary to be the Woman, the New Eve, who conquers the serpent, or the Devil (cf. Rv 12:9).

The *Catechism* cites both *Lumen Gentium*, 56 and St. Irenaeus in describing Mary's role as a New Eve:

> **494** As St. Irenaeus says, "Being obedient she became the cause of salvation for herself and for the whole human race."[255] Hence not a few of the early Fathers gladly assert....: "The knot of Eve's disobedience was untied by Mary's obedience; what the virgin Eve bound through her disbelief, Mary loosened by her faith."[256] Comparing her with Eve, they call Mary "the Mother of the living" and frequently claim: "Death through Eve, life through Mary."[257]

A summary statement about Mary's role as New Eve in the mission of her son is:

> **726** At the end of this mission of the Spirit, Mary became the Woman, the new Eve ("mother of the living"), the mother of the "whole Christ."[258] As such, she was present with the Twelve, who "with one accord devoted themselves to prayer,"[259] at the dawn of the "end time" which the Spirit was to inaugurate on the morning of Pentecost with the manifestation of the Church.

This same idea is expressed in paragraph 2618.

The final victory of Christ over the prince of this world occurs during the "hour" of Jesus, his death upon the Cross. Mary is present as the Woman *par excellence* who shares in this victory by her son, the one who conquers sin and death. Her gifts of the Immaculate Conception and the Assumption are mentioned as the signs of this victory over sin (cf. par. 2853).

The *Catechism of the Catholic Church* contains a compendium of teaching about Mary, the Mother of Jesus. Mary is present throughout the *Catechism* primarily as she is seen in the Scriptures and in the Conciliar document *Lumen Gentium*. It is especially through this scriptural and conciliar image of Mary that renewed knowledge, love, and devotion to Mary are enhanced and developed for the reader of the *Catechism*. There are no polemic overtones or innuendoes in this contextual synthesis surrounding the person of Mary. She is a courageous, generous, and loving woman and mother. Mary's total response to God makes of her a model for the believer whose response echoes her "May it be done to me according to your word" (Lk 1:38).

Mary's Life of Faith and Prayer

Mary, the Virgin mother of Jesus, is introduced in the *Catechism* in the first reflection on the Creed. She is the most perfect realization of free submission in faith just as Abraham was presented as the model of obedient faith. The response of Mary to the Word of God through her vibrant faith shows her as a courageous woman who believes in God as the ultimate truth who guaranteed the promises made in the Sacred Word of Scripture (cf. par. 144). It is significant that the Creed which expresses the human response to God is first presented in the context of the decree of Vatican II on Divine Revelation, and that the two models of such a human response to God with complete trust are found in Abraham and Mary. Twenty-five years later John Paul II introduced a similar parallel of Abraham and Mary in his encyclical, *Redemptoris Mater*. This complementarity of a man of faith and a woman of faith strengthens the relationship of God's revelatory message in the Hebrew Scriptures with that of the Christian Scriptures. Abraham is the father in faith of Judaism, while Christianity is likewise modeled in Mary's great response of "yes" to God. In a word, the First Testament is complemented in the Second Testament. The focusing on the persons of Mary and Abraham thus has an ecumenical nuance as well as a scriptural basis for our imitating the faith of both of our ancestors in faith — a father and a mother (cf. pars. 145-147).

Mary is declared as blessed, that is, a happy and fortunate person because she has believed in God's word (Lk 1:45). Abraham first heard the expression "nothing is impossible to God" (Gn 18:14) and Sarah his aged wife was so astonished that she laughed at the idea of conceiving a child. Mary had accepted and received the promise of the angel Gabriel. Mary's total decision and commitment to the word of God through the messenger is an absolutely free and unconditional response of love on the part of the servant of God (Lk 1:38). Elizabeth, the cousin of Mary, is the first to call Mary blessed because of her belief (cf. par. 148). The retelling of Mary's story by Luke is paralleled in the *Catechism* with the story of Abraham and Sarah. Again the scriptural witness to Mary's faith is attested; the Old and the New Testaments are seen as complementary. There is also a sensitivity to the Jewish heritage of Mary of Nazareth.

Mary's faith continued to grow steadily throughout her life, and in the supreme moment of witnessing the death of Jesus her faith did not vacillate. Mary never ceased in believing in the fulfillment of God's word. This is the reason for the Church venerating the most pristine realization of faith in a person (cf. par. 149). Once again the description of Mary and her faith is seen within the Scriptures (Lk 2:35, Jn 19:25-27). Together with the most recent instruction on Mary, the *Catechism* approaches Mary from a scriptural context. The Holy Scriptures are thus the soul of an authentic Mariology.

The final paragraph (165) of Article I, referring to the Apostles' Creed, returns to the faith of Abraham and Mary. Scripture again testifies to their faith: Abraham believes "hoping against hope" (Rm 4:18). The Virgin Mary, the preferred title for Mary in the *Catechism*, is a believing disciple despite the night of faith, the suffering of her Son, and the darkness of the tomb. The *Catechism* here is resonating the earliest Creed given in Paul's epistle to the Corinthians:

> For I handed on to you as of first importance what I also
> received: that Christ died for our sins in accordance with the
> Scriptures; that he was buried; that he was raised on the third
> day in accordance with the Scriptures; that he appeared to
> Kephas, then to the Twelve. After that, he appeared to more
> than five hundred brothers at once, most of whom are still
> living, though some have fallen asleep. After that he appeared
> to James, then to all the apostles. Last of all, as to one born
> abnormally, he appeared to me (1 Cor 15:3-8).

The overarching theme of Mary's courageous womanly faith
continues in the context of her being under the shadow of the Holy
Spirit. The section under her Immaculate Conception (pars. 490-
493) underlines that it was her faith in God that enabled her to give
her absolute free consent in a positive human act of loving response
to her call; however, this was possible because she was given the
grace of God. She was said to be "full of grace" (Lk 1:28). We know
from the philological study done by I. de la Potterie that this fullness
of grace is in reality the title the angel Gabriel calls her — you who
have been transformed and favored by the grace of God, *kécharitôménê*
(Lk 1:28).

Mary is always pointing to Jesus. This is an important principle
in the texts of the New Testament referring to her, especially in
those texts which deal with a faith dimension. In the Cana account,
Mary says, "Do whatever he [Jesus] tells you" (Jn 2:5). In the
Catechism (par. 165) a similar faith in Jesus is expressed through the
following text:

> Therefore, since we are surrounded by so great a cloud of
> witnesses, let us rid ourselves of every burden and sin that
> clings to us and persevere in running the race that lies before
> us while keeping our eyes fixed on Jesus, the leader and
> perfecter of faith. For the sake of the joy that lay before him
> he endured the cross, despising its shame, and has taken his
> seat at the right of the throne of God (Heb 12:1-2).

In the paradoxical mystery of the omnipotent God seemingly
lacking power in the tragedies of the world, such as war, disease,

suffering and death, Mary is presented again as a model of faith drawing us to Christ in his humanness. The faith response of Mary is seen in the context of the Annunciation (Lk 1:37) and in her faith-filled praise of God in her Magnificat (Lk 1:49). Our weaknesses are shared by Mary in the light of our relationship to Christ through faith:

> But he said to me, "My grace is sufficient for you, for power is made perfect in weakness." I will rather boast most gladly of my weaknesses, in order that the power of Christ may dwell with me (2 Cor 12:9).
>
> I have the strength for everything through him who empowers me (Ph 4:13).

The development of Mary's faith starts with the Annunciation Narrative which is both an announcement and a vocation account. Mary responds with her obedience of faith (*hypakoen pisteos;* Rm 1:5). Such a dynamic faith response is only possible through the influence of God's Holy Spirit upon Mary. This enables her to give a complete human response: "May it be done to me according to your word" (Lk 1:38). Again the *Catechism* places her response as a direct reply to the Word of God. Citing Irenaeus — the first Mariologist — Mary's obedience and her faith remove the obstacles of disobedience and incredulity (cf. par. 494). Perhaps, this obedience of faith can be understood in the Hebrew expression *leb shomeah;* that is, Mary responded with a "listening heart."

The crowning reference to Mary's faith is found under the title "The prayer of the Virgin Mary" in the fourth and final part of the *Catechism.*[260] The experience of Mary's practical prayer is seen at Cana when her solicitude and care result in an effective request of Jesus her son. This is also seen in the only other direct mention of Mary at the foot of the Cross, where she is seen as the "mother of the living" in the spiritual realm, that is, those who through their belief have become sons and daughters of God: "But to those who did accept him he gave power to become children of God, to those who believe in his name" (Jn 1:12).

The *Catechism* quite appropriately frames the prayer and faith of Mary with the two Marian texts of the Fourth Gospel, the contemplative Gospel: Jn 2:1-11 (par. 1613) and Jn 19:25-27 (pars. 762, 2618). Other paragraphs in the *Catechism* touching upon the faith of Mary are: 273, 506, 511, 534, 964, 967, 968, 972, 2617, 2619, 2622.

In three paragraphs (2617-2619) within the *Catechism of the Catholic Church* the prayer of Mary is mentioned. Once again, this Marian aspect is described in the Scriptures. The use of the revelatory texts is a guiding method for the *Catechism*. This is consistent with Vatican II's *Dei Verbum* (Divine Revelation), *Sacrosanctum Concilium* (Sacred Liturgy), and *Lumen Gentium* (Church).

Mary is a model for prayer within the life of the Church. The sections that describe her prayer are found in the concluding part of the *Catechism*: "Christian Life." Over 300 numbered articles are dedicated to prayer. The *Catechism* concludes with the Lord's Prayer and an explanation of each of its petitions (pars. 2558-2865).

The principal section on the prayer of Mary is found in Article 2 under the title "In the Fullness of Time."[261] Mary's prayer thereby is introduced into the earliest reference to her in the New Testament: "But when the fullness of time had come, God sent his Son, born of a woman, born under the law, to ransom those under the law, so that we might receive adoption" (Gal 4:4-5). According to St. Paul, Mary's prayer coincided with the benevolent plan of God's loving mercy. At the Annunciation, Mary articulated her prayer through a heart-filled "yes." She not only ponders over the events of her life in the light of her Jewish faith (Lk 2:19, 51), she is at the center of a community gathered in prayer in the upper room prior to the coming of the Holy Spirit at Pentecost. Her prayer embraces the time of expectant waiting, the event of the Incarnation, and the birth of the Church. Mary symbolizes the prayer life of the Church at every important moment of the Christ-event. Her "let it be" (*fiat*) is the soul of Christian prayer, that is, to be entirely oriented toward the Person of God. Her magnanimous response continues in her Magnificat which we, the People of God, pray each day in the universal prayer of the Church. The Johannine image of Mary is that of a woman interceding for the needy and who stands in strong faith at the moment of death (cf. Jn 2:1-11; 19:25-27).

The *Catechism* sums up the perfect expression of Mary's prayer:

> 2619 That is why the Canticle of Mary,[262] the *Magnificat* (Latin) or *Megalynei* (Byzantine) is the song both of the Mother of God and of the Church; the song of the Daughter of Zion and of the new People of God; the song of thanksgiving for the fullness of graces poured out in the economy of salvation and the song of the "poor" whose hope is met by the fulfillment of the promises made to our ancestors, "to Abraham and to his posterity for ever."

Mary is a model for the Church at prayer, and when we pray with her or to her we gather in spirit with the brothers and sisters, the apostles, and the holy women in the upper room awaiting the promise of Jesus, which is the Holy Spirit: "All these devoted themselves with one accord to prayer, together with some women, and Mary the mother of Jesus, and his brothers" (Ac 1:14).

In a fitting way, after the prayer to God, to the Second Person of the Trinity (Jesus), and to and through the Holy Spirit, Mary is included as one who prays with us and for us. It is Mary who is the model for the Church at prayer. In the final paragraph of the section on Marian prayer, this summary statement orients us in a Marian form of prayer:

> 2682 Because of Mary's singular cooperation with the action of the Holy Spirit, the Church loves to pray in communion with the Virgin Mary, to magnify with her the great things the Lord has done for her, and to entrust supplications and praises to her.

All Christian prayer is related to the prayer of Jesus Christ. This is a basic principle that influences all facets of our prayer life, including our Marian aspect of prayer and devotions. We see Christ as the way especially in our prayer life. We pray in the name of Jesus. The titles and description of Jesus both in the Scriptures and the

sacred liturgy are part of our invocation of him: Son of God, Word
of God, Lord, Savior, Lamb of God, King, Beloved Son, Son of the
Virgin, Good Shepherd, our Life, our Light, our Hope, our Resurrection, and our Friend (cf, par. 2665). Above all, it is the holy name
Jesus which contains all humanity, divinity, creation and redemption. In the East the Jesus Prayer is essential to what we are when we
pray, "Jesus, the Christ, Son of God, Lord, have pity on us sinners"
(cf. Ph 2:6-11). Among the devotions that entail this form of prayer
are devotion to the Sacred Heart of Jesus and the Way of the
Cross.[277] The invocation, "Come, Holy Spirit," enables us to pray,
for no one can say "Jesus is Lord" except under the power and action
of the Holy Spirit. Only after carefully treating of Prayer to the
Persons of the Holy Trinity does the *Catechism* introduce the section
on prayer, entitled "In communion with the holy Mother of God"
(pars. 2673-2682).

Mary is especially important in our prayer to help us understand the humanity of Jesus. Mary is totally transparent in the honor
and glory she renders God in her son Jesus. She shows us the way
to Jesus as the *hodoghitria*. There is within the Church's prayer to and
with Mary a double movement: the first glorifies God for the great
things that have been accomplished in Mary, the devoted handmaid
of the Lord, and also in us because of her role in the Incarnation; the
second entrusts to the Mother of God the supplications and praise
of the children of God because Jesus has taken his human flesh from
her.

This double movement of prayer is seen in the greatest prayer
dedicated to Mary, the "Hail Mary." This biblical prayer is identified
with Catholics probably more than the Lord's Prayer. The *Catechism*
addresses both the *Ave Maria* (pars. 2676-2677) and the *Pater Noster*
(pars. 2777-2802). The first section of the Hail Mary is directly from
the Gospel of Luke, a Gospel which emphasizes prayer on twenty-
two occasions. The *Ave Maria* is, therefore, to be seen within a
prayerful context. The atmosphere that surrounds Mary during the
angelic salutation is favorable to prayer and has been used as the
favorite prayer within the Catholic Church both through the

Angelus as well as the holy rosary. In a special way the rosary is a compendium of the whole Gospel (cf. par. 971).

God through Gabriel calls Mary to her special vocation. Mary responds totally to God with openness and with joy. In fact, she is told by the angel to rejoice because she has already found favor with God. As the salutation continues, the theme of the Daughter of Zion is recalled through words similar to those of the prophet Zephaniah (3:14-16). Mary like Judith is blessed among women. She is the person in Luke's Gospel who best exemplifies the beatitudes (Lk 6:20-22; cf. Mt 5:1-12). Elizabeth, her cousin, is the first to proclaim her blessed because of her belief (Lk 1:45). Just as Abraham was blessed with the promise of a progeny of believers (Gn 12:2-3), Mary, too, is the beginning of a new line of believers in the son she will bear.

In the conclusion of the prayer, the confidence we put in Mary's intercession is based on her own prayer: "May it be with me according to your word" (Lk 1:38). This is similar to Jesus' prayer during the agony in the Garden of Olives (Lk 22:42). The prayer is one of profound humility in which our present status is put into the perspective of our final hour: "now and at the hour of our death." Just as the Lord's Prayer is seen as an eschatological prayer (according to R.E. Brown[263]), so, too, is the Hail Mary an eschatological prayer helping us always to look toward the final moments and purpose of our lives in union with God's will.

The *Catechism* takes note of the various traditions in bringing this section to a close. Not only are the Roman or Western devotions to Mary mentioned but also those of the Byzantine, Coptic, Syrian, and Armenian Churches (cf. par. 2678). Thus the universal dimension of Christian prayer prevails.

The final mention of Mary in the *Catechism* sees her as an image and model of the Church at prayer. This is biblical, for the last mention of her is in the Acts of the Apostles:

> Then they returned to Jerusalem from the mount called Olivet, which is near Jerusalem, a Sabbath day's journey away. When they entered the city they went to the upper room

where they were staying, Peter and John and James and
Andrew, Philip and Thomas, Bartholomew and Matthew,
James son of Alphaeus, Simon the Zealot, and Judas son of
James. All these devoted themselves with one accord to
prayer, together with some women, and Mary the mother of
Jesus, and his brothers (Ac 1:12-14).

The *Catechism's* description of her is a commentary on Acts 1:12-24:

> **2679** Mary is the perfect *Orans* (pray-er), a figure of the
> Church. When we pray to her, we are adhering with her to the
> plan of the Father, who sends his Son to save all men. Like the
> beloved disciple we welcome Jesus' mother into our homes,[264]
> for she has become the mother of all the living. We can pray
> with and to her. The prayer of the Church is sustained by the
> prayer of Mary and united with it in hope.[265]

The sources used for depicting the mysteries of the birth, early
childhood and hidden life of Jesus are taken from the Infancy
Narratives of Matthew and Luke. Primarily, the *Catechism* is developing a Christology rather than a Mariology. Mary's life is connected
with that of her Child. Her life experiences are known precisely
because of Jesus her Son who is the center of both Infancy Narratives, and the *Catechism* (par. 525) celebrates her in a hymn taken
from Romanos the Melodist:

> The Virgin today brings into the world the Eternal
> And the earth offers a cave to the Inaccessible.
> The angels and shepherds praise him
> And the magi advance with the star,
> For you are born for us,
> Little Child, God eternal![266]

The nativity is presented as a mystery which leads us to humility and
acceptance of our human limits (par. 526).

Mary is related to the events of Jesus' infancy. With circumci-
sion he is fully under the Covenant and the prescriptions of the
Torah. By birth, religion, and culture Jesus is Jewish. In the Epiphany

Jesus is manifested to the Gentiles who find him with Mary and Joseph in their home in Bethlehem. The magi must first seek Jesus through the Jewish leaders and people before they can understand him as the Messiah promised through the Scriptures. Jesus is recognized as the promised one by Simeon and Anna who share in the glory of Israel. Mary, however, is forewarned that Jesus will be a sign of contradiction and that a sword of sorrow will pierce her heart. The flight into Egypt and his return to Israel recall the Exodus Event. Jesus is seen as a definitive liberator (par. 530).

The experiences of the hidden life of Jesus are presented in a setting that would be typical of any Jew during this epoch — day by day chores, manual labor, and a religious conduct guided by the Torah and its prescriptions. All of this is under the tutelage of his parents (Lk 2:51-52).

Likewise, his life of living out the fourth commandment — "honor your father and your mother" — announces and anticipates his submission to the will of God during his agony in the garden in Luke 22:42 (par. 532).

Pope Paul VI in a marvelous sermon for the feast of the Holy Family sums up the hidden years of Jesus:

> The home of Nazareth is the school where we begin to understand the life of Jesus — the school of the Gospel. First, then, a lesson of silence. May esteem for *silence*, that admirable and indispensable condition of mind, revive in us. . . . A lesson on *family life*. May Nazareth teach us what family life is, its communion of love, its austere and simple beauty, and its sacred and inviolable character. . . A lesson of *work*. Nazareth, home of the "Carpenter's Son," in you I would choose to understand and proclaim the severe and redeeming law of human work. . . . To conclude, I want to greet all the workers of the world, holding up to them their great pattern, their brother who is God.[267]

The only incident that breaks through the hidden life of Jesus is the finding of him in the Temple by Mary and Joseph. Here Mary's faith is again tested and strengthened by pondering over his unusual and mysterious words (Lk 2:51).

The *Catechism* shows us Mary's life through that of Christ's; it is always within the context of what we know from the Gospels of Matthew and Luke that we learn of Mary's life in relationship and dependence on what is being said of her son, Jesus. Her experiences are seen within the mission of the Son and Holy Spirit in the fullness of time (Gal 4:4). Mary is seen as the Seat of Wisdom precisely because of her cooperative effort in the history of salvation. Texts that are from Wisdom literature are accommodated to her life experiences (cf. Pr 8:1-9:6; Si 24). She is seen as the Daughter of Zion in Luke's Annunciation narrative. Her song of praise, the Magnificat, becomes the thanksgiving of the whole people of God (par. 722).

Mary continues throughout her life to be influenced and guided by God's Spirit of power and grace. This renders her virginity fruitful in the birth of Jesus. In her the Holy Spirit renders effective the merciful plan of God. The Spirit also manifests the Son of God become Son of Mary. Through her the Spirit begins to bring people into communion with Christ. The *Catechism* is clearly showing Mary as cooperative with all three Persons of the Holy Trinity. Through the Spirit she becomes the Woman, the new Eve, and mother of all living, the Mother of the whole Christ. We finally see her on the morning of Pentecost praying together with the Twelve as the Church is born. Mary's perfect response to God is expressed at the Annunciation and confirmed by her praise and adoration of God in the powerful sentiments of her Magnificat. This adoration renders her the absolute freedom of a liberated person who is bound by no form of slavery to sin nor any form of idolatry (par. 2097).

Endnotes

[212] *Fidei Depositum*, in *Catechism of the Catholic Church*, 2.

[213] Ibid., 5.

[214] Ibid., 6.

[215] The Marianum in Rome and the International Marian Research Institute located at the University of Dayton, Ohio.

[216] *Catechism*, 49.

[217] Ibid., 266.

[218] Cf. Lk 1:46-49.

[219] Cf. Gn 2:7, 22.

[220] Jn 14:30.

[221] Jn 12:31; Rv. 12:10.

[222] Rv. 12:13-16.

[223] Rv. 12:17.

[224] Rv. 22:17, 20.

[225] *Catechesi tradendi* 5.

[226] Ibid.

[227] Ibid.

[228] Council of Friuli (796): DS 619; cf. Lk 2:48-49.

[229] *Lumen Gentium* 62.

[230] Ibid., 60.

[231] Ibid., 62.

[232] Liturgy of St. John Chrysostom, Troparion "O Monogenes."

[233] *Gaudium et spes* 22.

[234] *Catechism*, 115.

[235] Ibid., 117.

[236] Ibid., 122.

[237] *Lumen Gentium*, 56; cf. 61.

[238] Ibid., 56.

[239] Ibid., 53, 63.

[240] Ibid., 62.

[241] Ibid.

[242] *Marialis cultus*, 56.

[243] *Lumen Gentium*, 68.

[244] 1 Cor 13:8; cf. *Lumen Gentium*, 48.

[245] John Paul II, *Mulieris dignitatem* 27.

[246] Eph 5:27.

[247] Cf. John Paul II, *Mulieris dignitatem* 27.

[248] *Lumen Gentium*, 65; cf. Eph 5:26-27.

[249] *Lumen Gentium*, 64; cf. 63.

[250] Clement of Alexandria, *Paedagogus* 1, 6, 42: PG 8, 300.

[251] *Lumen Gentium*, 69.

[252] Ibid., 68; cf. 2 P 3:10.

[253] *Lumen Gentium*, 57.

[254] Ibid., 58; cf. Jn 19:26-27.

[255] St. Irenaeus, *Adversus haereses* 3, 22, 4:PG 7/1, 959 A.

[256] Ibid.

[257] *Lumen Gentium*, 56; St. Epiphanius, *Panarion seu adversus LXXX haereses* 78, 18: PG 42, 728 CD-729 AB; St. Jerome, *Ep.* 22, 21: PL 22, 408.

[258] Cf. Jn 19:25-27.

[259] Ac 1:14.

[260] *Catechism*, 630.

[261] Ibid., 624.

[262] Cf. Lk 1:46-55.

[263] Raymond E. Brown, *New Testament Essays* (New York: Paulist, 1965), 217-253.

[264] Cf. Jn 19:27.

[265] Cf. *Lumen Gentium* 68-69.

[266] *Kontakion* of Romanos the Melodist.

[267] Paul VI at Nazareth, January 5, 1964. Cited in the *Catechism*, par. 533.

Appendix 1

Texts Presented in
Testi Mariani del Primo Millenio, Pages 56-98

Pentateuch

Genesis
1:1-2, 26-28
2:8-10
2:15-17
2:18-25
3:1-6, 13-15
3:1-7
3:8-13
3:9-15, 20
3:14-20
3:20
3:21-24
4:1-5, 8
6:5-8, 12
6:13-22
7:6-23
8:1, 6-17
9:8-17
12:1-3
12:1-7
14:17-20
17:1-7, 15-19
22:1-2, 8b-12
22:1-2, 9-13, 15-18
28:10-17
49:8-12

Exodus
3:1-8
3:1-8a
12:1-3, 5-6
13:1-2, 11-12, 13b
13:21-22
14:19, 21-24, 26
15:20-21
16:10-15, 33-34
17:5-7
19:3-8a
19:16-19
24:12, 15-18
25:10-16
25:17-22
25:23-30
25:31-32, 36-37
26:1, 7, 15, 26-29
26:31-34
27:1-2
30:1-2, 6-8
27:9-10
30:22-32
30:34-37
31:18, 3
32:15-16
40:1-10
40:34-38

Leviticus
12:1-4, 6-8

Numbers
9:15-23
17:16-26
20:7-11
24:15-17a
24:15-19
36:6-9

Deuteronomy
26:16-19

Joshua
3:5-6, 10a, 11-13, 17

Judges
6:11-17, 36-40
11:34-39a
13:2-7, 11-14, 24

Ruth
2:1-2, 8-11; 4:13-17

Historical Books

116:12-13, 15-16bc, 17-18
117:19-20
118:14-15, 16-17, 19-21
119:1-2, 10-11, 12 and 14, 15-16
122:1-2, 3-4, 8-9
126:3

131:1, 2, 3
131:6-8, 11, 13-14
132:11, 13-14, 17-18
138:13-16
145:1-2, 4-6, 8-9
147:12-13, 14-15, 19-20

Poetic & Wisdom Books

Proverbs
8:17-21, 34-35
8:22-31
9:1-2, 5-6

Song of Songs
2:8-14
4:6-7, 9, 12-15

Canticles
1 Samuel 2:1, 4-5, 6-7, 8abcd
Judith 13:18bcde, 19
Judith 16:13, 14, 15
Song of Songs 2:10bc and 14ef;
    4:8a and 9a, 11cd and 12, 15

Sirach 14:20, 21-22, 23-25
Isaiah 12:2-3, 4bcd, 5-6
Isaiah 61:10a-d and f, 11;
    62:2-3
Jeremiah 31:10, 11-12ab, 13-14

Wisdom
7:21, 8-2

Sirach
24:1ff
24:1-4, 8-12, 18-21
24:9-12, 18-21
24:17-21
51:13-18, 20-22

Prophetic Books

Isaiah
6:1-8
7:10-14; 8:10c
7:10-17
8:1-4
9:1, 5-6
9:1-3, 5-6
11:1-2, 10
11:1-5, 10
19:1, 19-21
53:1-2
53:1-5, 7-10
56:1, 6-7
60:1-6
61:1-3, 10-11
61:9-11
66:10-14

Ezekiel
10:18-19
44:1-4
47:1-2, 8-9, 12

Daniel
2:31-35

Micah
5:1-3
5:1-4a

Habakkuk
3:3-4

Zephaniah
3:14-18a
3:14-20

Zechariah
2:14-17
4:1-7
9:9-10

Malachi
3:1-3
3:1-4

BIBLICAL TEXTS IN PATRISTICS AND LITURGY ACCOMMODATED TO MARY

Genesis 1:1-2 In the beginning when God created the heavens and the earth, 2 the earth was a formless void and darkness covered the face of the deep, while a wind from God swept over the face of the waters.

Genesis 1:26-28 Then God said, "Let us make humankind in our image, according to our likeness; and let them have dominion over the fish of the sea, and over the birds of the air, and over the cattle, and over all the wild animals of the earth, and over every creeping thing that creeps upon the earth." 27 So God created humankind in his image, in the image of God he created them; male and female he created them. 28 God blessed them, and God said to them, "Be fruitful and multiply, and fill the earth and subdue it; and have dominion over the fish of the sea and over the birds of the air and over every living thing that moves upon the earth."

Genesis 2:4-10 These are the generations of the heavens and the earth when they were created. In the day that the LORD God made the earth and the heavens, 5 when no plant of the field was yet in the earth and no herb of the field had yet sprung up — for the LORD God had not caused it to rain upon the earth, and there was no one to till the ground; 6 but a stream would rise from the earth, and water the whole face of the ground — 7 then the LORD God formed man from the dust of the ground, and breathed into his nostrils the breath of life; and the man became a living being.8 And the LORD God planted a garden in Eden, in the east; and there he put the man whom he had formed. 9 Out of the ground the LORD God made to grow every tree that is pleasant to the sight and good for food, the tree of life also in the midst of the garden, and the tree of the knowledge of good and evil. 10 A river flows out of Eden to water the garden, and from there it divides and becomes four branches.

Genesis 2:15-25 The LORD God took the man and put him in the garden of Eden to till it and keep it. 16 And the LORD God commanded the man, "You may freely eat of every tree of the garden; 17 but of the tree of the knowledge of good and evil you shall not eat, for in the day that you eat of it you shall die." 18 Then the LORD God said, "It is not good that the man should be alone; I will make him a helper as his partner." 19 So out of the ground the LORD God formed every animal of the field and every bird of the air, and brought them to the man to see what he would call them; and whatever the man called every living creature, that was its name. 20 The man gave names to all cattle, and to the birds of the air, and to every animal of the field; but for the man there was not found a helper as his partner. 21 So the LORD God caused a deep sleep to fall upon the man, and he slept; then he took one of his ribs and closed up its place with flesh. 22 And the rib that the LORD God had taken from the man he made into a woman and brought her to the man. 23 Then the man said, "This at last is bone of my bones and flesh of my flesh; this one shall be called Woman, for out of Man this one was taken." 24 Therefore a man leaves his father and his mother and clings to his wife, and they become one flesh. 25 And the man and his wife were both naked, and were not ashamed.

Genesis 3:1-24 Now the serpent was more crafty than any other wild animal that the LORD God had made. He said to the woman, "Did God say, 'You shall not eat from any tree in the garden'?" 2 The woman said to the serpent, "We may eat of the fruit of the trees in the garden; 3 but God said, 'You shall not eat of the fruit of the tree that is in the middle of the garden, nor shall you touch it, or you shall die.'" 4 But the serpent said to the woman, "You will not die; 5 for God knows that when you eat of it your eyes will be opened, and you will be like God, knowing good and evil." 6 So when the woman saw that the tree was good for food, and that it was a delight to the eyes, and that the tree was to be desired to make one wise, she took of its fruit and ate; and she also gave some to her husband, who was with her, and he ate. 7 Then the eyes of both were opened, and they knew that they were naked; and they sewed fig leaves together and made loincloths for themselves. 8 They heard the sound of the LORD God walking in the garden at the time of the evening breeze, and the man and his wife hid themselves from the presence of the LORD God among the trees of the garden. 9 But the LORD God called to the man, and said to him, "Where are you?" 10 He said, "I heard the sound of you in the garden, and I was afraid, because I was naked; and I hid myself." 11 He said, "Who told you that you were naked? Have you eaten from the tree of which I commanded you not to eat?" 12 The man said, "The woman whom you gave to be with me, she gave me fruit from the tree, and I ate." 13 Then the LORD God said to the woman, "What is this that you have done?" The woman said, "The serpent tricked me, and I ate." 14 The

LORD God said to the serpent, "Because you have done this, cursed are you among all animals and among all wild creatures; upon your belly you shall go, and dust you shall eat all the days of your life. 15 I will put enmity between you and the woman, and between your offspring and hers; he will strike your head, and you will strike his heel." 16 To the woman he said, "I will greatly increase your pangs in childbearing; in pain you shall bring forth children, yet your desire shall be for your husband, and he shall rule over you." 17 And to the man he said, "Because you have listened to the voice of your wife, and have eaten of the tree about which I commanded you, 'You shall not eat of it,' cursed is the ground because of you; in toil you shall eat of it all the days of your life; 18 thorns and thistles it shall bring forth for you; and you shall eat the plants of the field. 19 By the sweat of your face you shall eat bread until you return to the ground, for out of it you were taken; you are dust, and to dust you shall return." 20 The man named his wife Eve, because she was the mother of all living. 21 And the LORD God made garments of skins for the man and for his wife, and clothed them. 22 Then the LORD God said, "See, the man has become like one of us, knowing good and evil; and now, he might reach out his hand and take also from the tree of life, and eat, and live forever" — 23 therefore the LORD God sent him forth from the garden of Eden, to till the ground from which he was taken. 24 He drove out the man; and at the east of the garden of Eden he placed the cherubim, and a sword flaming and turning to guard the way to the tree of life.

Genesis 4:1-5 Now the man knew his wife Eve, and she conceived and bore Cain, saying, "I have produced a man with the help of the LORD." 2 Next she bore his brother Abel. Now Abel was a keeper of sheep, and Cain a tiller of the ground. 3 In the course of time Cain brought to the LORD an offering of the fruit of the ground, 4 and Abel for his part brought of the firstlings of his flock, their fat portions. And the LORD had regard for Abel and his offering, 5 but for Cain and his offering he had no regard. So Cain was very angry, and his countenance fell.

Genesis 4:8 Cain said to his brother Abel, "Let us go out to the field." And when they were in the field, Cain rose up against his brother Abel, and killed him.

Genesis 6:5-8 The LORD saw that the wickedness of humankind was great in the earth, and that every inclination of the thoughts of their hearts was only evil continually. 6 And the LORD was sorry that he had made humankind on the earth, and it grieved him to his heart. 7 So the LORD said, "I will blot out from the earth the human beings I have created — people together with animals and creeping things and birds of the air, for I am sorry that I have made them." 8 But Noah found favor in the sight of the LORD.

Genesis 6:12-22 And God saw that the earth was corrupt; for all flesh had corrupted its ways upon the earth 13 And God said to Noah, "I have determined to make an end of all flesh, for the earth is filled with violence because of them; now I am going to destroy them along with the earth. 14 Make yourself an ark of cypress wood; make rooms in the ark, and cover it inside and out with pitch. 15 This is how you are to make it: the length of the ark three hundred cubits, its width fifty cubits, and its height thirty cubits. 16 Make a roof for the ark, and finish it to a cubit above; and put the door of the ark in its side; make it with lower, second, and third decks. 17 For my part, I am going to bring a flood of waters on the earth, to destroy from under heaven all flesh in which is the breath of life; everything that is on the earth shall die. 18 But I will establish my covenant with you; and you shall come into the ark, you, your sons, your wife, and your sons' wives with you. 19 And of every living thing, of all flesh, you shall bring two of every kind into the ark, to keep them alive with you; they shall be male and female. 20 Of the birds according to their kinds, and of the animals according to their kinds, of every creeping thing of the ground according to its kind, two of every kind shall come in to you, to keep them alive. 21 Also take with you every kind of food that is eaten, and store it up; and it shall serve as food for you and for them." 22 Noah did this; he did all that God commanded him.

Genesis 7:6-23 Noah was six hundred years old when the flood of waters came on the earth. 7 And Noah with his sons and his wife and his sons' wives went into the ark to escape the waters of the flood. 8 Of clean animals, and of animals that are not clean, and of birds, and of everything that creeps on the ground, 9 two and two, male and female, went into the ark with Noah, as God had commanded Noah. 10 And after seven days the waters of the flood came on the earth. 11 In the six hundredth year of Noah's life, in the second month, on the seventeenth day of the month, on that day all the fountains of the great deep burst forth, and the windows of the heavens were opened. 12 The rain fell on the earth forty days and forty nights. 13 On the very same day Noah with his sons, Shem and Ham and Japheth, and Noah's wife and the three wives of his sons entered the ark, 14 they and every wild animal of every kind, and all domestic animals of every kind, and every creeping thing that creeps on the earth, and every bird of every kind — every bird, every winged creature. 15 They went into the ark with Noah, two and two of all flesh in which there was the breath of life. 16 And those that entered, male and female of all flesh, went in as God had commanded him; and the LORD shut him in. 17 The flood continued forty days on the earth; and the waters increased, and bore up the ark, and it rose high above the earth. 18 The waters swelled and increased greatly on the earth; and the ark floated on the face of the waters. 19 The waters swelled so mightily on the earth that all the high mountains under the whole heaven were covered; 20

the waters swelled above the mountains, covering them fifteen cubits deep.
21 And all flesh died that moved on the earth, birds, domestic animals, wild
animals, all swarming creatures that swarm on the earth, and all human
beings; 22 everything on dry land in whose nostrils was the breath of life
died. 23 He blotted out every living thing that was on the face of the ground,
human beings and animals and creeping things and birds of the air; they were
blotted out from the earth. Only Noah was left, and those that were with him
in the ark.

Genesis 8:1 But God remembered Noah and all the wild animals and all the
domestic animals that were with him in the ark. And God made a wind blow
over the earth, and the waters subsided.

Genesis 8:6-17 At the end of forty days Noah opened the window of the
ark that he had made 7 and sent out the raven; and it went to and fro until
the waters were dried up from the earth. 8 Then he sent out the dove from
him, to see if the waters had subsided from the face of the ground; 9 but the
dove found no place to set its foot, and it returned to him to the ark, for the
waters were still on the face of the whole earth. So he put out his hand and
took it and brought it into the ark with him. 10 He waited another seven
days, and again he sent out the dove from the ark; 11 and the dove came back
to him in the evening, and there in its beak was a freshly plucked olive leaf;
so Noah knew that the waters had subsided from the earth. 12 Then he
waited another seven days, and sent out the dove; and it did not return to him
any more. 13 In the six hundred first year, in the first month, the first day of
the month, the waters were dried up from the earth; and Noah removed the
covering of the ark, and looked, and saw that the face of the ground was
drying. 14 In the second month, on the twenty-seventh day of the month,
the earth was dry. 15 Then God said to Noah, 16 "Go out of the ark, you and
your wife, and your sons and your sons' wives with you. 17 Bring out with
you every living thing that is with you of all flesh — birds and animals and
every creeping thing that creeps on the earth — so that they may abound
on the earth, and be fruitful and multiply on the earth."

Genesis 9:8-17 Then God said to Noah and to his sons with him, 9 "As for
me, I am establishing my covenant with you and your descendants after you,
10 and with every living creature that is with you, the birds, the domestic
animals, and every animal of the earth with you, as many as came out of the
ark. 11 I establish my covenant with you, that never again shall all flesh be
cut off by the waters of a flood, and never again shall there be a flood to
destroy the earth." 12 God said, "This is the sign of the covenant that I make
between me and you and every living creature that is with you, for all future
generations: 13 I have set my bow in the clouds, and it shall be a sign of the
covenant between me and the earth. 14 When I bring clouds over the earth

and the bow is seen in the clouds, 15 I will remember my covenant that is between me and you and every living creature of all flesh; and the waters shall never again become a flood to destroy all flesh. 16 When the bow is in the clouds, I will see it and remember the everlasting covenant between God and every living creature of all flesh that is on the earth." 17 God said to Noah, "This is the sign of the covenant that I have established between me and all flesh that is on the earth."

Genesis 12:1-7 Now the LORD said to Abram, "Go from your country and your kindred and your father's house to the land that I will show you. 2 I will make of you a great nation, and I will bless you, and make your name great, so that you will be a blessing. 3 I will bless those who bless you, and the one who curses you I will curse; and in you all the families of the earth shall be blessed." 4 So Abram went, as the LORD had told him; and Lot went with him. Abram was seventy-five years old when he departed from Haran. 5 Abram took his wife Sarai and his brother's son Lot, and all the possessions that they had gathered, and the persons whom they had acquired in Haran; and they set forth to go to the land of Canaan. When they had come to the land of Canaan, 6 Abram passed through the land to the place at Shechem, to the oak of Moreh. At that time the Canaanites were in the land. 7 Then the LORD appeared to Abram, and said, "To your offspring I will give this land." So he built there an altar to the LORD, who had appeared to him.

Genesis 14:17-20 After his return from the defeat of Chedorlaomer and the kings who were with him, the king of Sodom went out to meet him at the Valley of Shaveh (that is, the King's Valley). 18 And King Melchizedek of Salem brought out bread and wine; he was priest of God Most High. 19 He blessed him and said, "Blessed be Abram by God Most High, maker of heaven and earth; 20 and blessed be God Most High, who has delivered your enemies into your hand!" And Abram gave him one tenth of everything.

Genesis 17:1-7 When Abram was ninety-nine years old, the LORD appeared to Abram, and said to him, "I am God Almighty; walk before me, and be blameless. 2 And I will make my covenant between me and you, and will make you exceedingly numerous." 3 Then Abram fell on his face; and God said to him, 4 "As for me, this is my covenant with you: You shall be the ancestor of a multitude of nations. 5 No longer shall your name be Abram, but your name shall be Abraham; for I have made you the ancestor of a multitude of nations. 6 I will make you exceedingly fruitful; and I will make nations of you, and kings shall come from you. 7 I will establish my covenant between me and you, and your offspring after you throughout their generations, for an everlasting covenant, to be God to you and to your offspring after you.

Genesis 17:15-19 God said to Abraham, "As for Sarai your wife, you shall not call her Sarai, but Sarah shall be her name. 16 I will bless her, and moreover I will give you a son by her. I will bless her, and she shall give rise to nations; kings of peoples shall come from her." 17 Then Abraham fell on his face and laughed, and said to himself, "Can a child be born to a man who is a hundred years old? Can Sarah, who is ninety years old, bear a child?" 18 And Abraham said to God, "O that Ishmael might live in your sight!" 19 God said, "No, but your wife Sarah shall bear you a son, and you shall name him Isaac. I will establish my covenant with him as an everlasting covenant for his offspring after him.

Genesis 22:1-2 After these things God tested Abraham. He said to him, "Abraham!" And he said, "Here I am." 2 He said, "Take your son, your only son Isaac, whom you love, and go to the land of Moriah, and offer him there as a burnt offering on one of the mountains that I shall show you."

Genesis 22:8-13 Abraham said, "God himself will provide the lamb for a burnt offering, my son." So the two of them walked on together. 9 When they came to the place that God had shown him, Abraham built an altar there and laid the wood in order. He bound his son Isaac, and laid him on the altar, on top of the wood. 10 Then Abraham reached out his hand and took the knife to kill his son. 11 But the angel of the LORD called to him from heaven, and said, "Abraham, Abraham!" And he said, "Here I am." 12 He said, "Do not lay your hand on the boy or do anything to him; for now I know that you fear God, since you have not withheld your son, your only son, from me." 13 And Abraham looked up and saw a ram, caught in a thicket by its horns. Abraham went and took the ram and offered it up as a burnt offering instead of his son.

Genesis 22:15-18 The angel of the LORD called to Abraham a second time from heaven, 16 and said, "By myself I have sworn, says the LORD: Because you have done this, and have not withheld your son, your only son, 17 I will indeed bless you, and I will make your offspring as numerous as the stars of heaven and as the sand that is on the seashore. And your offspring shall possess the gate of their enemies, 18 and by your offspring shall all the nations of the earth gain blessing for themselves, because you have obeyed my voice."

Genesis 28:10-17 Jacob left Beer-sheba and went toward Haran. 11 He came to a certain place and stayed there for the night, because the sun had set. Taking one of the stones of the place, he put it under his head and lay down in that place. 12 And he dreamed that there was a ladder set up on the earth, the top of it reaching to heaven; and the angels of God were ascending and descending on it. 13 And the LORD stood beside him and said, "I am the LORD, the God of Abraham your father and the God of Isaac; the land on which you lie I will give to you and to your offspring; 14 and your offspring shall be like the dust of the earth, and you shall spread abroad to the west and to the east and to the north and to the south; and all the families of the earth shall be blessed in you and in your offspring. 15 Know that I am with you and will keep you wherever you go, and will bring you back to this land; for I will not leave you until I have done what I have promised you." 16 Then Jacob woke from his sleep and said, "Surely the LORD is in this place — and I did not know it!" 17 And he was afraid, and said, "How awesome is this place! This is none other than the house of God, and this is the gate of heaven."

Genesis 49:8-12 Judah, your brothers shall praise you; your hand shall be on the neck of your enemies; your father's sons shall bow down before you. 9 Judah is a lion's whelp; from the prey, my son, you have gone up. He crouches down, he stretches out like a lion, like a lioness — who dares rouse him up? 10 The scepter shall not depart from Judah, nor the ruler's staff from between his feet, until tribute comes to him; and the obedience of the peoples is his. 11 Binding his foal to the vine and his donkey's colt to the choice vine, he washes his garments in wine and his robe in the blood of grapes; 12 his eyes are darker than wine, and his teeth whiter than milk.

Exodus 3:1-8 Moses was keeping the flock of his father-in-law Jethro, the priest of Midian; he led his flock beyond the wilderness, and came to Horeb, the mountain of God. 2 There the angel of the LORD appeared to him in a flame of fire out of a bush; he looked, and the bush was blazing, yet it was not consumed. 3 Then Moses said, "I must turn aside and look at this great sight, and see why the bush is not burned up." 4 When the LORD saw that he had turned aside to see, God called to him out of the bush, "Moses, Moses!" And he said, "Here I am." 5 Then he said, "Come no closer! Remove the sandals from your feet, for the place on which you are standing is holy ground." 6 He said further, "I am the God of your father, the God of Abraham, the God of Isaac, and the God of Jacob." And Moses hid his face, for he was afraid to look at God. 7 Then the LORD said, "I have observed the misery of my people who are in Egypt; I have heard their cry on account of their taskmasters. Indeed, I know their sufferings, 8 and I have come down to deliver them from the Egyptians, and to bring them up out of that land to a good and broad land, a land flowing with milk and honey, to the country of the Canaanites, the Hittites, the Amorites, the Perizzites, the Hivites, and the Jebusites.

Exodus 12:1-3 The LORD said to Moses and Aaron in the land of Egypt: 2 This month shall mark for you the beginning of months; it shall be the first month of the year for you. 3 Tell the whole congregation of Israel that on the tenth of this month they are to take a lamb for each family, a lamb for each household.

Exodus 12:5-6 Your lamb shall be without blemish, a year-old male; you may take it from the sheep or from the goats. 6 You shall keep it until the fourteenth day of this month; then the whole assembled congregation of Israel shall slaughter it at twilight.

Exodus 13:1-2 The LORD said to Moses: 2 Consecrate to me all the firstborn; whatever is the first to open the womb among the Israelites, of human beings and animals, is mine.

Exodus 13:11-13 "When the LORD has brought you into the land of the Canaanites, as he swore to you and your ancestors, and has given it to you, 12 you shall set apart to the LORD all that first opens the womb. All the firstborn of your livestock that are males shall be the Lord's. 13 But every firstborn donkey you shall redeem with a sheep; if you do not redeem it, you must break its neck. Every firstborn male among your children you shall redeem.

Exodus 14:19 The angel of God who was going before the Israelite army moved and went behind them; and the pillar of cloud moved from in front of them and took its place behind them.

Exodus 14:21-24 Then Moses stretched out his hand over the sea. The LORD drove the sea back by a strong east wind all night, and turned the sea into dry land; and the waters were divided. 22 The Israelites went into the sea on dry ground, the waters forming a wall for them on their right and on their left. 23 The Egyptians pursued, and went into the sea after them, all of Pharaoh's horses, chariots, and chariot drivers. 24 At the morning watch the LORD in the pillar of fire and cloud looked down upon the Egyptian army, and threw the Egyptian army into panic.

Exodus 14:26 Then the LORD said to Moses, "Stretch out your hand over the sea, so that the water may come back upon the Egyptians, upon their chariots and chariot drivers."

Exodus 15:20-21 Then the prophet Miriam, Aaron's sister, took a tambourine in her hand; and all the women went out after her with tambourines and with dancing. 21 And Miriam sang to them: "Sing to the LORD, for he has triumphed gloriously; horse and rider he has thrown into the sea."

Exodus 16:10-15 And as Aaron spoke to the whole congregation of the Israelites, they looked toward the wilderness, and the glory of the LORD appeared in the cloud. 11 The LORD spoke to Moses and said, 12 "I have heard the complaining of the Israelites; say to them, 'At twilight you shall eat meat, and in the morning you shall have your fill of bread; then you shall know that I am the LORD your God.'" 13 In the evening quails came up and covered the camp; and in the morning there was a layer of dew around the camp. 14 When the layer of dew lifted, there on the surface of the wilderness was a fine flaky substance, as fine as frost on the ground. 15 When the Israelites saw it, they said to one another, "What is it?" For they did not know what it was. Moses said to them, "It is the bread that the LORD has given you to eat.

Exodus 16:33-34 And Moses said to Aaron, "Take a jar, and put an omer of manna in it, and place it before the LORD, to be kept throughout your generations." 34 As the LORD commanded Moses, so Aaron placed it before the covenant, for safekeeping.

Exodus 17:5-7 The LORD said to Moses, "Go on ahead of the people, and take some of the elders of Israel with you; take in your hand the staff with which you struck the Nile, and go. 6 I will be standing there in front of you on the rock at Horeb. Strike the rock, and water will come out of it, so that the people may drink." Moses did so, in the sight of the elders of Israel. 7 He called the place Massah and Meribah, because the Israelites quarreled and tested the LORD, saying, "Is the LORD among us or not?"

Exodus 19:3-8 Then Moses went up to God; the LORD called to him from the mountain, saying, "Thus you shall say to the house of Jacob, and tell the Israelites: 4 You have seen what I did to the Egyptians, and how I bore you on eagles' wings and brought you to myself. 5 Now therefore, if you obey my voice and keep my covenant, you shall be my treasured possession out of all the peoples. Indeed, the whole earth is mine, 6 but you shall be for me a priestly kingdom and a holy nation. These are the words that you shall speak to the Israelites." 7 So Moses came, summoned the elders of the people, and set before them all these words that the LORD had commanded him. 8 The people all answered as one: "Everything that the LORD has spoken we will do." Moses reported the words of the people to the LORD.

Exodus 19:16-19 On the morning of the third day there was thunder and lightning, as well as a thick cloud on the mountain, and a blast of a trumpet so loud that all the people who were in the camp trembled. 17 Moses brought the people out of the camp to meet God. They took their stand at the foot of the mountain. 18 Now Mount Sinai was wrapped in smoke, because the LORD had descended upon it in fire; the smoke went up like the smoke of a kiln, while the whole mountain shook violently. 19 As the blast of the trumpet grew louder and louder, Moses would speak and God would answer him in thunder.

Exodus 24:12 The LORD said to Moses, "Come up to me on the mountain, and wait there; and I will give you the tablets of stone, with the law and the commandment, which I have written for their instruction."

Exodus 24:15-18 Then Moses went up on the mountain, and the cloud covered the mountain. 16 The glory of the LORD settled on Mount Sinai, and the cloud covered it for six days; on the seventh day he called to Moses out of the cloud. 17 Now the appearance of the glory of the LORD was like a devouring fire on the top of the mountain in the sight of the people of Israel. 18 Moses entered the cloud, and went up on the mountain. Moses was on the mountain for forty days and forty nights.

Exodus 25:10-32 They shall make an ark of acacia wood; it shall be two and a half cubits long, a cubit and a half wide, and a cubit and a half high. 11 You shall overlay it with pure gold, inside and outside you shall overlay it, and you shall make a molding of gold upon it all around. 12 You shall cast four rings of gold for it and put them on its four feet, two rings on the one side of it, and two rings on the other side. 13 You shall make poles of acacia wood, and overlay them with gold. 14 And you shall put the poles into the rings on the sides of the ark, by which to carry the ark. 15 The poles shall remain in the rings of the ark; they shall not be taken from it. 16 You shall put into the ark the covenant that I shall give you. 17 Then you shall make a mercy seat of pure gold; two cubits and a half shall be its length, and a cubit and a half its width. 18 You shall make two cherubim of gold; you shall make them of hammered work, at the two ends of the mercy seat. 19 Make one cherub at the one end, and one cherub at the other; of one piece with the mercy seat you shall make the cherubim at its two ends. 20 The cherubim shall spread out their wings above, overshadowing the mercy seat with their wings. They shall face one to another; the faces of the cherubim shall be turned toward the mercy seat. 21 You shall put the mercy seat on the top of the ark; and in the ark you shall put the covenant that I shall give you. 22 There I will meet with you, and from above the mercy seat, from between the two cherubim that are on the ark of the covenant, I will deliver to you all my commands for the Israelites. 23 You shall make a table of acacia wood, two cubits long, one cubit wide, and a cubit and a half high. 24 You shall overlay it with pure gold, and make a molding of gold around it. 25 You shall make around it a rim a hand-breadth wide, and a molding of gold around the rim. 26 You shall make for it four rings of gold, and fasten the rings to the four corners at its four legs. 27 The rings that hold the poles used for carrying the table shall be close to the rim. 28 You shall make the poles of acacia wood, and overlay them with gold, and the table shall be carried with these. 29 You shall make its plates and dishes for incense, and its flagons and bowls with which to pour drink offerings; you shall make them of pure gold. 30 And you shall set the bread of the Presence on the table before me always. 31 You shall make a lampstand of pure gold. The base and the shaft of the lampstand shall be made of hammered work; its cups, its calyxes, and its petals shall be of one piece with it; 32 and there shall be six branches going out of its sides, three branches of the lampstand out of one side of it and three branches of the lampstand out of the other side of it.

Exodus 25:36-37 Their calyxes and their branches shall be of one piece with it, the whole of it one hammered piece of pure gold. 37 You shall make the seven lamps for it; and the lamps shall be set up so as to give light on the space in front of it.

Exodus 26:1 Moreover you shall make the tabernacle with ten curtains of fine twisted linen, and blue, purple, and crimson yarns; you shall make them with cherubim skillfully worked into them.

Exodus 26:7 You shall also make curtains of goats' hair for a tent over the tabernacle; you shall make eleven curtains.

Exodus 26:15 You shall make upright frames of acacia wood for the tabernacle.

Exodus 26:26-29 You shall make bars of acacia wood, five for the frames of the one side of the tabernacle, 27 and five bars for the frames of the other side of the tabernacle, and five bars for the frames of the side of the tabernacle at the rear westward. 28 The middle bar, halfway up the frames, shall pass through from end to end. 29 You shall overlay the frames with gold, and shall make their rings of gold to hold the bars; and you shall overlay the bars with gold.

Exodus 26:31-34 You shall make a curtain of blue, purple, and crimson yarns, and of fine twisted linen; it shall be made with cherubim skillfully worked into it. 32 You shall hang it on four pillars of acacia overlaid with gold, which have hooks of gold and rest on four bases of silver. 33 You shall hang the curtain under the clasps, and bring the ark of the covenant in there, within the curtain; and the curtain shall separate for you the holy place from the most holy. 34 You shall put the mercy seat on the ark of the covenant in the most holy place.

Exodus 27:1-2 You shall make the altar of acacia wood, five cubits long and five cubits wide; the altar shall be square, and it shall be three cubits high. 2 You shall make horns for it on its four corners; its horns shall be of one piece with it, and you shall overlay it with bronze.

Exodus 27:9-10 You shall make the court of the tabernacle. On the south side the court shall have hangings of fine twisted linen one hundred cubits long for that side; 10 its twenty pillars and their twenty bases shall be of bronze, but the hooks of the pillars and their bands shall be of silver.

Exodus 30:1-2 You shall make an altar on which to offer incense; you shall make it of acacia wood. 2 It shall be one cubit long, and one cubit wide; it shall be square, and shall be two cubits high; its horns shall be of one piece with it.

Exodus 30:6-8 You shall place it in front of the curtain that is above the ark of the covenant, in front of the mercy seat that is over the covenant, where I will meet with you. 7 Aaron shall offer fragrant incense on it; every morning when he dresses the lamps he shall offer it, 8 and when Aaron sets up the lamps in the evening, he shall offer it, a regular incense offering before the LORD throughout your generations.

Exodus 30:22-32 The LORD spoke to Moses: 23 Take the finest spices: of liquid myrrh five hundred shekels, and of sweet-smelling cinnamon half as much, that is, two hundred fifty, and two hundred fifty of aromatic cane, 24 and five hundred of cassia — measured by the sanctuary shekel — and a hin of olive oil; 25 and you shall make of these a sacred anointing oil blended as by the perfumer; it shall be a holy anointing oil. 26 With it you shall anoint the tent of meeting and the ark of the covenant, 27 and the table and all its utensils, and the lampstand and its utensils, and the altar of incense, 28 and the altar of burnt offering with all its utensils, and the basin with its stand; 29 you shall consecrate them, so that they may be most holy; whatever touches them will become holy. 30 You shall anoint Aaron and his sons, and consecrate them, in order that they may serve me as priests. 31 You shall say to the Israelites, "This shall be my holy anointing oil throughout your generations. 32 It shall not be used in any ordinary anointing of the body, and you shall make no other like it in composition; it is holy, and it shall be holy to you.

Exodus 30:34-37 The LORD said to Moses: Take sweet spices, stacte, and onycha, and galbanum, sweet spices with pure frankincense (an equal part of each), 35 and make an incense blended as by the perfumer, seasoned with salt, pure and holy; 36 and you shall beat some of it into powder, and put part of it before the covenant in the tent of meeting where I shall meet with you; it shall be for you most holy. 37 When you make incense according to this composition, you shall not make it for yourselves; it shall be regarded by you as holy to the LORD.

Exodus 31:3 and I have filled him with divine spirit, with ability, intelligence, and knowledge in every kind of craft.

Exodus 31:18 When God finished speaking with Moses on Mount Sinai, he gave him the two tablets of the covenant, tablets of stone, written with the finger of God.

Exodus 32:15-16 Then Moses turned and went down from the mountain, carrying the two tablets of the covenant in his hands, tablets that were written on both sides, written on the front and on the back. 16 The tablets were the work of God, and the writing was the writing of God, engraved upon the tablets.

Exodus 40:1-10 The LORD spoke to Moses: 2 On the first day of the first month you shall set up the tabernacle of the tent of meeting. 3 You shall put in it the ark of the covenant, and you shall screen the ark with the curtain. 4 You shall bring in the table, and arrange its setting; and you shall bring in the lampstand, and set up its lamps. 5 You shall put the golden altar for incense before the ark of the covenant, and set up the screen for the entrance of the tabernacle. 6 You shall set the altar of burnt offering before the entrance of the tabernacle of the tent of meeting, 7 and place the basin between the tent of meeting and the altar, and put water in it. 8 You shall set up the court all around, and hang up the screen for the gate of the court. 9 Then you shall take the anointing oil, and anoint the tabernacle and all that is in it, and consecrate it and all its furniture, so that it shall become holy. 10 You shall also anoint the altar of burnt offering and all its utensils, and consecrate the altar, so that the altar shall be most holy.

Exodus 40:34-38 Then the cloud covered the tent of meeting, and the glory of the LORD filled the tabernacle. 35 Moses was not able to enter the tent of meeting because the cloud settled upon it, and the glory of the LORD filled the tabernacle. 36 Whenever the cloud was taken up from the tabernacle, the Israelites would set out on each stage of their journey; 37 but if the cloud was not taken up, then they did not set out until the day that it was taken up. 38 For the cloud of the LORD was on the tabernacle by day, and fire was in the cloud by night, before the eyes of all the house of Israel at each stage of their journey.

Leviticus 12:1-4 The LORD spoke to Moses, saying: 2 Speak to the people of Israel, saying: If a woman conceives and bears a male child, she shall be ceremonially unclean seven days; as at the time of her menstruation, she shall be unclean. 3 On the eighth day the flesh of his foreskin shall be circumcised. 4 Her time of blood purification shall be thirty-three days; she shall not touch any holy thing, or come into the sanctuary, until the days of her purification are completed.

Leviticus 12:6-8 When the days of her purification are completed, whether for a son or for a daughter, she shall bring to the priest at the entrance of the tent of meeting a lamb in its first year for a burnt offering, and a pigeon or a turtledove for a sin offering. 7 He shall offer it before the LORD, and make atonement on her behalf; then she shall be clean from her flow of blood. This is the law for her who bears a child, male or female. 8 If she cannot afford a sheep, she shall take two turtledoves or two pigeons, one for a burnt offering and the other for a sin offering; and the priest shall make atonement on her behalf, and she shall be clean.

Numbers 9:15-23 On the day the tabernacle was set up, the cloud covered the tabernacle, the tent of the covenant; and from evening until morning it was over the tabernacle, having the appearance of fire. 16 It was always so: the cloud covered it by day and the appearance of fire by night. 17 Whenever the cloud lifted from over the tent, then the Israelites would set out; and in the place where the cloud settled down, there the Israelites would camp. 18 At the command of the LORD the Israelites would set out, and at the command of the LORD they would camp. As long as the cloud rested over the tabernacle, they would remain in camp. 19 Even when the cloud continued over the tabernacle many days, the Israelites would keep the charge of the LORD, and would not set out. 20 Sometimes the cloud would remain a few days over the tabernacle, and according to the command of the LORD they would remain in camp; then according to the command of the LORD they would set out. 21 Sometimes the cloud would remain from evening until morning; and when the cloud lifted in the morning, they would set out, or if it continued for a day and a night, when the cloud lifted they would set out. 22 Whether it was two days, or a month, or a longer time, that the cloud continued over the tabernacle, resting upon it, the Israelites would remain in camp and would not set out; but when it lifted they would set out. 23 At the command of the LORD they would camp, and at the command of the LORD they would set out. They kept the charge of the LORD, at the command of the LORD by Moses.

Numbers 17 The LORD spoke to Moses, saying: 2 Speak to the Israelites, and get twelve staffs from them, one for each ancestral house, from all the leaders of their ancestral houses. Write each man's name on his staff, 3 and write Aaron's name on the staff of Levi. For there shall be one staff for the head of each ancestral house. 4 Place them in the tent of meeting before the covenant, where I meet with you. 5 And the staff of the man whom I choose shall sprout; thus I will put a stop to the complaints of the Israelites that they continually make against you. 6 Moses spoke to the Israelites; and all their leaders gave him staffs, one for each leader, according to their ancestral houses, twelve staffs; and the staff of Aaron was among theirs. 7 So Moses placed the staffs before the LORD in the tent of the covenant. 8 When Moses went into the tent of the covenant on the next day, the staff of Aaron for the house of Levi had sprouted. It put forth buds, produced blossoms, and bore ripe almonds. 9 Then Moses brought out all the staffs from before the LORD to all the Israelites; and they looked, and each man took his staff. 10 And the LORD said to Moses, "Put back the staff of Aaron before the covenant, to be kept as a warning to rebels, so that you may make an end of their complaints against me, or else they will die." 11 Moses did so; just as the LORD commanded him, so he did. 12 The Israelites said to Moses, "We are perishing; we are lost, all of us are lost! 13 Everyone who approaches the tabernacle of the LORD will die. Are we all to perish?"

Numbers 24:15-19 So he uttered his oracle, saying: "The oracle of Balaam son of Beor, the oracle of the man whose eye is clear, 16 the oracle of one who hears the words of God, and knows the knowledge of the Most High, who sees the vision of the Almighty, who falls down, but with his eyes uncovered: 17 I see him, but not now; I behold him, but not near — a star shall come out of Jacob, and a scepter shall rise out of Israel; it shall crush the borderlands of Moab, and the territory of all the Shethites. 18 Edom will become a possession, Seir a possession of its enemies, while Israel does valiantly. 19 One out of Jacob shall rule, and destroy the survivors of Ir."

Numbers 36:6-9 This is what the LORD commands concerning the daughters of Zelophehad, 'Let them marry whom they think best; only it must be into a clan of their father's tribe that they are married, 7 so that no inheritance of the Israelites shall be transferred from one tribe to another; for all Israelites shall retain the inheritance of their ancestral tribes. 8 Every daughter who possesses an inheritance in any tribe of the Israelites shall marry one from the clan of her father's tribe, so that all Israelites may continue to possess their ancestral inheritance. 9 No inheritance shall be transferred from one tribe to another; for each of the tribes of the Israelites shall retain its own inheritance.'"

Deuteronomy 26:16-19 This very day the LORD your God is commanding you to observe these statutes and ordinances; so observe them diligently with all your heart and with all your soul. 17 Today you have obtained the Lord's agreement: to be your God; and for you to walk in his ways, to keep his statutes, his commandments, and his ordinances, and to obey him. 18 Today the LORD has obtained your agreement: to be his treasured people, as he promised you, and to keep his commandments; 19 for him to set you high above all nations that he has made, in praise and in fame and in honor; and for you to be a people holy to the LORD your God, as he promised.

Joshua 3:5-6 Then Joshua said to the people, "Sanctify yourselves; for tomorrow the LORD will do wonders among you." 6 To the priests Joshua said, "Take up the ark of the covenant, and pass on in front of the people." So they took up the ark of the covenant and went in front of the people.

Joshua 3:10-13 Joshua said, "By this you shall know that among you is the living God who without fail will drive out from before you the Canaanites, Hittites, Hivites, Perizzites, Girgashites, Amorites, and Jebusites: 11 the ark of the covenant of the Lord of all the earth is going to pass before you into the Jordan. 12 So now select twelve men from the tribes of Israel, one from each tribe. 13 When the soles of the feet of the priests who bear the ark of the LORD, the Lord of all the earth, rest in the waters of the Jordan, the waters of the Jordan flowing from above shall be cut off; they shall stand in a single heap."

Joshua 3:17 While all Israel were crossing over on dry ground, the priests who bore the ark of the covenant of the LORD stood on dry ground in the middle of the Jordan, until the entire nation finished crossing over the Jordan.

Judges 6:11-17 Now the angel of the LORD came and sat under the oak at Ophrah, which belonged to Joash the Abiezrite, as his son Gideon was beating out wheat in the wine press, to hide it from the Midianites. 12 The angel of the LORD appeared to him and said to him, "The LORD is with you, you mighty warrior." 13 Gideon answered him, "But sir, if the LORD is with us, why then has all this happened to us? And where are all his wonderful deeds that our ancestors recounted to us, saying, 'Did not the LORD bring us up from Egypt?' But now the LORD has cast us off, and given us into the hand of Midian." 14 Then the LORD turned to him and said, "Go in this might of yours and deliver Israel from the hand of Midian; I hereby commission you." 15 He responded, "But sir, how can I deliver Israel? My clan is the weakest in Manasseh, and I am the least in my family." 16 The LORD said to him, "But I will be with you, and you shall strike down the Midianites, every one of them." 17 Then he said to him, "If now I have found favor with you, then show me a sign that it is you who speak with me.

Judges 6:36-40 Then Gideon said to God, "In order to see whether you will deliver Israel by my hand, as you have said, 37 I am going to lay a fleece of wool on the threshing floor; if there is dew on the fleece alone, and it is dry on all the ground, then I shall know that you will deliver Israel by my hand, as you have said." 38 And it was so. When he rose early next morning and squeezed the fleece, he wrung enough dew from the fleece to fill a bowl with water. 39 Then Gideon said to God, "Do not let your anger burn against me, let me speak one more time; let me, please, make trial with the fleece just once more; let it be dry only on the fleece, and on all the ground let there be dew." 40 And God did so that night. It was dry on the fleece only, and on all the ground there was dew.

Judges 11:34-39 Then Jephthah came to his home at Mizpah; and there was his daughter coming out to meet him with timbrels and with dancing. She was his only child; he had no son or daughter except her. 35 When he saw her, he tore his clothes, and said, "Alas, my daughter! You have brought me very low; you have become the cause of great trouble to me. For I have opened my mouth to the LORD, and I cannot take back my vow." 36 She said to him, "My father, if you have opened your mouth to the LORD, do to me according to what has gone out of your mouth, now that the LORD has given you vengeance against your enemies, the Ammonites." 37 And she said to her father, "Let this thing be done for me: Grant me two months, so that I may go and wander on the mountains, and bewail my virginity, my companions and I." 38 "Go," he said and sent her away for two months. So she departed, she and her companions, and bewailed her virginity on the mountains. 39 At the end of two months, she returned to her father, who did with her according to the vow he had made. She had never slept with a man. So there arose an Israelite custom that. . . .

Judges 13:2-7 There was a certain man of Zorah, of the tribe of the Danites, whose name was Manoah. His wife was barren, having borne no children. 3 And the angel of the LORD appeared to the woman and said to her, "Although you are barren, having borne no children, you shall conceive and bear a son. 4 Now be careful not to drink wine or strong drink, or to eat anything unclean, 5 for you shall conceive and bear a son. No razor is to come on his head, for the boy shall be a nazirite to God from birth. It is he who shall begin to deliver Israel from the hand of the Philistines." 6 Then the woman came and told her husband, "A man of God came to me, and his appearance was like that of an angel of God, most awe-inspiring; I did not ask him where he came from, and he did not tell me his name; 7 but he said to me, 'You shall conceive and bear a son. So then drink no wine or strong drink, and eat nothing unclean, for the boy shall be a nazirite to God from birth to the day of his death.'"

Judges 13:11-14 Manoah got up and followed his wife, and came to the man and said to him, "Are you the man who spoke to this woman?" And he said, "I am." 12 Then Manoah said, "Now when your words come true, what is to be the boy's rule of life; what is he to do?" 13 The angel of the LORD said to Manoah, "Let the woman give heed to all that I said to her. 14 She may not eat of anything that comes from the vine. She is not to drink wine or strong drink, or eat any unclean thing. She is to observe everything that I commanded her."

Judges 13:24 The woman bore a son, and named him Samson. The boy grew, and the LORD blessed him.

Ruth 2:1-2 Now Naomi had a kinsman on her husband's side, a prominent rich man, of the family of Elimelech, whose name was Boaz. 2 And Ruth the Moabite said to Naomi, "Let me go to the field and glean among the ears of grain, behind someone in whose sight I may find favor." She said to her, "Go, my daughter."

Ruth 2:8-11 Then Boaz said to Ruth, "Now listen, my daughter, do not go to glean in another field or leave this one, but keep close to my young women. 9 Keep your eyes on the field that is being reaped, and follow behind them. I have ordered the young men not to bother you. If you get thirsty, go to the vessels and drink from what the young men have drawn." 10 Then she fell prostrate, with her face to the ground, and said to him, "Why have I found favor in your sight, that you should take notice of me, when I am a foreigner?" 11 But Boaz answered her, "All that you have done for your mother-in-law since the death of your husband has been fully told me, and how you left your father and mother and your native land and came to a people that you did not know before.

Ruth 4:13-17 So Boaz took Ruth and she became his wife. When they came together, the LORD made her conceive, and she bore a son. 14 Then the women said to Naomi, "Blessed be the LORD, who has not left you this day without next-of-kin; and may his name be renowned in Israel! 15 He shall be to you a restorer of life and a nourisher of your old age; for your daughter-in-law who loves you, who is more to you than seven sons, has borne him." 16 Then Naomi took the child and laid him in her bosom, and became his nurse. 17 The women of the neighborhood gave him a name, saying, "A son has been born to Naomi." They named him Obed; he became the father of Jesse, the father of David.

1 Samuel 1:9-28 After they had eaten and drunk at Shiloh, Hannah rose and presented herself before the LORD. Now Eli the priest was sitting on the seat beside the doorpost of the temple of the LORD. 10 She was deeply distressed and prayed to the LORD, and wept bitterly. 11 She made this vow: "O LORD of hosts, if only you will look on the misery of your servant, and remember me, and not forget your servant, but will give to your servant a male child, then I will set him before you as a nazirite until the day of his death. He shall drink neither wine nor intoxicants, and no razor shall touch his head." 12 As she continued praying before the LORD, Eli observed her mouth. 13 Hannah was praying silently; only her lips moved, but her voice was not heard; therefore Eli thought she was drunk. 14 So Eli said to her,

"How long will you make a drunken spectacle of yourself? Put away your wine." 15 But Hannah answered, "No, my lord, I am a woman deeply troubled; I have drunk neither wine nor strong drink, but I have been pouring out my soul before the LORD. 16 Do not regard your servant as a worthless woman, for I have been speaking out of my great anxiety and vexation all this time." 17 Then Eli answered, "Go in peace; the God of Israel grant the petition you have made to him." 18 And she said, "Let your servant find favor in your sight." Then the woman went to her quarters, ate and drank with her husband, and her countenance was sad no longer. 19 They rose early in the morning and worshiped before the LORD; then they went back to their house at Ramah. Elkanah knew his wife Hannah, and the LORD remembered her. 20 In due time Hannah conceived and bore a son. She named him Samuel, for she said, "I have asked him of the LORD." 21 The man Elkanah and all his household went up to offer to the LORD the yearly sacrifice, and to pay his vow. 22 But Hannah did not go up, for she said to her husband, "As soon as the child is weaned, I will bring him, that he may appear in the presence of the LORD, and remain there forever; I will offer him as a nazirite for all time." 23 Her husband Elkanah said to her, "Do what seems best to you, wait until you have weaned him; only — may the LORD establish his word." So the woman remained and nursed her son, until she weaned him. 24 When she had weaned him, she took him up with her, along with a three-year-old bull, an ephah of flour, and a skin of wine. She brought him to the house of the LORD at Shiloh; and the child was young. 25 Then they slaughtered the bull, and they brought the child to Eli. 26 And she said, "Oh, my lord! As you live, my lord, I am the woman who was standing here in your presence, praying to the LORD. 27 For this child I prayed; and the LORD has granted me the petition that I made to him. 28 Therefore I have lent him to the LORD; as long as he lives, he is given to the LORD." She left him there for the LORD.

1 Samuel 2:1-10 Hannah prayed and said, "My heart exults in the LORD; my strength is exalted in my God. My mouth derides my enemies, because I rejoice in my victory. 2 "There is no Holy One like the LORD, no one besides you; there is no Rock like our God. 3 Talk no more so very proudly, let not arrogance come from your mouth; for the LORD is a God of knowledge, and by him actions are weighed. 4 The bows of the mighty are broken, but the feeble gird on strength. 5 Those who were full have hired themselves out for bread, but those who were hungry are fat with spoil. The barren has borne seven, but she who has many children is forlorn. 6 The LORD kills and brings to life; he brings down to Sheol and raises up. 7 The LORD makes poor and makes rich; he brings low, he also exalts. 8 He raises up the poor from the dust; he lifts the needy from the ash heap, to make them sit with princes and inherit a seat of honor. For the pillars of the earth are the

Lord's, and on them he has set the world. 9 "He will guard the feet of his faithful ones, but the wicked shall be cut off in darkness; for not by might does one prevail. 10 The LORD! His adversaries shall be shattered; the Most High will thunder in heaven. The LORD will judge the ends of the earth; he will give strength to his king, and exalt the power of his anointed."

2 Samuel 7:1-5 Now when the king was settled in his house, and the LORD had given him rest from all his enemies around him, 2 the king said to the prophet Nathan, "See now, I am living in a house of cedar, but the ark of God stays in a tent." 3 Nathan said to the king, "Go, do all that you have in mind; for the LORD is with you." 4 But that same night the word of the LORD came to Nathan: 5 Go and tell my servant David: Thus says the LORD: Are you the one to build me a house to live in?

2 Samuel 7:8-13 Now therefore thus you shall say to my servant David: Thus says the LORD of hosts: I took you from the pasture, from following the sheep to be prince over my people Israel; 9 and I have been with you wherever you went, and have cut off all your enemies from before you; and I will make for you a great name, like the name of the great ones of the earth. 10 And I will appoint a place for my people Israel and will plant them, so that they may live in their own place, and be disturbed no more; and evildoers shall afflict them no more, as formerly, 11 from the time that I appointed judges over my people Israel; and I will give you rest from all your enemies. Moreover the LORD declares to you that the LORD will make you a house. 12 When your days are fulfilled and you lie down with your ancestors, I will raise up your offspring after you, who shall come forth from your body, and I will establish his kingdom. 13 He shall build a house for my name, and I will establish the throne of his kingdom forever.

2 Samuel 7:16 Your house and your kingdom shall be made sure forever before me; your throne shall be established forever.

1 Kings 8:1-13 Then Solomon assembled the elders of Israel and all the heads of the tribes, the leaders of the ancestral houses of the Israelites, before King Solomon in Jerusalem, to bring up the ark of the covenant of the LORD out of the city of David, which is Zion. 2 All the people of Israel assembled to King Solomon at the festival in the month Ethanim, which is the seventh month. 3 And all the elders of Israel came, and the priests carried the ark. 4 So they brought up the ark of the LORD, the tent of meeting, and all the holy vessels that were in the tent; the priests and the Levites brought them up. 5 King Solomon and all the congregation of Israel, who had assembled before him, were with him before the ark, sacrificing so many sheep and oxen that they could not be counted or numbered. 6 Then the priests brought the ark of the covenant of the LORD to its place, in the inner sanctuary of the house, in the most holy place, underneath the wings of the cherubim. 7 For the cherubim spread out their wings over the place of the ark, so that the cherubim made a covering above the ark and its poles. 8 The poles were so long that the ends of the poles were seen from the holy place in front of the inner sanctuary; but they could not be seen from outside; they are there to this day. 9 There was nothing in the ark except the two tablets of stone that Moses had placed there at Horeb, where the LORD made a covenant with the Israelites, when they came out of the land of Egypt. 10 And when the priests came out of the holy place, a cloud filled the house of the LORD, 11 so that the priests could not stand to minister because of the cloud; for the glory of the LORD filled the house of the LORD. 12 Then Solomon said, "The LORD has said that he would dwell in thick darkness. 13 I have built you an exalted house, a place for you to dwell in forever."

1 Kings 8:27-30 "But will God indeed dwell on the earth? Even heaven and the highest heaven cannot contain you, much less this house that I have built! 28 Regard your servant's prayer and his plea, O LORD my God, heeding the cry and the prayer that your servant prays to you today; 29 that your eyes may be open night and day toward this house, the place of which you said, 'My name shall be there,' that you may heed the prayer that your servant prays toward this place. 30 Hear the plea of your servant and of your people Israel when they pray toward this place; O hear in heaven your dwelling place; heed and forgive.

1 Kings 9:3 The LORD said to him, "I have heard your prayer and your plea, which you made before me; I have consecrated this house that you have built, and put my name there forever; my eyes and my heart will be there for all time.

1 Chronicles 15:3-4 David assembled all Israel in Jerusalem to bring up the ark of the LORD to its place, which he had prepared for it. 4 Then David gathered together the descendants of Aaron and the Levites:

1 Chronicles 15:14-16 So the priests and the Levites sanctified themselves to bring up the ark of the LORD, the God of Israel. 15 And the Levites carried the ark of God on their shoulders with the poles, as Moses had commanded according to the word of the LORD. 16 David also commanded the chiefs of the Levites to appoint their kindred as the singers to play on musical instruments, on harps and lyres and cymbals, to raise loud sounds of joy.

1 Chronicles 15:25 So David and the elders of Israel, and the commanders of the thousands, went to bring up the ark of the covenant of the LORD from the house of Obed-edom with rejoicing.

1 **Chronicles 15:28** So all Israel brought up the ark of the covenant of the LORD with shouting, to the sound of the horn, trumpets, and cymbals, and made loud music on harps and lyres.

1 **Chronicles 16:1-2** They brought in the ark of God, and set it inside the tent that David had pitched for it; and they offered burnt offerings and offerings of well-being before God. 2 When David had finished offering the burnt offerings and the offerings of well-being, he blessed the people in the name of the LORD.

Judith 13:14 Then she said to them with a loud voice, "Praise God, O praise him! Praise God, who has not withdrawn his mercy from the house of Israel, but has destroyed our enemies by my hand this very night!"

Judith 13:17-20 All the people were greatly astonished. They bowed down and worshiped God, and said with one accord, "Blessed are you our God, who have this day humiliated the enemies of your people." 18 Then Uzziah said to her, "O daughter, you are blessed by the Most High God above all other women on earth; and blessed be the Lord God, who created the heavens and the earth, who has guided you to cut off the head of the leader of our enemies. 19 Your praise will never depart from the hearts of those who remember the power of God.

Judith 15:8-10 Then the high priest Joakim and the elders of the Israelites who lived in Jerusalem came to witness the good things that the Lord had done for Israel, and to see Judith and to wish her well. 9 When they met her, they all blessed her with one accord and said to her. "You are the glory of Jerusalem, you are the great boast of Israel, you are the great pride of our nation! 10 You have done all this with your own hand; you have done great good to Israel, and God is well pleased with it. May the Almighty Lord bless you forever!" And all the people said, "Amen."

Judith 16:13-15 "A new hymn I will sing to my God. O Lord, great are you and glorious, wonderful in power and unsurpassable. 14 Let your every creature serve you; for you spoke, and they were made, You sent forth your spirit, and they were created; no one can resist your word. 15 The mountains to their bases, and the seas, are shaken; the rocks, like wax, melt before your glance. "But to those who fear you, you are very merciful.

Esther 2:16-18 When Esther was taken to King Ahasuerus in his royal palace in the tenth month, which is the month of Tebeth, in the seventh year of his reign, 17 the king loved Esther more than all the other women; of all the virgins she won his favor and devotion, so that he set the royal crown on her head and made her queen instead of Vashti. 18 Then the king gave a great banquet to all his officials and ministers — " Esther's banquet." He also granted a holiday to the provinces, and gave gifts with royal liberality.

Esther 8:3-8 Then Esther spoke again to the king; she fell at his feet, weeping and pleading with him to avert the evil design of Haman the Agagite and the plot that he had devised against the Jews. 4 The king held out the golden scepter to Esther, 5 and Esther rose and stood before the king. She said, "If it pleases the king, and if I have won his favor, and if the thing seems right before the king, and I have his approval, let an order be written to revoke the letters devised by Haman son of Hammedatha the Agagite, which he wrote giving orders to destroy the Jews who are in all the provinces of the king. 6 For how can I bear to see the calamity that is coming on my people? Or how can I bear to see the destruction of my kindred?" 7 Then King Ahasuerus said to Queen Esther and to the Jew Mordecai, "See, I have given Esther the house of Haman, and they have hanged him on the gallows, because he plotted to lay hands on the Jews. 8 You may write as you please with regard to the Jews, in the name of the king, and seal it with the king's ring; for an edict written in the name of the king and sealed with the king's ring cannot be revoked."

Esther 8:16-17 For the Jews there was light and gladness, joy and honor. 17 In every province and in every city, wherever the king's command and his edict came, there was gladness and joy among the Jews, a festival and a holiday. Furthermore, many of the peoples of the country professed to be Jews, because the fear of the Jews had fallen upon them.

Esther C:14:1 Then Queen Esther, seized with deadly anxiety, fled to the Lord.

Esther C:14:3-4 She prayed to the Lord God of Israel, and said: "O my Lord, you only are our king; help me, who am alone and have no helper but you, 4 for my danger is in my hand.

Esther C:14:14 But save us by your hand, and help me, who am alone and have no helper but you, O Lord.

Esther C:14:19 O God, whose might is over all, hear the voice of the despairing, and save us from the hands of evildoers. And save me from my fear!

2 Maccabees 7:1 It happened also that seven brothers and their mother were arrested and were being compelled by the king, under torture with whips and thongs, to take of unlawful swine's flesh.

2 Maccabees 7:20-29 The mother was especially admirable and worthy of honorable memory. Although she saw her sons perish within a single day, she bore it with good courage because of her hope in the Lord. 21 She encouraged each of them in the language of their ancestors. Filled with a noble spirit, she reinforced her woman's reasoning with a man's courage, and said to them, 22 "I do not know how you came into being in my womb. It was not I who gave you life and breath, nor I who set in order the elements within each of you. 23 Therefore the Creator of the world, who shaped the beginning of humankind and devised the origin of all things, will in his mercy give life and breath back to you again, since you now forget yourselves for the sake of his laws." 24 Antiochus felt that he was being treated with contempt, and he was suspicious of her reproachful tone. The youngest brother being still alive, Antiochus not only appealed to him in words, but promised with oaths that he would make him rich and enviable if he would turn from the ways of his ancestors, and that he would take him for his Friend and entrust him with public affairs. 25 Since the young man would not listen to him at all, the king called the mother to him and urged her to advise the youth to save himself. 26 After much urging on his part, she undertook to persuade her son. 27 But, leaning close to him, she spoke in their native language as follows, deriding the cruel tyrant: "My son, have pity on me. I carried you nine months in my womb, and nursed you for three years, and have reared you and brought you up to this point in your life, and have taken care of you. 28 I beg you, my child, to look at the heaven and the earth and see everything that is in them, and recognize that God did not make them out of things that existed. And in the same way the human race came into being. 29 Do not fear this butcher, but prove worthy of your brothers. Accept death, so that in God's mercy I may get you back again along with your brothers."

Psalm 2:7-11 I will tell of the decree of the LORD: He said to me, "You are my son; today I have begotten you. 8 Ask of me, and I will make the nations your heritage, and the ends of the earth your possession. 9 You shall break them with a rod of iron, and dash them in pieces like a potter's vessel." 10 Now therefore, O kings, be wise; be warned, O rulers of the earth. 11 Serve the LORD with fear, with trembling.

Psalm 7 O LORD my God, in you I take refuge; save me from all my pursuers, and deliver me, 2 or like a lion they will tear me apart; they will drag me away, with no one to rescue. 3 O LORD my God, if I have done this, if there is wrong in my hands, 4 if I have repaid my ally with harm or plundered my foe without cause, 5 then let the enemy pursue and overtake me, trample my life to the ground, and lay my soul in the dust. Selah 6 Rise up, O LORD, in your anger; lift yourself up against the fury of my enemies; awake, O my God; you have appointed a judgment. 7 Let the assembly of the peoples be gathered around you, and over it take your seat on high. 8 The LORD judges the peoples; judge me, O LORD, according to my righteousness and according to the integrity that is in me. 9 O let the evil of the wicked come to an end, but establish the righteous, you who test the minds and hearts, O righteous God. 10 God is my shield, who saves the upright in heart. 11 God is a righteous judge, and a God who has indignation every day. 12 If one does not repent, God will whet his sword; he has bent and strung his bow; 13 he has prepared his deadly weapons, making his arrows fiery shafts. 14 See how they conceive evil, and are pregnant with mischief, and bring forth lies. 15 They make a pit, digging it out, and fall into the hole that they have made. 16 Their mischief returns upon their own heads, and on their own heads their violence descends. 17 I will give to the LORD the thanks due to his righteousness, and sing praise to the name of the LORD, the Most High.

Psalm 8 O LORD, our Sovereign, how majestic is your name in all the earth! You have set your glory above the heavens. 2 Out of the mouths of babes and infants you have founded a bulwark because of your foes, to silence the enemy and the avenger. 3 When I look at your heavens, the work of your fingers, the moon and the stars that you have established; 4 what are human beings that you are mindful of them, mortals that you care for them? 5 Yet you have made them a little lower than God, and crowned them with glory and honor. 6 You have given them dominion over the works of your hands; you have put all things under their feet, 7 all sheep and oxen, and also the beasts of the field, 8 the birds of the air, and the fish of the sea, whatever passes along the paths of the seas. 9 O LORD, our Sovereign, how majestic is your name in all the earth!

Psalm 9 I will give thanks to the LORD with my whole heart; I will tell of all your wonderful deeds. 2 I will be glad and exult in you; I will sing praise to your name, O Most High. 3 When my enemies turned back, they stumbled and perished before you. 4 For you have maintained my just cause; you have sat on the throne giving righteous judgment. 5 You have rebuked the nations, you have destroyed the wicked; you have blotted out their name forever and ever. 6 The enemies have vanished in everlasting ruins; their cities you have rooted out; the very memory of them has perished. 7 But the LORD sits enthroned forever, he has established his throne for judgment. 8 He judges the world with righteousness; he judges the peoples with equity. 9 The LORD is a stronghold for the oppressed, a stronghold in times of trouble. 10 And those who know your name put their trust in you, for you, O LORD, have not forsaken those who seek you. 11 Sing praises to the LORD, who dwells in Zion. Declare his deeds among the peoples. 12 For he who avenges blood is mindful of them; he does not forget the cry of the afflicted. 13 Be gracious to me, O LORD. See what I suffer from those who hate me; you are the one who lifts me up from the gates of death, 14 so that

I may recount all your praises, and, in the gates of daughter Zion, rejoice in your deliverance. 15 The nations have sunk in the pit that they made; in the net that they hid has their own foot been caught. 16 The LORD has made himself known, he has executed judgment; the wicked are snared in the work of their own hands. Higgaion. Selah 17 The wicked shall depart to Sheol, all the nations that forget God. 18 For the needy shall not always be forgotten, nor the hope of the poor perish forever. 19 Rise up, O LORD! Do not let mortals prevail; let the nations be judged before you. 20 Put them in fear, O LORD; let the nations know that they are only human. Selah

Psalm 10 Why, O LORD, do you stand far off? Why do you hide yourself in times of trouble? 2 In arrogance the wicked persecute the poor — let them be caught in the schemes they have devised. 3 For the wicked boast of the desires of their heart, those greedy for gain curse and renounce the LORD. 4 In the pride of their countenance the wicked say, "God will not seek it out"; all their thoughts are, "There is no God." 5 Their ways prosper at all times; your judgments are on high, out of their sight; as for their foes, they scoff at them. 6 They think in their heart, "We shall not be moved; throughout all generations we shall not meet adversity." 7 Their mouths are filled with cursing and deceit and oppression; under their tongues are mischief and iniquity. 8 They sit in ambush in the villages; in hiding places they murder the innocent. Their eyes stealthily watch for the helpless; 9 they lurk in secret like a lion in its covert; they lurk that they may seize the poor; they seize the poor and drag them off in their net. 10 They stoop, they crouch, and the helpless fall by their might. 11 They think in their heart, "God has forgotten, he has hidden his face, he will never see it." 12 Rise up, O LORD; O God, lift up your hand; do not forget the oppressed. 13 Why do the wicked renounce God, and say in their hearts, "You will not call us to account"? 14 But you do see! Indeed you note trouble and grief, that you may take it into your hands; the helpless commit themselves to you; you have been the helper of the orphan. 15 Break the arm of the wicked and evildoers; seek out their wickedness until you find none. 16 The LORD is king forever and ever; the nations shall perish from his land. 17 O LORD, you will hear the desire of the meek; you will strengthen their heart, you will incline your ear 18 to do justice for the orphan and the oppressed, so that those from earth may strike terror no more.

Psalm 15:2-5 Those who walk blamelessly, and do what is right, and speak the truth from their heart; 3 who do not slander with their tongue, and do no evil to their friends, nor take up a reproach against their neighbors; 4 in whose eyes the wicked are despised, but who honor those who fear the LORD; who stand by their oath even to their hurt; 5 who do not lend money at interest, and do not take a bribe against the innocent. Those who do these things shall never be moved.

Psalm 16:5-11 The LORD is my chosen portion and my cup; you hold my lot. 6 The boundary lines have fallen for me in pleasant places; I have a goodly heritage. 7 I bless the LORD who gives me counsel; in the night also my heart instructs me. 8 I keep the LORD always before me; because he is at my right hand, I shall not be moved. 9 Therefore my heart is glad, and my soul rejoices; my body also rests secure. 10 For you do not give me up to Sheol, or let your faithful one see the Pit. 11 You show me the path of life. In your presence there is fullness of joy; in your right hand are pleasures forevermore.

Psalm 18:2-7 The LORD is my rock, my fortress, and my deliverer, my God, my rock in whom I take refuge, my shield, and the horn of my salvation, my stronghold. 3 I call upon the LORD, who is worthy to be praised, so I shall be saved from my enemies. 4 The cords of death encompassed me; the torrents of perdition assailed me; 5 the cords of Sheol entangled me; the snares of death confronted me. 6 In my distress I called upon the LORD; to my God I cried for help. From his temple he heard my voice, and my cry to him reached his ears. 7 Then the earth reeled and rocked; the foundations also of the mountains trembled and quaked, because he was angry.

Psalm 18:19-20 He brought me out into a broad place; he delivered me, because he delighted in me. 20 The LORD rewarded me according to my righteousness; according to the cleanness of my hands he recompensed me.

Psalm 19:8-14 The precepts of the LORD are right, rejoicing the heart; the commandment of the LORD is clear, enlightening the eyes; 9 the fear of the LORD is pure, enduring forever; the ordinances of the LORD are true and righteous altogether. 10 More to be desired are they than gold, even much fine gold; sweeter also than honey, and drippings of the honeycomb. 11 Moreover by them is your servant warned; in keeping them there is great reward. 12 But who can detect their errors? Clear me from hidden faults. 13 Keep back your servant also from the insolent; do not let them have dominion over me. Then I shall be blameless, and innocent of great transgression. 14 Let the words of my mouth and the meditation of my heart be acceptable to you, O LORD, my rock and my redeemer.

Psalm 21:10-11 You will destroy their offspring from the earth, and their children from among humankind. 11 If they plan evil against you, if they devise mischief, they will not succeed.

Psalm 22:4-6 In you our ancestors trusted; they trusted, and you delivered them. 5 To you they cried, and were saved; in you they trusted, and were not put to shame. 6 But I am a worm, and not human; scorned by others, and despised by the people.

Psalm 22:10-11 On you I was cast from my birth, and since my mother bore me you have been my God. 11 Do not be far from me, for trouble is near and there is no one to help.

Psalm 22:23-24 You who fear the LORD, praise him! All you offspring of Jacob, glorify him; stand in awe of him, all you offspring of Israel! 24 For he did not despise or abhor the affliction of the afflicted; he did not hide his face from me, but heard when I cried to him.

Psalm 23 The LORD is my shepherd, I shall not want. 2 He makes me lie down in green pastures; he leads me beside still waters; 3 he restores my soul. He leads me in right paths for his name's sake. 4 Even though I walk through the darkest valley, I fear no evil; for you are with me; your rod and your staff — they comfort me. 5 You prepare a table before me in the presence of my enemies; you anoint my head with oil; my cup overflows. 6 Surely goodness and mercy shall follow me all the days of my life, and I shall dwell in the house of the LORD my whole life long.

Psalm 24 The earth is the Lord's and all that is in it, the world, and those who live in it; 2 for he has founded it on the seas, and established it on the rivers. 3 Who shall ascend the hill of the LORD? And who shall stand in his holy place? 4 Those who have clean hands and pure hearts, who do not lift up their souls to what is false, and do not swear deceitfully. 5 They will receive blessing from the LORD, and vindication from the God of their salvation. 6 Such is the company of those who seek him, who seek the face of the God of Jacob. Selah 7 Lift up your heads, O gates! and be lifted up, O ancient doors! that the King of glory may come in. 8 Who is the King of glory? The LORD, strong and mighty, the LORD, mighty in battle. 9 Lift up your heads, O gates! and be lifted up, O ancient doors! that the King of glory may come in. 10 Who is this King of glory? The LORD of hosts, he is the King of glory. Selah

Psalm 27:1-5 The LORD is my light and my salvation; whom shall I fear? The LORD is the stronghold of my life; of whom shall I be afraid? 2 When evildoers assail me to devour my flesh — my adversaries and foes — they shall stumble and fall. 3 Though an army encamp against me, my heart shall not fear; though war rise up against me, yet I will be confident. 4 One thing I asked of the LORD, that will I seek after: to live in the house of the LORD all the days of my life, to behold the beauty of the LORD, and to inquire in his temple. 5 For he will hide me in his shelter in the day of trouble; he will conceal me under the cover of his tent; he will set me high on a rock.

Psalm 31:2-6 Incline your ear to me; rescue me speedily. Be a rock of refuge for me, a strong fortress to save me. 3 You are indeed my rock and my fortress; for your name's sake lead me and guide me, 4 take me out of the net that is hidden for me, for you are my refuge. 5 Into your hand I commit my spirit; you have redeemed me, O LORD, faithful God. 6 You hate those who pay regard to worthless idols, but I trust in the LORD.

Psalm 31:15-16 My times are in your hand; deliver me from the hand of my enemies and persecutors. 16 Let your face shine upon your servant; save me in your steadfast love.

Psalm 31:20 In the shelter of your presence you hide them from human plots; you hold them safe under your shelter from contentious tongues.

Psalm 34:2-3 My soul makes its boast in the LORD; let the humble hear and be glad. 3 O magnify the LORD with me, and let us exalt his name together.

Psalm 34:6-9 This poor soul cried, and was heard by the LORD, and was saved from every trouble. 7 The angel of the LORD encamps around those who fear him, and delivers them. 8 O taste and see that the LORD is good; happy are those who take refuge in him. 9 O fear the LORD, you his holy ones, for those who fear him have no want.

Psalm 40:7-11 Then I said, "Here I am; in the scroll of the book it is written of me. 8 I delight to do your will, O my God; your law is within my heart." 9 I have told the glad news of deliverance in the great congregation; see, I have not restrained my lips, as you know, O LORD. 10 I have not hidden your saving help within my heart, I have spoken of your faithfulness and your salvation; I have not concealed your steadfast love and your faithfulness from the great congregation. 11 Do not, O LORD, withhold your mercy from me; let your steadfast love and your faithfulness keep me safe forever.

Psalm 44:2-3 you with your own hand drove out the nations, but them you planted; you afflicted the peoples, but them you set free; 3 for not by their own sword did they win the land, nor did their own arm give them victory; but your right hand, and your arm, and the light of your countenance, for you delighted in them.

Psalm 44:10-18 You made us turn back from the foe, and our enemies have gotten spoil. 11 You have made us like sheep for slaughter, and have scattered us among the nations. 12 You have sold your people for a trifle, demanding no high price for them. 13 You have made us the taunt of our neighbors, the derision and scorn of those around us. 14 You have made us a byword among the nations, a laughingstock among the peoples. 15 All day long my disgrace is before me, and shame has covered my face 16 at the words of the taunters and revilers, at the sight of the enemy and the avenger.

17 All this has come upon us, yet we have not forgotten you, or been false to your covenant. 18 Our heart has not turned back, nor have our steps departed from your way,

Psalm 45:11-12 and the king will desire your beauty. Since he is your lord, bow to him; 12 the people of Tyre will seek your favor with gifts, the richest of the people.

Psalm 45:14-17 in many-colored robes she is led to the king; behind her the virgins, her companions, follow. 15 With joy and gladness they are led along as they enter the palace of the king. 16 In the place of ancestors you, O king, shall have sons; you will make them princes in all the earth. 17 I will cause your name to be celebrated in all generations; therefore the peoples will praise you forever and ever.

Psalm 46:5 God is in the midst of the city; it shall not be moved; God will help it when the morning dawns.

Psalm 46:9 He makes wars cease to the end of the earth; he breaks the bow, and shatters the spear; he burns the shields with fire.

Psalm 47:2-4 For the LORD, the Most High, is awesome, a great king over all the earth. 3 He subdued peoples under us, and nations under our feet. 4 He chose our heritage for us, the pride of Jacob whom he loves. Selah

Psalm 47:9 The princes of the peoples gather as the people of the God of Abraham. For the shields of the earth belong to God; he is highly exalted.

Psalm 66:7-8 who rules by his might forever, whose eyes keep watch on the nations — let the rebellious not exalt themselves. Selah 8 Bless our God, O peoples, let the sound of his praise be heard.

Psalm 67:2-7 that your way may be known upon earth, your saving power among all nations. 3 Let the peoples praise you, O God; let all the peoples praise you. 4 Let the nations be glad and sing for joy, for you judge the peoples with equity and guide the nations upon earth. Selah 5 Let the peoples praise you, O God; let all the peoples praise you. 6 The earth has yielded its increase; God, our God, has blessed us. 7 May God continue to bless us; let all the ends of the earth revere him.

Psalm 70:5 But I am poor and needy; hasten to me, O God! You are my help and my deliverer; O LORD, do not delay!

Psalm 71:6-7 Upon you I have leaned from my birth; it was you who took me from my mother's womb. My praise is continually of you. 7 I have been like a portent to many, but you are my strong refuge.

Psalm 72:1-2 Give the king your justice, O God, and your righteousness to a king's son. 2 May he judge your people with righteousness, and your poor with justice.

Psalm 72:7-8 In his days may righteousness flourish and peace abound, until the moon is no more. 8 May he have dominion from sea to sea, and from the River to the ends of the earth.

Psalm 72:10-13 May the kings of Tarshish and of the isles render him tribute, may the kings of Sheba and Seba bring gifts. 11 May all kings fall down before him, all nations give him service. 12 For he delivers the needy when they call, the poor and those who have no helper. 13 He has pity on the weak and the needy, and saves the lives of the needy.

Psalm 72:17 May his name endure forever, his fame continue as long as the sun. May all nations be blessed in him; may they pronounce him happy.

Psalm 75:2-3 At the set time that I appoint I will judge with equity. 3 When the earth totters, with all its inhabitants, it is I who keep its pillars steady. Selah

Psalm 77:14 You are the God who works wonders; you have displayed your might among the peoples.

Psalm 84:2-6 My soul longs, indeed it faints for the courts of the LORD; my heart and my flesh sing for joy to the living God. 3 Even the sparrow finds a home, and the swallow a nest for herself, where she may lay her young, at your altars, O LORD of hosts, my King and my God. 4 Happy are those who live in your house, ever singing your praise. Selah 5 Happy are those whose strength is in you, in whose heart are the highways to Zion. 6 As they go through the valley of Baca they make it a place of springs; the early rain also covers it with pools.

Psalm 84:9-11 Behold our shield, O God; look on the face of your anointed. 10 For a day in your courts is better than a thousand elsewhere. I would rather be a doorkeeper in the house of my God than live in the tents of wickedness. 11 For the LORD God is a sun and shield; he bestows favor and honor. No good thing does the LORD withhold from those who walk uprightly.

Psalm 85:9-13 Surely his salvation is at hand for those who fear him, that his glory may dwell in our land. 10 Steadfast love and faithfulness will meet; righteousness and peace will kiss each other. 11 Faithfulness will spring up from the ground, and righteousness will look down from the sky. 12 The LORD will give what is good, and our land will yield its increase. 13 Righteousness will go before him, and will make a path for his steps.

Psalm 86:1-3 Incline your ear, O LORD, and answer me, for I am poor and needy. 2 Preserve my life, for I am devoted to you; save your servant who trusts in you. You are my God; 3 be gracious to me, O Lord, for to you do I cry all day long.

Psalm 86:5-7 For you, O Lord, are good and forgiving, abounding in steadfast love to all who call on you. 6 Give ear, O LORD, to my prayer; listen to my cry of supplication. 7 In the day of my trouble I call on you, for you will answer me.

Psalm 87:1-3 On the holy mount stands the city he founded; 2 the LORD loves the gates of Zion more than all the dwellings of Jacob. 3 Glorious things are spoken of you, O city of God. Selah

Psalm 87:5-7 And of Zion it shall be said, "This one and that one were born in it"; for the Most High himself will establish it. 6 The LORD records, as he registers the peoples, "This one was born there." Selah 7 Singers and dancers alike say, "All my springs are in you."

Psalm 96:1-3 O sing to the LORD a new song; sing to the LORD, all the earth. 2 Sing to the LORD, bless his name; tell of his salvation from day to day. 3 Declare his glory among the nations, his marvelous works among all the peoples.

Psalm 96:11-13 Let the heavens be glad, and let the earth rejoice; let the sea roar, and all that fills it; 12 let the field exult, and everything in it. Then shall all the trees of the forest sing for joy 13 before the LORD; for he is coming, for he is coming to judge the earth. He will judge the world with righteousness, and the peoples with his truth.

Psalm 103:1-4 Bless the LORD, O my soul, and all that is within me, bless his holy name. 2 Bless the LORD, O my soul, and do not forget all his benefits — 3 who forgives all your iniquity, who heals all your diseases, 4 who redeems your life from the Pit, who crowns you with steadfast love and mercy,

Psalm 103:6-11 The LORD works vindication and justice for all who are oppressed. 7 He made known his ways to Moses, his acts to the people of Israel. 8 The LORD is merciful and gracious, slow to anger and abounding in steadfast love. 9 He will not always accuse, nor will he keep his anger forever. 10 He does not deal with us according to our sins, nor repay us according to our iniquities. 11 For as the heavens are high above the earth, so great is his steadfast love toward those who fear him;

Psalm 103:13-14 As a father has compassion for his children, so the LORD has compassion for those who fear him. 14 For he knows how we were made; he remembers that we are dust.

Psalm 103:17-18 But the steadfast love of the LORD is from everlasting to everlasting on those who fear him, and his righteousness to children's children, 18 to those who keep his covenant and remember to do his commandments.

Psalm 110:2-3 The LORD sends out from Zion your mighty scepter. Rule in the midst of your foes. 3 Your people will offer themselves willingly on the day you lead your forces on the holy mountains. From the womb of the morning, like dew, your youth will come to you.

Psalm 113:1-8 Praise the LORD! Praise, O servants of the LORD; praise the name of the LORD. 2 Blessed be the name of the LORD from this time on and forevermore. 3 From the rising of the sun to its setting the name of the LORD is to be praised. 4 The LORD is high above all nations, and his glory above the heavens. 5 Who is like the LORD our God, who is seated on high, 6 who looks far down on the heavens and the earth? 7 He raises the poor from the dust, and lifts the needy from the ash heap, 8 to make them sit with princes, with the princes of his people.

Psalm 115:16 The heavens are the Lord's heavens, but the earth he has given to human beings.

Psalm 116:12-13 What shall I return to the LORD for all his bounty to me? 13 I will lift up the cup of salvation and call on the name of the LORD,

Psalm 116:15-18 Precious in the sight of the LORD is the death of his faithful ones. 16 O LORD, I am your servant; I am your servant, the child of your serving girl. You have loosed my bonds. 17 I will offer to you a thanksgiving sacrifice and call on the name of the LORD. 18 I will pay my vows to the LORD in the presence of all his people,

Psalm 117 Praise the LORD, all you nations! Extol him, all you peoples! 2 For great is his steadfast love toward us, and the faithfulness of the LORD endures forever. Praise the LORD!

Psalm 118:14-21 The LORD is my strength and my might; he has become my salvation. 15 There are glad songs of victory in the tents of the righteous: "The right hand of the LORD does valiantly; 16 the right hand of the LORD is exalted; the right hand of the LORD does valiantly." 17 I shall not die, but I shall live, and recount the deeds of the LORD. 18 The LORD has punished me severely, but he did not give me over to death. 19 Open to me the gates of righteousness, that I may enter through them and give thanks to the

LORD. 20 This is the gate of the LORD; the righteous shall enter through it. 21 I thank you that you have answered me and have become my salvation.

Psalm 119:1-2 Happy are those whose way is blameless, who walk in the law of the LORD. 2 Happy are those who keep his decrees, who seek him with their whole heart,

Psalm 119:10-16 With my whole heart I seek you; do not let me stray from your commandments. 11 I treasure your word in my heart, so that I may not sin against you. 12 Blessed are you, O LORD; teach me your statutes. 13 With my lips I declare all the ordinances of your mouth. 14 I delight in the way of your decrees as much as in all riches. 15 I will meditate on your precepts, and fix my eyes on your ways. 16 I will delight in your statutes; I will not forget your word.

Psalm 122:1-4 I was glad when they said to me, "Let us go to the house of the LORD!" 2 Our feet are standing within your gates, O Jerusalem. 3 Jerusalem — built as a city that is bound firmly together. 4 To it the tribes go up, the tribes of the LORD, as was decreed for Israel, to give thanks to the name of the LORD.

Psalm 122:8-9 For the sake of my relatives and friends I will say, "Peace be within you." 9 For the sake of the house of the LORD our God, I will seek your good.

Psalm 126:3 The LORD has done great things for us, and we rejoiced.

Psalm 131 O LORD, my heart is not lifted up, my eyes are not raised too high; I do not occupy myself with things too great and too marvelous for me. 2 But I have calmed and quieted my soul, like a weaned child with its mother; my soul is like the weaned child that is with me. 3 O Israel, hope in the LORD from this time on and forevermore.

Psalm 132:11 The LORD swore to David a sure oath from which he will not turn back: "One of the sons of your body I will set on your throne.

Psalm 132:13-14 For the LORD has chosen Zion; he has desired it for his habitation: 14 "This is my resting place forever; here I will reside, for I have desired it.

Psalm 132:17-18 There I will cause a horn to sprout up for David; I have prepared a lamp for my anointed one. 18 His enemies I will clothe with disgrace, but on him, his crown will gleam."

Psalm 139:13-15 For it was you who formed my inward parts; you knit me together in my mother's womb. 14 I praise you, for I am fearfully and wonderfully made. Wonderful are your works; that I know very well. 15 My frame was not hidden from you, when I was being made in secret, intricately woven in the depths of the earth.

Psalm 139:16 Your eyes beheld my unformed substance. In your book were written all the days that were formed for me, when none of them as yet existed.

Psalm 145:1-2 I will extol you, my God and King, and bless your name forever and ever. 2 Every day I will bless you, and praise your name forever and ever.

Psalm 145:4-6 One generation shall laud your works to another, and shall declare your mighty acts. 5 On the glorious splendor of your majesty, and on your wondrous works, I will meditate. 6 The might of your awesome deeds shall be proclaimed, and I will declare your greatness.

Psalm 145:8-9 The LORD is gracious and merciful, slow to anger and abounding in steadfast love. 9 The LORD is good to all, and his compassion is over all that he has made.

Psalm 147:12-15 Praise the LORD, O Jerusalem! Praise your God, O Zion! 13 For he strengthens the bars of your gates; he blesses your children within you. 14 He grants peace within your borders; he fills you with the finest of wheat. 15 He sends out his command to the earth; his word runs swiftly.

Psalm 147:19-20 He declares his word to Jacob, his statutes and ordinances to Israel. 20 He has not dealt thus with any other nation; they do not know his ordinances. Praise the LORD!

Proverbs 8:17-35 I love those who love me, and those who seek me diligently find me. 18 Riches and honor are with me, enduring wealth and prosperity. 19 My fruit is better than gold, even fine gold, and my yield than choice silver. 20 I walk in the way of righteousness, along the paths of justice, 21 endowing with wealth those who love me, and filling their treasuries. 22 The LORD created me at the beginning of his work, the first of his acts of long ago. 23 Ages ago I was set up, at the first, before the beginning of the earth. 24 When there were no depths I was brought forth, when there were no springs abounding with water. 25 Before the mountains had been shaped, before the hills, I was brought forth — 26 when he had not yet made earth and fields, or the world's first bits of soil. 27 When he established the heavens, I was there, when he drew a circle on the face of the deep, 28 when he made firm the skies above, when he established the fountains of the deep, 29 when he assigned to the sea its limit, so that the waters might not transgress his command, when he marked out the foundations of the earth, 30 then I was beside him, like a master worker; and I was daily his delight, rejoicing before him always, 31 rejoicing in his inhabited world and delighting in the human race. 32 And now, my children, listen to me: happy are those who keep my ways. 33 Hear instruction and be wise, and do not neglect it. 34 Happy is the one who listens to me, watching daily at my gates, waiting beside my doors. 35 For whoever finds me finds life and obtains favor from the LORD;

Proverbs 9:1-2 Wisdom has built her house, she has hewn her seven pillars. 2 She has slaughtered her animals, she has mixed her wine, she has also set her table.

Proverbs 9:5-6 "Come, eat of my bread and drink of the wine I have mixed. 6 Lay aside immaturity, and live, and walk in the way of insight."

Song of Songs 2:8-14 The voice of my beloved! Look, he comes, leaping upon the mountains, bounding over the hills. 9 My beloved is like a gazelle or a young stag. Look, there he stands behind our wall, gazing in at the windows, looking through the lattice. 10 My beloved speaks and says to me: "Arise, my love, my fair one, and come away; 11 for now the winter is past, the rain is over and gone. 12 The flowers appear on the earth; the time of singing has come, and the voice of the turtledove is heard in our land. 13 The fig tree puts forth its figs, and the vines are in blossom; they give forth fragrance. Arise, my love, my fair one, and come away. 14 O my dove, in the clefts of the rock, in the covert of the cliff, let me see your face, let me hear your voice; for your voice is sweet, and your face is lovely.

Song of Songs 4:6-7 Until the day breathes and the shadows flee, I will hasten to the mountain of myrrh and the hill of frankincense. 7 You are altogether beautiful, my love; there is no flaw in you.

Song of Songs 4:9 You have ravished my heart, my sister, my bride, you have ravished my heart with a glance of your eyes, with one jewel of your necklace.

Song of Songs 4:12-15 A garden locked is my sister, my bride, a garden locked, a fountain sealed. 13 Your channel is an orchard of pomegranates with all choicest fruits, henna with nard, 14 nard and saffron, calamus and cinnamon, with all trees of frankincense, myrrh and aloes, with all chief spices — 15 a garden fountain, a well of living water, and flowing streams from Lebanon.

Wisdom 7:21 — 8:2 I learned both what is secret and what is manifest, 22 for wisdom, the fashioner of all things, taught me. There is in her a spirit that is intelligent, holy, unique, manifold, subtle, mobile, clear, unpolluted, distinct, invulnerable, loving the good, keen, irresistible, 23 beneficent, humane, steadfast, sure, free from anxiety, all-powerful, overseeing all, and penetrating through all spirits that are intelligent, pure, and altogether subtle. 24 For wisdom is more mobile than any motion; because of her pureness she pervades and penetrates all things. 25 For she is a breath of the power of God, and a pure emanation of the glory of the Almighty; therefore nothing defiled gains entrance into her. 26 For she is a reflection of eternal light, a spotless mirror of the working of God, and an image of his goodness. 27 Although she is but one, she can do all things, and while remaining in herself, she renews all things; in every generation she passes into holy souls and makes them friends of God, and prophets; 28 for God loves nothing so much as the person who lives with wisdom. 29 She is more beautiful than the sun, and excels every constellation of the stars. Compared with the light she is found to be superior, 30 for it is succeeded by the night, but against wisdom evil does not prevail. 1 She reaches mightily from one end of the earth to the other, and she orders all things well. 2 I loved her and sought her from my youth; I desired to take her for my bride, and became enamored of her beauty.

Sirach 14:20-25 Happy is the person who meditates on wisdom and reasons intelligently, 21 who reflects in his heart on her ways and ponders her secrets, 22 pursuing her like a hunter, and lying in wait on her paths; 23 who peers through her windows and listens at her doors; 24 who camps near her house and fastens his tent peg to her walls; 25 who pitches his tent near her, and so occupies an excellent lodging place.

Sirach 24:1-34 Wisdom praises herself, and tells of her glory in the midst of her people. 2 In the assembly of the Most High she opens her mouth, and in the presence of his hosts she tells of her glory: 3 "I came forth from the mouth of the Most High, and covered the earth like a mist. 4 I dwelt in the highest heavens, and my throne was in a pillar of cloud. 5 Alone I compassed the vault of heaven and traversed the depths of the abyss. 6 Over waves of the sea, over all the earth, and over every people and nation I have held sway. 7 Among all these I sought a resting place; in whose territory should I abide? 8 "Then the Creator of all things gave me a command, and my Creator chose the place for my tent. He said, 'Make your dwelling in Jacob, and in Israel receive your inheritance.' 9 Before the ages, in the beginning, he created me, and for all the ages I shall not cease to be. 10 In the holy tent I ministered before him, and so I was established in Zion. 11 Thus in the beloved city he gave me a resting place, and in Jerusalem was my domain. 12 I took root in an honored people, in the portion of the Lord, his heritage. 13 "I grew tall like a cedar in Lebanon, and like a cypress on the heights of Hermon. 14 I grew tall like a palm tree in En-gedi, and like rosebushes in Jericho; like a fair olive tree in the field, and like a plane tree beside water I grew tall. 15 Like cassia and camel's thorn I gave forth perfume, and like choice myrrh I spread my fragrance, like galbanum, onycha, and stacte, and like the odor of incense in the tent. 16 Like a terebinth I spread out my branches, and my branches are glorious and graceful. 17 Like the vine I bud forth delights, and my blossoms become glorious and abundant fruit. 19 "Come to me, you who desire me, and eat your fill of my fruits. 20 For the memory of me is sweeter than honey, and the possession of me sweeter than the honeycomb. 21 Those who eat of me will hunger for more, and those who drink of me will thirst for more. 22 Whoever obeys me will not be put to shame, and those who work with me will not sin." 23 All this is the book of the covenant of the Most High God, the law that Moses commanded us as an inheritance for the congregations of Jacob. 25 It overflows, like the Pishon, with wisdom, and like the Tigris at the time of the first fruits. 26 It runs over like the Euphrates, with understanding, and like the Jordan at harvest time. 27 It pours forth instruction like the Nile, like the Gihon at the time of vintage. 28 The first man did not know wisdom fully, nor will the last one fathom her. 29 For her thoughts are more abundant than the sea, and her counsel deeper than the great abyss. 30 As for me, I was like a canal from a river, like a water channel into a garden. 31 I said, "I will water my garden and drench my flower-beds." And lo, my canal became a river, and my river a sea. 32 I will again make instruction shine forth like the dawn, and I will make it clear from far away. 33 I will again pour out teaching like prophecy, and leave it to all future generations. 34 Observe that I have not labored for myself alone, but for all who seek wisdom.

Sirach 51:13-18 While I was still young, before I went on my travels, I sought wisdom openly in my prayer. 14 Before the temple I asked for her, and I will search for her until the end. 15 From the first blossom to the ripening grape my heart delighted in her; my foot walked on the straight path; from my youth I followed her steps. 16 I inclined my ear a little and received her, and I found for myself much instruction. 17 I made progress in her; to him who gives wisdom I will give glory. 18 For I resolved to live according to wisdom, and I was zealous for the good, and I shall never be disappointed. 19 My soul grappled with wisdom, and in my conduct I was strict; I spread out my hands to the heavens, and lamented my ignorance of her. 20 I directed my soul to her, and in purity I found her. With her I gained understanding from the first; therefore I will never be forsaken. 21 My heart was stirred to seek her; therefore I have gained a prize possession. 22 The Lord gave me my tongue as a reward, and I will praise him with it.

Isaiah 6:1-8 In the year that King Uzziah died, I saw the Lord sitting on a throne, high and lofty; and the hem of his robe filled the temple. 2 Seraphs were in attendance above him; each had six wings: with two they covered their faces, and with two they covered their feet, and with two they flew. 3 And one called to another and said: "Holy, holy, holy is the LORD of hosts;

the whole earth is full of his glory." 4 The pivots on the thresholds shook at the voices of those who called, and the house filled with smoke. 5 And I said: "Woe is me! I am lost, for I am a man of unclean lips, and I live among a people of unclean lips; yet my eyes have seen the King, the LORD of hosts!" 6 Then one of the seraphs flew to me, holding a live coal that had been taken from the altar with a pair of tongs. 7 The seraph touched my mouth with it and said: "Now that this has touched your lips, your guilt has departed and your sin is blotted out." 8 Then I heard the voice of the Lord saying, "Whom shall I send, and who will go for us?" And I said, "Here am I; send me!"

Isaiah 7:10-14 Again the LORD spoke to Ahaz, saying, 11 Ask a sign of the LORD your God; let it be deep as Sheol or high as heaven. 12 But Ahaz said, I will not ask, and I will not put the LORD to the test. 13 Then Isaiah said: "Hear then, O house of David! Is it too little for you to weary mortals, that you weary my God also? 14 Therefore the Lord himself will give you a sign. Look, the young woman is with child and shall bear a son, and shall name him Immanuel.

Isaiah 7:15-17 He shall eat curds and honey by the time he knows how to refuse the evil and choose the good. 16 For before the child knows how to refuse the evil and choose the good, the land before whose two kings you are in dread will be deserted. 17 The LORD will bring on you and on your people and on your ancestral house such days as have not come since the day that Ephraim departed from Judah — the king of Assyria."

Isaiah 8:1-4 Then the LORD said to me, Take a large tablet and write on it in common characters, "Belonging to Maher-shalal-hash-baz," 2 and have it attested for me by reliable witnesses, the priest Uriah and Zechariah son of Jeberechiah. 3 And I went to the prophetess, and she conceived and bore a son. Then the LORD said to me, Name him Maher-shalal-hash-baz; 4 for before the child knows how to call "My father" or "My mother," the wealth of Damascus and the spoil of Samaria will be carried away by the king of Assyria.

Isaiah 8:10 Take counsel together, but it shall be brought to naught; speak a word, but it will not stand, for God is with us.

Isaiah 9:1-6 But there will be no gloom for those who were in anguish. In the former time he brought into contempt the land of Zebulun and the land of Naphtali, but in the latter time he will make glorious the way of the sea, the land beyond the Jordan, Galilee of the nations. 2 The people who walked in darkness have seen a great light; those who lived in a land of deep darkness — on them light has shined. 3 You have multiplied the nation, you have increased its joy; they rejoice before you as with joy at the harvest, as people exult when dividing plunder. 4 For the yoke of their burden, and the bar across their shoulders, the rod of their oppressor, you have broken as on the day of Midian. 5 For all the boots of the tramping warriors and all the garments rolled in blood shall be burned as fuel for the fire. 6 For a child has been born for us, a son given to us; authority rests upon his shoulders; and he is named Wonderful Counselor, Mighty God, Everlasting Father, Prince of Peace.

Isaiah 11:1-5, 10 A shoot shall come out from the stump of Jesse, and a branch shall grow out of his roots. 2 The spirit of the LORD shall rest on him, the spirit of wisdom and understanding, the spirit of counsel and might, the spirit of knowledge and the fear of the LORD. 3 His delight shall be in the fear of the LORD. He shall not judge by what his eyes see, or decide by what his ears hear; 4 but with righteousness he shall judge the poor, and decide with equity for the meek of the earth; he shall strike the earth with the rod of his mouth, and with the breath of his lips he shall kill the wicked. 5 Righteousness shall be the belt around his waist, and faithfulness the belt around his loins. 10 On that day the root of Jesse shall stand as a signal to the peoples; the nations shall inquire of him, and his dwelling shall be glorious.

Isaiah 12 You will say in that day: I will give thanks to you, O LORD, for though you were angry with me, your anger turned away, and you comforted me. 2 Surely God is my salvation; I will trust, and will not be afraid, for the LORD GOD is my strength and my might; he has become my salvation. 3 With joy you will draw water from the wells of salvation. 4 And you will say in that day: Give thanks to the LORD, call on his name; make known his deeds among the nations; proclaim that his name is exalted. 5 Sing praises to the LORD, for he has done gloriously; let this be known in all the earth. 6 Shout aloud and sing for joy, O royal Zion, for great in your midst is the Holy One of Israel.

Isaiah 19:1 An oracle concerning Egypt. See, the LORD is riding on a swift cloud and comes to Egypt; the idols of Egypt will tremble at his presence, and the heart of the Egyptians will melt within them.

Isaiah 19:19-21 On that day there will be an altar to the LORD in the center of the land of Egypt, and a pillar to the LORD at its border. 20 It will be a sign and a witness to the LORD of hosts in the land of Egypt; when they cry to the LORD because of oppressors, he will send them a savior, and will defend and deliver them. 21 The LORD will make himself known to the Egyptians; and the Egyptians will know the LORD on that day, and will worship with sacrifice and burnt offering, and they will make vows to the LORD and perform them.

Isaiah 53:1-5 Who has believed what we have heard? And to whom has the arm of the LORD been revealed? 2 For he grew up before him like a young plant, and like a root out of dry ground; he had no form or majesty that we should look at him, nothing in his appearance that we should desire him. 3 He was despised and rejected by others; a man of suffering and acquainted with infirmity; and as one from whom others hide their faces he was despised, and we held him of no account. 4 Surely he has borne our infirmities and carried our diseases; yet we accounted him stricken, struck down by God, and afflicted. 5 But he was wounded for our transgressions, crushed for our iniquities; upon him was the punishment that made us whole, and by his bruises we are healed.

Isaiah 53:7-10 He was oppressed, and he was afflicted, yet he did not open his mouth; like a lamb that is led to the slaughter, and like a sheep that before its shearers is silent, so he did not open his mouth. 8 By a perversion of justice he was taken away. Who could have imagined his future? For he was cut off from the land of the living, stricken for the transgression of my people. 9 They made his grave with the wicked and his tomb with the rich, although he had done no violence, and there was no deceit in his mouth. 10 Yet it was the will of the LORD to crush him with pain. When you make his life an offering for sin, he shall see his offspring, and shall prolong his days; through him the will of the LORD shall prosper.

Isaiah 56:1 Thus says the LORD: Maintain justice, and do what is right, for soon my salvation will come, and my deliverance be revealed.

Isaiah 56:6-7 And the foreigners who join themselves to the LORD, to minister to him, to love the name of the LORD, and to be his servants, all who keep the Sabbath, and do not profane it, and hold fast my covenant — 7 these I will bring to my holy mountain, and make them joyful in my house of prayer; their burnt offerings and their sacrifices will be accepted on my altar; for my house shall be called a house of prayer for all peoples.

Isaiah 60:1-6 Arise, shine; for your light has come, and the glory of the LORD has risen upon you. 2 For darkness shall cover the earth, and thick darkness the peoples; but the LORD will arise upon you, and his glory will appear over you. 3 Nations shall come to your light, and kings to the brightness of your dawn. 4 Lift up your eyes and look around; they all gather together, they come to you; your sons shall come from far away, and your daughters shall be carried on their nurses' arms. 5 Then you shall see and be radiant; your heart shall thrill and rejoice, because the abundance of the sea shall be brought to you, the wealth of the nations shall come to you. 6 A multitude of camels shall cover you, the young camels of Midian and Ephah;

all those from Sheba shall come. They shall bring gold and frankincense, and shall proclaim the praise of the LORD.

Isaiah 61:1-3 The spirit of the Lord GOD is upon me, because the LORD has anointed me; he has sent me to bring good news to the oppressed, to bind up the brokenhearted, to proclaim liberty to the captives, and release to the prisoners; 2 to proclaim the year of the Lord's favor, and the day of vengeance of our God; to comfort all who mourn; 3 to provide for those who mourn in Zion — to give them a garland instead of ashes, the oil of gladness instead of mourning, the mantle of praise instead of a faint spirit. They will be called oaks of righteousness, the planting of the LORD, to display his glory.

Isaiah 61:10-11 I will greatly rejoice in the LORD, my whole being shall exult in my God; for he has clothed me with the garments of salvation, he has covered me with the robe of righteousness, as a bridegroom decks himself with a garland, and as a bride adorns herself with her jewels. 11 For as the earth brings forth its shoots, and as a garden causes what is sown in it to spring up, so the Lord GOD will cause righteousness and praise to spring up before all the nations.

Isaiah 62:1-3 For Zion's sake I will not keep silent, and for Jerusalem's sake I will not rest, until her vindication shines out like the dawn, and her salvation like a burning torch. 2 The nations shall see your vindication, and all the kings your glory; and you shall be called by a new name that the mouth of the LORD will give. 3 You shall be a crown of beauty in the hand of the LORD, and a royal diadem in the hand of your God.

Isaiah 66:10-14 Rejoice with Jerusalem, and be glad for her, all you who love her; rejoice with her in joy, all you who mourn over her — 11 that you may nurse and be satisfied from her consoling breast; that you may drink deeply with delight from her glorious bosom. 12 For thus says the LORD: I will extend prosperity to her like a river, and the wealth of the nations like an overflowing stream; and you shall nurse and be carried on her arm, and dandled on her knees. 13 As a mother comforts her child, so I will comfort you; you shall be comforted in Jerusalem. 14 You shall see, and your heart shall rejoice; your bodies shall flourish like the grass; and it shall be known that the hand of the LORD is with his servants, and his indignation is against his enemies.

Baruch 3:36-37 Such is our God; no other is to be compared to him: 37 He has traced out all the way of understanding, and has given her to Jacob, his servant, to Israel, his beloved son. 38 Since then she has appeared on earth, and moved among men.

Ezekiel 10:18-19 Then the glory of the LORD went out from the threshold of the house and stopped above the cherubim. 19 The cherubim lifted up their wings and rose up from the earth in my sight as they went out with the wheels beside them. They stopped at the entrance of the east gate of the house of the LORD; and the glory of the God of Israel was above them.

Ezekiel 44:1-4 Then he brought me back to the outer gate of the sanctuary, which faces east; and it was shut. 2 The LORD said to me: This gate shall remain shut; it shall not be opened, and no one shall enter by it; for the LORD, the God of Israel, has entered by it; therefore it shall remain shut. 3 Only the prince, because he is a prince, may sit in it to eat food before the LORD; he shall enter by way of the vestibule of the gate, and shall go out by the same way. 4 Then he brought me by way of the north gate to the front of the temple; and I looked, and lo! the glory of the LORD filled the temple of the LORD; and I fell upon my face.

Ezekiel 47:1-2 Then he brought me back to the entrance of the temple; there, water was flowing from below the threshold of the temple toward the east (for the temple faced east); and the water was flowing down from below the south end of the threshold of the temple, south of the altar. 2 Then he brought me out by way of the north gate, and led me around on the outside to the outer gate that faces toward the east; and the water was coming out on the south side.

Ezekiel 47:8-9 He said to me, "This water flows toward the eastern region and goes down into the Arabah; and when it enters the sea, the sea of stagnant waters, the water will become fresh. 9 Wherever the river goes, every living creature that swarms will live, and there will be very many fish, once these waters reach there. It will become fresh; and everything will live where the river goes.

Ezekiel 47:12 On the banks, on both sides of the river, there will grow all kinds of trees for food. Their leaves will not wither nor their fruit fail, but they will bear fresh fruit every month, because the water for them flows from the sanctuary. Their fruit will be for food, and their leaves for healing."

Daniel 2:31-35 "In your vision, O king, you saw a statue, very large and exceedingly bright, terrifying in appearance as it stood before you. 32 The head of the statue was pure gold, its chest and arms were silver, its belly and thighs bronze, 33 the legs iron, its feet partly iron and partly tile. 34 While you looked at the statue, a stone which was hewn from a mountain without a hand being put to it, struck its iron and tile feet, breaking them in pieces. 35 The iron, tile, bronze, silver, and gold all crumbled at once, fine as the chaff on the threshing floor in summer, and the wind blew them away without leaving a trace. But the stone that struck the statue became a great mountain and filled the whole earth.

Micah 5:1-4 Now you are walled around with a wall; siege is laid against us; with a rod they strike the ruler of Israel upon the cheek. 2 But you, O Bethlehem of Ephrathah, who are one of the little clans of Judah, from you shall come forth for me one who is to rule in Israel, whose origin is from of old, from ancient days. 3 Therefore he shall give them up until the time when she who is in labor has brought forth; then the rest of his kindred shall return to the people of Israel. 4 And he shall stand and feed his flock in the strength of the LORD, in the majesty of the name of the LORD his God. And they shall live secure, for now he shall be great to the ends of the earth;

Habakkuk 3:3-4 God came from Teman, the Holy One from Mount Paran. Selah His glory covered the heavens, and the earth was full of his praise. 4 The brightness was like the sun; rays came forth from his hand, where his power lay hidden.

Zephaniah 3:14-20 Sing aloud, O daughter Zion; shout, O Israel! Rejoice and exult with all your heart, O daughter Jerusalem! 15 The LORD has taken away the judgments against you, he has turned away your enemies. The king of Israel, the LORD, is in your midst; you shall fear disaster no more. 16 On that day it shall be said to Jerusalem: Do not fear, O Zion; do not let your hands grow weak. 17 The LORD, your God, is in your midst, a warrior who gives victory; he will rejoice over you with gladness, he will renew you in his love; he will exult over you with loud singing 18 as on a day of festival. I will remove disaster from you, so that you will not bear reproach for it. 19 I will deal with all your oppressors at that time. And I will save the lame and gather the outcast, and I will change their shame into praise and renown in all the earth. 20 At that time I will bring you home, at the time when I gather you; for I will make you renowned and praised among all the peoples of the earth, when I restore your fortunes before your eyes, says the LORD.

Zechariah 2:10-12 Sing and rejoice, O daughter Zion! For lo, I will come and dwell in your midst, says the LORD. 11 Many nations shall join themselves to the LORD on that day, and shall be my people; and I will dwell in your midst. And you shall know that the LORD of hosts has sent me to you. 12 The LORD will inherit Judah as his portion in the holy land, and will again choose Jerusalem.

Zechariah 4:1-7 The angel who talked with me came again, and wakened me, as one is wakened from sleep. 2 He said to me, "What do you see?" And I said, "I see a lampstand all of gold, with a bowl on the top of it; there are seven lamps on it, with seven lips on each of the lamps that are on the top of it. 3 And by it there are two olive trees, one on the right of the bowl and the other on its left." 4 I said to the angel who talked with me, "What are these, my lord?" 5 Then the angel who talked with me answered me, "Do you not know what these are?" I said, "No, my lord." 6 He said to me, "This is the word of the LORD to Zerubbabel: Not by might, nor by power, but by my spirit, says the LORD of hosts. 7 What are you, O great mountain? Before Zerubbabel you shall become a plain; and he shall bring out the top stone amid shouts of 'Grace, grace to it!'"

Zechariah 9:9-10 Rejoice greatly, O daughter Zion! Shout aloud, O daughter Jerusalem! Lo, your king comes to you; triumphant and victorious is he, humble and riding on a donkey, on a colt, the foal of a donkey. 10 He will cut off the chariot from Ephraim and the war horse from Jerusalem; and the battle bow shall be cut off, and he shall command peace to the nations; his dominion shall be from sea to sea, and from the River to the ends of the earth.

Malachi 3:1-4 See, I am sending my messenger to prepare the way before me, and the Lord whom you seek will suddenly come to his temple. The messenger of the covenant in whom you delight — indeed, he is coming, says the LORD of hosts. 2 But who can endure the day of his coming, and who can stand when he appears? For he is like a refiner's fire and like fullers' soap; 3 he will sit as a refiner and purifier of silver, and he will purify the descendants of Levi and refine them like gold and silver, until they present offerings to the LORD in righteousness. 4 Then the offering of Judah and Jerusalem will be pleasing to the LORD as in the days of old and as in former years.

Appendix 3

References to the Blessed Virgin Mary in the Catechism of the Catholic Church and the Apostolic Constitution *Fidei Depositum*

The approval and publication of the *Catechism of the Catholic Church* represent a service which the Successor of Peter wishes to offer to the Holy Catholic Church, to all the particular Churches in peace and communion with the Apostolic See: the service, that is, of supporting and confirming the faith of all the Lord Jesus' disciples (cf. Lk 22:32), as well as of strengthening the bonds of unity in the same apostolic faith.

Therefore, I ask all the Church's Pastors and the Christian faithful to receive this catechism in a spirit of communion and to use it assiduously in fulfilling their mission of proclaiming the faith and calling people to the Gospel life. This catechism is given to them that it may be a sure and authentic reference text for teaching Catholic doctrine and particularly for preparing local catechisms. It is also offered to all the faithful who wish to deepen their knowledge of the unfathomable riches of salvation (cf. Eph 3:8). It is meant to support ecumenical efforts that are moved by the holy desire for the unity of all Christians, showing carefully the content and wondrous harmony of the Catholic faith. The *Catechism of the Catholic Church*, lastly, is offered to every individual who asks us to give an account of the hope that is in us (cf. 1 P 3:15) and who wants to know what the Catholic Church believes.

This catechism is not intended to replace the local catechisms duly approved by the ecclesiastical authorities, the diocesan Bishops and the Episcopal Conferences, especially if they have been approved by the Apostolic See. It is meant to encourage and assist in the writing of new local catechisms, which take into account various situations and cultures, while carefully preserving the unity of faith and fidelity to Catholic doctrine.

At the conclusion of this document presenting the *Catechism of the Catholic Church*, I beseech the Blessed Virgin Mary, Mother of the Incarnate

Word and Mother of the Church, to support with her powerful intercession the catechetical work of the entire Church on every level, at this time when she is called to a new effort of evangelization. May the light of the true faith free humanity from the ignorance and slavery of sin in order to lead it to the only freedom worthy of the name (cf. Jn 8:32): that of life in Jesus Christ under the guidance of the Holy Spirit, here below and in the Kingdom of heaven, in the fullness of the blessed vision of God face to face (cf. 1 Cor 13:12; 2 Cor 5:6-8)!

Beverly Stoller

Fragment of a fresco from the catacomb of Priscilla in Rome, dating from the beginning of the third century A.D. It is the most ancient image of the Blessed Virgin.

This image, among the most ancient in Christian art, expresses a theme that lies at the heart of the Christian faith: the mystery of the incarnation of the Son of God born of the Virgin Mary.

— At the left, the figure of a man pointing to a star, located above the Virgin with the child: a prophet, probably Balaam, who announced that "a star shall come forth out of Jacob, and a scepter shall rise out of Israel" (Nb 24:17). This is the whole expectation of the Old Covenant and the cry of a fallen humanity for a savior and redeemer (cf. 27; 528).

— This prophecy was fulfilled in the birth of Jesus, the incarnate Son of God, conceived by the power of the Holy Spirit and born of the Virgin Mary (cf. §§27; 53; 422; 488). Mary brought him into the world and gave him to all mankind. For this reason she is the purest image of the Church (cf. §967).

64 Through the prophets, God forms his people in the hope of salvation, in the expectation of a new and everlasting Covenant intended for all, to be written on their hearts.[1] The prophets proclaim a radical redemption of the People of God, purification from all their infidelities, a salvation which will include all the nations.[2] Above all, the poor and humble of the Lord will bear this hope. Such holy women as Sarah, Rebecca, Rachel, Miriam, Deborah, Hannah, Judith, and Esther kept alive the hope of Israel's salvation. The purest figure among them is Mary.[3]

148 The Virgin Mary most perfectly embodies the obedience of faith. By faith Mary welcomes the tidings and promise brought by the angel Gabriel, believing that "with God nothing will be impossible" and so giving her assent: "Behold I am the handmaid of the Lord; let it be [done] to me according to your word."[4] Elizabeth greeted her: "Blessed is she who believed that there would be a fulfillment of what was spoken to her from the Lord."[5] It is for this faith that all generations have called Mary blessed.[6]

149 Throughout her life and until her last ordeal[7] when Jesus her son died on the cross, Mary's faith never wavered. She never ceased to believe in the fulfillment of God's word. And so the Church venerates in Mary the purest realization of faith.

165 It is then we must turn to the *witnesses of faith*: to Abraham, who "in hope ... believed against hope";[8] to the Virgin Mary, who, in "her pilgrimage of faith," walked into the "night of faith"[9] in sharing the darkness of her son's suffering and death; and to so many others: "Therefore, since we are surrounded by so great a cloud of witnesses, let us also lay aside every weight, and sin which clings so closely, and let us run with perseverance the race that is set before us, looking to Jesus the pioneer and perfecter of our faith."[10]

The Apostles' Creed: He was conceived by the power of the Holy Spirit and born of the Virgin Mary.

The Nicene Creed: by the power of the Holy Spirit he was born of the Virgin Mary, and became man.

273 Only faith can embrace the mysterious ways of God's almighty power. This faith glories in its weaknesses in order to draw to itself Christ's power.[11] The Virgin Mary is the supreme model of this faith, for she believed that "nothing will be impossible with God," and was able to magnify the Lord: "For he who is mighty has done great things for me, and holy is his name."[12]

369 Man and woman have been *created*, which is to say, *willed* by God: on the one hand, in perfect equality as human persons; on the other, in their respective beings as man and woman. "Being man" or "being woman" is a reality which is good and willed by God: man and woman possess an inalienable dignity which comes to them immediately from God their Creator.[13] Man and woman are both with one and the same dignity "in the image of God." In their "being-man" and "being-woman," they reflect the Creator's wisdom and goodness.

410 After his fall, man was not abandoned by God. On the contrary, God calls him and in a mysterious way heralds the coming victory over evil and his restoration from his fall.[14] This passage in Genesis is called the *Protoevangelium* ("first gospel"): the first announcement of the Messiah and Redeemer, of a battle between the serpent and the Woman, and of the final victory of a descendant of hers.

411 The Christian tradition sees in this passage an announcement of the "New Adam" who, because he "became obedient unto death, even death on a cross," makes amends superabundantly for the disobedience of Adam.[15] Furthermore many Fathers and Doctors of the Church have seen the woman announced in the *Protoevangelium* as Mary, the mother of Christ, the "new Eve." Mary benefited first of all and uniquely from Christ's victory over sin: she was preserved from all stain of original sin and by a special grace of God committed no sin of any kind during her whole earthly life.[16]

423 We believe and confess that Jesus of Nazareth, born a Jew of a daughter of Israel at Bethlehem at the time of King Herod the Great and the emperor Caesar Augustus, a carpenter by trade, who died crucified in Jerusalem under the procurator Pontius Pilate during the reign of the emperor Tiberius, is the eternal Son of God made man. He "came from God,"[17] "descended from heaven,"[18] and "came in the flesh."[19] For "the Word became flesh and dwelt among us, full of grace and truth; we have beheld his glory, glory as of the only Son from the Father. . . . And from his fullness have we all received, grace upon grace."[20]

430 Jesus means in Hebrew: "God saves." At the annunciation, the angel Gabriel gave him the name Jesus as his proper name, which expresses both his identity and his mission.[21] Since God alone can forgive sins, it is God who, in Jesus his eternal Son made man, "will save his people from their sins."[22] In Jesus, God recapitulates all of his history of salvation on behalf of men.

435 The name of Jesus is at the heart of Christian prayer. All liturgical prayers conclude with the words "through our Lord Jesus Christ." The *Hail Mary* reaches its high point in the words "blessed is the fruit of thy womb, Jesus." The Eastern prayer of the heart, the *Jesus Prayer*, says: "Lord Jesus Christ, Son of God, have mercy on me, a sinner." Many Christians, such as St. Joan of Arc, have died with the one word "Jesus" on their lips.

437 To the shepherds, the angel announced the birth of Jesus as the Messiah promised to Israel: "To you is born this day in the city of David a Savior, who is Christ the Lord."[23] From the beginning he was "the one whom the Father consecrated and sent into the world," conceived as "holy" in Mary's virginal womb.[24] God called Joseph to "take Mary as your wife, for that which is conceived in her is of the Holy Spirit," so that Jesus, "who is called Christ," should be born of Joseph's spouse into the messianic lineage of David.[25]

452 The name Jesus means "God saves." The child born of the Virgin Mary is called Jesus, "for he will save his people from their sins" (Mt 1:21): "there is no other name under heaven given among men by which we must be saved" (Acts 4:12).

456 With the Nicene Creed, we answer by confessing: "For us men and for our salvation he came down from heaven; by the power of the Holy Spirit, he became incarnate of the Virgin Mary, and was made man."

461 Taking up St. John's expression, "The Word became flesh,"[26] the Church calls "Incarnation" the fact that the Son of God assumed a human nature in order to accomplish our salvation in it. In a hymn cited by St. Paul, the Church sings the mystery of the Incarnation:

> Have this mind among yourselves, which is yours in Christ Jesus, who, though he was in the form of God, did not count equality with God a thing to be grasped, but emptied himself, taking the form of a servant, being born in the likeness of men. And being found in human form he humbled himself and became obedient unto death, even death on a cross.[27]

466 The Nestorian heresy regarded Christ as a human person joined to the divine person of God's Son. Opposing this heresy, St. Cyril of Alexandria and the third ecumenical council at Ephesus in 431 confessed "that the Word, uniting to himself in his person the flesh animated by a rational soul, became man."[28] Christ's humanity has no other subject than the divine person of the Son of God, who assumed it and made it his own, from his conception. For this reason the Council of Ephesus proclaimed in 431 that Mary truly became the Mother of God by the human conception of the Son of God in her womb: "Mother of God, not that the nature of the Word or his divinity received the beginning of its existence from the holy Virgin, but that, since the holy body, animated by a rational soul, which the Word of God united to himself according to the hypostasis, was born from her, the Word is said to be born according to the flesh."[29]

467 The Monophysites affirmed that the human nature had ceased to exist as such in Christ when the divine person of God's Son assumed it. Faced with this heresy, the fourth ecumenical council, at Chalcedon in 451, confessed:

> Following the holy Fathers, we unanimously teach and confess one and the same Son, our Lord Jesus Christ; the same perfect in divinity and perfect in humanity, the same truly God and truly man, composed of rational soul and body; consubstantial with the Father as to his divinity and consubstantial with us as to his humanity; "like us in all things but sin." He was begotten from the Father before all ages as to his divinity and in these last days, for us and for our salvation, was born as to his humanity of the virgin Mary, the Mother of God.[30]

> We confess that one and the same Christ, Lord, and only-begotten Son, is to be acknowledged in two natures without confusion, change, division, or separation. The distinction between the natures was never abolished by their union, but rather the character proper to each of the two natures was preserved as they came together in one person (*prosopon*) and one hypostasis.[31]

469 The Church thus confesses that Jesus is inseparably true God and true man. He is truly the Son of God who, without ceasing to be God and Lord, became a man and our brother:

> "What he was, he remained and what he was not, he assumed," sings the Roman Liturgy.[32] And the liturgy of St. John Chrysostom proclaims and sings: "O only-begotten Son and Word of God, immortal being, you who deigned for our salvation to become incarnate of the holy Mother of God and ever-virgin Mary, you who without change became man and were crucified, O Christ our God, you who by your death have crushed death, you who are

one of the Holy Trinity, glorified with the Father and the Holy
Spirit, save us!"[33]

470 Because "human nature was assumed, not absorbed,"[34] in the mysterious union of the Incarnation, the Church was led over the course of centuries
to confess the full reality of Christ's human soul, with its operations of
intellect and will, and of his human body. In parallel fashion, she had to recall
on each occasion that Christ's human nature belongs, as his own, to the
divine person of the Son of God, who assumed it. Everything that Christ is
and does in this nature derives from "one of the Trinity." The Son of God
therefore communicates to his humanity his own personal mode of existence
in the Trinity. In his soul as in his body, Christ thus expresses humanly the
divine ways of the Trinity:[35]

> The Son of God. . . worked with human hands; he thought with
> a human mind. He acted with a human will, and with a human
> heart he loved. Born of the Virgin Mary, he has truly been made
> one of us, like to us in all things except sin.[36]

490 To become the mother of the Savior, Mary "was enriched by God with
gifts appropriate to such a role."[37] The angel Gabriel at the moment of the
annunciation salutes her as "full of grace."[38] In fact, in order for Mary to be
able to give the free assent of her faith to the announcement of her vocation,
it was necessary that she be wholly born by God's grace.

491 Through the centuries the Church has become ever more aware that
Mary, "full of grace" through God,[39] was redeemed from the moment of her
conception. That is what the dogma of the Immaculate Conception confesses, as Pope Pius IX proclaimed in 1854:

> The most Blessed Virgin Mary was, from the first moment of her
> conception, by a singular grace and privilege of almighty God
> and by virtue of the merits of Jesus Christ, Savior of the human
> race, preserved immune from all stain of original sin.[40]

492 The "splendor of an entirely unique holiness" by which Mary is
"enriched from the first instant of her conception" comes wholly from
Christ: she is "redeemed, in a more exalted fashion, by reason of the merits
of her Son."[41] The Father blessed Mary more than any other created person
"in Christ with every spiritual blessing in the heavenly places" and chose her
"in Christ before the foundation of the world, to be holy and blameless
before him in love."[42]

493 The Fathers of the Eastern tradition call the Mother of God "the All-
Holy" (*Panagia*) and celebrate her as "free from any stain of sin, as though

fashioned by the Holy Spirit and formed as a new creature."[43] By the grace of God Mary remained free of every personal sin her whole life long.

494 At the announcement that she would give birth to "the Son of the Most High" without knowing man, by the power of the Holy Spirit, Mary responded with the obedience of faith, certain that "with God nothing will be impossible": "Behold, I am the handmaid of the Lord; let it be [done] to me according to your word."[44] Thus, giving her consent to God's word, Mary becomes the mother of Jesus. Espousing the divine will for salvation wholeheartedly, without a single sin to restrain her, she gave herself entirely to the person and to the work of her Son; she did so in order to serve the mystery of redemption with him and dependent on him, by God's grace:[45]

> As St. Irenaeus says, "Being obedient she became the cause of salvation for herself and for the whole human race."[46] Hence not a few of the early Fathers gladly assert. . . : "The knot of Eve's disobedience was untied by Mary's obedience: what the virgin Eve bound through her disbelief, Mary loosened by her faith."[47] Comparing her with Eve, they call Mary "the Mother of the living" and frequently claim: "Death through Eve, life through Mary."[48]

495 Called in the Gospels "the mother of Jesus," Mary is acclaimed by Elizabeth, at the prompting of the Spirit and even before the birth of her son, as "the mother of my Lord."[49] In fact, the One whom she conceived as man by the Holy Spirit, who truly became her Son according to the flesh, was none other than the Father's eternal Son, the second person of the Holy Trinity. Hence the Church confesses that Mary is truly "Mother of God" (*Theotokos*).[50]

501 Jesus is Mary's only son, but her spiritual motherhood extends to all men whom indeed he came to save: "The Son whom she brought forth is he whom God placed as the first-born among many brethren, that is, the faithful in whose generation and formulation she cooperates with a mother's love."[51]

502 The eyes of faith can discover in the context of the whole of Revelation the mysterious reasons why God in his saving plan wanted his Son to be born of a virgin. These reasons touch both on the person of Christ and his redemptive mission, and on the welcome Mary gave that mission on behalf of all men.

503 Mary's virginity manifests God's absolute initiative in the Incarnation. Jesus has only God as Father. "He was never estranged from the Father because of the human nature which he assumed. . . . He is naturally Son of the Father as to his divinity and naturally son of his mother as to his humanity, but properly Son of the Father in both natures."[52]

504 Jesus is conceived by the Holy Spirit in the Virgin Mary's womb because he is the New Adam, who inaugurates the new creation: "The first man was from the earth, a man of dust; the second man is from heaven."[53] From his conception, Christ's humanity is filled with the Holy Spirit, for God "gives him the Spirit without measure."[54] From "his fullness" as the head of redeemed humanity "we have all received, grace upon grace."[55]

505 By his virginal conception, Jesus, the New Adam, ushers in *the new birth* of children adopted in the Holy Spirit through faith. "How can this be?"[56] Participation in the divine life arises "not of blood nor of the will of the flesh nor of the will of man, but of God."[57] The acceptance of this life is virginal because it is entirely the Spirit's gift to man. The spousal character of the human vocation in relation to God[58] is fulfilled perfectly in Mary's virginal motherhood.

506 Mary is a virgin because her virginity is *the sign of her faith* "unadulterated by any doubt," and of her undivided gift of herself to God's will.[59] It is her faith that enables her to become the mother of the Savior: "Mary is more blessed because she embraces faith in Christ than because she conceives the flesh of Christ."[60]

507 At once virgin and mother, Mary is the symbol and the most perfect realization of the Church: "the Church indeed. . . by receiving the word of God in faith becomes herself a mother. By preaching and Baptism she brings forth sons, who are conceived by the Holy Spirit and born of God, to a new and immortal life. She herself is a virgin, who keeps in its entirety and purity the faith she pledged to her spouse."[61]

508 From among the descendants of Eve, God chose the Virgin Mary to be the mother of his Son. "Full of grace," Mary is "the most excellent fruit of redemption" (SC 103): from the first instant of her conception, she was totally preserved from the stain of original sin and she remained pure from all personal sin throughout her life.

509 Mary is truly "Mother of God" since she is the mother of the eternal Son of God made man, who is God himself.

510 Mary "remained a virgin in conceiving her Son, a virgin in giving birth to him, a virgin in carrying him, a virgin in nursing him at her breast, always a virgin" (St. Augustine, *Serm.* 186, 1:PL 38, 999): with her whole being she is "the handmaid of the Lord" (Lk 1:38).

511 The Virgin Mary "cooperated through free faith and obedience in human salvation" (LG 56). She uttered her yes "in the name of all human nature" (St. Thomas Aquinas, *STh* III, 30, 1). By her obedience she became the new Eve, mother of the living.

525 Jesus was born in a humble stable, into a poor family.[62] Simple shepherds were the first witnesses to this event. In this poverty heaven's glory was made manifest.[63] The Church never tires of singing the glory of this night:

> The Virgin today brings into the world the Eternal / And the earth offers a cave to the Inaccessible. / The angels and shepherds praise him / And the magi advance with the star, / For you are born for us, / Little Child, God eternal![64]

526 To become a child in relation to God is the condition for entering the kingdom.[65] For this, we must humble ourselves and become little. Even more: to become "children of God" we must be "born from above" or "born of God."[66] Only when Christ is formed in us will the mystery of Christmas be fulfilled in us.[67] Christmas is the mystery of this "marvelous exchange":

> O marvelous exchange! Man's Creator has become man, born of the Virgin. We have been made sharers in the divinity of Christ who humbled himself to share our humanity.[68]

528 The *Epiphany* is the manifestation of Jesus as Messiah of Israel, Son of God and Savior of the world. The great feast of Epiphany celebrates the adoration of Jesus by the wise men (*magi*) from the East, together with his baptism in the Jordan and the wedding feast at Cana in Galilee.[69] In the magi, representatives of the neighboring pagan religions, the Gospel sees the first-fruits of the nations, who welcome the good news of salvation through the Incarnation. The magi's coming to Jerusalem in order to pay homage to the king of the Jews shows that they seek in Israel, in the messianic light of the star of David, the one who will be king of the nations.[70] Their coming means that pagans can discover Jesus and worship him as Son of God and Savior of the world only by turning toward the Jews and receiving from them the messianic promise as contained in the Old Testament.[71] The Epiphany shows that "the full number of the nations" now takes its "place in the family of the patriarchs," and acquires *Israelitica dignitas*[72] (are made "worthy of the heritage of Israel").

529 The *presentation of Jesus in the temple* shows him to be the firstborn Son who belongs to the Lord.[73] With Simeon and Anna, all Israel awaits its *encounter* with the Savior — the name given to this event in the Byzantine tradition. Jesus is recognized as the long-expected Messiah, the "light to the nations" and the "glory of Israel," but also "a sign that is spoken against." The sword of sorrow predicted for Mary announces Christ's perfect and unique oblation on the cross that will impart the salvation God had "prepared in the presence of all peoples."

531 During the greater part of his life Jesus shared the condition of the vast majority of human beings: a daily life spent without evident greatness, a life of manual labor. His religious life was that of a Jew obedient to the law of God,[74] a life in the community. From this whole period it is revealed to us that Jesus was "obedient" to his parents and that he "increased in wisdom and in stature, and in favor with God and man."[75]

532 Jesus' obedience to his mother and legal father fulfills the fourth commandment perfectly and was the temporal image of his filial obedience to his Father in heaven. The everyday obedience of Jesus to Joseph and Mary both announced and anticipated the obedience of Holy Thursday: "Not my will. . . ."[76] The obedience of Christ in the daily routine of his hidden life was already inaugurating his work of restoring what the disobedience of Adam had destroyed.[77]

533 The hidden life at Nazareth allows everyone to enter into fellowship with Jesus by the most ordinary events of daily life:

> The home of Nazareth is the school where we begin to understand the life of Jesus — the school of the Gospel. First, then, a lesson of silence. May esteem for *silence*, that admirable and indispensable condition of mind, revive in us. . . A lesson on *family life*. May Nazareth teach us what family life is, its communion of love, its austere and simple beauty, and its sacred and inviolable character. . . A lesson of *work*. Nazareth, home of the "Carpenter's Son," in you I would choose to understand and proclaim the severe and redeeming law of human work. . . . To conclude, I want to greet all the workers of the world, holding up to them their great pattern, their brother who is God.[78]

534 The *finding of Jesus in the temple* is the only event that breaks the silence of the Gospels about the hidden years of Jesus.[79] Here Jesus lets us catch a glimpse of the mystery of his total consecration to a mission that flows from his divine sonship: "Did you not know that I must be about my Father's work?"[80] Mary and Joseph did not understand these words, but they accepted them in faith. Mary "kept all these things in her heart" during the years Jesus remained hidden in the silence of an ordinary life.

554 From the day Peter confessed that Jesus is the Christ, the Son of the living God, the Master "began to show his disciples that he must go to

Jerusalem and suffer many things. . . and be killed, and on the third day be raised."[81] Peter scorns this prediction, nor do the others understand it any better than he.[82] In this context the mysterious episode of Jesus' Transfiguration takes place on a high mountain,[83] before three witnesses chosen by himself: Peter, James, and John. Jesus' face and clothes become dazzling with light, and Moses and Elijah appear, speaking "of his departure, which he was to accomplish at Jerusalem."[84] A cloud covers him and a voice from heaven says: "This is my Son, my Chosen; listen to him!"[85]

559 How will Jerusalem welcome her Messiah? Although Jesus had always refused popular attempts to make him king, he chooses the time and prepares the details for his messianic entry into the city of "his father David."[86] Acclaimed as son of David, as the one who brings salvation (*Hosanna* means "Save!" or "Give salvation!"), the "King of glory" enters his City "riding on an ass."[87] Jesus conquers the Daughter of Zion, a figure of his Church, neither by ruse nor by violence, but by the humility that bears witness to the truth.[88] And so the subjects of his kingdom on that day are children and the God's poor, who acclaim him as had the angels when they announced him to the shepherds.[89] Their acclamation, "Blessed be he who comes in the name of the LORD,"[90] is taken up by the Church in the "*Sanctus*" of the Eucharistic liturgy that introduces the memorial of the Lord's Passover.

563 No one, whether shepherd or wise man, can approach God here below except by kneeling before the manger at Bethlehem and adoring him hidden in the weakness of a new-born child.

564 By his obedience to Mary and Joseph, as well as by his humble work during the long years in Nazareth, Jesus gives us the example of holiness in the daily life of family and work.

583 Like the prophets before him Jesus expressed the deepest respect for the Temple in Jerusalem. It was in the Temple that Joseph and Mary presented him forty days after his birth.[91] At the age of twelve he decided to remain in the Temple to remind his parents that he must be about his Father's business.[92] He went there each year during his hidden life at least for Passover.[93] His public ministry itself was patterned by his pilgrimages to Jerusalem for the great Jewish feasts.[94]

593 Jesus venerated the Temple by going up to it for the Jewish feasts of pilgrimage, and with a jealous love he loved this dwelling of God among men. The Temple prefigures his own mystery. When he announces its destruction, it is as a manifestation of his own execution and of the entry into a new age in the history of salvation, when his Body would be the definitive Temple.

602 Consequently, St. Peter can formulate the apostolic faith in the divine plan of salvation in this way: "You were ransomed from the futile ways inherited from your fathers...with the precious blood of Christ, like that of a lamb without blemish or spot. He was destined before the foundation of the world but was made manifest at the end of the times for your sake."[95] Man's sins, following on original sin, are punishable by death.[96] By sending his own Son in the form of a slave, in the form of a fallen humanity, on account of sin, God "made him to be sin who knew no sin, so that in him we might become the righteousness of God."[97]

695 *Anointing*. The symbolism of anointing with oil also signifies the Holy Spirit,[98] to the point of becoming a synonym for the Holy Spirit. In Christian initiation, anointing is the sacramental sign of Confirmation, called "chrismation" in the Churches of the East. Its full force can be grasped only in relation to the primary anointing accomplished by the Holy Spirit, that of Jesus. Christ (in Hebrew *"messiah"*) means the one "anointed" by God's spirit. There were several anointed ones of the Lord in the Old Covenant, pre-eminently King David.[99] But Jesus is God's Anointed in a unique way: the humanity the Son assumed was entirely anointed by the Holy Spirit. The Holy Spirit established him as "Christ."[100] The Virgin Mary conceived Christ by the Holy Spirit who, through the angel, proclaimed him the Christ at his birth, and prompted Simeon to come to the temple to see the Christ of the Lord.[101] The Spirit filled Christ and the power of the Spirit went out from him in his acts of healing and saving.[102] Finally, it was the Spirit who raised Jesus from the dead.[103] Now, fully established as "Christ" in his humanity victorious over death, Jesus pours out the Holy Spirit abundantly until "the saints" constitute — in their union with the humanity of the Son of God — that perfect man "to the measure of the stature of the fullness of Christ":[104] "the whole Christ," in St. Augustine's expression.

697 *Cloud and light*. These two images occur together in the manifestations of the Holy Spirit. In the theophanies of the Old Testament, the cloud, now obscure, now luminous, reveals the living and saving God, while veiling the transcendence of his glory — with Moses on Mount Sinai,[105] at the tent of meeting,[106] and during the wandering in the desert,[107] and with Solomon at the dedication of the Temple.[108] In the Holy Spirit, Christ fulfills these figures. The Spirit comes upon the Virgin Mary and "overshadows" her, so that she might conceive and give birth to Jesus.[109] On the mountain of Transfiguration, the Spirit in the "cloud came and overshadowed" Jesus, Moses and Elijah, Peter, James and John, and "a voice came out of the cloud,

saying, 'This is my Son, my Chosen; listen to him!'"[110] Finally, the cloud took Jesus out of the sight of the disciples on the day of his ascension and will reveal him as Son of man in glory on the day of his final coming.[111]

711 "Behold, I am doing a new thing."[112] Two prophetic lines were to develop, one leading to the expectation of the Messiah, the other pointing to the announcement of a new Spirit. They converge in the small Remnant, the people of the poor, who await in hope the "consolation of Israel" and "the redemption of Jerusalem."[113].

> We have seen earlier how Jesus fulfills the prophecies concerning himself. We limit ourselves here to those in which the relationship of the Messiah and his Spirit appears more clearly.

717 "There was a man sent from God, whose name was John."[114] John was "filled with the Holy Spirit even from his mother's womb"[115] by Christ himself, whom the Virgin Mary had just conceived by the Holy Spirit. Mary's visitation to Elizabeth thus became a visit from God to his people.[116]

721 Mary, the all-holy ever-virgin Mother of God, is the masterwork of the mission of the Son and the Spirit in the fullness of time. For the first time in the plan of salvation and because his Spirit had prepared her, the Father found the *dwelling place* where his Son and his Spirit could dwell among men. In this sense the Church's Tradition has often read the most beautiful texts on wisdom in relation to Mary.[117] Mary is acclaimed and represented in the liturgy as the "Seat of Wisdom."

In her, the "wonders of God" that the Spirit was to fulfill in Christ and the Church began to be manifested:

722 The Holy Spirit *prepared* Mary by his grace. It was fitting that the mother of him in whom "the whole fullness of deity dwells bodily"[118] should herself be "full of grace." She was, by sheer grace, conceived without sin as the most humble of creatures, the most capable of welcoming the inexpressible gift of the Almighty. It was quite correct for the angel Gabriel to greet her as the "Daughter of Zion": "Rejoice."[119] It is the thanksgiving of the whole People of God, and thus of the Church, which Mary in her canticle[120] lifts up to the Father in the Holy Spirit while carrying within her the eternal Son.

723 In Mary, the Holy Spirit *fulfills* the plan of the Father's loving goodness. With and through the Holy Spirit, the Virgin conceives and gives birth to the Son of God. By the Holy Spirit's power and her faith, her virginity became uniquely fruitful.[121]

724 In Mary, the Holy Spirit *manifests* the Son of the Father, now become the Son of the Virgin. She is the burning bush of the definitive theophany. Filled with the Holy Spirit she makes the Word visible in the humility of his flesh. It is to the poor and the first representatives of the gentiles that she makes him known.[122]

725 Finally, through Mary, the Holy Spirit begins to bring men, the objects of God's merciful love,[123] *into communion* with Christ. And the humble are always the first to accept him: shepherds, magi, Simeon and Anna, the bride and groom at Cana, and the first disciples.

726 At the end of this mission of the Spirit, Mary became the Woman, the new Eve ("mother of the living"), the mother of the "whole Christ."[124] As such, she was present with the Twelve, who "with one accord devoted themselves to prayer,"[125] at the dawn of the "end time" which the Spirit was to inaugurate on the morning of Pentecost with the manifestation of the Church.

744 In the fullness of time the Holy Spirit completes in Mary all the preparations for Christ's coming among the People of God. By the action of the Holy Spirit in her, the Father gives the world Emmanuel, "God-with-us" (Mt 1:23).

766 The Church is born primarily of Christ's total self-giving for our salvation, anticipated in the institution of the Eucharist and fulfilled on the cross. "The origin and growth of the Church are symbolized by the blood and water which flowed from the open side of the crucified Jesus."[126] "For it was from the side of Christ as he slept the sleep of death upon the cross that there came forth the 'wondrous sacrament of the whole Church.'"[127] As Eve was formed from the sleeping Adam's side, so the Church was born from the pierced heart of Christ hanging dead on the cross.

773 In the Church this communion of men with God, in the "love [that] never ends," is the purpose which governs everything in her that is a sacramental means, tied to this passing world.[128] "[The Church's] structure is totally ordered to the holiness of Christ's members. And holiness is measured according to the 'great mystery' in which the Bride responds with the gift of love to the gift of the Bridegroom."[129] Mary goes before us all in the holiness that is the Church's mystery as "the bride without spot or wrinkle."[130] This is why the "Marian" dimension of the Church precedes the "Petrine."[131]

813 *The Church is one because of her source:* "the highest exemplar and source of this mystery is the unity, in the Trinity of Persons, of one God, the Father and the Son in the Holy Spirit."[132] The Church is one *because of her founder:* for "the Word made flesh, the prince of peace, reconciled all men to God by the cross,...restoring the unity of all in one people and one body."[133] The Church is one *because of her "soul"*: "It is the Holy Spirit, dwelling in those who believe and pervading and ruling over the entire Church, who brings about that wonderful communion of the faithful and joins them together so intimately in Christ that he is the principle of the Church's unity."[134] Unity is of the essence of the Church:

> What an astonishing mystery! There is one Father of the universe, one Logos of the universe, and also one Holy Spirit, everywhere one and the same; there is also one virgin become mother, and I should like to call her "Church."[135]

829   "But while in the most Blessed Virgin the Church has already reached that perfection whereby she exists without spot or wrinkle, the faithful still strive to conquer sin and increase in holiness. And so they turn their eyes to Mary":[136] in her, the Church is already the "all-holy."

867   The Church is holy: the Most Holy God is her author; Christ, her bridegroom, gave himself up to make her holy; the Spirit of holiness gives her life. Since she still includes sinners, she is "the sinless one made up of sinners." Her holiness shines in the saints; in Mary she is already all-holy.

963   Since the Virgin Mary's role in the mystery of Christ and the Spirit has been treated, it is fitting now to consider her place in the mystery of the Church. "The Virgin Mary. . . is acknowledged and honored as being truly the Mother of God and of the redeemer. . . . She is 'clearly the mother of the members of Christ'. . . since she has by her charity joined in bringing about the birth of believers in the Church, who are members of its head."[137] "Mary, Mother of Christ, Mother of the Church."[138]

964   Mary's role in the Church is inseparable from her union with Christ and flows directly from it. "This union of the mother with the Son in the work of salvation is made manifest from the time of Christ's virginal conception up to his death";[139] it is made manifest above all at the hour of his Passion:

> Thus the Blessed Virgin advanced in her pilgrimage of faith, and faithfully persevered in her union with her Son unto the cross. There she stood, in keeping with the divine plan, enduring with her only begotten Son the intensity of his suffering, joining herself with his sacrifice in her mother's heart, and lovingly consenting to the immolation of this victim, born of her: to be given, by the same Christ Jesus dying on the cross, as a mother to his disciple, with these words: "Woman, behold your son."[140]

965   After her Son's Ascension, Mary "aided the beginnings of the Church by her prayers."[141] In her association with the apostles and several women, "we also see Mary by her prayers imploring the gift of the Spirit, who had already overshadowed her in the Annunciation."[142]

966   "Finally the Immaculate Virgin, preserved free from all stain of original sin, when the course of her earthly life was finished, was taken up body and soul into heavenly glory, and exalted by the Lord as Queen over all things, so that she might be the more fully conformed to her Son, the Lord of lords and conqueror of sin and death."[143] The Assumption of the Blessed Virgin is a singular participation in her Son's Resurrection and an anticipation of the resurrection of other Christians:

> In giving birth you kept your virginity; in your Dormition you did not leave the world, O Mother of God, but were joined to the source of Life. You conceived the living God and, by your prayers, will deliver our souls from death.[144]

967   By her complete adherence to the Father's will, to his Son's redemptive work, and to every prompting of the Holy Spirit, the Virgin Mary is the Church's model of faith and charity. Thus she is a "preeminent and...wholly unique member of the Church"; indeed, she is the "exemplary realization" (*typus*)[145] of the Church.

968   Her role in relation to the Church and to all humanity goes still further. "In a wholly singular way she cooperated by her obedience, faith, hope, and burning charity in the Savior's work of restoring supernatural life to souls. For this reason she is a mother to us in the order of grace."[146]

969   "This motherhood of Mary in the order of grace continues uninterruptedly from the consent which she loyally gave at the Annunciation and which she sustained without wavering beneath the cross, until the eternal fulfillment of all the elect. Taken up to heaven she did not lay aside this saving office but by her manifold intercession continues to bring us the gifts of eternal salvation. . . . Therefore the Blessed Virgin is invoked in the Church under the titles of Advocate, Helper, Benefactress, and Mediatrix."[147]

970   Mary's function as mother of men in no way obscures or diminishes this unique mediation of Christ, but rather shows its power. But the Blessed Virgin's salutary influence on men. . . "flows forth from the superabundance of the merits of Christ, rests on his mediation, depends entirely on it, and draws all its power from it."[148] "No creature could ever be counted along with the Incarnate Word and Redeemer; but just as the priesthood of Christ is shared in various ways both by his ministers and the faithful, and as the one goodness of God is radiated in different ways among his creatures, so also the unique mediation of the Redeemer does not exclude but rather gives rise to a manifold cooperation which is but a sharing in this one source."[149]

971 *"All generations will call me blessed"*: "The Church's devotion to the Blessed Virgin is intrinsic to Christian worship."[150] The Church rightly honors "the Blessed Virgin with special devotion. From the most ancient times the Blessed Virgin has been honored with the title of 'Mother of God,' to whose protection the faithful fly in all their dangers and needs. . . . This very special devotion. . . differs essentially from the adoration which is given to the incarnate Word and equally to the Father and the Holy Spirit, and greatly fosters this adoration.[151]" The liturgical feasts dedicated to the Mother of God and Marian prayer, such as the rosary, an "epitome of the whole Gospel," expresses this devotion to the Virgin Mary.[152]

972 After speaking of the Church, her origin, mission, and destiny, we can find no better way to conclude than by looking to Mary. In her we contemplate what the Church already is in her mystery on her own "pilgrimage of faith," and what she will be in the homeland at the end of her journey. There, "in the glory of the Most Holy and Undivided Trinity," "in the communion of all the saints,"[153] the Church is awaited by the one she venerates as Mother of her Lord and as her own mother.

> In the meantime the Mother of Jesus, in the glory which she possesses in body and soul in heaven, is the image and beginning of the Church as it is to be perfected in the world to come. Likewise she shines forth on earth, until the day of the Lord shall come, a sign of certain hope and comfort to the pilgrim People of God.[154]

973 By pronouncing her "fiat" at the Annunciation and giving her consent to the Incarnation, Mary was already collaborating with the whole work her Son was to accomplish. She is mother wherever he is Savior and head of the Mystical Body.

974 The most Blessed Virgin Mary, when the course of her earthly life was completed, was taken up body and soul into the glory of heaven, where she already shares in the glory of her Son's Resurrection, anticipating the resurrection of all members of his Body.

975 "We believe that the Holy Mother of God, the new Eve, Mother of the Church, continues in heaven to exercise her maternal role on behalf of the members of Christ" (Paul VI, *CPG* § 15).

1014 The Church encourages us to prepare ourselves for the hour of our death. In the litany of the saints, for instance, she has us pray: "From a sudden and unforeseen death, deliver us, O Lord";[155] to ask the Mother of God to intercede for us "at the hour of our death" in the *Hail Mary*; and to entrust ourselves to St. Joseph, the patron of a happy death.

> Every action of yours, every thought, should be those of one
> who expects to die before the day is out. Death would have
> no great terrors for you if you had a quiet conscience....
> Then why not keep clear of sin instead of running away from
> death? If you aren't fit to face death today, it's very unlikely
> you will be tomorrow....[156]

> Praised are you, my Lord, for our sister bodily Death,
> from whom no living man can escape.
> Woe on those who will die in mortal sin!
> Blessed are they who will be found
> in your most holy will,
> for the second death will not harm them.[157]

1020 The Christian who unites his own death to that of Jesus views it as a step towards him and an entrance into everlasting life. When the Church for the last time speaks Christ's words of pardon and absolution over the dying Christian, seals him for the last time with a strengthening anointing, and gives him Christ in viaticum as nourishment for the journey, she speaks with gentle assurance:

> Go forth, Christian soul, from this world
> in the name of God the almighty Father,
> who created you,
> in the name of Jesus Christ, the Son of the living God,
> who suffered for you,
> in the name of the Holy Spirit,
> who was poured out upon you.
> Go forth, faithful Christian!

> May you live in peace this day,
> may your home be with God in Zion,
> with Mary, the virgin Mother of God,
> with Joseph, and all the angels and saints....

> May you return to [your Creator]
> who formed you from the dust of the earth.
> May holy Mary, the angels, and all the saints
> come to meet you as you go forth from this life....
> May you see your Redeemer face to face....[158]

1024 This perfect life with the Most Holy Trinity — this communion of life and love with the Trinity, with the Virgin Mary, the angels and all the blessed — is called "heaven." Heaven is the ultimate end and fulfillment of the deepest human longings, the state of supreme, definitive happiness.

1053 "We believe that the multitude of those gathered around Jesus and Mary in Paradise forms the Church of heaven, where in eternal blessedness they see God as he is and where they are also, to various degrees, associated with the holy angels in the divine governance exercised by Christ in glory, by interceding for us and helping our weakness by their fraternal concern" (Paul VI, *CPG* § 29).

1106 Together with the anamnesis, the epiclesis is at the heart of each sacramental celebration, most especially of the Eucharist:

> You ask how the bread becomes the Body of Christ, and the wine . . . the Blood of Christ. I shall tell you: the Holy Spirit comes upon them and accomplishes what surpasses every word and thought. . . . Let it be enough for you to understand that it is by the Holy Spirit, just as it was of the Holy Virgin and by the Holy Spirit that the Lord, through and in himself, took flesh.[159]

1138 "Recapitulated in Christ," these are the ones who take part in the service of the praise of God and the fulfillment of his plan: the heavenly powers, all creation (the four living beings), the servants of the Old and New Covenants (the twenty-four elders), the new People of God (the one hundred and forty-four thousand),[160] especially the martyrs "slain for the word of God," and the all-holy Mother of God (the Woman), the Bride of the Lamb,[161] and finally "a great multitude which no one could number, from every nation, from all tribes, and peoples and tongues."[162]

1161 All the signs in the liturgical celebrations are related to Christ: as are sacred images of the holy Mother of God and of the saints as well. They truly signify Christ, who is glorified in them. They make manifest the "cloud of witnesses"[163] who continue to participate in the salvation of the world and to whom we are united, above all in sacramental celebrations. Through their icons, it is man "in the image of God," finally transfigured "into his likeness,"[164] who is revealed to our faith. So too are the angels, who also are recapitulated in Christ:

> Following the divinely inspired teaching of our holy Fathers and the tradition of the Catholic Church (for we know that this tradition comes from the Holy Spirit who dwells in her) we rightly define with full certainty and correctness that, like the figure of the precious and life-giving cross, venerable and holy images of our Lord and God and Savior, Jesus Christ, our inviolate Lady, the holy Mother of God, and the venerated angels, all the saints and the just, whether painted or made of mosaic or another suitable material, are to be exhibited in the holy churches of God, on sacred vessels and vestments, walls and panels, in houses and on streets.[165]

1172 "In celebrating this annual cycle of the mysteries of Christ, Holy Church honors the Blessed Mary, Mother of God, with a special love. She is inseparably linked with the saving work of her Son. In her the Church admires and exalts the most excellent fruit of redemption and joyfully contemplates, as in a faultless image, that which she herself desires and hopes wholly to be."[166]

1187 The liturgy is the work of the whole Christ, head and body. Our high priest celebrates it unceasingly in the heavenly liturgy, with the holy Mother of God, the apostles, all the saints, and the multitude of those who have already entered the kingdom.

1192 Sacred images in our churches and homes are intended to awaken and nourish our faith in the mystery of Christ. Through the icon of Christ and his works of salvation, it is he whom we adore. Through sacred images of the holy Mother of God, of the angels and of the saints, we venerate the persons represented.

1195 By keeping the memorials of the saints — first of all the holy Mother of God, then the apostles, the martyrs, and other saints — on fixed days of the liturgical year, the Church on earth shows that she is united with the liturgy of heaven. She gives glory to Christ for having accomplished his salvation in his glorified members; their example encourages her on her way to the Father.

1370 To the offering of Christ are united not only the members still here on earth, but also those already *in the glory of heaven.* In communion with and commemorating the Blessed Virgin Mary and all the saints, the Church offers the Eucharistic sacrifice. In the Eucharist the Church is as it were at the foot of the cross with Mary, united with the offering and intercession of Christ.

1419 Having passed from this world to the Father, Christ gives us in the Eucharist the pledge of glory with him. Participation in the Holy Sacrifice identifies us with his Heart, sustains our strength along the pilgrimage of this life, makes us long for eternal life, and unites us even now to the Church in heaven, the Blessed Virgin Mary, and all the saints.

1477 "This treasury includes as well the prayers and good works of the Blessed Virgin Mary. They are truly immense, unfathomable, and even pristine in their value before God. In the treasury, too, are the prayers and good works of all the saints, all those who have followed in the footsteps of Christ the Lord and by his grace have made their lives holy and carried out the mission the Father entrusted to them. In this way they attained their own salvation and at the same time cooperated in saving their brothers in the unity of the Mystical Body."[167]

1613 On the threshold of his public life Jesus performs his first sign — at his mother's request — during a wedding feast.[168] The Church attaches great importance to Jesus' presence at the wedding at Cana. She sees in it the confirmation of the goodness of marriage and the proclamation that thenceforth marriage will be an efficacious sign of Christ's presence.

1655 Christ chose to be born and grow up in the bosom of the holy family of Joseph and Mary. The Church is nothing other than "the family of God." From the beginning, the core of the Church was often constituted by those who had become believers "together with all [their] household."[169] When they were converted, they desired that "their whole household" should also be saved.[170] These families who became believers were islands of Christian life in an unbelieving world.

1717 The Beatitudes depict the countenance of Jesus Christ and portray his charity. They express the vocation of the faithful associated with the glory of his Passion and Resurrection; they shed light on the actions and attitudes characteristic of the Christian life; they are the paradoxical promises that sustain hope in the midst of tribulations; they proclaim the blessings and rewards already secured, however dimly, for Christ's disciples; they have begun in the lives of the Virgin Mary and all the saints.

2030 It is in the Church, in communion with all the baptized, that the Christian fulfills his vocation. From the Church he receives the Word of God containing the teachings of "the law of Christ."[171] From the Church he receives the grace of the sacraments that sustains him on the "way." From the Church he learns the *example of holiness* and recognizes its model and source in the all-holy Virgin Mary; he discerns it in the authentic witness of those who live it; he discovers it in the spiritual tradition and long history of the saints who have gone before him and whom the liturgy celebrates in the rhythms of the sanctoral cycle.

2097 To adore God is to acknowledge, in respect and absolute submission, the "nothingness of the creature" who would not exist but for God. To adore God is to praise and exalt him and to humble oneself, as Mary did in the Magnificat, confessing with gratitude that he has done great things and holy is his name.[172] The worship of the one God sets man free from turning in on himself, from the slavery of sin and the idolatry of the world.

2146 The second commandment *forbids the abuse of God's name*, i.e., every improper use of the names of God, Jesus Christ, but also of the Virgin Mary and all the saints.

2162 The second commandment forbids every improper use of God's name. Blasphemy is the use of the name of God, of Jesus Christ, of the Virgin Mary, and of the saints in an offensive way.

2177 The Sunday celebration of the Lord's Day and his Eucharist is at the heart of the Church's life. "Sunday is the day on which the paschal mystery is celebrated in light of the apostolic tradition and is to be observed as the foremost holy day of obligation in the universal Church."[173]

> "Also to be observed are the day of the Nativity of Our Lord Jesus Christ, the Epiphany, the Ascension of Christ, the feast of the Body and Blood of Christ, the feast of Mary the Mother of God, her Immaculate Conception, her Assumption, the feast of Saint Joseph, the feast of the Apostles Saints Peter and Paul, and the feast of All Saints."[174]

2502 *Sacred art* is true and beautiful when its form corresponds to its particular vocation: evoking and glorifying, in faith and adoration, the transcendent mystery of God — the surpassing invisible beauty of truth and love visible in Christ, who "reflects the glory of God and bears the very stamp of his nature," in whom "the whole fullness of deity dwells bodily."[175] This spiritual beauty of God is reflected in the most holy Virgin Mother of God, the angels, and saints. Genuine sacred art draws man to adoration, to prayer, and to the love of God, Creator and Savior, the Holy One and Sanctifier.

2599 The Son of God who became Son of the Virgin learned to pray in his human heart. He learns to pray from his mother, who kept all the great things the Almighty had done and treasured them in her heart.[176] He learns to pray in the words and rhythms of the prayer of his people, in the synagogue at Nazareth and the Temple at Jerusalem. But his prayer springs from an otherwise secret source, as he intimates at the age of twelve: "I must be in my Father's house."[177] Here the newness of prayer in the fullness of time begins to be revealed: his *filial prayer*, which the Father awaits from his children, is finally going to be lived out by the only Son in his humanity, with and for men.

2617 Mary's prayer is revealed to us at the dawning of the fullness of time. Before the incarnation of the Son of God, and before the outpouring of the Holy Spirit, her prayer cooperates in a unique way with the Father's plan of loving kindness: at the Annunciation, for Christ's conception; at Pentecost, for the formation of the Church, his Body.[178] In the faith of his humble handmaid, the Gift of God found the acceptance he had awaited from the beginning of time. She whom the Almighty made "full of grace" responds by offering her whole being: "Behold I am the handmaid of the Lord; let it be

[done] to me according to your word." "Fiat": this is Christian prayer: to be wholly God's, because he is wholly ours.

2618 The Gospel reveals to us how Mary prays and intercedes in faith. At Cana,[179] the mother of Jesus asks her son for the needs of a wedding feast; this is the sign of another feast — that of the wedding of the Lamb where he gives his body and blood at the request of the Church, his Bride. It is at the hour of the New Covenant, at the foot of the cross,[180] that Mary is heard as the Woman, the new Eve, the true "Mother of all the living."

2619 That is why the Canticle of Mary,[181] the *Magnificat* (Latin) or *Megalynei* (Byzantine) is the song both of the Mother of God and of the Church; the song of the Daughter of Zion and of the new People of God; the song of thanksgiving for the fullness of graces poured out in the economy of salvation and the song of the "poor" whose hope is met by the fulfillment of the promises made to our ancestors, "to Abraham and to his posterity for ever."

2622 The prayers of the Virgin Mary, in her Fiat and Magnificat, are characterized by the generous offering of her whole being in faith.

2665 The prayer of the Church, nourished by the Word of God and the celebration of the liturgy, teaches us to pray to the Lord Jesus. Even though her prayer is addressed above all to the Father, it includes in all the liturgical traditions forms of prayer addressed to Christ. Certain psalms, given their use in the Prayer of the Church and the New Testament, place on our lips and engrave in our hearts prayer to Christ in the form of invocations: Son of God, Word of God, Lord, Savior, Lamb of God, King, Beloved Son, Son of the Virgin, Good Shepherd, our Life, our Light, our Hope, our Resurrection, Friend of mankind. . . .

2673 In prayer the Holy Spirit unites us to the person of the only Son, in his glorified humanity, through which and in which our filial prayer unites us in the Church with the Mother of Jesus.[182]

2674 Mary gave her consent in faith at the Annunciation and maintained it without hesitation at the foot of the Cross. Ever since, her motherhood has extended to the brothers and sisters of her Son "who still journey on earth surrounded by dangers and difficulties."[183] Jesus, the only mediator, is the way of our prayer; Mary, his mother and ours, is wholly transparent to him: she "shows the way" (*hodigitria*), and is herself "the Sign" of the way, according to the traditional iconography of East and West.

2675 Beginning with Mary's unique cooperation with the working of the Holy Spirit, the Churches developed their prayer to the holy Mother of

God, centering it on the person of Christ manifested in his mysteries. In countless hymns and antiphons expressing this prayer, two movements usually alternate with one another: the first "magnifies" the Lord for the "great things" he did for his lowly servant and through her for all human beings;[184] the second entrusts the supplications and praises of the children of God to the Mother of Jesus, because she now knows the humanity which, in her, the Son of God espoused.

2676 This twofold movement of prayer to Mary has found a privileged expression in the *Ave Maria*:

> *Hail Mary* [or *Rejoice, Mary*]: the greeting of the angel Gabriel opens this prayer. It is God himself who, through his angel as intermediary, greets Mary. Our prayer dares to take up this greeting to Mary with the regard God had for the lowliness of his humble servant and to exult in the joy he finds in her.[185]

> *Full of grace, the Lord is with thee:* These two phrases of the angel's greeting shed light on one another. Mary is full of grace because the Lord is with her. The grace with which she is filled is the presence of him who is the source of all grace. "Rejoice. . . O Daughter of Jerusalem. . . the Lord your God is in your midst."[186] Mary, in whom the Lord himself has just made his dwelling, is the daughter of Zion in person, the ark of the covenant; the place where the glory of the Lord dwells. She is "the dwelling of God . . . with men."[187] Full of grace, Mary is wholly given over to him who has come to dwell in her and whom she is about to give to the world.

> *Blessed art thou among women and blessed is the fruit of thy womb, Jesus.* After the angel's greeting, we make Elizabeth's greeting our own. "Filled with the Holy Spirit," Elizabeth is the first in the long succession of generations who have called Mary "blessed."[188] "Blessed is she who believed. . . ."[189] Mary is "blessed among women" because she believed in the fulfillment of the Lord's word. Abraham, because of his faith, became a blessing for all the nations of the earth.[190] Mary, because of her faith, became the mother of believers, through whom all nations of the earth receive him who is God's own blessing: Jesus, the "fruit of thy womb."

2677 *Holy Mary, Mother of God:* With Elizabeth we marvel, "And why is this granted me, that the mother of my Lord should come to me?"[191] Because she gives us Jesus, her son, Mary is Mother of God and our mother; we can entrust all our cares and petitions to her: she prays for us as she prayed for herself: "Let it be to me according to your word."[192] By entrusting ourselves to her prayer, we abandon ourselves to the will of God together with her: "Thy will be done."

Pray for us sinners, now and at the hour of our death: By asking Mary to pray for us, we acknowledge ourselves to be poor sinners and we address ourselves to the "Mother of Mercy," the All-Holy One. We give ourselves over to her now, in the Today of our lives. And our trust broadens further, already at the present moment, to surrender "the hour of our death" wholly to her care. May she be there as she was at her son's death on the cross. May she welcome us as our mother at the hour of our passing[193] to lead us to her son, Jesus, in paradise.

2678 Medieval piety in the West developed the prayer of the rosary as a popular substitute for the Liturgy of the Hours. In the East, the litany called the *Akathistos* and the *Paraclesis* remained closer to the choral office in the Byzantine churches, while the Armenian, Coptic, and Syriac traditions preferred popular hymns and songs to the Mother of God. But in the *Ave Maria*, the *theotokia*, the hymns of St. Ephrem or St. Gregory of Narek, the tradition of prayer is basically the same.

2679 Mary is the perfect *Orans* (pray-er), a figure of the Church. When we pray to her, we are adhering with her to the plan of the Father, who sends his Son to save all men. Like the beloved disciple we welcome Jesus' mother into our homes,[194] for she has become the mother of all the living. We can pray with and to her. The prayer of the Church is sustained by the prayer of Mary and united with it in hope.[195]

2682 Because of Mary's singular cooperation with the action of the Holy Spirit, the Church loves to pray in communion with the Virgin Mary, to magnify with her the great things the Lord has done for her, and to entrust supplications and praises to her.

2725 Prayer is both a gift of grace and a determined response on our part. It always presupposes effort. The great figures of prayer of the Old Covenant before Christ, as well as the Mother of God, the saints, and he himself, all teach us this: prayer is a battle. Against whom? Against ourselves and against the wiles of the tempter who does all he can to turn man away from prayer, away from union with God. We pray as we live, because we live as we pray. If we do not want to act habitually according to the Spirit of Christ, neither can we pray habitually in his name. The "spiritual battle" of the Christian's new life is inseparable from the battle of prayer.

2827 "If any one is a worshiper of God and does his will, God listens to him."[196] Such is the power of the Church's prayer in the name of her Lord, above all in the Eucharist: Her prayer is also a communion of intercession with the all-holy Mother of God[197] and all the saints who have been pleasing to the Lord because they willed his will alone:

> It would not be inconsistent with the truth to understand the words, "Thy will be done on earth as it is in heaven," to mean: "in the Church as in our Lord Jesus Christ himself"; or "in the Bride who has been betrothed, just as in the Bridegroom who has accomplished the will of the Father."[198]

2837 "Daily" (*epiousios*) occurs nowhere else in the New Testament. Taken in a temporal sense, this word is a pedagogical repetition of "this day,"[199] to confirm us in trust "without reservation." Taken in the qualitative sense, it signifies what is necessary for life, and more broadly every good thing sufficient for subsistence.[200] Taken literally (*epi-ousios*: "super-essential"), it refers directly to the Bread of Life, the Body of Christ, the "medicine of immortality," without which we have no life within us.[201] Finally in this connection, its heavenly meaning is evident: "this day" is the Day of the Lord, the day of the feast of the kingdom, anticipated in the Eucharist that is already the foretaste of the kingdom to come. For this reason it is fitting for the Eucharistic liturgy to be celebrated each day.

> The Eucharist is our daily bread. The power belonging to this divine food makes it a bond of union. Its effect is then understood as unity, so that, gathered into his Body and made members of him, we may become what we receive. . . . This also is our daily bread: the readings you hear each day in church and the hymns you hear and sing. All these are necessities for our pilgrimage.[202]

> The Father in heaven urges us, as children of heaven, to ask for the bread of heaven. [Christ] himself is the bread who, sown in the Virgin, raised up in the flesh, kneaded in the Passion, baked in the oven of the tomb, reserved in churches, brought to altars, furnishes the faithful each day with food from heaven.[203]

2853 Victory over the "prince of this world"[204] was won once for all at the Hour when Jesus freely gave himself up to death to give us his life. This is the judgment of this world, and the prince of this world is "cast out."[205] "He pursued the woman"[206] but had no hold on her: the new Eve, "full of grace" of the Holy Spirit, is preserved from sin and the corruption of death (the Immaculate Conception and the Assumption of the Most Holy Mother of God, Mary, ever virgin). "Then the dragon was angry with the woman, and went off to make war on the rest of her offspring."[207] Therefore the Spirit and the Church pray: "Come, Lord Jesus,"[208] since his coming will deliver us from the Evil One.

Endnotes

[1] Cf. Is 2:2-4; Jr 31:31-34; Heb 10:16.

[2] Cf. Ezk 36; Is 49:5-6; 53:11.

[3] Cf. Zp 2:3; Lk 1:38.

[4] Lk 1:37-38; cf. Gn 18:14.

[5] Lk 1:45.

[6] Cf. Lk 1:48.

[7] Cf. Lk 2:35.

[8] Rm 4:18.

[9] *Lumen Gentium* 58; John Paul II, *Redemptoris Mater* 18.

[10] Heb 12:1-2.

[11] Cf. 2 Cor 12:9; Ph 4:13.

[12] Lk 1:37, 49.

[13] Cf. Gn 2:7, 22.

[14] Cf. Gn 3:9, 15.

[15] Cf. 1 Cor 15:21-22, 45; Ph 2:8; Rm 5:19-20.

[16] Cf. Pius IX, *Ineffabilis Deus*: DS 2803; Council of Trent: DS 1573.

[17] Jn 13:3.

[18] Jn 3:13; 6:33.

[19] 1 Jn 4:2.

[20] Jn 1:14, 16.

[21] Cf. Lk 1:31.

[22] Mt 1:21; cf. 2:7.

[23] Lk 2:11.

[24] Jn 10:36; cf. Lk 1:35.

[25] Mt 1:20; cf. Mt 1:16; Rm 1:1; 2 Tm 2:8; Rv 22:16.

[26] Jn 1:14.

[27] Ph 2:5-8; cf. *Liturgy of the Hours*, Saturday, Canticle at Evening Prayer.

[28] Council of Ephesus (431): DS 250.

[29] Council of Ephesus: DS 251.

[30] Council of Chalcedon (451): DS 301; cf. Heb 4:15.

[31] Council of Chalcedon: DS 302.

[32] *Liturgy of the Hours*, January 1, Antiphon for Morning Prayer; cf. St. Leo the Great, *Sermo in nat. Dom.* 1, 2; PL 54, 191-192.

[33] Liturgy of St. John Chrysostom, Troparion "O *monogenes.*"

[34] *Gaudium et spes* 22 § 2.

[35] Cf. Jn 14:9-10.

[36] *Gaudium et spes* 22 § 2.

[37] *Lumen Gentium* 56.

[38] Lk 1:28.

[39] Lk 1:28.

[40] Pius IX, *Ineffabilis Deus*, 1854: DS 2803.

[41] *Lumen Gentium* 53, 56

[42] Cf. Eph 1:3-4.

[43] *Lumen Gentium* 56.

[44] Lk 1:28-38; cf. Rm 1:5.

[45] Cf. *Lumen Gentium* 56.

[46] St. Irenaeus, *Adversus haereses* 3, 22, 4: PG 7/1, 959 A.

[47] Ibid.

[48] *Lumen Gentium* 56; Epiphanius, *Panarion seu adversus LXXX haereses* 78, 18: PG 42, 728 CD - 729 AB; St. Jerome, *Ep.* 22, 21: PL 22, 408.

[49] Lk 1:43; Jn 2:1; 19:25; cf. Mt 13:55; *et al.*

[50] Council of Ephesus (431): DS 251.

[51] *Lumen Gentium* 63; cf. Jn 19:26-27; Rm 8:29; Rv 12:17.

[52] Council of Friuli (796): DS 619; cf. Lk 2:48-49.

[53] 1 Cor 15:45, 47.

[54] Jn 3:34.

[55] Jn 1:16; cf. Col 1:18.

[56] Lk 1:34; cf. Jn 3:9.

[57] Jn 1:13.

[58] Cf. 2 Cor 11:2.

[59] *Lumen Gentium* 63; cf. 1 Cor 7:34-35.

[60] St. Augustine, *De virg.* 3: PL 40, 398.

[61] *Lumen Gentium* 64; cf. 63.

[62] Cf. Lk 2:6-7.

[63] Cf. Lk 2:8-20.

[64] *Kontakion* of Romanos the Melodist.

[65] Cf. Mt 18:3-4

[66] Jn 3:7; 1:13; 1:12; cf. Mt 23:12.

[67] Cf. Gal 4:19.

[68] *Liturgy of the Hours*, Antiphon I of Evening Prayer for January 1st.

[69] Mt. 2:1; cf. *Liturgy of the Hours*, Epiphany, Evening Prayer II, Antiphon at the Canticle of Mary.

[70] Cf. Mt 2:2; Nb 24:17-19; Rv 22:16.

[71] Cf. Jn 4:22; Mt 2:4-6.

[72] St. Leo the Great, *Sermo 3 in epiphania Domini* 1-3, 5: PL 54, 242; *Liturgy of the Hours*, Epiphany, Office of Readings; *Roman Missal*, Easter Vigil 26, Prayer after the Third Reading.

[73] Cf. Lk 2:22-39; Ex 13:2; 12-13.

[74] Cf. Gal 4:4.

[75] Lk 2:51-52.

[76] Lk 22:42.

[77] Cf. Rm 5:19.

[78] Paul VI at Nazareth, January 5, 1964: *Liturgy of the Hours*, Feast of the Holy Family, Office of Readings.

[79] Cf. Lk 2:41-52.

[80] Lk 2:49 alt.

[81] Mt 16:21.

[82] Cf. Mt 16:22-23; Mt 17:23; Lk 9:45.

[83] Cf. Mt 17:1-8 and parallels; 2 P 1:16-18.

[84] Lk 9:31.

[85] Lk 9:35.

[86] Lk 1:32; cf. Mt 21:1-11; Jn 6:15.

[87] Ps 24:7-10; Zc 9:9.

[88] Cf. Jn 18:37.

[89] Cf. Mt 21:15-16; cf. Ps 8:3; Lk 19:38; 2:14.

[90] Cf. Ps 118:26.

[91] Lk 2:22-39.

[92] Cf. Lk 2:46-49.

[93] Cf. Lk 2:41.

[94] Cf. Jn 2:13-14; 5:1, 14; 7:1, 10, 14; 8:2; 10:22-23.

[95] 1 P 1:18-20.

[96] Cf. Rm 5:12; 1 Cor 15:56.

[97] 2 Cor 5:21; cf. Ph 2:7; Rm 8:3.

[98] Cf. 1 Jn 2:20, 27; 2 Cor 1:21.

[99] Cf. Ex 30:22-32; 1 S 16:13.

[100] Cf. Lk 4:18-19; Is 61:1.

[101] Cf. Lk 2:11, 26-27.

[102] Cf. Lk 4:1; 6:19; 8:46.

[103] Cf. Rm 1:4; 8:11.

[104] Eph 4:13; cf. Ac 2:36.

[105] Cf. Ex 24:15-18.

[106] Cf. Ex 33:9-10.

[107] Cf. Ex 40:36-38; 1 Cor 10:1-2.

[108] Cf. 1 K 8:10-12.

[109] Lk 1:35.

[110] Lk 9:34-35.

[111] Cf. Ac 1:9; cf. Lk 21:27.

[112] Is 43:19.

[113] Cf. Zp 2:3; Lk 2:25, 38.

[114] Jn 1:6.

[115] Lk 1:15, 41.

[116] Cf. Lk 1:68.

[117] Cf. Pr 8:1-9:6; Si 24.

[118] Col 2:9.

[119] Cf. Zp 3:14; Zc 2:14.

[120] Cf. Lk 1:46-55.

[121] Cf. Lk 1:26-38; Rm 4:18-21; Gal 4:26-28.

[122] Cf. Lk 1:15-19; Mt 2:11.

[123] Cf. Lk 2:14.

[124] Cf. Jn 19:25-27.

[125] Ac 1:14.

[126] *Lumen Gentium* 3: cf. Jn 19:34.

[127] *Sacrosanctum concilium* 5.

[128] 1 Cor 13:8; *Lumen Gentium* 48.

[129] John Paul II, *Mulieris dignitatem* 27.

[130] Eph 5:27.

[131] Cf. John Paul II, *Mulieris dignitatem* 27.

[132] *Unitatis redintegratio* 2 § 5.

[133] *Gaudium et spes* 78 § 3.

[134] *Unitatis redintegratio* 2 § 2.

[135] Clement of Alexandria, *Paedagogus* 1, 6, 42: PG 8, 300.

[136] *Lumen Gentium* 65; cf. Eph 5:26-27.

[137] *Lumen Gentium* 53; cf. St. Augustine, *De virg.* 6: PL 40, 399.

[138] Paul VI, Discourse, November 21, 1964.

[139] *Lumen Gentium* 57.

[140] *Lumen Gentium* 58; cf. Jn 19:26-27.

[141] *Lumen Gentium* 69.

[142] *Lumen Gentium* 59.

[143] *Lumen Gentium* 59; cf. Pius XII, *Munificentissimus Deus* (1950): DS 3903; cf. Rv. 19:16.

[144] Byzantine Liturgy, *Troparion*, Feast of the Dormition, August 15th.

[145] *Lumen Gentium* 53; 63.

[146] *Lumen Gentium* 61.

[147] *Lumen Gentium* 62.

[148] *Lumen Gentium* 60.

[149] *Lumen Gentium* 62.

[150] Lk 1:48; Paul VI, *Marialis cultus* 56.

[151] *Lumen Gentium* 66.

[152] Cf. Paul VI, *Marialis cultus* 42; *Sacrosanctum concilium* 103.

[153] *Lumen Gentium* 69.

[154] *Lumen Gentium* 68; cf. 2 P 3:10.

[155] *Roman Missal*, Litany of the Saints.

[156] *The Imitation of Christ*, I, 23, 1.

[157] St. Francis of Assisi, *Canticle of the Creatures*.

158 *Order of Christian Funerals*, Prayer of Commendation.
159 St. John Damascene, *De fide orthodoxa* 4, 13: PG 94, 1145 A.
160 Cf. Rv 4-5; 7:1-8; 14:1; Is 6:2-3.
161 Rv 6:9-11; Rv 21:9; cf. 12.
162 Rv 7:9.
163 Heb 12:1.
164 Cf. Rm 8:29; 1 Jn 3:2.
165 Council of Nicaea II: DS 600.
166 *Sacrosanctum concilium* 103.
167 *Indulgentiarum doctrina* 5.
168 Cf. Jn 2:1-11.
169 Cf. Ac 18:8.
170 Cf. Ac 16:31; Ac 11:14.
171 Gal 6:2.
172 Cf. Lk 1:46-49.
173 *Codex Iuris Canonici*, can. 1246 § 1.
174 *Codex Iuris Canonici*, can. 1246 § 2: "The conference of bishops can abolish certain holy days of obligation or transfer them to a Sunday with prior approval of the Apostolic See."
175 Heb 1:3; Col 2:9.
176 Cf. Lk 1:49; 2:19; 2:51.
177 Lk 2:49.
178 Cf. Lk 1:38; Ac 1:14.
179 Cf. Jn 2:1-12.
180 Cf. Jn 19:25-27.
181 Cf. Lk 1:46-55.
182 Cf. Ac 1:14.
183 *Lumen Gentium* 62.
184 Cf. Lk 1:46-55.
185 Cf. Lk 1:48; Zp 3:17b.
186 Zp 3:14, 17a.
187 Rv 21:3.
188 Lk 1:41, 48.
189 Lk 1:45.
190 Cf. Gn 12:3.
191 Lk 1:43.
192 Lk 1:38.
193 Cf. Jn 19:27.
194 Cf. Jn 19:27.
195 Cf. *Lumen Gentium* 68-69.
196 Jn 9:31; cf. 1 Jn 5:14.
197 Cf. Lk 1:38, 49.

[198] St. Augustine, *De sermone Domini in monte* 2, 6, 24: PL 34, 1279.

[199] Cf. Ex 16:19-21.

[200] Cf. 1 Tm 6:8.

[201] St. Ignatius of Antioch, *Epistula ad Ephesios* 20, 2: PG 5, 661; Jn 6:53-56.

[202] St. Augustine, *Sermo* 57, 7: PL 38, 389.

[203] St. Peter Chrysologus, *Sermo* 67: PL 52, 392; cf. Jn 6:51.

[204] Jn 14:30.

[205] Jn 21:31; Rv 12:10.

[206] Rv 12:13-16.

[207] Rv 12:17.

[208] Rv. 22:17, 20

Appendix 4

ALPHABETICAL LISTING OF
REFERENCES TO MARIAN THEMES IN
THE CATECHISM OF THE CATHOLIC CHURCH

(**Bold** indicates key articles for theme)

Annunciation (vocation): 430, **484**, **490**, **491**, 492, 493, 508, **721**,
2097

Assumption (queenship): **966**, **974**, 2177, 2853

Christ and Mary: **437**, 467, 469, 726, **970**, 1138, 2162, 2665

Church and Mary: 507, **766**, **773**, 813, 829, 867, 963, 964, **967**, 968,
969, **972**, 973, 974, 975, 1138, 1172, 1370, 1419, 1477, 1655,
1717, 2030, **2679**, 2827

Daughter of Zion: 559, 583, 593, 722, 2619, 2676

Economy of Salvation/Plan of God and Mary:
Fidei Depositum, p. 5; 2 paragraphs
426, 502, 503, 969

Eve and Mary: 410, 411, 494, 511, **726**, 975, 2853

Faith of Mary: 144, 148, 149, **165**, 273, **494**, 506, 511, 534, 964, 967,
968, 972, 2617, 2622, 2719

Holy Spirit and Mary: 485, 486, **504**, 695, 697, **722**, 723, 724, 725,
726, 744, 2673, 2676, 2682

Image/Icon of Mary:
prologue between pp. 12-13
476, **972**, 1161, 1172, 1192, 2502, 2674

Appendix 5

Alphabetical Index of Masses
of the Blessed Virgin Mary

(See Chapter Six)

Appendix 6

MARIAN THEMES
AND MARIAN ASPECTS IN
ROMAN CATHOLIC CATECHISMS
1555-1966

Name	Motherhood	Virginity	Salvation	Church	Prayer	Particularites
Canisius 1555	I Mother of God: Conceived by Holy Spirit	I Virgin: Born of Virgin Mary	I Center of Salvation, backstage, presence		II Greeted as Virginal Mother - Angel's salutation: Hail Mary - Mother of Mercy: protection, consolation Prayer to Mary in Scripture and tradition	• Mary sign of God • No controversy, theological speculation • Not IC and Ass.
Roman 1566	I Mother of God: Conceived by the Spirit	I Virgin: Born of the Virgin: Virginity untarnished (Spirit protector) Complementarity of divine fecundity and permanent virginity	I Close cooperation in salvation: - parallelism: E–M		IV Devotion of Saints: - Angelus (Thanksgiving) - Salve Regina (Queen-sinner) - Helplessness: protection	• Strong scriptural basis, not patristic • not IC and Ass.
Deharbe 1847	Virginal Mother (Bethlehem, Egypt) - Relation to Trinity - Daughter of Father - Mother of Sion - Bride of Spirit	Virgin: Born of the Virgin Mary	Church as Institution of Salvation: - peripheral role of Mary - Cana, Calvary and Pentecost not mentioned		Power of Mary's intercession - Prayer for happy death - Angelus	• objective presentation sufficient to produce conviction • English translation of 1908 does not mention IC and Ass.
German 1955	I Mother of Redeemer: Mystery of Mary - chosen by God - undefiled by sin	I No strong affirmation of virginity IC — Feast Dogma	II Our Mother — Our Queen - governs the whole world with Christ - Queen of Angels Spiritual Motherhood (parallel to Christ our brother) Participation in the sacrifice of the Cross	II Mother of Christians - Presence, participation in Spirit Event and young Church	II Salve Regina Mother of Sorrows - refuge of sinners - comforter of the Afflicted	• Dogma of Assumption (Feast doctrine)
Dutch 1966	Mother of the Lord - Daughter of Sion	Born from God, Born from Virgin Mary - Jesus first born of Mary		- Archetype of the Church (first realization) - Mary our sister - Sorrows of Mary (existential dimension)	Liturgical Feast - Pentecost - Assumption - Immaculate Conception	• IC added after requested • biblical, existential, less doctrinal

Minor Texts

64	Bearers of hope in OT:	Mary purest of these figures
144	Obedience of faith:	Mary most perfect realization
148/149	Obedience of faith:	Mary purest realization of faith
165	Witness of faith in darkness:	Mary witness of faith in the night of pilgrimage
273	Power in weakness:	Mary supreme model of faith that in God nothing is impossible
411	Genesis 3:15 applied to Mary:	Many fathers and doctors apply text to Mary as Mother of Christ and New Eve (1) preservation from original sin (2) sinlessness through grace
512-570	Infancy and hidden life:	Nativity: Virgin gave birth to the Eternal. (Romans) Presentation: Mary's sword announcing Christ's passion Jesus' obedience to Mary and Joseph Temple scene: Joseph and Mary receive declaration in faith and Mary ponders them in her heart
623	Christ self-giving (offering) to the Father:	Our participation in Christ's sacrifice (association) supremely accomplished in His Mother who was associated more intimately than any other (Lk 2:35)
773	Mystery of the Church (mystery of Union = Holiness):	Marian dimension of the Church precedes the Petrine Dimension (MD 27), because Mary precedes in Holiness all members of Church; is thus assimilated to Spouse without stain nor wrinkle (Eph 5:27)
829	Holiness of Church:	In Mary Church has attained holiness, is all holy and thus model of holiness
1,014	Preparation for Death:	Intercession of Mary, Mother of God: Comes to meet faithful
1,172	Sanctoral in liturgical year:	Mary, Mother of God, venerated with special love, because united to her Son in work of salvation (indissoluble link); she is very pure image in which Church contemplates most excellent fruit of redemption
1,370	Sacramental Sacrifice:	Church acts in communion with Blessed Virgin Mary and all Saints. Church is, with Mary, as if standing at the foot of the Cross united to sacrifice and intercession of Christ

1,477	Indulgences (reconciliation):	Prayers and good works of BVM and Saints contribute to spiritual treasures of Communion of Saints
1,655	Domestic Church (Marriage)	Christ wanted to be born and raised in the Holy Family of Joseph and Mary; Family beginning of Church; Church is family of God
1,717	Human vocation is a vocation to beatitudes (Beatitudes paint the face of Christ):	Beatitudes have been inaugurated in the life of the Virgin Mary and in the family
2,043	Commandments of the Church (4th):	Sunday obligation completed by partaking in principal liturgical feast knowing the Lord, Mary and the Saints
2,097	1st Commandment (Adoration to God alone):	To adore God means, as Mary did in the Magnificat, to praise, exalt him and to "humiliate" oneself (Lk 1:46-49)
2,146	2nd Commandment:	Prohibits unsuitable usage of the name of God, Jesus Christ, Virgin Mary and the Saints
2,177	3rd Commandment:	Sunday Eucharist to be observed in the whole Church. Ten days of obligation, of which Mother of God, Immaculate Conception and Assumption
2,502	8th Commandment (Sacred Art):	Sacred Art is true and beautiful if it evokes and glorifies (in faith and adoration) the transcendent mystery of God, that is: (1) Invisible beauty of truth and love in Christ (2) Spiritual beauty in Mother of God, Angels, Saints
2,599	Jesus' Prayer:	(1) Son of Man born Son of Virgin learned to pray according to his human heart (2) He learned it from his Mother, who kept the *Magnalia Dei* in her heart and meditated them (Lk 1:49; 2:19; 2:51) (Other sources: his people, especially his Father)
2,665	Prayer addressed to Jesus:	Among many other titles mentioned (Son of God, Word of God, Lord, Redeemer) also: Son of the Virgin
2,827	Our Father (3) (Your will be done):	God answers prayers of those who do his will: This is the power of the Church's prayer said in the name of the Lord and in the Communion of intercession with the All Holy Mother of God, (Lk 1:38-49) and of all Saints
2,853	Our Father (7) (Deliver us from evil):	Christ is victor over the Prince of this world. Prince pursues the Woman (Rv 12:13-14), but has no power over her: the New Eve, full of the grace of the Spirit, is liberated/freed from sin and corruption of death (IC and Ass. of Saint Mary, Mother of God, ever Virgin)

MARIAN TEXTS IN THE
CATECHISM OF THE CATHOLIC CHURCH (1992)

Major Texts

1. I believe in Jesus Christ, the only Son of God

   1) Born of a woman (Gal 4:4) [422]

   2) Jewishness of Jesus: born a Jew of a Maid of Israel [423]

   3) True God, true Man (Christological debate)
      — Ephesus 431 (no juxtaposition-Nestorius): truly Mother of God
      — Chalcedon 451 (no monophysitism): Virgin Mary, Mother of God
      — V Constantinople 553 (One of the Trinity): Mother of God, ever Virgin
      — [GS 22, 2]

   4) Conceived by the Holy Spirit, born of the Virgin Mary [484-512]
      Event — Agent — Fruit: Christ
      1) Predestination
      2) Immaculate Conception
      3) Annunciation (Fiat)
      4) Divine Motherhood
      5) Virginity of Mary
      6) Mary — ever Virgin
      7) Virginal Maternity of Mary in God's plan of salvation

2. I believe in the Holy Spirit [721-726]

   Spirit of Christ (= Holy Spirit) in the fullness of time (NT, as opposed to OT = time of promise)

   1) Mary = masterpiece of joint mission of Spirit and Son

   2) Mary = Dwelling place, temple of Son and Spirit offered to Father

   3) Thus Mary understood as Seat of Wisdom

   4) Beginning manifestation of God's marvelous deeds in Mary through Spirit:
      — Spirit prepares Mary by his grace
      — Spirit accomplishes in Mary the plan of God
      — Spirit manifests Son of Father who became Son of the Virgin

— In Mary, Spirit establishes relation/communion between Jesus
  Christ and representatives of humanity in need of redemption
— In the Spirit, Mary becomes Woman, New Eve ("mother of
  the living"), Mother of the "total Christ"

3. I believe in the holy Catholic Church [963-975]

Church in the Plan of God, major images, attributes, organization,
communion of Saints. . . .
Mary, Mother of Christ, Mother of the Church (VI)
  — True Mother of God, redeemer
  — Mother of members of Christ
  — Mother of the Church

1) Mary's maternity of/for the Church
  — Totally united to her Son in her life
  — Totally united to her Son in her Assumption
  — Mary is our mother in the order of grace
  — Model of faith and charity for Church
  — Through cooperation in Christ's salvific work, she becomes, in
    the order of grace, our Mother
  — Mary's maternity in economy of salvation until consummation

2) Cult (devotion to) of the Holy Spirit
  — Integral part of Christian worship — legitimate special
    devotion
  — Virgin honored as mother of God; protection, refuge
  — Essentially different from cult of adoration (Trinity); Marian
    devotion in the service of divine worship
  — expressed in liturgical celebration and Marian prayer (rosary)

3) Mary — eschatological icon
  — We contemplate in Mary mystery of the Church:

(1) now and

(2) at the end of her pilgrimage
  — Mother of the Lord, Mother of the Church inaugurates
    ultimate achievement of heavenly Church
  — Sign of Hope and consolation

4. The Prayer of Mary [2617-2619]

In the fullness of time,
  Jesus prays
  Jesus teaches how to pray
  Jesus listens and acts on behalf of our prayer
  The prayer of Mary

1) Mary's prayer revealed at the Annunciation and Pentecost as unique cooperation in God's plan
   — Fiat in the Christian prayer: to be completely God's, since he is completely ours

2) Mary's prayer of intercession in faith expressed in Cana and Calvary

3) Mary's Magnificat is both canticle of the Mother of God and of the Church, whose hope has been fulfilled

5. Prayer in communion with the Holy Mother of God [2673-2679]

In "Ways of prayer" (prayer to the Father, to Jesus, with [as the Holy Spirit], we are told how to pray in communion with the Holy Mother of God

1) Mary the *Hodegetria*: She points the way to Jesus, who is the way of our prayer
   Spiritual maternity

2) Mary is the sign, transparence unto Jesus, the way of our prayer

3) Prayer to Mary is centered on Christ's person as manifested in his mysteries
   Double movement:
   (1) Praise for great things the Lord accomplishes in/for his humble servant (= Hail Mary)
   (2) Entrusting to Mary all praise/supplication of God's children (= Holy Mary)

4) Mary is the perfect *Orans*, figure of the Church:
   (1) assent to God's plan
   (2) inviting Mary into "our being"
   — We pray with Mary, and we pray to Mary
   — Mary's prayer sustains, supports the prayer of the Church

BIBLIOGRAPHY

Andreasen, Niels-Erik A. "The Role of the Queen Mother in Israelite Society." *The Catholic Biblical Quarterly* 45 (1983): 179-194.

Aubineau, Michel. *Les Homélies Festales d'Hésychius de Jérusalem.* Vol. I. Bruxelles: Société des Bollandistes, 1978.

Bardenhewer, O. *Der Name Maria: Geschichte der Deutung Desselben.* Fribourg im Breisgau, 1895.

Bea, Cardinal Agostino. "Maria SS. nel Protoevangelo (Gen 3.15)." *Marianum* XV (1953): 1-21.

Beinert, Wolfgang. *Parlare di Maria oggi?* Italy: Edizioni Paoline Catania, 1975.

Billot Louis. *De Verbo Incarnato,* 6th ed., Rome, 1922, 380.

Black, Matthew and H. H. Rowley, eds. *Peake's Commentary on the Bible.* London: Nelson, 1964.

Bloch, Renée. "Midrash." *Dictionnaire de la Bible.* Suppl. Vol. V. Paris: Letouzey, 1957.

Botterweck, G. Johannes and Helmer Ringgren, eds. *Theological Dictionary of the Old Testament.* Vol. II. Trans. John T. Willis. Grand Rapids, MI: Eerdmans, 1975.

Brennan, Walter. *The Sacred Memory of Mary.* New York: Paulist, 1988.

Brown, Raymond E. *The Birth of the Messiah: A Commentary on the*

Infancy Narratives in the Gospels of Matthew and Luke. New updated ed. New York: Doubleday, 1993.

_____. *The Gospel According to John* (xiii-xxi), Anchor Bible 29A. Garden City, NY: Doubleday, 1966.

_____. *New Testament Essays.* New York: Paulist, 1965.

Brown, Raymond E., Joseph A. Fitzmyer, and Roland E. Murphy, eds. *The Jerome Biblical Commentary.* Englewood Cliffs, NJ: Prentice, 1968.

_____. *The New Jerome Biblical Commentary.* Englewood Cliffs, NJ: Prentice, 1990.

Buby, Bertrand. "The Biblical Prayer of Mary (Luke 2:19, 51)." *Review for Religious* 39 (1980): 577-581.

_____. "A New Testament Passover Haggadah." *The Bible Today* 29 (1967): 2010-2016.

_____. "Research on the Biblical Approach and the Method of Exegesis Appearing in the Greek Homiletic Texts of the Late Fourth and Early Fifth Centuries, Emphasizing the Incarnation Especially the Nativity and Mary's Place Within It." *Marian Library Studies* 13-14 (1981-82): 223-394.

Bultmann, Rudolph. *The Gospel of John.* Philadelphia: Westminster, 1971.

Buttrick, George Arthur, ed. *The Interpreter's Dictionary of the Bible: An Illustrated Encyclopedia.* 5 vols. New York: Abingdon, 1962.

Catechism of the Catholic Church. Boston, MA: St. Paul Books & Media, 1994.

Charlesworth, James H. *The Old Testament Pseudepigrapha.* Vol. 2. New York: Doubleday, 1985.

Cohen, A. *The Psalms.* London: Soncino, 1971.

_____. ed. *The Soncino Chumash: The Five Books of Moses with Haphtaroth.* London: Soncino, 1966.

Collection of Masses of the Blessed Virgin Mary. Vol. 2. New York: Catholic Book Publishing Co., 1992.

Craghan, John F. "Esther: A Fully Liberated Woman." *The Bible Today* 24 (1986): 6-11.

_____. *Yesterday's Word Today.* Collegeville, MN: Liturgical Press, 1982.

Crim, Keith, gen. ed. *The Interpreters Dictionary of the Bible: An Illustrated Encyclopedia.* Suppl. vol. New York: Abingdon, 1992.

Cross, Frank M., Jr., and David Noel Freedman. "The Song of Miriam." *Journal of Near Eastern Studies* 14 (1955): 237-250.

Daube, David. *The New Testament and Rabbinic Judaism.* London: University of London, 1956.

De Fiores, Stefano, and Salvatore Meo. *Nuovo Dizionario di Mariologia.* 2a ed. Milano: Edizioni Paoline, 1986.

de Fraine, J. *Women of the Old Testament.* Trans. Forrest L. Ingram. De Pere, WI: St. Norbert Abbey Press, 1968.

de la Potterie, Ignace. "La mère de Jésus et la conception virginale du Fils Dieu." *Marianum* XL (1978): 41-90.

_____. *Mary in the Mystery of the Covenant.* Trans. Bertrand Buby. New York: Alba House, 1992.

Flannery, Austin, gen. ed. *Vatican Council II: The Conciliar and Post-Conciliar Documents.* New rev. ed. Collegeville, MN: Liturgical Press, 1992.

Flusser, David. "Mary and Israel." *Mary: Images of the Mother of Jesus in Jewish and Christian Perspective.* Philadelphia: Fortress, 1986.

Ford, J. Massyngberde [Massingberd]. "The Mother of Jesus and the Authorship of the Epistle to the Hebrews." *The Bible Today* 82 (1976): 683-694.

_____. "Mary's Virginitas Post-Partum and Jewish Law." *Biblica* 54 (1973): 269-272.

Freedman, David Noel, ed-in-chief. *The Anchor Bible Dictionary.* Vol. 5. New York: Doubleday, 1992.

Fuller, Reginald C., gen. ed. *A New Catholic Commentary on Holy Scripture.* Rev. and updated. Nashville: Thomas Nelson, 1975.

Gharib, Georges, Ermanno M. Toniolo, Luigi Gambero, and Gerardo Di Nola, eds. *Testi Mariani del Primo Millennio.* 4 vols. Roma: Città Nuova Editrice, 1988-1991.

Gittens, Peter Winston. "Magistra Apostolorum in the Writings of Rupert of Deutz." Diss. Pontifical Theological Faculty, The Marianum, Rome, and International Marianum Research Institute, University of Dayton, 1991.

Gutmann, Joseph. *The Synagogue: Studies in Origins, Archaeology and Architecture.* New York: KTAV, 1975.

John Paul II, Pope. *Mother of the Redeemer (Redemptoris Mater).* Boston: St. Paul Books and Media, 1987.

Johnson, Ann. *Miryam of Judah: Witness in Truth & Tradition.* Notre Dame, IN: Ave Maria, 1987.

Kirwin, George F. [Francis]. "*Lumen Gentium*, Nos. 66 to 69 — Twenty Years Later." *Marian Studies* XXXVII (1986): 143-164.

_____. "The Nature of the Queenship of Mary." Diss. Catholic University of America, 1973.

Koehler, Theodore. "Les principales interprétations traditionelles de Jn. 19, 25-27 pendant les douze premiers siècles." *Etudes Mariales* 16 (1959): 119-155.

Laurentin, René. *A Short Treatise on the Blessed Virgin Mary.* Washington, NJ: AMI, 1991.

_____. *Structure et Théologie de Luc I-II.* Paris: Gabalda, 1957.

_____. *The Truth of Christmas Beyond the Myths: The Gospels of the Infancy of Christ.* Petersham, MA: Bede, 1986.

Lazor, Bernard A. "Mary in the Mysteries of Christ from Advent to the Baptism of the Lord: Biblical References." *Marian Studies* XLI (1990): 31-48.

Le Déaut, Roger. "Judaisme" in *Dictionnaire de Spiritualité.* Vol. VIII. Paris: Beauchesne, 1974.

_____. "Miryam, soeur de Moise, et Marie, mère du Messie." *Biblica* 45 (1964): 198-219.

Learsi, Rufus. *Israel: A History of the Jewish People.* New York: Meridian, 1966.

Lemmo, Nunzio. "Maria, 'Figlia di Sion,' a partire da Lc 1, 26-38, Bilancio esegetico dal 1939 al 1982." *Marianum* XLV (1983): 175-258.

Levine, Lee I. *The Galilee in Late Antiquity.* Cambridge, MA: Harvard University Press, 1992.

Lockyer, Herbert. *All the Women of the Bible.* Grand Rapids, MI: Zondervan, n.d.

Lyonnet, Stanislaus. "Chaire Kécharitôméné." *Biblica* 20 (1939): 131-141.

MacKenzie, R.A.F. *Sirach.* Wilmington, DE: Glazier, 1983.

Macquarrie, John. *Mary for All Christians.* Grand Rapids, MI: Eerdmans, 1990.

"Mary — Woman of the Mediterranean: A Special Issue." *Biblical Theological Bulletin* 20 (1990): 45-94.

McKenzie, John L. *Dictionary of the Bible.* New York: Macmillan, 1965.

Ménard, J.-E. *Evangile selon Philippe.* Paris: Letouzey, 1967.

Metzger, Bruce. *A Textual Commentary on the Greek New Testament.* New York: United Bible Societies, 1971.

Meyer, Ben F. "But Mary Kept All These Things . . ." (Lk 2, 19. 51). *Catholic Biblical Quarterly* 26 (1964): 31-49.

Meyers, Carol [L]. *Discovering Eve: Ancient Israelite Women in Context.* New York: Oxford University Press, 1988.

_____. "Everyday Life: Women in the Period of the Hebrew Bible." *The Women's Bible Commentary*. Eds. Carol A. Newsom and Sharon H. Ringe. Louisville: Westminster/John Knox, 1992.

Miller, Charles H. *"As It Is Written": The Use of Old Testament References in the Documents of Vatican Council II*. St Louis, MO: Marianist Communications Center, 1973.

Monteore, C.G. and H. Loewe. *A Rabbinic Anthology*. New York: Schocken, 1974.

Mowinckel, S. [Sigmund]. *He That Cometh*. Trans. G.W. Anderson. New York: Abingdon, n.d.

Nelson, Richard D. "David: A Model for Mary in Luke?" *Biblical Theology Bulletin* 18 (1988): 138-142.

Neusner, Jacob. "Can People Who Believe in Different Religions Talk Together?" *Journal of Ecumenical Studies* 28 (1991): 88-100.

_____. *Midrash in Context: Exegesis in Formative Judaism*. Philadelphia: Fortress, 1983.

New American Bible. Collins World, 1970.

Niditch, Susan. "Genesis." *The Women's Bible Commentary*. Eds. Carol A. Newsom and Sharon H. Ringe. Louisville, KY: Westminster/John Knox, 1992.

O'Carroll, Michael. *Theotokos: A Theological Encyclopedia of the Blessed Virgin Mary*. Wilmington, DE: Glazier, 1982.

O'Connor, Kathleen M. *The Wisdom Literature*. Wilmington, DE: Glazier, 1988.

Okure, Teresa. "Women in the Bible." *With Passion and Compassion: Third World Women Doing Theology*. New York: Maryknoll, 1988.

Paul VI, Pope. *Devotion to the Blessed Virgin Mary (Marialis cultus)*. 2 Feb. 1974.

Peretto, Elio. "Ricerche su Mt 1-2." *Marianum* XXXI (1969): 140-247.

Pixner, Bargil. "Church of the Apostles Found on Mount Zion." *Biblical Archaeological Review* 16:3 (1990): 16+.

Renaud, B. [Bernard]. "Cahiers de la Revue Bibliques." *Structure et Attaches Littéraires de Michée IV-V.* Vol. 2. Paris: Gabalda, 1964.

Senior, Donald, gen. ed. *The Catholic Study Bible: New American Bible.* New York: Oxford University Press, 1990.

Serra, Aristide. *E C'era la Madre di Gesù. . . (Gv 2, 1): saggi di esegesi biblico-mariana* (1978-1988). Roma: Edizioni Cens-Marianum, 1989.

Smith, Eustace. "The Scriptural Basis for Mary's Queenship." *Marian Studies* IV (1953): 109-117.

Smith, W. Robertson. *The Religion of the Semites: The Fundamental Institutions.* New York: Schocken, 1972.

Stock, Klemens. "La Vocazione di Maria Luke 1:26-38." *Marianum* XLV (1983): 112-113n41.

Stuhlmueller, Carroll. *Biblical Meditations for Advent and the Christmas Season.* New York: Paulist, 1980.

_____. "Old Testament Settings for Mary in the Liturgy." *Bible Today* 24 (No. 3, May 1986): 159-166.

Suenens, Léon Joseph Cardinal. *A New Pentecost.* New York: Seabury, 1975.

Thompson, Thomas A. "The Virgin Mary in the Liturgy: 1963-1988." *Marian Studies* XL (1989): 77-104.

Trible, Phyllis. "Bringing Miriam Out of the Shadows." *Bible Review* 5.1 (1989): 14-34.

_____. "Depatriarchalizing in Bibical Interpretation," *Journal of the American Academy of Religion* 41 (1973): 30-48.

_____. *God and the Rhetoric of Sexuality.* Philadelphia: Fortress, 1978.

Turro, James C. "Mary in Ordinary Time: Biblical References." *Marian Studies* XLIII (1992): 60-71.

Wainwright, Elaine Mary. "But Who Do *You* Say That I Am?" Unpublished, p. 24.

_____. *Towards a Feminist Critical Reading of the Gospel According to Matthew*. New York: Walter de Gruyter, 1991.

Wohlmann, Avital. "Mary of Nazareth." *Sidic* 20.2 (1987): 9-14.

Wright, Addison G. *Midrash*. New York: Alba House, 1967.

Zorrell, F. "Maria, soror Moysis, et Maria, Mater Dei." *Verbum Domini* 6 (1926): 257-263.

UNIVERSITY OF DAYTON
ROESCH LIBRARY

1 JAN 30	11
2	12
3	13
4	14
5	15
6	16
7	17
8	18
9	19
10	20